Munich 1972

Also by David Clay Large

Nazi Games: The Olympics of 1936
And the World Closed Its Doors: One Family's Abandonment to the Holocaust
Berlin
Where Ghosts Walked: Munich's Road to the Third Reich
Germans to the Front: West German Rearmament in the Adenauer Era
Contending with Hitler: Varieties of Resistance in the Third Reich (editor)
The End of the European Era: 1890 to the Present (with Felix Gilbert)
Between Two Fires: Europe's Path in the 1930s
Wagnerism in European Culture and Politics (coeditor)
*The Politics of Law and Order: A History of the Bavarian Einwohnerwehr,
1918–1921*

Munich 1972

Tragedy, Terror, and Triumph at the Olympic Games

David Clay Large

ROWMAN & LITTLEFIELD PUBLISHERS, INC.
Lanham • Boulder • New York • Toronto • Plymouth, UK

Published by Rowman & Littlefield Publishers, Inc.
A wholly owned subsidary of The Rowman & Littlefield Publishing Group, Inc.
4501 Forbes Boulevard, Suite 200, Lanham, Maryland 20706
http://www.rowmanlittlefield.com

Estover Road, Plymouth PL6 7PY, United Kingdom

Distributed by NATIONAL BOOK NETWORK

British Library Cataloguing in Publication Information Available

Library of Congress Cataloging-in-Publication Data
Large, David Clay.
  Munich 1972 : tragedy, terror, and triumph at the Olympic Games / David Clay
Large.
    p. cm.
  Includes index.
  ISBN 978-0-7425-6739-9 (hardback) — ISBN 978-0-7425-6741-2 (electronic)
  1. Terrorism—Germany—Munich. 2. Athletes—Violence against—Germany—
Munich. 3. Israelis—Violence against—Germany—Munich. 4. Olympic Games
(20th : 1972 : Munich, Germany). 5. Munazzamat Aylul al-Aswad. I. Title.
HV6433.G32L37 2012
364.152′30943364—dc23
2011036165

♾™ The paper used in this publication meets the minimum requirements of
American National Standard for Information Sciences—Permanence of Paper for
Printed Library Materials, ANSI/NISO Z39.48-1992.

Printed in the United States of America

To Howard J. De Nike

Contents

Acknowledgments

Writing a book can be rather like completing an endurance run over hilly terrain, and now, having come to the end of another long slog, I get to break out the cold beer and drink to those institutions and individuals who helped me stay the course.

Montana State University, my academic home for the past quarter century, provided a grant in support of research for this book early on. MSU's History and Philosophy Department also helped fund the procurement of photographs. Sven Riepe at Süddeutsche Zeitung Photo helped me comb through his institution's extensive collection for appropriate images. My editor at Rowman & Littlefield, Susan McEachern, encouraged this project from its inception and offered useful advice all along the way. The staffs of the various archives and libraries where I conducted my research also deserve a tip of the glass: Bayerisches Hauptstaatsarchiv, Munich; British Library, London; Bundesarchiv Berlin; Bundesarchiv Koblenz; Deutsche Sporthochschule, Cologne; Doe Library, University of California, Berkeley; Friedrich-Ebert-Stiftung, Bonn; German National Olympic Committee (NOK), Frankfurt; Hoover Institution, Stanford; Institut für Zeitgeschichte, Munich; International Olympic Committee Archive, Lausanne; LA '84 Foundation, Los Angeles; Monacensia Library, Munich; Montana State University Library, Bozeman (especially Interlibrary Loan); National Archives, College Park; Politisches Archiv im Auswärtigen Amt, Berlin; Staatsarchiv, Munich; Stadtarchiv, Munich; Stadtbibliothek, Cologne; Sterling Library, Yale University; University of Illinois Archive (Avery Brundage Collection); Widener Library, Harvard University; and Willy-Brandt-Haus, Berlin.

I am especially grateful to colleagues and friends who consented to read over drafts of my manuscript in part or in its entirety. (Some of those pressed into service, I can well imagine, greeted this task in the spirit of Dorothy Parker's famous lament, "What fresh hell is this?") My beleaguered helpmates include Andreas W. Daum, Howard De Nike, Brian Ladd, Dale Martin, Frank Rettenberg, Jonathan Schneer, Billy G. Smith, Hans R. Vaget, and Brett Walker. Lawrence "Monk" Terry, on oarsman on the U.S. Olympic rowing teams at Mexico City and Munich, shared his recollections of Munich '72 from the athlete's point of view. Despite painstaking vetting from all the above, I am, of course, solely responsible for any inaccuracies or imbecilities that remain in the final product.

Finally, I need to thank my long-suffering wife, Margaret, who, once again, had to endure considerable surliness and bitchiness on the part of her partner during the completion of a long writing project. And many thanks also to eight-year-old Alma, who, justifiably, would have preferred that her daddy play games with her rather than write about them for others.

San Francisco, California, 2011

Munich 1972

Introduction

I am always amazed when I hear people saying that sport creates
goodwill between the nations, and that if only the common peoples
of the world could meet one another at football or cricket, they would
have no inclination to meet on the battlefield. Even if one didn't know
from concrete examples (the 1936 Olympic Games, for instance) that
international sporting contests lead to orgies of hatred, one could
deduce it from general principles.

—George Orwell, "The Sporting Spirit" (1945)

A thing I never know, when I'm starting out to tell a story . . .
is how much explanation to bung in at the outset.

—Bertie Wooster in P. G. Wodehouse, *The Code of the Woosters* (1938)

When the XX Summer Olympic Games opened on August 26,
1972, in Munich, West Germany, the host city was brimming
with pride and (generally) good spirits. Visitors arriving in this
beautiful Bavarian metropolis on the Isar River, with its famous museums,
beer halls, and views of the nearby Alps, were struck by how earnestly the
locals were working to appear "laid back" and "charming" (not, perhaps,
the first adjectives that leap from the lips in connection with the word
German). For their part, the politicians and officials who had taken on the
mighty task of organizing these Munich Games were doing their utmost
to make everything about their show different from the Berlin Olympics
of 1936, the last time an Olympic festival had taken place on German soil.

Then, of course, Adolf Hitler had been in power, and the "Nazi Games" had helped advertise and promote the Third Reich.

The planners of the 1972 Games had good reason to worry about Nazi associations. Munich itself had been the birthplace of Nazism and the site of Hitler's first attempt to seize power, the "Beer Hall Putsch" of November 1923. After their most famous citizen had become Reich Chancellor in January 1933, city fathers christened Munich "Capital of the [Nazi] Movement" and added a swastika to the town's coat of arms. Hitler personally commissioned a new museum in Munich, the House of German Art, for the display of ideologically acceptable artwork. In 1937, Munich opened the Exhibition of Degenerate Art, a traveling display of some 650 works by artists identified with the avant-garde. Assembled by Adolf Ziegler, a Nazi arts official and hack painter known for his recumbent nudes of striking verisimilitude (which specialty earned him the sobriquet *Reichsschamhaarpinsler*—official pubic hair painter of the Reich), the collection contained works by Max Ernst, Paul Klee, Oskar Kokoschka, Georg Grosz, and Otto Dix, to name a few. Citizens were encouraged to compare the works in this show with those in the nearby House of German Art so that they might better understand the urgency of Hitler's "renewal" of German culture. Munich also pioneered in the regime's program of mass incarceration and political terror: Dachau, Nazi Germany's "pilot" concentration camp, lay just up the road. In September 1938, Munich played host to the infamous conference between Hitler, Benito Mussolini, Neville Chamberlain, and Édouard Daladier that ceded the Czech Sudetenland to Germany and helped set the stage for World War II (making "Munich" a byword for appeasement ever after). But in 1972, twenty-seven years after the collapse of the Third Reich, Germany's second chance at hosting a summer Olympic festival would showcase a new Munich and a new (West) Germany—a kinder and gentler Germany that had arisen from the ashes of Hitler's Reich. In short, Munich would put on the most carefree and happy-go-lucky Olympics in history: *die heiteren Spiele* (the "Cheerful Games"), as the catchy slogan of the day had it.

Whereas visitors to Nazi Berlin in 1936 had found a city awash in swastika flags, Munich in the summer of '72 offered a sea of fluttering Olympic banners in tranquil pastels—the strident reds, blacks, and purples of Nazi and Imperial Germany having been explicitly *verboten*. In marked contrast to the bombastic neo-classical Olympic architecture of 1936, Munich offered modernistic structures designed to remind the world that the Bavarian capital was a forward-looking metropolis, open to the new and innovative. The Olympic Stadium and an adjoining sports complex were covered by a swooping tent-like glass roof, meant to symbolize transparency and inclusiveness. The sprawling grounds featured bucolic walkways and a hilltop "shrine to peace" shaded by Cypress trees donated by Lebanon. Berlin '36 had had no official mascot, but Munich '72 emphatically did—indeed, it effectively launched this ludicrous practice. The creature in question was a Bavarian Dachshund named "Waldi," available in a cuddly stuffed version in all the local souvenir shops. Impressed by the lengths to which Munich's Olympic impresarios had gone to "efface lingering memories of Berlin 1936," a visiting reporter for America's *Ramparts* magazine gushed after opening day: "Then [in 1936] it had been the Teutonic gods of war that were being supplicated; but now, thirty-six years later, it was to be the milder deities of Mount Olympus as thousands of the world's greatest athletes gathered in gentle Bavarian surroundings to return the Olympic ideal to German soil."

As strikingly "un-Berlin" as Munich '72's stylistic regime undoubtedly was, it was in the realm of *security*, not aesthetics or even atmospherics, where the Bavarian festival departed most significantly, and fatefully, from Germany's previous Olympic experience. Although the Nazis downplayed their militarism during the Berlin Games, there were plenty of uniformed police, soldiers, and SS-men stationed around town and the Reichssportfeld. At Munich's sprawling Olympic Park, by contrast, the primary keepers of order consisted of civilian volunteers dressed in leisure-suit-like outfits of a pale blue hue said to evoke "the azure skies of Bavaria." Rather than pistols or rifles (or even nightsticks), these pastel-clad guardians of the Olympic peace carried walkie-talkies, and they had been trained in the latest techniques of crowd control and anger management. Whereas Berlin's Olympic Village had been located on a military base many miles away from the main Olympic complex, Munich's lay within walking distance of the stadium. The 1972 Village had a chain-link fence around it, but said fence was only six and a half feet tall and had no menacing coils of barbed wire running along the top. The fence was patrolled by guards on foot and in vehicles, but after the first two or three days of competition the patrols were scaled back, especially at night. "Nothing happens at night," observed an Olympic security official.

The opening days of the Munich Games were by no means all sweetness and light—there were protest demonstrations in the streets and some displays of rancor on the athletic field. Yet, on the whole, the festival got off to a promising start. The meticulously orchestrated opening ceremony proved a tour de force of lighthearted fun. In the futuristic main stadium and Aquatic Center, athletes set a host of new Olympic and world records.

America's Mark Spitz swam his way to *seven* gold medals, itself an Olympic record. Foreign visitors seemed gratifyingly impressed by Bavaria's big show. West German radio boasted of a "wave of international praise" emanating from Munich. "Here is a new, changed Germany of which nothing is reminiscent of the National Socialist dictatorship that politically misused the Olympics thirty-six years ago in Berlin. Munich need not fear comparisons."

Then, on September 5, day 10 of the competitions, came the horrific terrorist attack on Israeli athletes and coaches at the Olympic Village. In the wee hours of the morning, eight heavily armed men climbed over the unguarded fence surrounding the Olympic Village to gain access to the Israeli compound. The operation was carried out by "Black September," an arm of the Palestine Liberation Organization's Fatah group. In the course of seizing and confining a group of hostages, the Palestinians killed two Israelis. Now television coverage from Munich alternated between the athletic events—amazingly, these were not suspended until seven hours after the attack had begun—and hooded gunmen holding an unspecified number of Israeli Olympians captive in the team's two-story compound at the Village. On the following morning, TV coverage switched to a grim-faced Bavarian official announcing that an attempt to rescue the remaining hostages at a nearby airfield called Fürstenfeldbruck had gone terribly awry and resulted in fifteen deaths—all nine of the hostages, five of the eight terrorists, and one German policeman. Although the killers were not German, the fact that the murders had taken place on German soil seemed to compound the horror—as did the peaceful setting: an Olympic festival designed to promote international brotherhood and understanding. Added to the horror was a bitter irony: the very effort to make Munich '72 so different from Berlin '36, and thereby to replace ugly associations with positive ones, seemed to have helped facilitate a brutal terrorist attack whose outcome ended up rekindling memories of the bad old days. One can certainly say that, within the context of modern German history, and modern sports history, no road to hell was ever paved with nobler intentions.

It is, of course, for the events of September 5 and 6 that the Munich Games are largely remembered today. This is understandable: the "Munich Massacre" (as the terror episode came to be called) was the greatest tragedy to befall the modern Olympic Games; it was also the most lethal terrorist attack in the history of postwar Germany. Yet, it is one of the central premises of this study that there is a host of other good reasons why Munich '72 merits our continuing interest—and, more to the point, why it warrants a comprehensive historical treatment.

Contrary to the claims of the International Olympic Committee (IOC), the modern Olympics have always been "political," and Munich's version was the most intensely political of all the modern Games—even more so than those Nazi Games of 1936. Far from providing an "Olympic Truce"—a temporary suspension of all the rancor and acrimony afflicting the world outside the sacred precincts of play—Munich '72 acted like a malign magnet, drawing into its powerful force-field most of the major tensions, conflicts, and bitter rivalries of the day. Or, to deploy a pair of additional metaphors, the West German Olympic boosters' project of bringing "the youth of the world" to Munich in the summer of '72 turned this comfortable Bavarian town into a seething cockpit of world events—a socio-political seismic zone.

The opening day smiles on the faces of the Olympic organizers were largely expressions of profound relief. The long run-up to the Games had been anything but "carefree" or "cheerful." Given Munich's problematical past, the IOC's decision in 1966 to award the '72 Summer Games to this city was highly controversial. Many commentators asked how, a mere twenty-one years after the end of World War II and the demise of Hitler's Reich, a *German* city, and especially *this* German city, could be tapped to host the most prestigious athletic festival in the world. The promoters of the Munich Games were obliged to spend much time and effort making the case that, as Willi Daume, president of the Munich Organizing Committee (OC) put it, the "gift of the world's trust" was "not undeserved."

The choice of Munich was contentious not only because of factors rooted in the municipal and national past—all that weighty historical baggage—but also due to controversies grounded firmly in the present. West Germany in general and Munich in particular were on the front line of the Cold War. The Bavarian capital was home to thousands of militantly anti-communist and anti-Soviet refugees from Eastern European lands that had fallen under Moscow's sway in the wake of World War II. Munich housed offices of Radio Liberty and Radio Free Europe—American-funded broadcasters that beamed Western-oriented news and entertainment programs into Eastern Europe and the Soviet Union. As if that were not enough, West Germany's foreign intelligence agency, the Bundesnachrichten Dienst (BND), which focused its attention mainly on the Communist East, was headquartered in a small town just south of Munich. In the eyes of the Soviets and their Eastern European allies, Munich was the very epicenter of Western "revanchism" and "neo-imperialism" and therefore singularly unsuited to host an "internationalist" and "peace-promoting" enterprise like the Olympics. It took many months of hard lobbying by Willi Daume to bring the USSR, which had briefly contemplated entering its own capital in the race for the '72 Summer Games, into the Munich camp.

Moscow's opposition to Munich turned out to be mild compared to the fuss put up by that "other Germany"—the German Democratic Republic (GDR). East Berlin saw the IOC's selection of Munich as emblematic of a bias on the part of the Olympic establishment in favor of the capitalist West. Although, shortly before selecting Munich, the IOC had decided that the GDR, along with its West German rival, could appear in all future Olympics as a fully sovereign entity under its own national flag, East German officials and pundits insisted loudly that the "neo-fascist" hate-mongers in Munich would invariably discriminate against athletes from Socialist lands and in general "misuse" the Games for nefarious political purposes, just as the Nazis had done.

In reality, the Munich OC was determined to provide equal treatment for the Eastern Europeans and to lay on an especially warm welcome for their "German brothers" on the other side of the Iron Curtain. What is more, Chancellor Willy Brandt, as of 1969 the new leader in Bonn, saw the Munich Games as an excellent opportunity to further his ongoing policy of *Ostpolitik*—his campaign to mend fences with the Socialist East, including the GDR. Yet, it was precisely this double-barreled charm offensive from the West that unnerved the leadership of the GDR, which worried that too much intra-German fraternization might undermine the ideological division between the two states—a division that the GDR government (with uncertain backing from Moscow) had recently buttressed by building the Berlin Wall. But after venting much spleen over the very idea of a Munich Olympiad, the GDR's political and Olympic establishment gradually came to understand that in these Games the East could showcase its separate political identity, not to mention its superior athletic prowess.

For a time, the animosity toward Munich from Eastern Europe had been so virulent that the IOC, and the Munich planners, worried about the possibility of an extensive East-bloc boycott. We know now that the Eastern powers never seriously intended to shun Munich—after all, if they wanted to demonstrate their athletic superiority over the West, they had to show up—but this does not mean that Munich '72 lacked for genuine boycott threats. On the eve of the Games, a threatened boycott by a large number of Black African states was narrowly averted. The Africans were deeply aggrieved over an invitation from the Munich OC to white-ruled Rhodesia, an invitation that had been strongly backed by the IOC. Only a last-minute decision by this same IOC (over the vehement objections of committee-president Avery Brundage, a crusty old American who had run the committee with an iron hand since 1952) to exclude Rhodesia mollified the Black Africans and ensured their presence in Munich. As this bitter dispute made clear, Munich '72 was caught up not only in the politics of the Cold War but also in those of the new Africa emerging from colonial rule.

The threat of a boycott by Black African nations carried with it a possible no-show on the part of African Americans belonging to the huge U.S. team scheduled to compete in Munich. Several American black athletes had indicated that, if their African brothers stayed away from Bavaria, they would as well. Of course, the IOC's last-minute cave-in on Rhodesia allowed the Munich organizers to strike this particular worry from their long list of anxieties. Yet, it also guaranteed the retention of another nagging worry: the fear that American blacks might do in Munich what the African American sprinters John Carlos and Tommie Smith had done in Mexico City in 1968—stage some sort of "Black Power" demonstration during the competitions. Rumblings from the American camp in the run-up to the Games gave the impression that, when it came to displays of African American grievance, Munich might make Mexico City look like child's play.

A related anxiety, even scarier, involved the possibility that African American GIs stationed in West Germany (of which a sizeable contingent happened to be headquartered right in Bavaria) might descend on Munich during the Games to wreak some kind of mayhem. According to Bavarian intelligence sources, "radicalized" African American soldiers, high on the rhetoric of Black Nationalism, posed perhaps the single greatest threat to the "order" and tranquility of the Munich Games.

Beyond the threat of black militancy was a considerably more diffuse danger of disruptions to the Games deriving from the ever-increasing friction over the Vietnam War. For years, West German cities, including Munich, had been the scene of protests, many of them violent, against U.S. "genocide" in Vietnam. In the three years preceding the Games, outrage in Germany over the war had intensified as the Nixon administration attempted to "end" the conflict by escalating it: mining North Vietnam's Haiphong Harbor; bombing Northern cities, including Hanoi; and invading Cambodia. In short, Vietnam might be far from Munich geographically, but the '72 Olympics offered an enticing arena in which anti-war activists might bring the war "home" to the visiting Americans and their West German hosts. Indeed, the above-mentioned street demonstrations at the opening of the Games were all about Vietnam—and the fact that American bombs were raining down on that small Asian country just as "doves of peace" were being released into the air at the Olympic Stadium in Munich.

The array of tensions afflicting the globe in the years leading up to the '72 Games weighed heavily on Munich's Olympic planners, especially on those responsible for keeping the festival safe. The lack of armed guards and high, barbwire-topped fences on the Olympic grounds has given rise to the canard that the organizers were blasé about security in general, relegating the whole issue to the back burner. I will argue in this book that the reality was more complex. True, security was not the Munich planners' top priority, but they did order extensive studies of global "threat zones" in advance of the Games with an eye to being prepared for all manner of contingencies. Alas, there were so many sources of possible trouble that it was quite difficult to know where to focus one's defenses. To the extent that the Munich OC *did* focus its resources, this concentration was understandably directed at the threats that seemed most pressing at the time: hostilities related to the Cold War, Vietnam War, Third World anticolonialism, domestic radicalism (mostly left, but also right), and African American militancy. The forces of order also tried to gird their loins for an expected upsurge in ordinary criminality.

And what of the ever-volatile Middle East? Munich's security experts were by no means unmindful of dangers emanating from this quarter—even, quite specifically, from Black September—but the "Palestinian problem" constituted at best a small blip on the security planners' radar screen. Looking back at the data available to those planners, one can argue that this blip should have been considerably larger, but that argument would be based in part on knowledge of what was to come—that is, on ever-trusty hindsight. In my discussion of the events of September 5 and 6 I certainly have no intention of mounting any kind of "apology" for the glaring security inadequacies at Munich '72, but I also hope that by putting this miserable affair in a broader historical context I can make some headway toward a satisfactory explanation of what went down on this darkest day of modern Olympic history.

It will already be apparent that in talking about this tragic episode I readily deploy the terms "terror" and "terrorist." This was standard practice at the time and has remained so ever since. I have elected to retain this usage in full awareness that, the weight of convention here notwithstanding, these terms are notoriously slippery and tendentious. We are all familiar with the cliché that "one man's terrorist is another man's freedom-fighter." Not surprisingly, the Palestinians who seized the Israeli compound at Munich and ended up butchering eleven Olympians saw themselves in the latter category, emphatically rejecting the term "terrorist." The denial is as questionable as it is understandable. Terrorism is generally defined as the deployment of violence against innocent non-combatants in the pursuit of a political goal, often that of compelling a more powerful entity to act in a particular way. This definition pretty well sums up the Black September operation at Munich, though of course, once again, apologists for this particular instance of terror will undoubtedly deny the claim "innocence" for the Israeli Olympians on grounds that *no* Israeli could ever be innocent.

One can, I think, categorize the Munich murders as terrorist while still being mindful of the legitimacy of the Palestinian grievances and also of the undeniable fact that the Zionists who fought to create a Jewish state in Palestine had frequently resorted to terror tactics of their own in that struggle. The Irgun's bombing of the King David Hotel in Jerusalem on July 22, 1946, comes to mind as just one example of this deplorable practice.*

Finally, one can deploy the term "terror" for the Munich episode without losing sight of the additional fact that this concept covers an awful lot of ground and that individual instances of terror differ widely in scope, motivation, and operational tactics. The Munich action was certainly much smaller in scope than the most infamous recent terrorist outrage, the Al-Qaida-sponsored attacks in the United States on September 11, 2001. "9/11" also differed significantly from Munich in motivation and method. As I hope to make clear in my discussion of the Munich attack, the Black September operatives should not be lumped together indiscriminately with the death-infatuated religious maniacs who flew passenger planes into the World Trade Center and Pentagon in that later and much bigger September massacre. Yet, none of these differences in scope, method, and motivation should obscure the more fundamental fact that, for the *victims* of terror, the size of the killing fields, the choice of weaponry, and the finer points of motivation don't matter very much.

---

* The Irgun, a right-wing underground Zionist group led by Menachem Begin, targeted the King David Hotel because it housed, in addition to ordinary guests, the offices of the British Mandatory Authority in Palestine, the headquarters of British military forces in the region, and the Secretariat of the Government of Palestine. The Irgun telephoned warnings to the hotel before their huge bomb went off, but the hotel was not evacuated, mainly because there had been a string of false alarms previously. The ensuing explosion collapsed one wing of the hotel and killed ninety-one people, most of them hotel staff or workers for the Secretariat. The majority of fatalities were Arab; twenty-one were British. Another forty-six people were injured. Although the Zionist political leadership condemned the bombing, Israeli leaders later found reasons to justify it. On the sixtieth anniversary of the attack, Binyamin Netanyahu, leader of the right-wing Likud (and later prime minister), described the bombing as a legitimate operation with a military target, not an act of terror.

The terror attack of September 5 and 6 disrupted the athletic competitions at the Munich Games but did not halt them for good. After a twenty-four-hour interval and brief memorial service, the Games resumed. The decision to continue the competitions was made by the IOC and announced by President Brundage at the memorial service. This decision, immortalized in Brundage's famous phrase "The Games Must Go On," drew heated criticism not just from political figures and journalists but also from some of the athletes, for whom these Olympics constituted the greatest moment in their sporting lives. The controversial decision to resume play at Munich '72 deserves our scrutiny.

The play itself should also be examined. This might seem to be a given (after all, aren't the Olympics about sports?), but in actuality Olympic festivals are often so caught up in off-the-field controversies that the athletes and athletic events seem to get lost in the shuffle. This was certainly the case with Munich '72. Perhaps not surprisingly, the few studies presently available on Munich '72 downplay or ignore the competitions entirely, focusing exclusively on the terror attack or the German political and cultural issues at stake. Yet, I believe the athletic events at the Munich Games *are* of great interest. They are of interest not only in the way that most sporting contests are—as little pieces of high drama—but also, like the festival in general, as reflections of tensions and conflicts outside the athletic arena. This is especially true of the contests at Munich between athletes from the United States and the USSR, which often amounted to a continuation of the Cold War by other means. Events pitting the two Germanys against each other also carried a lot of political baggage, not least because these battles were taking place on German turf.

The importance of this intra-German rivalry notwithstanding, in my treatment of the athletic events at Munich '72, I devote more attention to the U.S./USSR matchups and to the American performances in general. Apart from the fact that American men and women were involved in some of the most dramatic athletic contests at these Games, the Americans brought with them to Munich an ongoing (and revealing) internal struggle over race. It is well known that issues of race were "in the air" at the Mexico City Games of 1968. It is less well known that racial turmoil, especially among the Americans, clouded the atmosphere in Munich as well.

To the degree that the athletic side of the Munich festival has achieved any long-term resonance, this historical longevity applies only to a few very special moments or achievements: Mark Spitz's aforementioned seven gold medals in swimming; Russian gymnast Olga Korbut's dazzling victories and tearful defeat; the endlessly disputed basketball final between the United States and the USSR. But like all Olympic festivals, the one in Munich featured a host of brilliant performances that might also be classed as "memorable" if only they were more widely remembered. Sports cognoscenti specializing on the Olympic Games may be familiar with the achievements in 1972 by figures like Shane Gould, Ulrike Meyfarth, Lasse Virén, Valery Borzov, Dan Gable, Heidi Rosendahl, Mykola Avilov, Mary Peters, and Frank Shorter, but most of us will come up blank, or nearly so. Once again, the stellar performances by athletes like these merit revisiting not only because of their inherent drama but also, in some cases, due to their social significance. As we shall see, this pertains as well to a number of performances and contests that were not so stellar.

Among the Munich '72 athletes who did not become, shall we say, a household name is the American swimmer Rick DeMont. He won a gold medal only to have it revoked by the IOC on grounds that he had ingested a banned substance prior to his event. In his sad case, the accusation of using a performance-enhancing drug was off the mark, but "doping" by athletes was a genuine issue at the Munich Games—as it would be, ever more prominently, at Olympic festivals to come. In the realm of Olympic doping, Munich '72 is of particular interest because it was the first Olympics at which local experts and the IOC made a serious effort to address this problem. In the end, though, the anti-doping procedures introduced at Munich were inadequate, to put it mildly. Munich's failure on this front set the stage for an ongoing soap opera that seems to become tawdrier with each Olympic installment.

For a final note on my treatment of the athletic dimensions of the Munich Olympics, there were 196 events conducted in 21 sports spread over 16 days: my "coverage" of this vast athletic panorama is selective and idiosyncratic, the selection determined in part by considerations of larger interest, in part by personal preference. I care about boxing, track, and swimming, for example; I don't give a fig about fencing or air-rifle shooting. Also, since it is the *Munich* festival that is at the center of my interest here—the Bavarian capital itself being one of my chief actors—I am not concerned with the '72 whitewater canoeing events that took place in Augsburg, or with the sailing up in Kiel. If one is looking for a complete account of all the athletic events that transpired during the XX Summer Games, one should turn to an encyclopedia, not to this book.

If most of the athletic performances at Munich '72—the core of the festival—have been long forgotten, or remembered only dimly, this is even more true of organizational matters like funding, physical plant construction, advertising and promotion, reportage (print and broadcast), and ceremony. In my view, these matters are of genuine importance in the assessment of any Olympic festival, but they merit particular attention in the case of Munich, given all the acrimony surrounding that city's selection as an Olympic host and corresponding pressures on the organizers to put on a truly special show. A major component of Munich's special show involved culture—that is, enlisting all the city's vaunted cultural assets behind an effort to enlighten and entertain Olympic guests. Here also was yet another way for Munich to focus attention on the most edifying parts of its historical legacy at the expense of those rather less compelling bits.

I devote considerable space to questions of cost, physical plant aesthetics, promotion, commerce, and details of ceremony because these apparently mundane matters open a revealing window on a particular place and time—Munich in the late sixties and early seventies—and also because they can tell us much about how the modern Olympic movement works, or doesn't work. This book is by no means a case study in the pitfalls of putting on an Olympic festival in the modern era, but it may help us better understand why so many citizens of potential host cities are not all that anxious to "win" the Olympics—or why, when the Games finally come to town, so many folks head for the hills.*

In the end, it was not only because of the terror attack that the Munich Games raised fundamental questions about the nature and purpose of the Olympic Games. Were they worth all the cost and bother? Whom did they serve—*cui bono*? Could they go on? If they did go on, how should they be changed?

Of course, they did go on, but they came in for some very hard times in subsequent years, due in part to repeated boycotts. At the Montreal Games in 1976, twenty-eight African states ordered their Olympic teams home because New Zealand, which maintained rugby ties to South Africa, was allowed to participate. In retaliation for the Soviet invasion of Afghanistan in 1979, President Jimmy Carter required the U.S. Olympic Committee to boycott the Moscow Summer Games in 1980. Under pressure from

---

* The IOC awarded the 1976 Winter Games to Denver, Colorado, but the citizens of that state voted to abandon the Games, which were then picked up by Innsbruck, Austria, host of the 1964 Winter Games. In 1993, Berlin, having recently been named capital of newly reunified Germany, bid for the 2000 Summer Games, but that move generated a fierce anti-Olympic protest in the city, which, along with a host of miscues by Berlin's Olympic Committee, helped sink the city's bid. In 2009, some 84 percent of the residents of Chicago said they opposed the idea of hosting the 2016 Summer Games in their city if it meant that even one dime would come out of municipal coffers. Chicago, of course, did not get those Games.

Washington, sixty-one other nations, including West Germany and Israel, also stayed away (though, much to Carter's consternation, Britain, France, and Italy refused to follow America's example). With the American team a no-show at Moscow, NBC Television exercised a clause in its contract that allowed it to cancel its planned coverage of the 1980 Games. The Soviets exacted their revenge four years later by boycotting the Los Angeles Games, taking most of their Eastern European allies with them. These boycotts did little or nothing to affect the domestic or foreign policies of the targeted nations, but of course, they grievously hurt the athletes, who lost their opportunity to compete, and they dealt a serious blow to the Olympics enterprise, revealing more painfully than ever the hollowness of the movement's claim to stand above politics.

But boycotts were not the only source of the Olympic movement's difficulties in the post-Munich era. There were huge cost overruns (Montreal in particular was a financial disaster); more doping scandals; more "professionalism" exposés; and even more venue-selection acrimony. Matters were not helped by shaky stewardship in Lausanne. Lord Killanin, an Irish grandee who took over for Brundage directly following the Munich Games, was so inept that many IOC members actually began to miss the cranky old martinet (variously decried as "Slavery Avery" and "Avery Umbrage"). William E. Simon of the U.S. Olympic Committee was particularly unhappy with the new president, of whom he said, "Explaining something sensible to Lord Killanin is akin to explaining something to a cauliflower. The advantage of the cauliflower is that if all else fails, you can cover it with melted cheese and eat it."

Whatever he personally thought of Lord Killanin, Avery Brundage was convinced that the organization he was turning over to him in 1972 did not have much of a future. As he handed his successor the symbolic keys to the IOC presidency he said, "You won't have much use for these. I believe the Olympic movement will not last more than a few years." The next few years seemed to bear Brundage out. In 1980, when Juan Antonio Samaranch replaced Killanin as president of the IOC, the organization had only $200,000 in liquid cash and $2 million in assets. "Everybody was writing the Olympic obituary," recalls a former IOC official. In some ways, it's quite odd that—in the manner of Mark Twain—reports of the Olympic movement's death proved exaggerated.

Although the Olympic movement obviously managed to muddle through its tough times—the IOC is a wealthy institution again, due largely to its share in the sale of ever more lucrative TV rights and commercial licensing—every Olympic festival since Munich '72 has been haunted by memories of that particular Olympiad. I close my book with a discussion of how memories of the Munich Games, particularly the terror attack, have played out in the Olympic movement and elsewhere over the years. But I have not saved the subject of "memory" for my epilogue. The reader will notice that it is a persistent and recurring theme throughout the book: memories of Germans regarding their recent past and recovery after the war; memories of Israelis regarding the Holocaust and their campaign to create a Jewish state in Palestine; memories of the Palestinians, those "victims of the victims," regarding their own struggles for survival and dignity under Israeli occupation; memories of athletes regarding a high point in their sporting lives, albeit one tinged with sorrow; and memories of the citizens of Munich regarding what should have been the greatest moment in their city's postwar history—but that ended up being something rather more complicated than that.

CHAPTER **One**

The Decision for Munich

What could one say about Munich,
except that it was a German paradise?
—Thomas Wolfe, *The Web and the Rock* (1925)

The dozens of tired and sweaty dignitaries gathered in Rome's opulent Hotel Excelsior on a muggy afternoon in late April 1966 were getting restless. Representing the municipalities competing for the honor of hosting the Summer and Winter Olympic Games to be held in 1972, they had been cooling their heels for hours in a stuffy anteroom outside the conference hall where the International Olympic Committee (IOC) was set to determine its venue decisions for that year's Olympic festivals.

The four cities still in contention for the '72 Summer Games were Montreal, Munich, Detroit, and Madrid. (Montreal was bidding for the fourth time; Detroit, for the *seventh*. Madrid had withdrawn a few weeks earlier, only to jump back in.) Speculating among themselves over which of their cities might get the nod, these rival Olympic aspirants could not help but be reminded of another secretive and tension-ridden Roman lottery—that involving the selection of a new pope by the College of Cardinals, which by hallowed tradition involved the release of a puff of white smoke over the Sistine Chapel to announce "*Habemus Papam*." The IOC, then less than a century old, lacked such hoary customs, but it certainly had learned over time how to milk its much-anticipated venue decisions for all the publicity value they were worth.

Finally, after a six-hour wait, the delegations from the four competing cities were invited into the inner sanctum. IOC president Avery Brundage, the seventy-eight-year-old former Olympian and Chicago construction magnate who had been running the committee for the past fourteen years, stepped to the microphone and growled, "The Games of the Twentieth Summer Olympiad are awarded to . . . Munich!" Allowing for a few seconds of audible gasps and scattered applause, Brundage then pronounced that the '72 Winter Games would go to Sapporo, Japan. Thus, roughly two decades after the end of World War II, the IOC had entrusted the world's most prestigious international athletic festival to the principal losers in that epochal conflict.*

Like most of the IOC's venue decisions over the years, the 1966 decision for Munich (we are not concerned here with Sapporo) had a complicated background, rife with political intrigue and mutual back-scratching and back-stabbing. But in the case of Munich's selection, there was even more political infighting and controversy than usual. As noted above, the Bavarian city had a troubling Nazi past, and it also occupied a prominent place on the front line of the Cold War. To understand how, on April 26, 1966, the IOC chose Munich, West Germany, of all places, to host the 1972 Summer Olympics requires that we flesh out this complicated back story.

Will the Real Germany Please Stand Up? The FRG-GDR Struggle for Olympic Representation

When the modern Olympic Games resumed in 1948 after a twelve-year hiatus occasioned by World War II, virtually no one connected to the Olympic movement could have imagined that a *German* city would host an Olympic festival in the foreseeable future, much less host one a mere twenty-four years hence. (But then, in view of the horrors inflicted upon the world by the Germans during the war, it would have been equally difficult to fathom that those same Germans, on both sides of the Iron Curtain, would once again have major military arms at their disposal within a mere decade of the war's conclusion.)

No Germans (or Japanese) were allowed to participate in the first post–World War II Olympics in 1948—the St. Moritz Winter Games and

---

* In the final round of voting for the Summer Games venue in 1972, Munich received thirty-one votes; Montreal and Madrid, sixteen each; and Detroit, zero. Poor Motown!

the London Summer Games—just as Germans had been banned from the first two post–World War I Olympic festivals in Antwerp (1920) and Paris (1924). Although Germany was obliged after World War II to sit out only one Olympic season, returning to the Olympic fold in 1952 at the Oslo Winter Games and the Helsinki Summer Games, the "Germany" in question consisted solely of West Germany, formally known as the Federal Republic of Germany (FRG), with its capital in the small and unprepossessing university town of Bonn. (True, there was also a team at Helsinki from the ethnic German Saarland, but at that time the Saarland, lying on the Franco-German border, was officially a protectorate of France, and its presence at the Games was simply a function of *folie de grandeur* on the part of Paris.) As for that other product of Germany's Cold War division in 1949, the Communist-ruled German Democratic Republic (GDR), it could have sent athletes to Oslo and Helsinki only under the auspices of the "German" national team organized by the Olympic committee of the FRG, which, tellingly, called itself the National Olympic Committee for Germany (NOCG). At that time the NOCG was the only German Olympic agency recognized by the IOC.

Not surprisingly, GDR sports officials protested vehemently against this arrangement, and formally sought accreditation for their own national Olympic committee, formed in 1951. The IOC, however, insisted it could recognize only one committee per nation, thereby implying that the GDR was not a nation at all. This was exactly the line taken by the FRG, which claimed to be the sole legal representative of German sovereignty and nationhood. The then-president of the NOCG, Ritter von Halt, a wealthy banker, Brundage confidant, and former Nazi Party member who had helped organize "Hitler's Games" in 1936, argued also that the IOC must not recognize the East German committee on grounds that this would introduce "politics" into the Olympic movement. Thus, in 1952, it certainly looked as if the IOC was happily doing its part to strengthen the Western side in the crucial German theater of the dawning Cold War. This seemed only to confirm the committee's long-established image as an archconservative club for superannuated sporting men from the lower aristocracy and global plutocracy—what George Orwell called "the Blimp Class."

And yet, while the IOC in the early 1950s definitely favored the Western side in the German-German struggle over Olympic representation, the committee was not really satisfied with an arrangement that effectively excluded the East Germans from any Olympic competition. Ever since its foundation in the late nineteenth century, the IOC had always liked to think of itself as an "apolitical" organization that stood airily above the petty quarrels between nations. On the other hand, the modern Olympic movement had never lived up to its "Olympian" pretentions. Its principal founder, Baron Pierre de Coubertin, was guided by distinctly national principles, with participation in the Games based solely on national affiliation and a set of rituals emphasizing national pathos. Indeed, the Olympics had emerged over the years as yet another kind of measuring stick for national prowess, its quadrennial athletic competitions displays less of international togetherness than of "warfare without weapons." And yet, in the wake of World War II, the most destructive conflict in modern history, leaders of the Olympic movement, even its patriarch Avery Brundage, were anxious to do more to live up to Olympism's putative universalist principles.

This aspiration explains why the IOC finally welcomed the Soviet Union into the Olympic movement in 1951 (for participation in the '52 Games), and why the committee at least *tried* to admit both new Chinas, the Republic of China (Taiwan) and the People's Republic of China (Beijing), to the Games of 1952 and 1956. Alas, since neither China was satisfied with the IOC's "two-China" policy, *no* team from China appeared in 1952, and Taiwan participated in 1956 only after Beijing elected to boycott that festival.

Unable to have its way with the two Chinas, the IOC was determined to impose its will on the two Germanys. Thus, in 1952, the committee decreed that, in all future Olympics beginning in 1956, the two German states must be represented in Olympic competition by a common, *unified* team. In other words, the IOC would make the Germans behave as one, whether they liked it or not. For Brundage, achieving this result would demonstrate to the world that sport, at least Olympic sport, could indeed "triumph over politics." Or, as he put the matter with characteristic grandiloquence, "Under the symbol of the five Olympic rings political problems could be resolved in the realm of sport that politicians had failed to master." With time, Brundage became so infatuated with the concept of a single, unified German team that he referred to it as "my baby." He became as protective of this ungainly infant as any doting parent.

Although, for the time being, the IOC continued to grant full recognition only to West Germany's Olympic committee (East Germany's committee received "provisional" status), the committee also decided, after much deliberation, that the FRG's national symbols, its flag and anthem, would not be appropriate for the new unified team. Instead, Germany's squad would henceforth participate in the Games under a "neutral" set of symbols emblematic of the "idea of Germany" but not specific to either of the two rival German states.

So just what kind of unifying Olympic symbolism did the luminaries of Lausanne come up with for the Germans? For the 1956 Olympics in Cortina, Italy, and Melbourne, Australia, a new neutral flag was not necessary because, until 1959, both Germanys used the same black-red-gold banner associated with the short-lived German republican movement of 1848–1849 and the ill-fated "Weimar Republic" of 1918–1933. In 1959, however, things became complicated, for at that point the GDR introduced a new national flag of its own, employing the old republican German colors but with a central emblem consisting of a hammer and draftsman's compass. Called to action, the IOC decreed that for the impending Games of 1960, to be held in Squaw Valley, California, and Rome, Italy, the unified German team would appear under a replacement banner featuring the standard black-red-gold bars with Olympism's five linked rings adorning the center.

Troublesome from the beginning was the question of a common anthem, for each new German state had its own national hymn. The FRG used a stirring composition whose melody had been written by Josef Haydn for the Austrian emperor in 1797, with a German nationalist text added by Hoffmann von Fallersleben in 1841. This so-called Deutschlandlied was adopted for the first time as German's national anthem by the Weimar Republic in 1922 and then, with some reluctance, carried over by the Nazis during the Third Reich. When the West German parliament decided in 1952 to enshrine the "Deutschlandlied" as the infant FRG's own anthem, it stipulated that only the unobjectionable third stanza emphasizing "unity, justice and freedom" should be retained, while the first stanza evoking a "Germany above everything" and stretching "from the Meuse to the Neman" must go. (Alas, the politically correct third stanza never really caught on with the West German public, many citizens not even bothering to learn the words. At sporting events, most fans continued to sing the first stanza.) The GDR, for its part, had commissioned an entirely new hymn, "Risen from the Ruins," with earnestly inspirational lyrics by the Communist poet Johannes R. Becher ("Let us plough, let us build, let us learn and create as never before") and rousing music by Hanns Eisler. Since neither Germany could stand to hear the other Germany's anthem, and most people outside Germany had little use for either national hymn, the IOC came up with a perfectly anodyne (and predictable) replacement: the Choral Section of Beethoven's Ninth Symphony, "Ode to Joy," with words by Friedrich Schiller.

Not surprisingly, neither side was entirely happy with this setup, which ensured that *none* of the German athletes participating in the greatest athletic show on earth would be allowed to parade around under their own national flag or hear their own national anthem trilling from the stadium sound system as they collected their gold medals on the victory podium.

Early on, it was mainly the Bonn government that felt aggrieved over the new arrangement because the admittance of East German athletes to the Games and the creation of neutral symbolism for the unified teams obviously compromised the FRG's claim to be the only true and legally sovereign Germany. In 1955, Bonn reinforced this claim with the so-called Hallstein Doctrine, which derived its name from Walter Hallstein, a prominent foreign policy advisor to Chancellor Konrad Adenauer. This doctrine stated that the FRG would retain diplomatic relations solely with nations that did not recognize the GDR (excepting only the USSR, with which Bonn itself started exchanging ambassadors in 1955). While this move helped for a time to keep East Germany diplomatically cut off from much of the world, it also circumscribed Bonn's influence in the world because it prevented the FRG from maintaining relations with the Communist-ruled Eastern European governments, all of which recognized the GDR.

To Bonn's dismay, the Hallstein Doctrine cut little ice with the IOC, which essentially ignored it. For anticommunist hardliners in the FRG government, including Adenauer himself, the notion that an august international body like the IOC would accord *any* form of recognition to the GDR was shocking. On the eve of the Melbourne Olympics of 1956, Adenauer's government even contemplated boycotting these Games rather than going along with the unified team concept. Had Bonn taken this route, it would not have been entirely alone, for, in protest against the USSR's brutal suppression of the Hungarian Uprising in that year, Spain and The Netherlands pulled their teams from Melbourne rather than compete alongside the Soviets. But of course, in Bonn's case a boycott would have been entirely counterproductive because East German athletes would certainly have joined their Soviet comrades, making the GDR, not the FRG, look like the real German state. Gritting his teeth, Adenauer sanctioned the appearance of a unified German team in Melbourne after all.

Adenauer and the West German conservatives were even more distraught four years later on the eve of the Rome Games, for the GDR had just introduced its new flag, dubbed by Bonn the "Spalterfahne" (splitter flag). To the West German leaders, this innovation opened the horrible possibility that their nation's athletes and supporters in Rome might be compelled to see the GDR's reviled hammer and compass hoisted over the stadium. When the IOC jumped in at the last minute with its five-ring solution, Bonn was not much mollified, for it saw the traditional German banner, now exclusively Bonn's banner, as the only legitimate symbol for the German nation. To Adenauer, the flag compromise showed the IOC at its craven worst. The next thing you knew, he groused to Willi Daume, the committee would be allowing the Sarrasani Circus "to put an elephant on the flag," while the butchers' guild might be permitted to add its trademark "pig's head." Declaring that it would be "beneath the dignity of a German citizen to march under [the five-ringed flag]," the chancellor once again threatened a boycott. However, cooler heads in the NOCG managed yet again to convince the chancellor that a boycott would benefit only the GDR, and the unified German team, per IOC decree, marched into the Rome stadium bearing the multicolored five-ringed emblem that Baron de Coubertin himself had designed (in 1914!) as a symbol of Olympism's ability to unite all five continents.

In October 1963, eighty-seven-year-old Konrad Adenauer, whose government was mired in scandal and whose own personal welcome was wearing thin after fourteen years of imperious rule, stepped aside for a fellow Conservative, Ludwig Erhard. An expert on economics, the portly and affable Erhard was inclined to break away from Adenauer's self-isolating hard-line stance against the GDR and Eastern Europe. Yet, in the end, the replacement of "Der Alte" (the old man) by "Der Dicke" (the fat man) did not significantly improve relations with the East, either in politics or in sport.

The reason for this, of course, was that roughly two years before the changeover in Bonn a concrete wall had been thrown up by the GDR government around West Berlin to prevent East German citizens from continuing to use the now capitalist, western part of the former Reich capital as an avenue of escape to West Germany. For Bonn, the construction of the Berlin Wall made it impossible, at least for the time being, to even think of improving or normalizing relations with the East. How could one do normal business with a government that walled in its own citizens, while justifying its new (in GDR terminology) "Anti-Fascist Protective Barrier" as a necessary measure to prevent *Westerners* from moving east to subvert the "Socialist Workers' and Peasants' Paradise"?

In the realm of high-level sport outside the Olympic context, the erection of the Berlin Wall had a particularly profound impact because in previous years, despite great enmity between the two rival German governments, individual athletes and sporting associations from East and West had managed to maintain contacts with one another, especially in divided Berlin. Now, however, Bonn and the West Berlin municipal government ordered that such contacts be terminated forthwith. At a hastily convened meeting of West Germany's Deutscher Sportbund (German Sport Federation—DSB) in Düsseldorf on August 16, 1961, officials passed a resolution disallowing, so long as the Berlin barrier stood, ties between the DSB and East Germany's equivalent athletic associations, while also banning West German athletes from participating in international competitions "on the territory of the Soviet Occupation Zone [i.e., the GDR]." As additional punishment for the GDR, Bonn not only banned display of the East German "splitter flag" at international sporting events on West German territory but also embarked on a crusade to induce all other Western states to do the same.

At the Olympic level, however, the Wall had a less dramatic effect, at least for the moment. The IOC, true to its ideal of standing above politics, refused to abandon the unified German team concept for the next round of Olympics to be held in 1964 in Innsbruck, Austria, and Tokyo, Japan. Although Avery Brundage conceded that, in light of the Wall, cooperation between the two sides might be difficult, he nonetheless ordered officials from both sides of the barrier to sit down and work out a modus vivendi for the upcoming Games.

Neither side was happy with the arrangements that eventually emerged from a series of wearisome meetings, nor did they stop quarreling. The GDR, backed by Moscow, tried to convince the IOC to classify West Berlin as a separate political entity, forcing it to have its own Olympic committee and Olympic teams. West German officials not only rejected this effort to isolate West Berlin but also insisted that the walled city be allowed to host Olympic qualification rounds for the common German team. Furthermore, they said, any Eastern athletes who had fled to the West must be able to participate on the common team with no fear of retribution. The IOC ruled in the FRG's favor on these issues in October 1962.

Yet Bonn had good reason to resent the IOC's insistence on retaining the common German team for the next round of Olympics in 1964. The Summer Games in Tokyo proved to be especially problematical. Not only did the West Germans once again have to march side by side with East Germans under the common Olympic flag, as if Germany were one big happy family and the Wall did not exist, but in this instance they also had to march in a team that contained more Easterners than Westerners—194 versus 182. (In the qualifying competitions for the common team, Easterners had significantly outperformed Westerners for the first time.) For Bonn, this startling development was but a harbinger of worse things to come.

For the GDR, being able to outpace the much larger FRG in the production of Olympic athletes represented a significant milestone in that young state's struggle to be taken seriously as a sports factory. Oddly enough, though, high achievement in Olympic sport had not been a priority for East

Berlin's leadership at the time of the GDR's foundation in 1949. In that era, GDR sports officials and commentators echoed the older Communist line that big-time spectator sports, especially the Olympics, should actually be avoided by socialist nations because the primary function of these spectacles was to serve "capitalist exploiters" around the world as a tool to distract the toiling masses from their true class interests. As one GDR sporting publication put it, "The Olympic Games constitute a narcotic [to mask] the gray misery of everyday life for the workers." However, when the USSR elected to join the Olympic movement in 1951, and with Bonn staking its own (exclusive) claim to Olympic representation, East Berlin decided that it too should seek a place at the Olympic table.

As we have seen, pressure from Bonn helped to keep GDR athletes out of the Oslo and Helsinki Games of 1952, but the IOC's mandate for a unified German team thereafter came as a godsend to East Berlin because, as Communist Party chairman Walter Ulbricht quickly grasped, Olympic sport offered a golden opportunity for the GDR to challenge Bonn's preemptory claim to be the only legitimate Germany. In Ulbricht's eyes, the GDR was the *real* Germany, and it was time to stand up and say so. Thus, although on the very first unified German team—the one that appeared in the Cortina Winter Games of 1956—Easterners were outnumbered by Westerners fifty-one to twelve, the East German Communist newspaper *Neues Deutschland* crowed on opening day: "After many years of struggle for just recognition, the GDR steps for the first time into the Olympic forum. In the group of [German] athletes marching behind the officials we see more than a few who in their exceptional accomplishments supported our fight for Olympic recognition, who helped to bring glory and respect to the name of our Republic." In truth, real "glory" for GDR athletes would have to wait until the Melbourne Summer Games, since at Cortina, East German athletes won no medals at all, whereas at Melbourne they won six, including one gold (in boxing). Still, *Neues Deutschland* was not wrong to see that opening day ceremony at Cortina as a genuine breakthrough for the GDR.

Although, due to the IOC's compromise on symbolism for the combined German team, GDR athletes did not get to hear their own national anthem played at Melbourne or any subsequent Olympics through 1968, they started hearing "Risen from the Ruins" soon enough at other international athletic contests. Unlike the IOC, most international sports federations, including the prestigious International Amateur Athletic Federation (IAAF), recognized the GDR as a separate entity early on, allowing East German competitors to appear not only with their own national symbols but also in their own distinct uniforms. In order to maximize the number of times that athletes wearing these uniforms would appear on victory podiums around the world, Ulbricht's regime embarked on a concentrated program of sports development. In 1950 alone, some nineteen new training facilities and stadia were constructed as part of a national youth-development initiative. In the same year, Ulbricht opened the Hochschule für Körperkultur und Sport (German College of Physical Culture and Sport) in Leipzig, which soon turned into one of the world's premier nurseries of athletic talent. Here, young people who had shown exceptional promise in government-mandated sports programs could develop and refine their athletic skills free from any outside distractions. (That the blessings of this development program eventually included extensive experimentation with performance-enhancing drugs became evident only later.)

Along with its crusade to turn the GDR into a world-class athletic power, the Ulbricht regime embarked on an equally ambitious effort to enhance its political clout via the "glory" derived from growing sporting prowess. More specifically, the GDR leadership came to believe, at least for a brief period in the mid-1950s, that sport might prove to be a lever whereby the East might gain the upper hand in its bitter competition with the West for political stature and influence within the boundaries of the old German Reich. Might not sport even help facilitate a German reunification process in which *East Berlin*, not Bonn, called the shots? Hence, at a time when Bonn was complaining vociferously about being obliged to cooperate with East Berlin in unified Olympic teams, East German officials coined the motto "All Germans at a common table." Soon, they hoped, they would be sitting at the head of that table.

Of course, this was not to be—at least not in the political realm. In fact, sporting success at the international level turned out to have no discernible effect at all on the GDR's political stature in the FRG, where the powerful West German mark, not athletic medals, stood out as the chief emblem of national prowess. Once it became apparent to Ulbricht and the East German Socialist Unity Party that their "All Germans at a common table" idea did not provide them with a useful avenue for political penetration of the FRG, they abandoned it with as much alacrity as they had initially embraced it. Beginning in the late 1950s and early 1960s, GDR political leaders and sports bureaucrats demanded a separate Olympic team and the right to appear in Olympic competition with their own national symbols. To reinforce this demand, they insisted that the GDR was a far better steward of Olympic ideals than the FRG. More specifically, East Berlin claimed that, while West Germany deployed "professionals" on its Olympic teams and used the Olympics to buttress its nationalistic agenda, the GDR fully embraced Baron de Coubertin's emphasis on amateurism and on using Olympic sport to promote international peace and brotherhood.

In line with the GDR's growing effort to cultivate a separate East German identity and national pride among its citizenry, the state-controlled media began hailing the East German athletes on Germany's unified Olympic teams as heroes of the Workers' and Peasants' State. If an Eastern athlete achieved a victory, that victory was celebrated not as a success for "Germany" but strictly for the GDR and its socialist system. Thus, when the Dresden native Ingrid Kraemer unexpectedly won the 3-meter diving competition in the Rome Games, *Neues Deutschland* devoted reams of purple prose to her accomplishment, dubbing her the "golden girl from the German Democratic Republic."

If the GDR media coverage of the Rome Games gave the impression that, for all practical purposes, there were *two* Germanys engaged in Olympic competition, that impression was essentially correct. Genuine unity in the German Olympic program had been dubious from the moment the IOC had mandated it, and it became more so as time went on. West and East German athletes may have worn the same uniforms and competed under common colors, but their political minders made sure that they did not become too cozy with one another. During the 1956 Olympics, they did not even share living quarters or train together. At the 1960 Rome Games, the IOC insisted that all members of the unified German squad live together and train together, and the chief of mission for the German delegation, Gerhard Stöck (gold medalist in the javelin at the 1936 Berlin Games), claimed that his athletes were "getting along well with each other." But in fact, officials from the two states accompanying the team discouraged off-the-field socializing among their respective charges, and for the most part the athletes seem to have followed this non-fraternization order. (About the only thing that officials from the two Germanys could agree on in Rome was that the Italians had been very remiss in allowing Leni Riefenstahl's famous film about the Berlin Games, *Olympia*, to play in the Olympic Village.) At all the Olympic festivals involving "unified" German delegations, participation in major team sports, such as basketball, soccer, and ice hockey, provided no avenue for intra-German cooperation because separate qualification rounds in each state ensured homogeneous teams from *either* the East or the West. And of course, after 1961, the Berlin Wall made the two Germanys' purported Olympic "unity" even more strained. Brundage's "baby" had been ungainly as an infant, but by the early 1960s it had grown into a veritable freak.

A Bridge across the Wall?

By the early 1960s, many members of the IOC were increasingly fed up with the committee's quixotic experiment in German Olympic unity. Brundage, however, was not yet prepared to jettison his belief that Olympic sport could triumph over political divisions. In his view, even the building of the Berlin Wall was not proof that the two Germanys could not act as one on the field of Olympic play. On the contrary, he saw the Wall as simply a new challenge for the Olympic movement, another political obstacle to be overcome by the supposedly unifying power of international sport. For him, the only real question was exactly *how* the Olympic movement might subdue this latest political menace—and in the process salvage the IOC's much-maligned experiment in German Olympic togetherness.

Interestingly enough, a possible answer to this question—Berlin-Berlin Olympic Games transpiring on both sides of the Wall—did not originate with Brundage himself, though the alacrity with which the IOC president embraced this notion, along with that notion's imperial disregard of mundane political realities, gave it the stamp of a patented Brundage project, another Brundage baby.

The actual author of this bizarre idea was West Germany's own Willi Daume, the man who, as a German member of the IOC and also president of the West German Olympic Committee, would later lead the NOCG's campaign to bring the Olympics to Munich.

Born on May 24, 1913, Wilhelm "Willi" Karl August Ferdinand Daume grew up in a well-heeled Catholic family in the industrial city of Dortmund. His father owed an iron foundry and was a major figure in the town's social establishment. Young Willi showed a passion for sports early on, joining a local athletic club at the age of six. In high school and college he became such a star in handball and basketball that he played for the German national team in both sports. The high point of his sporting career came in 1936, when he was selected as a member of Germany's basketball squad for the Berlin Games—though, alas, he was only a substitute and never actually got to play in a game.

Although Willi Daume's background in athletics was well known when he later came to prominence as a sports administrator in postwar West Germany, another aspect of his biography received no attention whatsoever—his career during the Third Reich. After serving briefly in the Wehrmacht, Daume joined the Nazi Party on December 20, 1937. On the strength of his athletic credentials, he became a leader in various government-sponsored programs to develop sporting skills and fitness among the nation's youth.

For the Nazis, sport was crucial as an incubator of martial vigor and ideological zealotry. Daume fully subscribed to the notion that young people must pursue not just athletic excellence but also ideological purity and zest for battle. Thus, in 1940, he wrote in his sport club's bulletin: "The task is set, our idea is pure and clear. And for that idea we are willing to go through fire! But one does not go through fire cautiously, lest one get burned. No, one has to storm right through! To this end we demand of you great enthusiasm, great forcefulness, and great loyalty."

Along with his role as a sports functionary, Daume kept his hand in his family's foundry business, a domain where he could also serve the Nazi regime. In 1940, after the German occupation of Belgium, he ran an iron foundry in Antwerp that had been incorporated into his family's iron empire. While supplying the Reich with much-needed iron and steel, Daume's firm employed some sixty-five slave laborers. As of 1943, Daume added yet another dimension to his service to the Nazi system: he became an informer for the SD (the security arm of the SS), supplying information to Berlin on the political atmosphere in occupied Belgium. Daume's service as a snoop for the SD had the added advantage of keeping him out of the Wehrmacht and possible service on the Eastern Front, a fate which, despite all his talk about going through fire for the Führer, he desperately wanted to avoid.

Following the collapse of the Third Reich, Daume returned to Dortmund, where he divided his time between helping rebuild community sports programs and working in the family foundry business. In November 1945, he filled out a British Military Government de-Nazification questionnaire, which required respondents to specify what they had done during the Hitler era. Not surprisingly, like virtually every other German with a "brown past," Daume significantly downplayed his involvement in the Nazi system. The British authorities, with whom the personable young industrialist had developed quite cordial relations, allowed him to continue on with his activities, both in sport development and in business.

In spring 1948, however, Daume was forced to fill out another questionnaire and undergo a formal de-Nazification hearing. Once again, he airbrushed his past, admitting his service in the Wehrmacht but saying nothing about his Nazi Party membership or informant work for the SD. Furthermore, he claimed that in his role as a sports functionary he had restricted himself to "technical issues" and entirely avoided "the political realm." He even went so far as to portray himself as a "victim" of National Socialism, claiming that local party bosses in Dortmund had made "difficulties" for him because he had stood up for people opposed to the Nazi system. Alas, he could offer no credible documentation for his supposed victim status, and the British authorities ended up placing him in category IV ("Mitläufer"—collaborator) and fining him DM 1000.

Although this punishment was a mere slap on the wrist, it was too harsh for Daume to accept. In January 1949, he appealed the ruling to a special court established for this purpose. His lawyers promised to bring in evidence of "active resistance" on his part against the Third Reich. Even though, once again, no exculpating evidence was actually produced, the appeals court, now manned exclusively by Germans, reclassified him in category V as *unbelastet*—untainted. As justification for this decision, the court argued that Daume had clearly "rejected Nazism in his heart."

Equipped with what his contemporaries mockingly called a *Persils-chein*—that is, a whitewash, named after a popular detergent—Daume did not need to worry very much about his role in the Third Reich as he expanded the family business and worked his way up the ladder of the West German sports establishment. Nobody wanted to talk much about the recent past—the focus was all on rebuilding for the present and the future. But even if Daume had not been able to reinvent himself as an opponent of National Socialism, his actual service to the Hitler state would not have been too great a liability in an era when Soviet Communism, not vanquished Nazism, was perceived as the primary threat to the Western world.

As it happened, Daume owed his biggest break as a sports functionary in postwar Germany—his election to the IOC in 1956—largely to the help of another former Nazi who had reinvented himself as a convinced democrat in the new era: Ritter von Halt. Having worked extensively with Daume in West Germany's embryonic sports establishment, von Halt in 1953 recommended the younger man enthusiastically to his old drinking buddy, Avery Brundage (with whom Halt had traveled around Germany in 1934):

> Willi Daume, an industrialist, owner of an iron foundry, is also a man of extraordinary winning manners and possesses a well-founded knowledge in sports administrations. He is the president of the German Sports Federation, the roof [umbrella] organization of all specialized sports organizations in Germany, and a presidential member of the German National Olympic Committee. He used to be a handball and basketball player and as such was in the German team at the Olympic Games in Berlin. Daume can also hold his own and does not let himself be used by anybody—so that he will meet Olympic standards in this respect, too. He is 38 years old and speaks French and English. He has a young and charming wife.

Through his work in the West German Olympic Committee and the IOC, Daume had always supported Brundage's project of a unified German Olympic team, though once the Berlin Wall went up he had severe doubts about the viability of this experiment. He also believed, however, that Bonn's freeze on German-German sporting ties in the wake of the Wall was dangerously isolating West Germany in the world of international sport. Knowing of his friend Brundage's almost mystical belief in the power of high-level sport to work political miracles, Daume asked the president in early 1963 what he thought about the notion of both West and East Berlin submitting a joint bid for the 1968 Summer Olympic Games. As he explained the idea, each half of the divided city would host a share of the competitions and ancillary events, thereby, in effect, throwing a sporting bridge over the Berlin Wall. For the pragmatic Daume, this proposal had the added advantage of making the FRG look open and flexible, while forcing the GDR either to negate the power of its Wall or to come clean about that barrier's imprisoning rationale. As Daume expected, Brundage embraced the proposal enthusiastically, calling it, according to the German functionary, "an excellent idea."

Another early advocate of Daume's—and now Brundage's—Wall-transcending idea was West Berlin's ruling mayor, the Social Democrat Willy Brandt, then still a darling of the United States' Cold War establishment. Increasingly desperate for ways to make the wall around his city more porous, Brandt signed on to the "sporting bridge" gambit as one such possibility. For him, another obvious selling point was the opportunity to showcase the Western half of the old Reich capital as a completely "new" Berlin—a bastion of freedom and democracy different not only from the "old" Berlin but also from that other Berlin across the Wall.

Enticing as a Berlin-Berlin Olympiad may have been to its principal advocates, it never got much beyond the talking stage because virtually no one else found anything to like in this project. Crucially, both the FRG and GDR governments objected vehemently to the proposal on political grounds. Bonn worried that an Olympic festival held partly in West Berlin would emphasize that city's unique status as an entity that was not fully integrated into the Federal Republic, perhaps even leading to its transformation into an autonomous "free city" decoupled entirely from the FRG, an idea Moscow was then pushing. Bonn's conservatives also worried that Berlin-Berlin Olympics could elevate the influence and clout of the Social Democrat Willy Brandt, who was known to have political ambitions beyond his walled city. The GDR government, for its part, understood full well that a Berlin-Berlin Olympiad would either open big holes in its new

"Anti-Fascist Protective Barrier" or place the Wall's true imprisoning function in the glare of the world spotlight, neither of which was desirable from its point of view.

In early June 1963, East Berlin sent a delegation to Lausanne with the goal of "exposing" Daume's proposal as "a great provocation." In Lausanne, the GDR officials pointed out that they had never been consulted on the Berlin-Berlin Olympic project, nor had anyone contacted the GDR government, whose permission to use its territory for any Olympic events was obviously necessary. The delegates took this opportunity also to complain about Bonn's continuing "discrimination" against GDR athletes, citing recent visa denials to Eastern sportsmen as cases in point. Clearly, a country like the FRG, intent only on pursuing its "narrow chauvinistic" agenda, could not genuinely be interested in intra-German cooperation. Under no conditions, then, would the GDR consent to be part of Willi Daume's "deceptive charade."

Even Brundage, who was present in Lausanne at the IOC meeting with the GDR delegation, could see that there was no hope for a Berlin-Berlin Olympics in 1968: this particular baby was stillborn.

And yet, if the notion of a Berlin-Berlin Olympiad in 1968 ended up going nowhere, this episode was not without consequence for the future of the Olympic movement; for Germany's role within that movement; and, more specifically, for the Munich Games of 1972. For the IOC, abandoning the Berlin project meant burying the dream of overcoming Germany's division via a unified Olympic team. For Willi Daume and the NOCG, the ill-fated Berlin gambit constituted the springboard from which they would soon leap forth with an alternative Olympic venue proposal: Munich.

"A German Paradise": Munich's Olympic Application

At a meeting in Madrid on October 5, 1965, the IOC voted overwhelmingly to end its troubled experiment in German unity at the Olympic Games. At the upcoming 1968 Olympic festivals in Grenoble, France, and Mexico City, Mexico, Germany would be represented by *two* teams, one from the FRG and one from the GDR. As if alarmed by its own daring move, however, the committee also ruled at Madrid that, at least for the '68 Games, the two German teams would still have to appear with the common Olympic symbolism deployed in earlier festivals. East Germany, moreover, would not be listed under its official name, Deutsche Demokratische Republik, but as "Ostdeutschland."

West Germany's National Olympic Committee might have been expected to be up in arms over the IOC's Madrid decision, but Willi Daume thought he saw in it a possible opportunity rather than a clear setback. Freed from its imposed coupling with the prickly East Germans, the NOCG could shift its focus from German-German cohabitation to a very different enterprise: attracting the Games to a West German city—something Daume had dreamed of achieving since becoming president of the committee in 1960. The ambitious functionary saw hosting the Olympics as an excellent means of showing off a new political system—West Germany's fledgling parliamentary democracy. As he later wrote concerning this ambition, "In the end, the best way of showing the world what the new Germany really is like, what it has to offer in terms of humane values and culture, is to invite the youth of the world to the free part of Germany [to participate] in Olympic Games." Daume further believed that this particular moment, the post-Madrid moment, was especially propitious for a West German Olympic bid because the IOC, having just made a major concession to the East, would be of a mind to compensate the West.

As for possible West German host cities, Daume quickly settled on Munich as the strongest possible candidate. In recent years, with divided Berlin a mere shadow of its former self and provincial Bonn no more than a political ghetto (John Le Carré's *Small Town in Germany*), Munich had emerged as Germany's "secret capital"—the city most West Germans considered their nation's best answer to London, Paris, and Rome. Not only was Munich West Germany's fastest growing city, adding about fifty thousand residents each year, it also had become the FRG's wealthiest and most economically vibrant metropolis, having attracted from Berlin major commercial enterprises like Siemens and Allianz Insurance. In 1964, Hamburg's *Der Spiegel*, the FRG's most prominent newsmagazine, could say of Munich that it was "the only city in Germany that Hitler promised to make great—and that became great nonetheless." If *The Times* (London) could be believed, Munich even had "the prettiest and best-dressed girls in Germany." Perhaps most important, as Daume well knew, the handsome Bavarian capital, with its boisterous beer halls and annual Oktoberfest, along with its lively culture, laid-back atmosphere, and scenic surroundings, was internationally the best loved of all German cities, attracting by far the largest number of foreign tourists. But as he contemplated Munich's prospects in the immediate wake of the Madrid meeting, Daume also knew that, if he was to get his candidate city's feathered alpine hat into the ring for '72, he would have to work very fast: the application deadline, December 31, 1965, was less than three months away.

At the end of October 1965, Daume strode into the office of Hans-Jochen Vogel, Munich's popular Social Democratic mayor, and asked him out of the blue what he thought about the idea of a Munich bid for the 1972 Olympics. Vogel almost fell out of his chair. As he wrote in his memoirs, "No one would have even dreamed that Munich might one day host the Olympic Games." As soon as he had recovered his composure, Vogel asked Daume if he was aware that Munich was completely bereft of the athletic facilities necessary to host a modern Olympic festival. Above all, it lacked a large multi-purpose stadium of the kind that had become a sine-qua-non for the Games. He also reminded Daume (as if the latter needed such reminding) of the bitter fights between the FRG and GDR over status and clout in the Olympic movement—a long and tedious quarrel that he was sure would predispose the IOC against *any* German city. Finally, there was the inconvenient fact of Munich's problematical past—its highly prominent role as "Capital of the Nazi Movement" during the Third Reich. Who could forget that?

Of course, Daume was well aware of all these drawbacks, but he quickly made clear to Vogel that he did not think they posed insurmountable barriers to a successful application. The FRG, he reported coyly, had "many friends" on the IOC—friends who, in the wake of the Madrid decision, were "anxious to do something for the West Germans." His friend Avery Brundage, having been obliged to drop the idea of a Berlin-Berlin Olympiad, had discreetly let it be known that he might "look with favor" on a bid from Munich. (Brundage, we should note, had "fallen in love with Munich" during the 1936 Winter Olympics in Garmisch-Partenkirchen, for which nearby Munich had hosted most of the cultural events.) As for Munich's lack of existing facilities, said Daume, the IOC actually *preferred* it when host cities were obliged to build brand new Olympic arenas; this ensured state-of-the-art facilities and guaranteed major Olympic legacies in those cities. Munich's Nazi past was not really much of a problem either, Daume opined. After all, Brundage himself continued to tout the Nazi-sponsored 1936 Berlin Games as "a great success" and remained openly proud that as head of the American Olympic Committee in those days he had helped to avert a U.S. boycott of Berlin. And finally, confided Daume, the competition for summer '72 was relatively weak, there being as yet no "serious contenders."

With his insider confidence and ebullient enthusiasm for Munich, Daume managed to leave Mayor Vogel "half-convinced" that his town had "an outside chance" for the Games after all. And yet, considering this idea more fully, Mayor Vogel worried that a plethora of other impediments might turn out to be "almost insurmountable." Would the Soviets and other Eastern Europeans accept Munich, he asked himself? Would Bonn allow the GDR flag to be hoisted on West German territory, as the IOC would undoubtedly demand? Could Munich complete its ambitious new public transportation system (the metro and metropolitan railway, or U-Bahn and S-Bahn) in a mere seven years rather than in the projected twelve years? And above all, how would the necessary Olympic facilities be financed? Munich, he knew, could not undertake this task on its own despite its relative prosperity: Would the national and Bavarian state governments be prepared to jump in and help? Turning these questions around in his head hour after hour, Vogel finally came to the conclusion that the prospect of outside funding for Munich's necessary infrastructure improvements was strong enough to warrant making a bid for the Games. He decided then and there to start working on an Olympic application.

Although Vogel knew that Munich's candidacy could not go forward without backing from Bonn, his first sales trip took him not to the Rhine but to West Berlin—and to the office of Mayor Willy Brandt. Why Brandt? Support from Brandt was crucial, Vogel believed, because if Brandt concluded that an Olympic bid from Munich would add to the difficulties for his beleaguered half-city, he would undoubtedly act to kill the enterprise. As it happened, Vogel caught his colleague at a propitious moment. Having seen the quixotic Daume-Brundage idea of a Berlin-Berlin Olympics quickly come to grief, Brandt was looking for new ways to improve the relations between the two Germanys—thereby, perhaps, relieving the isolation of West Berlin. Instead of seeing a Munich Olympiad as injurious to that endeavor, Brandt saw it as possibly beneficial. After all, to secure the Games in the first place, Munich and Bonn would have to assure the IOC that East German athletes and visitors to the Games would be welcomed and cordially treated in the FRG. As for those thorny matters of national symbolism, Brandt suggested to Vogel that they might not even be an issue by 1972. (Here Brandt turned out to be right, but he could not have known at the time he made this prophecy that it would be proven correct in large part because by then he himself would have become the West German chancellor.)

Relieved that Brandt was on board, Vogel sought the blessing of the Bavarian state government. Perhaps surprisingly, this was not a given. The "Freistaat Bayern" (Free State of Bavaria) was dominated by the arch-conservative Christian Social Union (CSU), which had run the state since the creation of the Federal Republic in 1949. The state government tended to look with some suspicion on Munich, which had a Socialist in the mayor's office and a Social Democratic Party (SPD) majority on its city council. Then, too, Munich possessed a reputation for louche worldliness and bohemian flair that sometimes put it at odds with the staunchly conservative Bavarian heartland—the *Ur-Bayern* of small towns and prosperous farms. On the other hand, Vogel himself was anything but a bohemian—he belonged to the right wing of the Bavarian SPD—and he got along well with Bavaria's CSU leadership, whose commitment to economic growth and modernization he shared. Over time, in fact, the mayor grew increasingly impatient with those among his fellow citizens for whom, in his words, "Munich" still meant "the Munich of 1914," or perhaps even a static imaginary city that "had never existed at all."

Thus, when Vogel broached the question of a Munich bid for the '72 Olympics to Alfons Goppel (CSU), Bavaria's minister-president, the Conservative leader immediately promised his support. Bavarian minister of culture Ludwig Huber (likewise CSU) also jumped on board, which was important because Vogel and Daume planned to make Munich's vaunted cultural richness a key ingredient in their campaign for the Games. Decidedly less enthusiastic were various middle-level bureaucrats from the Finance Ministry, who, like bean counters everywhere, worried about costs and budgets. They did not think Bavaria could afford an "extravagance" like the Olympics, even if help from Bonn was forthcoming. In the end, however, Goppel was able to overcome the doubters, in no small part because he found a crucial ally in Franz Josef Strauß, the powerful CSU chairman who was also to become federal finance minister in late 1966. Strauß foresaw significant political and economic gains for Bavaria and West Germany through hosting an Olympic festival. On December 14, 1965, the Bavarian Landtag voted unanimously to support Munich's Olympic bid and to cover one-third of the costs of putting on the '72 Summer Games.

Even before the Landtag gave its nod of approval, Vogel and Daume prepared to take Munich's case to the federal government. Their task in Bonn, they feared, would be considerably more difficult. The biggest stumbling block involved Bonn's continuous policy of non-recognition of the GDR, which the conservative FRG government stubbornly persisted in referring to as the "Soviet Occupation Zone." Believing that the IOC was likely in the near future to allow both Germanys to participate in Olympic competition as fully sovereign states, Daume knew that if Bonn retained its hard-line stance vis-à-vis the GDR, Munich's chances for the Games were virtually zero.

Another problem involved financial support from the Bund (federal government). After a number of boom years, the West German economy had begun to turn sour in the mid-1960s, resulting in unprecedented budget deficits. In his campaign to be confirmed as chancellor in the September 1965 Bundestag elections, Ludwig Erhard had promised to cut government spending significantly in order to balance the budget. Clearly, it would be hard to square this promise with a decision to provide financial backing for a Munich Olympic festival.

On November 29, 1965, Vogel, Daume, and a small delegation of fellow Olympic petitioners arrived in Bonn for their crucial meeting with Erhard's government. Vogel, who led the delegation, was determined to make the strongest possible case for his city, but he was doubtful about his prospects. Hoping at the outset to undercut possible financial objections to Munich's candidacy, he laid out a quite modest budget estimate of DM 550 million, of which Bonn would need to contribute only one-third, since the Bavarian state and the Munich municipality would together cover the other two-thirds. Just as Vogel had feared, one of Erhard's advisors, chief of the Chancellor's Office Ludger Westrick, cast doubt (legitimately, as it turned out) on the reliability of the cost estimate, while reminding his boss of his campaign promise to cut government expenditures. Westrick also harped on the flag and anthem issue, observing that Bonn could hardly continue asking other NATO nations to disallow GDR symbols at international sporting events on their soil if the FRG did not follow this practice itself.

Just as Erhard seemed to be tilting in the direction of his ministerial naysayer, Vogel and Daume launched one last plea, focusing on the political benefits that would surely accrue to the FRG if the Games were to return to German soil after a thirty-six-year absence. Here was a chance, they said, for the Germans (at least the West Germans) to show the world how much they had changed since the end of the Third Reich!

But if Erhard was impressed by this argument, he apparently did not show it, at least initially. Thus, when he suddenly announced, after yet more discussion, that he actually stood *in favor* of the Munich bid, the shock was great on all sides, according to Vogel. The chancellor's justification for his stance was also unexpected. This strict fiscal conservative declared that, precisely in a time of economic difficulty, it was not useful "to keep blowing on the horn of distress." The fact was, he said, people needed some "good news" on occasion. In short, why not let Munich have a try at bringing home the Olympic bacon?

With Erhard's imprimatur, the Finance Committee of the Bundestag duly voted to support Munich's Olympic bid, though with the caveat that, if costs turned out to exceed DM 520 million, an additional vote would be required. On November 30, the full house of the Bundestag accepted the Finance Committee recommendation, following a peroration from Franz Josef Strauß extolling the bid and insisting that Bonn "could certainly afford [to host the Games] despite its budgetary situation."

Even more importantly, Chancellor Erhard, over the objections of Westrick and other hardliners, agreed not to impose visa restrictions on any Olympic participants, including those from the GDR. Yet, there still remained the question of whether, with respect to the GDR, Bonn would relax its ban on the "splitter flag" or "Becher-Hymn" on FRG soil. Knowing that Erhard would have trouble conceding any ground here, Daume and Vogel simply avoided saying anything about their plans for ceremony and national symbolism in Munich. This issue would have to be tackled later, if and when their bid passed muster with the IOC.

Tellingly, Munich's Olympic bid encountered skepticism not only in Bonn but also in some of the larger West German cities—rival metropolises that had not taken kindly to Munich's self-proclaimed "secret capital" status. Hamburg, the FRG's largest city (and also one of its eleven federal states), had long looked down its patrician nose at the rustic Bavarian capital. Thus, the announcement of Munich's Olympic bid provoked withering condescension from Hamburg's leading sports official, Gerhard Stöck (the ex-Olympian who had presided over the unified German team at Rome in 1960), who jeered, "[Munich's application] for the 1972 Games surprises me greatly. I had never expected it. For me, *Berlin* is the only German city that is Olympia-worthy." As for his own home town, Hamburg, Stöck insisted that local officials had never even contemplated an Olympic bid because the port city's lack of adequate athletic facilities would have made such a move presumptuous. Stöck did concede that Munich, with its many charms, might be attractive to outsiders, but he harbored "the suspicion" that the actual motive behind its Olympic campaign was a hope of finally securing "representative" athletic facilities at someone else's expense. Meanwhile, the Lower Saxon capital of Hanover, which called itself "Germany's Sports-City Number One," was equally miffed. Its leading sports official noted that his town, like Munich, might have had an interest in hosting the Olympics, but unlike Munich it had the good sense to realize that such a task was "beyond its financial resources."

Even some prominent West German athletes were flabbergasted by the sheer chutzpa of the Munich bid. West German hurdles champion Inge Schell told the *Münchner Merkur* newspaper, "Oh my, oh my, this is just a fairy tale!" Rainer Schubert, the German 400-meter champion, asked, "Can this [the application] really be serious? The idea is completely improbable."

Meanwhile, newspaper commentary around the country generally took the line "We wish the Münchners luck; they're certainly going to need it!"

In the hectic period while still working to secure a green light from Bavaria and the Bund, and to overcome the internal German sniping, Vogel and Daume also rushed to put together a formal written proposal they could present to the IOC before the rapidly approaching deadline. Amazingly, they managed to craft a polished, and indeed quite brilliant, application in a matter of a few weeks. The bid profited from excellent salesmanship skills on the part of its authors but also from Willi Daume's keen understanding of just what the IOC was looking for in a host city at that particular historical juncture.

By the mid-1960s, as Daume well knew, the IOC (especially Brundage) had become exasperated with ever larger, ever more expensive Olympic extravaganzas. Most recently, Rome and Tokyo had hosted Summer Games as big, sprawling, and unwieldy as those cities were themselves. Mexico City promised to be even worse. Among other drawbacks, the recent festivals had turned out to be transportation nightmares for Olympic visitors and even athletes, who because of long distances between venues and gargantuan traffic jams sometimes arrived late for the events they hoped to see or, worse yet, participate in. Wasn't it time to downsize a bit, to make the Games more manageable and civilized for both athletes and spectators?

Munich's application directly addressed this issue. It promised an Olympics of "kurze Wege" (short distances)—easily walkable routes between most of the relevant venues, which would be concentrated in one part of the city. (As was the case with the 1936 Berlin Games, however, the sailing events, which required serious water, would have to take place up in Kiel, on the North Sea. It also became necessary to stage the whitewater canoeing events in nearby Augsburg.) At Munich, athletes would also be able to stroll from the principal training and competition sites to their housing units in the Olympic Village, where the Olympic Press Center would be located as well. The entire Olympic complex would be quite close to downtown, quickly and conveniently reachable by surface roads or by a brand new subway line. Although the proposal guaranteed up-to-date and technically sophisticated facilities for athletes, journalists, and spectators, it also, quite cleverly, promised to keep costs and size in check—to put on an Olympic festival reflecting the "sensible modesty" of a mid-sized Northern European metropolis.

Another crotchet harbored by Brundage's IOC in the mid-1960s had to do with culture—or, more precisely, with an excess of cultural hoopla at recent Olympic festivals. The ancient Games had involved an inspirational melding of athletic play, religious ritual, and cultural creativity, a mixture of mind and muscle that Baron de Coubertin had hoped to revive in the modern Games. For much of the modern Games' early history, however, the festivals had been woefully short of serious culture, offering a bit of kitschy folklore here, a bit of light entertainment there. Interestingly enough, one exception to this rule had been the 1936 Berlin Games, where the organizers had made a concerted effort to emulate the ancient Greek example. Although the IOC under Brundage continued to believe that culture was important—Brundage himself, after all, was a serious collector of Oriental art—the committee also felt that Rome and Tokyo had gone overboard with their cultural offerings, and Mexico City, which promised a *full year* of international cultural events, was taking Coubertin's marriage of sport and spirit way too far. Cautioned by the IOC to keep Munich's cultural ambitions in check, and to focus exclusively on national and local assets, Daume promised to abide by the committee's strictures. In reality, however, he and Vogel were not about to be one-upped in the cultural domain by the Italians and Japanese, much less the Mexicans. Germany, after all, was the land of *Dichter und Denker* (poets and thinkers), and Munich itself was nothing if not a *Kulturstadt* extraordinaire. Moreover, as we shall see, the Munich organizers proved quite unwilling to restrict their cultural show to local and national attractions, something they believed that Germans above all could not afford to do.

Cleverly, however, the cultural component in Munich's Olympic bid did focus on home-ground attributes. Opening with a specific pledge "to finally fulfill the International Olympic Committee's long-held desire for a unique demonstration of the unity of sport and art," the application's detailed sub-section on culture reminded IOC voters that "Munich possesses countless valuable cultural monuments, artistic institutions, and splendid artworks deriving from an 800-year-old history spanning the Romanesque and Gothic, the Baroque and Rococo, Classicism and Romanticism, and the modern civilization of the twentieth century." More specifically, Munich boasted one of the world's greatest opera houses, three world-class philharmonic orchestras, seventeen major theaters, and twenty-three museums. Above all, the petition emphasized, Munich's culture was a *living* culture, cultivated not just as a bridge to the glorious past but also as a vehicle of education and character-formation, an ongoing enterprise attracting "hundreds of thousands of visitors each year from the entire civilized world."

Of course, as Daume and Vogel well understood, those international hordes descending on Munich every year did not come merely, or even primarily, to worship at the altar of high culture: they came to party down and gluttonize. Fitting for a city that hosted the annual Oktoberfest bacchanal, a kind of Olympics of boozing and eating, Munich harbored dozens of beer halls, wine cellars, and "traditional" Bavarian restaurants, where patrons consumed heroic portions of Sauerbraten, Weisswurst, and Ochsenfleisch, all washed down with liter-sized steins of Löwenbräu. The town's bohemian quarter, Schwabing, harbored over three hundred cabarets, bars, and coffee-houses sporting names like Ba-ba-lu, Captain Cook, and the Love Story Club. Naturally, the city also boasted a plethora of hotels, inns, and pensions, running from the very grand to the "merely comfortable" (translation: barely habitable). Already a world leader in tourism, Munich was busily building more hostelries and would be able by the time of the '72 Games to accommodate "one hundred thousand guests in a fully satisfactory manner."

Lest IOC voters conclude that Munich lived *too much* on its hospitality industry—on catering to sensual tastes both high and low—the application also emphasized Munich's importance as a leading center of industry, commerce, and technology. In part, this status derived from Munich's strategic location on Germany's main Autobahn routes and primary European rail corridors, as well as from its international airport, which served "practically all the large world airlines." Also key to Munich's global industrial clout were cutting-edge manufacturing firms like BMW, Siemens, and MAN (a major builder of diesel trucks, busses, and other utility vehicles). Then, too, Munich had succeeded Berlin as Germany's new movie capital, its Bavaria Studios producing films of international renown. (Even Billy Wilder had been forced to move the final shooting in 1963 for his Cold War comedy *One, Two, Three* from Berlin to Munich in order to avoid complications due to the presence of the Berlin Wall.) Equally noteworthy were the city's higher education institutions like the famed Ludwig-Maximilium Universität and its younger, but no less prestigious, counterpart, the Technical University. The rich history of Germany's and Munich's technological and scientific achievement was on grand display at the Deutsches Museum, a mammoth facility situated on an island in the Isar River.

Proud as they were of Munich's manufacturing, educational, and entertainment-industry attainments, Daume and Vogel understood that other assets, those in the form of natural beauty, tranquility, clean air, and a salubrious climate, were probably more important to Olympic visitors than factories or universities. And in this domain, they knew that the Bavarian capital was especially blessed, a distinction they were not about to let go unnoticed. Thus, their written bid contained another long sub-section pointing up Munich's proximity to the towering Bavarian Alps and to a host of beautiful sub-Alpine lakes, all of which offered "many opportunities for relaxation and scenic enjoyment." Picturesque mountain villages like Garmisch-Partenkirchen, Ettal, Oberammergau, and Berchtesgaden were all "quickly and conveniently reachable by private auto or train from Munich." In the city itself, visitors could find natural balm for their souls in beautiful parks like the Englischer Garten, a huge oasis of greens, small hills, streams, and ponds adjacent to the historic town center. Of course, the Alps-fed Isar River flowed right through the town. As for climate, here too Munich could hardly be topped. Its altitude (510 meters above sea level) and latitude (48 degrees, 7 minutes) helped provide very favorable temperatures and humidity levels during the summer months. In recent years, the temperature in July and August had averaged 17.2 degrees Celsius, with an average humidity of 68 percent. What was more, in the summer months Munich typically experienced 7.7 hours of sunshine every day!

Contemplating all these riches, natural and manmade, historical and contemporary, Munich's boosters found it fitting to conclude their petition by echoing the praises of their city sung by the American writer Thomas Wolfe, who had visited the town in the early 1920s. In his 1925 novel *The Web and the Rock*, Wolfe gushed, "What could one say about Munich, except that it was a kind of German paradise?"

Selling Munich

Even before Daume and Vogel had officially handed in Munich's bid to the IOC, exactly one day before the deadline, voices of opposition to an Olympic host role for the erstwhile "Capital of the [Nazi] Movement" made themselves heard around the world. The situation was a little reminiscent of the mid-1930s, when the IOC's decision to allow the 1936 Summer Games to go forward in Nazi-governed Berlin had ignited a global protest movement. At a press conference on November 30, 1965, where Mayor Vogel announced Munich's Olympic bid to the public, various foreign journalists could not help but bring up the specter of 1936. How, they asked, could a country that had so recently hosted "Hitler's Games" expect the Olympics to return to German soil, especially when the soil in question concerned the *very heart* of the old German evil?

The heavy legacy of the past even weighed on the discussions of the Olympic bid held in Munich's City Council. While most Council members believed the Games offered an excellent opportunity to show the world a new Munich and a new Germany, at least one delegate cautioned against getting puffed up over the "honor" and "prestige" that might come with hosting an Olympic festival. It was dangerous to speak of "national prestige," he said, because "in the era prior to 1945 far too much suffering" had come from pursuing this will-of-the-wisp. Tellingly, with an eye to the "political reservations" being raised outside Germany to the prospect of an Olympiad in the former "Capital of the Nazi Movement," the *Süddeutsche Zeitung*, Munich's most respected newspaper, suggested that perhaps "we [Germans] are the only ones who are continually astonished at [the persistence of] such reminiscences, having become world champions of forgetting."

Sensing Munich's particular vulnerability growing out of its "tainted past," a coalition of cities in the industrial Ruhr District suddenly offered their region to the NOCG as a better option than the Bavarian capital, arguing, rather dubiously, that this aging rust belt not only would attract less foreign antagonism than Munich but also had greater need of a financial shot in the arm due to its terribly distressed economic condition. But this last-minute petition got nowhere, since the IOC made clear that it could consider bids only from single cities.

A more serious threat came from Vienna, whose mayor sought to put together an eleventh-hour bid for '72. Fortunately for Munich, that idea came to naught because the Austrian government refused to back it on financial grounds. For a brief moment, it looked like Moscow might also apply, a prospect that threw panic into the Munich ranks. But in the end, Moscow had to back off largely because, as a Russian sports official conceded to the IOC, the Soviet capital was not yet physically prepared to host the Games; its immediate priority was the construction of new housing. Moreover, although this was not stated publicly, the Soviet government was unwilling to guarantee free and equal access to its territory to all Olympic participants. In particular, worried over offending Beijing, the Soviets were not prepared "to allow a team from Taiwan to appear with sovereign rights in Moscow."

Among the remaining contenders, Montreal was generally regarded as the most serious threat, although one German commentator insisted that *Detroit* was Munich's most dangerous rival. After all, as this journalist noted, the Michigan city was applying for the *seventh* time: might not this Yankee tenacity finally win over the hard-to-get hearts of the IOC? Moreover, noted the journalist, Detroit was "the greatest automobile city in the world" and enjoyed solid backing from General Motors, Ford, and Chrysler, not to mention the U.S. government. How could Munich stand up to such industrial and political firepower? (In fact, not only did Detroit never stand a chance to win the '72 Games, but those Games, as we shall see, perhaps contributed in a roundabout way to Detroit's loss of dominance in the world auto industry.)

No sooner had Munich submitted its bid in Lausanne than a new band of critics cropped up—signaling the onset of a fierce resistance that would persist up to and even beyond the moment when the IOC selected the Bavarian capital as its host city for summer '72.

One of those early shots across Munich's bow came from within Bavaria itself. A group of disgruntled CSU Bavarian Landtag delegates, despite having already voted to approve state funding for a Munich Olympic festival, telegrammed Vogel on March 24, 1966, stating that, because of the "extremely straightened financial situation" prevailing in Bavaria, the NOCG "must withdraw its Olympic bid forthwith." But it wasn't just the economic angle that vexed these in-house critics. Hosting the Games, they warned, would mean "more noise and traffic chaos" for Munich, "more population growth and price increases," and, perhaps worst of all, "more foreign guest workers." And why in God's name was Munich trying to get the Games when the city and surrounding region desperately needed more classrooms, hospitals, water services, science research facilities, and athletic grounds for young people? "We in Bavaria can't have everything," they declared, "and we must not bite off more than we can chew."

From our point of view today, what is especially interesting about this catalogue of complaints is how similar it sounds to the objections that regularly crop up in some quarters every time a city makes itself a candidate to host the Olympic Games. These days, the prospect of putting on an Olympic show invariably generates a good deal of internal protest. In 1966, however, this kind of internecine carping was not yet widespread, and for Vogel it represented little more than a minor irritation. He brushed off these in-house critics with reassurances that Munich had tendered its Olympic bid "only after carefully weighing all the factors involved." In any event, he pointedly asked, if these parliamentarians were so opposed to this enterprise, why had they not voiced their objections during the recent Landtag debates on the issue?

Vogel had little difficulty dispatching this weak and belated challenge from the home front, but he and Daume faced a much more dangerous and tenacious opponent in the GDR, which turned out to be vehemently opposed to a Munich Olympiad and was prepared to pull out all the stops to prevent such an outrage from materializing.

In a secret assessment of Munich's Olympic application compiled in mid-March 1966, officials from the top GDR sports association warned that Munich's prospects for landing the '72 Games looked alarmingly good, especially since Vienna and Moscow had opted out of the race. Avery Brundage was known "to have reacted positively" to Munich's bid, as had an influential Swiss IOC delegate, Marc Holder, who reportedly argued that the committee must bring the Games back to the heart of Europe after their recent sojourn in Asia and their impending visit to Latin America (Mexico City). Munich's emphasis in its application on connecting sport with culture (on a modest scale) had "also gone down well with the IOC," echoing as it did de Coubertin's vision of a merger of mind and muscle. But the *real* grand strategy behind Munich's bid, insisted these GDR observers, was "to allow the West German imperialists to enlist the Olympic Games in a campaign to elevate the political prestige of the FRG." More specifically, Bonn hoped by bringing the Games to Munich to improve Bonn's "hitherto weak status among the young nations of Africa and Asia" and to strengthen its "political offensive against the GDR." These nefarious aspirations for Munich, concluded the GDR officials, suggested "ominous parallels" with those harbored by the "German fascists" in 1936, when the Nazis had misused the Berlin and Garmisch Olympics to promote "their criminal political agenda."

But it was precisely this echo of 1936, opined these same officials, which offered some hope that Munich's Olympic candidacy might be nipped in the bud. After all, "many people in Germany and elsewhere" had taken note of the "parallels" between what West Germany hoped to do in 1972 and what Nazi Germany had done in 1936. Moreover, and equally encouraging, people around the world seemed to understand that the IOC, by awarding the Games to Munich, would vastly "add to the political difficulties connected to the German division." On the other hand, one could by no means count on the IOC's doing the right thing in this matter; there was a real danger that the committee might give the Olympics to Munich after all, thereby handing "the West German militarists [a golden opportunity] to camouflage their aggressive goals under the cover of peaceful Olympic play." What was required, therefore, was "an energetic international campaign against the selection of Munich."

(The East German observers were right, of course, to worry that the IOC would do the "wrong" thing from their point of view. In fact, it seems that for some IOC voters the supposed bugaboo of Berlin '36 was actually a plus, since that festival was generally seen as a model of organizational efficiency. Thus, a Brazilian IOC member who had participated in the Berlin Games assured Vogel that he intended to support Munich because "German organizational talent" was "very familiar" to him. Sensing that the

'36 example might be helpful in some circles, Munich boosters themselves occasionally cited it as proof that the Germans had "sufficient experience" to put on a successful show.)

Another GDR report compiled at the same time took up the matter of why, of all West German cities, *Munich* in particular was unfit to act as an Olympic host. The reasons for this went beyond Munich's past role in the Third Reich, damning as that was. In the GDR view, Munich's *present* political complexion was even more troubling, for the Bavarian capital had emerged in the postwar era as a hive of anticommunist activity and agitation. (GDR commentators fully endorsed their Soviet colleagues' term of abuse for Munich: *diversionnyi tsentr*—center of subversion.)

One of the factors that made Munich so "subversive" in GDR and Soviet eyes was its status as a major gathering point for thousands of ethnic German refugees from those parts of Hitler's Reich that had been overrun by the Red Army and incorporated into the Soviet Union's new Eastern European empire. The self-described Vertriebene (expellees) from the Sudetenland region of Czechoslovakia and the exiles from Silesia and East Prussia had formed potent lobby groups dedicated to the recovery of their "lost" homelands. The vast majority of the Sudeten-Germans had settled in Bavaria, where they found a staunch advocate in the CSU. Munich had also attracted many embittered veterans of pro-Nazi collaborationist groups like the Croatian Ustaše, Hungarian Arrow Cross, and Romanian Iron Guard. The Bavarian city even housed sizeable contingents of mostly Muslim refugees from the Caucasus and Central Asia—Tatars, Georgians, Kazakhs, and Uzbeks. During the war, these bitterly anticommunist Islamic peoples had been happy to fight against Stalinist Russia on the side of the Nazis, who assiduously recruited and trained them in a little-known operation called Tiger B. (This group was the nucleus of an Islamic faction in Munich that maintained its own mosque in the city. Backed by the CIA and the Islamic Brotherhood, this group became in the 1960s a pioneering beachhead of fundamentalist politicized Islamism in Europe.)

On the propaganda front, Munich housed Radio Free Europe, a Washington-financed broadcast service that, in the words of the GDR report, "is used as a mouthpiece of imperialist policies against the Socialist lands." Yet another "imperialist mouthpiece" in Munich was Radio Liberty. It had been set up in 1951 by prominent American anticommunists who wished, as they put it, to make a radio station available "to democratic elements among the emigration from the Soviet Union so that they could talk to their fellow countrymen in the homeland." Radio Liberty was located in the very building at the old Oberwiesenfeld Airport where Hitler had greeted Neville Chamberlain and Édouard Daladier upon their arrival for the Munich Conference in 1938. The surrounding grounds would later become the principal site for the '72 Olympic Games.

From the point of view of the GDR, all these "revanchist" and "imperialist" agencies, fully backed by Washington and its West German lackey, could be counted upon to take advantage of a Munich Olympiad to whip up nationalistic and anticommunist hysteria. Citing recent examples of "fascist terror" in the FRG, most prominently the murder of a Yugoslav diplomat in Bonn and the burning of the Yugoslav flag at a football match in Bremen, the GDR officials warned that a West German–hosted Olympic festival would undoubtedly produce a host of "new scandals."

In their interpretation of Munich's campaign for the '72 Games, the East Germans clearly assumed that the West German Olympic Committee was operating in perfect harmony with Bonn. This, of course, was not the case. Bonn had agreed to back Munich's bid financially, but hardliners in Erhard's cabinet continued to resist making the political accommodations with the GDR that Daume and Vogel were urgently lobbying for. However, in the latters' view, changing Bonn's stance on the GDR had to take a back seat for the moment to winning over the IOC for Munich.

To this end, Munich's promoters resorted to the time-honored tactics of cajolery, flattery, and implicit bribery. Daume, with his insider's knowledge of the IOC and long-standing friendship with Brundage, whom he had known since 1936, took the lead here. He grasped every opportunity to butter up his old friend, praising the American's stance against opening the Games to professionals and his crusade against excessive commercialization. He even attended Brundage's eightieth birthday party in 1967.

Ever the political pragmatist, Daume also turned his attention to Germany's old foe, the Soviet Union. Aware that the USSR government, like that of the GDR, opposed Munich as a potential host city for the Games, he worked to reverse this posture by promising, under the table, to put up the Soviet IOC delegate Konstantin Andrianov for vice president of the IOC. Flattered by the German courtship, Andrianov eventually came around. Having initially spoken out against Munich's Olympic aspirations, the Russian gradually moderated his tone—and in the end actually voted *for* the West German city. What Daume could *not* manage, on the other hand, was an immediate halt in the Soviet media's disparagement of Munich as an acceptable host for the Games. However, as we shall see, by spring 1971 Daume had also turned this situation around by promising to support a bid from Moscow for the 1980 Summer Games.

Daume tried to work a similar magic with the GDR. Hoping to stop or at least weaken East Berlin's campaign to derail Munich, he offered to support the application of Heinz Schöbel, a prominent GDR sports official, for membership in the IOC. (Schöbel won admittance in 1967.) Although Daume's intercession in this case did not prevent the GDR from carping against Munich, Schöbel himself was not active in the attacks and came to work amicably with his West German Olympic colleagues.

As for Vogel, he too embarked on a charm offensive aimed at the IOC, particularly Brundage. In December 1965, the mayor dispatched a book about Munich to Brundage, along with some strategic lines: "Of course, the city of Munich already has the privilege of knowing you as a friend. In any case, I have often heard from our mutual acquaintance, the late Dr. Karl Ritter von Halt, that you have always been glad to visit Munich, and that you always feel at home here." Vogel added that he and his vice mayor, Georg Brauchle, hoped to pay a personal visit to Brundage in Chicago very soon in order "to discuss our plans with you thoroughly" and "to hear from you your special wishes for the application and receive your valuable advice."

In fact, Vogel and Brauchle did undertake a forty-eight-hour "Blitz-trip" to Chicago, where the Bavarians paid court to Brundage at his penthouse office in the La Salle Hotel. During this brief meeting, Vogel shamelessly flattered the American mogul, comparing him to Germany's ancient cold warrior, Konrad Adenauer. Brundage, noted Vogel with satisfaction, duly appreciated the comparison, though the American could not resist pointing out that he was eleven years younger than the former chancellor.

In their fervent courtship of the IOC, the Bavarians did not neglect lesser lights on the committee. Vogel saw to it that any IOC delegate who happened to show up in Munich on a "fact-finding" mission was lavishly lodged, wined, and dined, generally at the opulent Vier Jahreszeiten Hotel. The city of Munich and the NOCG also dispatched representatives to Africa, South America, and Asia for private meetings with those IOC members who, despite offers of paid passage to Europe, had been unable or unwilling to make the junket to Munich. New IOC rules forbade candidate-city officials from inviting IOC delegates to their prospective Olympic sites during the month prior to a venue vote, but Munich extended generous hospitality to committee members right up to the deadline.

In addition to courting the IOC, the Munich boosters also wooed the international fraternity of sports journalists, believing their reporting to be influential in the shaping of IOC venue decisions. Because the

IOC meeting to decide the '72 site would transpire in Rome, the Bavarians paid particular attention to the Italian press, whose members were invited to personally inspect the attractions of the Bavarian metropolis. Vogel saw with gratification that the Italians seemed to favor Munich, not least because the Bavarian city was a lot closer to Italy than were Montreal and Detroit. (As for Madrid, Vogel did not consider it much of a threat because the Spanish capital itself seemed highly ambivalent about its bid; moreover, though Vogel did not mention this factor, whereas Munich had put its anti-democratic past behind it, Madrid and Spain were still under the thumb of the fascist Franco regime.)

As the moment for the crucial IOC vote drew nigh, Vogel and Daume knew that the main hurdle for Munich remained Bonn's problematical policies governing the appearance of GDR state symbolism on FRG soil. East Berlin was exploiting Bonn's intransigence in an effort to persuade its allies in the IOC to "shoot down" Munich in Rome. No sooner had the IOC delegates gathered in the Italian capital than Brundage himself, pressured by Moscow, demanded a written guarantee from Bonn that GDR Olympians would be treated in exactly the same fashion as all other Olympic participants. (The IOC had not yet formally decided to accord the GDR team full sovereign rights for the '72 Games, but Brundage was aware that they would probably do so soon; and in fact, they did just that at their Mexico City meeting in 1968.) In a desperate appeal to Chancellor Erhard for a written statement guaranteeing equal treatment for all Olympic visitors to Munich, the Bavarian delegation in Rome pointed out that even the Nazis had made substantial concessions to the IOC, including a promise—subsequently fulfilled—to enroll at least one Jew on their German Olympic team for Berlin in 1936. (Germany had named a half-Jewish fencer, Helene Mayer, to its team in 1936.)

At the last minute, Chancellor Erhard dispatched a telegram saying contradictorily that, while Bonn would honor all the IOC's guidelines, it would also continue to enforce its status as the sole representative of German sovereignty. Unable to achieve a modification of this stance, which of course was inadequate for the IOC's purposes, the Munich delegation opted for a bit of subterfuge. Instead of putting Erhard's impossible statement before Brundage, Vogel and Daume presented the IOC president with an English translation of an earlier statement by Interior Minister Paul Lücke, which took a softer line on the representation question. Of course, the earlier date on Lücke's original statement failed to appear on the translation presented to Brundage. To the Germans' great relief,

Brundage pronounced himself satisfied with Bonn's apparent accommodation.

All that remained now for the men from Munich was to make their final sales pitches to the IOC. The various contenders in Rome all followed a similar procedure in this matter. First, they put elaborate scale models of their projected Olympic facilities on display in the main exhibition hall at the Foro Italico, a Mussolini-built complex that had been the principal site of the 1960 Rome Games. A representative from each delegation guided IOC members through his town's exhibit, touting its glories. Mayor Vogel took on this duty for Munich, feeling in the process "like a concession-booth proprietor at Oktoberfest." Not surprisingly, Vogel came away from this task with the belief that Munich's little Olympia, which boasted a miniature chestnut tree and real grass, was by far the most impressive. Then, on the following day, delegations were invited to sum up the virtues of their entries through two formal addresses to the committee, one by the respective mayor and one by the national Olympic committee head. The contenders also showed short films in praise of their cities.

Munich's team had managed in record time to put together a glitzy promotional film entitled *Munich: A City Applies*. Produced by the city's Press and Information Service, the thirteen-minute film showcased Munich's scenic beauty, rich cultural attractions, generously endowed Fräuleins, and fun-loving atmosphere (Oktoberfest!). The production turned out to be, in Vogel's humble opinion, a "masterpiece . . . perfectly attuned to the mentality of the IOC."

The Germans' oral presentations were also effective. Daume was able to give his five-minute peroration in fluent French, an important asset given the fact that French and English were the two official languages of the IOC, and not all the committee members knew English. Vogel, speaking in serviceable English, also kept his comments brief, and in his fifteen-minute talk, he apparently managed to strike all the proper chords in his audience's emotional register. The mayor emphasized once again that Munich would depart from the recent practice whereby candidate cities tried to outdo previous municipal hosts in terms of size and cost.

> I wish to state that the City of Munich has neither the desire nor the ability to outshine the Rome or Tokyo Games in matters of material expense, and that we prefer to take the scale of the Helsinki [Olympics] as a suitable model for Olympic Games in Munich. This also applies to the cost of maintaining teams in Munich, which at current price levels would not exceed seven dollars per day per competitor.

As a way of obliquely addressing a touchy issue that he feared might still trouble some of the IOC voters—namely, Munich's Nazi past—Vogel pointed out that the Bavarian capital was an especially "youthful" city, with "more than a fifth of [its] population born after 1945." In other words, Munich's contemporary mindset was largely a product of younger folks who had had no role in the crimes of the Third Reich. And finally, after taking care of what might have been Munich's greatest weakness as a candidate city, Vogel reemphasized what he saw as his town's greatest strength: its desire and ability to stage an Olympic festival combining technical flawlessness (what else could one expect from the headquarters of BMW and Siemens?) with cultural vitality and human warmth (what else could one expect from a metropolis that called itself *"Die Weltstadt mit Herz"* (The World City with Heart)? Continuing, Vogel said,

> The City of Munich aspires to be more than a municipal machine, ensuring the efficient technical execution of the Olympic program. We should like to see the Games furnish the opportunity for a great encounter between competitors and visitors, and between these and the townspeople. We should also like to lay special stress on the cultural aspect of the Olympic Games. . . . With all [its splendid cultural] resources at hand, Munich has proposed that the Games should be accompanied by an extensive cultural program, which should form a unit together with the sporting program.

In short, Munich would finally realize Baron de Coubertin's "Olympic idea for modern times" by achieving a perfect "synthesis of cultural, ritual and athletic elements"—and it would do all this without adding to the recent Olympic record of bloat and excess.

The bloat and excess of municipal hyperbole finally having come to an end, the Olympic aspirants had nothing further to do but retreat to their stuffy anteroom in the Hotel Excelsior (itself, by the way, a monument to Felliniesque bloat and excess) to await the IOC's equivalent of a puff of white smoke.

CHAPTER Two

"We Just Slid Into It": Planning and Building for Munich '72

> If [the planned Olympic Stadium] is built, the Olympic ideal
> will achieve unprecedented architectural representation.
> And it must be built. . . . No other solution would be sensible.
>
> —Frei Otto, designer (1968)

The period between securing the right to host an Olympic festival and actually putting the big event on resembles in some ways the transition between winning a major elective office—say, that of the presidency of the United States—and actually taking office. In both cases, promises and plans made on the campaign trail are often significantly changed even before the additional pressures of doing the job kick in. Moreover, the task of laying the groundwork for the happy winner's impending time in the sun often generates challenges unforeseen during the period of candidacy. With the modern Olympics, however, the period of preparation is apt to be even more trying than a presidential transition because the duration involved is considerably longer—roughly six years—and yet it is often barely long enough to complete all the work that needs to be done.

This was especially true of the protracted planning and building program for Munich '72. As we have seen, Munich had promised in its bid for the Games to reverse a trend toward ever more elaborate and costly Olympic festivals. In the end, however, Munich managed to construct the most expansive (and expensive) Olympic stage to date. How did this happen? "We just slid into it," protested the chief of Munich's Olympic construction program. But, of course, the reality was rather more complicated.

"The Invisible Stopwatch Has Started to Tick"

At an International Olympic Committee (IOC)–sponsored party in Rome on April 27, 1966, honoring the prospective host cities for 1972 (Munich and Sapporo), West Germany's ambassador to Italy, Hans-Heinrich Herwarth von Bittenfeld, went out of his way to congratulate East Germany's Heinz Schöbel on his recent election to the IOC. Herwarth von Bittenfeld did not make this gesture on instructions from the Foreign Office in Bonn. On the contrary, his action represented a violation of Bonn's protocol regarding treatment of German Democratic Republic (GDR) dignitaries (they were to be cold-shouldered). But a West German city had just been tapped to host the Olympics in 1972, and the ambassador apparently felt obliged to act a bit "Olympian" himself.

Back in Munich, people celebrated their city's selection as an Olympic host with their own parties in the streets. Upon returning to his city from Rome, Mayor Hans-Jochen Vogel tried to inject a note of sobriety into the party atmosphere. He advised a crowd at the airport that the good burghers of Munich would themselves have to lend a hand in the preparations for '72, so that the world's high expectations for those Games might be fulfilled. Some "mistakes and disappointments" were inevitable, he cautioned. Moreover, the work had to commence immediately, for an "invisible stopwatch has already started to tick."

Willi Daume, too, stressed the responsibilities that Munich's selection as an Olympic host brought with it for both the city and the nation. The decision in Rome, he said in an interview on April 29, constituted a "moral victory" for the Federal Republic of Germany (FRG) because there had been lots of "resentments" against the Germans. "We Germans don't have it easy." Now, the entire world expected much from the Germans not just in terms of organizational efficiency but also in the realm of politics: the Munich Games had to transpire "entirely within the spirit of cooperation between East and West."

As soon as the beery celebrations over the IOC decision subsided, many Münchners themselves seemed uncomfortably aware that getting the Games might not be an unalloyed blessing for their city. They woke up the next morning with a nasty "hangover," observed one local commentator, not just because of all the beer they'd knocked back but also because of a dawning realization that, when it came to the physical plant and infra-structural requirements for putting on an Olympic show, their town was indeed sorely lacking. Bringing Munich up to Olympic speed in six short years would inevitably entail all sorts of burdens and pressures, even for ordinary folk. "Drunken joy followed by painful sobriety—is this going to be a symbol for the entire business?" asked the local observer, with some prescience.

Mindful of that "ticking stopwatch" cited by Vogel, West Germany's Olympic Committee moved quickly to establish the agencies necessary to plan and build the stage for '72. Like most national Olympic committees in the past, the National Olympic Committee for Germany (NOCG) opted to create a special body for this purpose, the "Organizing Committee for the Twentieth Olympic Games" (OC). Meeting for the first time on July 3, 1966, this body comprised leading figures from West Germany's political, sporting, and business establishments. Not surprisingly, Willi Daume as-sumed the presidency, while Vogel occupied one of the vice presidential slots. The crucial post of general secretary of the Munich OC was assumed by a Bavarian civil servant named Herbert Kunze. A hard-driving tax law-yer, Kunze had joined the Nazi Party in May 1933 and was briefly a member of the SS. Hans ("Johnny") Klein, an affable journalist and former govern-mental press attaché in the Middle East, handled the OC's press relations. Ebullient and outgoing, Klein boasted that his office door was "open to all—anybody can come in." Klein was assisted by Guido von Mengden, a veteran German sports theorist who, in an earlier incarnation as press sec-retary for the organizing committee behind the Berlin Games of 1936, had done his best to interpret high-level sport and the Olympics according to Nazi principles. Like his new boss, Willi Daume, Mengden had effectively changed his political spots and now touted the Olympics as a force for international understanding.

One of the OC's first decisions was to set up a separate agency, the Olympia Bau-Gesellschaft (Olympic Building Corporation), to handle all the construction operations for the Games. Like the OC, this body in-cluded top bureaucrats from all branches of government, as well as selected heavyweights from the building and banking industries. The corporation's work was monitored by an even more select "Board of Directors," whose chairmanship was entrusted to Franz Josef Strauß, the powerful Chris-tian Social Union (CSU) chairman and (as of December 12, 1966) federal finance minister. The portly Bavarian's dynamism and clout undoubtedly made him a valuable addition to Munich's organizational team. On the other hand, Strauß's imperious style and penchant for scandal also made his appointment highly controversial.*

In early planning discussions for Munich's Olympic festival, especially for its physical plant, it quickly became apparent that many of the original aspirations and ideals would fall by the wayside. Notions about scope, design, and (above all) cost underwent drastic revision. Put simply, it soon became clear that there would be nothing "modest" about Munich '72.

According to a defensive Mayor Vogel, the main fault for the changes to the original scheme lay with the various international sports federations that typically set the rules and regulations for their respective disciplines in Olympic play. Undoubtedly, Vogel had a point here. The federations made all sorts of demands to the OC regarding the facilities for 1972. For example, the basketball and volleyball federations demanded self-standing, made-to-order arenas, while the boxing, judo, and wrestling federations insisted on separate, uniquely designed spaces for each of their disciplines. Accommodating these agencies proved to be extremely expensive. The basketball arena alone ended up costing DM 23 million. A state-of-the-art riding stadium demanded by the Equestrian Federation consumed DM 51 million, ten times more than the original estimate. A fancy new artificial rowing course, built to the specifications of the International Rowing Federation, cost DM 69 million, another ten-fold overrun. As the international federations' demands poured in, requiring repeated returns to the drawing board, it gradually dawned on the OC that in the eyes of these foreign sports bureaucrats Munich's hopes for "modest" Games meant nothing: for them, an Olympic festival in the FRG offered a unique opportunity to take full advantage of "German perfectionism" in the realm of high-tech engineering and construction.

It was not only the sports federations that imposed expensive changes on the OC. The IOC itself, ignoring its own calls for downsized Games, forced the Munich organizers to add a brand new event to the competitive

* As Bonn's defense minister between 1956 and 1962, Strauß had managed the buildup of West Germany's new army, the Bundeswehr, with great vigor but little regard for diplomatic niceties. Moreover, an official of the Lockheed Aircraft Company accused him of taking bribes from his company to ensure the purchase of Lockheed Starfighter jets for the German air force. The charges were never proven, but Strauß was forced to step down in 1962 in the wake of a different scandal involving the newsmagazine *Der Spiegel*, whose editor, Rudolf Augstein, Strauß ordered jailed for publishing an article contesting the battle worthiness of Bonn's armed forces. Later on, Strauß made headlines by losing his wallet to a prostitute in New York City; she had mugged him, he claimed.

program, the whitewater canoe slalom, which necessitated the construction of an elaborate artificial course incorporating all the latest bells and whistles. Lacking space for such a facility at the projected Olympic complex in Munich, and unable to find a suitable location near the city, the organizers ended up situating the canoe course near the town of Augsburg, some eighty kilometers away. Meanwhile, executives from the TV and radio networks stepped in with their own sets of ambitious design specifications for Munich's broadcast facilities. Tellingly, the OC felt compelled to accommodate these and other demands from powerful outside interests at a time when the GDR and its Eastern European allies were heaping criticism on the prospective host city.

Pressure from outside actors, however, was not the only reason, or even the main one, that the plans for Munich '72 soon lost all semblance of frugality. Once Munich's Olympic boosters had safely landed this important show, they were no longer sure they wanted to keep it modest and unassuming. Echoing planners for the 1936 Berlin Games some thirty-five years earlier, Munich '72 organizers began asking themselves why they should go to all the trouble of inviting the world to dinner unless they intended to lay on a seriously impressive banquet. And, of course, they were convinced that they had much to show off. The diligent, hardworking West Germans had pulled off a remarkable feat in the postwar era by transforming their rubble-strewn cities, Munich especially, into vibrant centers of commerce and the arts. The FRG as a whole had become, in a few short years, one of the world's leading economies, a king of exports. The Olympics offered a perfect opportunity to make the world acquainted with that new (West) Germany—with a society that was not only politically healthy but economically vibrant as well.

For some West Germans, indeed, their nation's socioeconomic accomplishments were reason enough to cast off, as they saw it, the prickly hairshirt they had been obliged to wear since 1945 as penance for the crimes of the Third Reich. Franz Josef Strauß himself articulated a sentiment shared by many of his countrymen when he declared in 1969, "A people who have delivered such [great] economic achievements have the right not to hear about Auschwitz any longer." And if West Germans no longer needed to agonize over Auschwitz, perhaps they also no longer needed to be quite so humble and self-effacing in the ways they represented themselves to the outside world. True, they could not afford to come across as bombastic or grandiose (nor did they want to), but a little stylistic ambition couldn't hurt.

Vogel and Daume, architects of Munich's winning Olympic bid, were themselves instrumental in this rethinking process. As an industrialist,

Daume was proud of the FRG's astonishing postwar growth in manufacturing and technology. He thus proved highly susceptible to pleas from his friends in the building sector to use the Games as a showcase for West German industrial and technological prowess. (He gave an early hint of this inclination when, right after Munich won the Games, he told reporters that, for him, "modesty" did not mean "small-mindedness.") Vogel, in his capacity as mayor of West Germany's "secret capital," began to see the Games as an opportunity to put Munich on the map as a global player, especially in the architectural realm. The Olympics, he understood, represented a unique chance to make an indelible architectural statement. Both he and Daume were familiar with the dazzling structures designed by Kenzo Tange for the Tokyo Games of 1964. Never mind that he, Vogel, had earlier disclaimed any intention of one-upping Tange. Now he realized that, courtesy of the '72 Games, Munich might not only accelerate necessary infrastructural improvements but also catch the world's aesthetic eye, as Tange had clearly done. Vogel also well knew that in the first half of the nineteenth century Munich had stood at the center of world architectural interest when Bavaria's first king, Ludwig I, had commissioned a host of new buildings and monuments that had turned his unassuming capital into something like a Florence of the North. Might not the Olympic Games provide the seedbed for another great architectural flowering, but one that was sui generis, in keeping with Munich's emergence as a world cultural capital in its own right? (We should add that Vogel's term of office was set to expire in June 1972, and he did not plan to run again; if he were to emerge as a latter-day Ludwig I, the construction of Munich's Olympic complex offered his best—and last—chance to do so.)

From the outset, the huge task of planning and building for Munich '72 was marked not only by broad philosophical disputes over questions of scope and style but also by endless battles over turf between politicians and artists, bean counters and builders, and staff architects and outside experts called in to consult on the various projects. At times, it almost seemed as if the Olympic designers and builders, in their heated rivalries and struggles for supremacy, were trying to set an example for the sporting competitions to come—that is, if the athletic facilities ever actually materialized out of the heat and smoke of the planning process.

"Rainbow Games"

To a large degree, the original promise of a low-key, relaxed, and environmentally sensitive Olympic festival in '72 was embedded in the man tapped by the OC to shape the overall aesthetic design for the Games: Otl Aicher. Aicher's job encompassed everything from the fundamental architectural philosophy for the Games through emblems, flags, signage, uniforms, programs, posters, and official invitations. Vogel later claimed that Aicher proved to be such a demanding and difficult partner that it was all he could do to keep him from being fired. (For some of Aicher's critics, the fact that he didn't come from Bavaria was reason enough to distrust him.)

Nonetheless, Aicher seemed to be the perfect man for the job he'd been appointed to do. Unlike many of those connected with the planning of Munich '72, he brought to the table an extremely honorable—and present-able—past, for as a youth he had been a member of the famous White Rose opposition to Hitler and had even married a sister of Hans and Sophie Scholl, the martyred leaders of that resistance group. On the professional front, Aicher boasted an equally impressive résumé. A professor at West Germany's leading graphic arts institute, the neo-Bauhaus Hochschule für Gestaltung (College of Design) in Ulm, which he had helped to found, Aicher had previously designed arresting corporate images for the chemical giant BASF and the national airline, Lufthansa. A critical left-leaning Catholic, he knew enough about orthodoxy, religious and political, to believe that change was healthy. As a politically engaged artist, he thought he could achieve the necessary changes through the power of aesthetics. "One can make politics with color," he liked to say, and he set out to do just that by establishing a color scheme for Munich '72 that (he hoped) might convey the progressive political mindset behind the enterprise while inspiring properly enlightened thinking among all those who came to bask in the benign aura of what he called the "Rainbow Games." Aicher summarily decreed that there must be no red, black, gold, or purple at Munich because these were the favored colors of dictatorships, old and new, as well as signifiers of German nationalism, past and present. Monomaniacally, he insisted that only six muted pastels—two tones each of blue, green, and yellow-orange, plus a light silver—could be used on the flags, uniforms, programs, posters, and advertising material for the Munich Games.

Valuable as Aicher's ideas undoubtedly were for setting the desired tone at the Games, they would turn out to contain certain drawbacks in their practical application. For example, the leisure suit–like outfits he came up with for the on-the-ground Olympic security personnel—baby blue polyester pant/jacket ensembles complemented by baseball-style hats and white canvas shoes—definitely ensured that the people wearing this garb would never be confused with the German police forces of old (which was the main point), but who could take seriously security men who were dead ringers for vacationing seniors from Cleveland, Ohio? The childlike stick-figure "pictogram" system Aicher designed for directional signage at the Games also presented problems. The geometric symbols (somewhat similar to those invented by Masaru Katsumie for the Tokyo Games) were meant to serve as a handy non-verbal Esperanto, decipherable to all, but in reality, like actual Esperanto, the signs were often quite Delphic. Some of them resisted interpretation entirely; others were just weird. An American journalist was totally baffled by the pictograph on the doors of the women's bathrooms: the figure had symmetrical arcs suggestive of a skirt, but, just like the figure for the men's johns, "she" stood with her arms crossed in front of her at crotch level. Now just what the devil could she be doing? Finally, Aicher's pastel-colored Olympic banners, which were displayed all around town in place of the plethora of national flags that usually bedecked host cities, probably did little to heighten the spirit of "Olympism" (whatever that was) at the expense of nationalism, which was Aicher's intention; in any event, their lollipop hues seemed more evocative of Miami Beach's Art Deco District in its prime than of an eight-hundred-year-old Germanic metropolis in the heart of Central Europe.

Aicher's proposal for the Games' official logo, a sunlike ring encircled by vague stellar and floral motifs, eventually met with rejection by the OC because it was thought to resemble too closely the official emblems of the Tokyo and Mexico City Games. Moreover, it seemed too vulnerable to forgery by counterfeiters. After rejecting Aicher's emblem design, the committee held a competition to come up with a replacement. The winner turned out to be a very complex spiral arrangement—looking, perhaps, like a cross between a dart board, bicycle wheel, and stylized sun. Whatever it was supposed to be, the committee had a tough time defending it from its many critics, not least because looking at it for very long tended to induce vertigo and a deep sense of unease. Daume was distinctly unconvincing when he pronounced Munich's official Olympic emblem to be "the most beautiful design in the world."

Munich '72's representation in poster art also became a subject of controversy. Willi Daume, who fancied himself an art connoisseur, came up with the idea for a poster series called Edition Olympia, which involved twenty-eight separate images, each to be drawn by a world-famous artist. With the lure of generous honoraria, Daume was able to attract a few big names, including Oskar Kokoschka, that aging star of Germany's early twentieth-century Expressionist avant-garde. "OK," however, ended up producing a wavy-line drawing of a naked Greek Kouros with slack musculature and bowed head—an anti-Greek athletic god if there ever was one. The artistic community loved the work, and so did Otl Aicher, but local sports-writers, along with many ordinary Münchners, found the drawing distinctly inappropriate. (One outraged commentator said Kokoschka's figure looked like some piss-ant weakling who'd spent way too much time at a desk.)

Undaunted by the tepid public response to Edition Olympia, the OC turned again to the international art community in order to come up with an iconic "official poster" for the '72 Games. Daume and company sponsored a limited competition for the poster design involving ten renowned graphic artists from around the world. But the jury charged with selecting the winning design was sharply divided between an artistic faction looking for something innovative and a group of traditionalist officials and politicians favoring a conventional depiction of local landmarks like the twin-domed Frauenkirche. In the end, the jury did settle on a winner, but that poster was not the one eventually approved by the OC in 1970 as the official poster of the '72 Games and reproduced in 190,000 copies. This committee-endorsed work, put out by a local advertising company, involved a more or less representational scheme featuring the tented Olympic complex and television tower, along with the vertigo-inducing Olympic emblem. Hamburg's weekly *Die Zeit* derided the grass-green and pale-blue poster as "an embarrassing compromise" whose original colored version was "quite a bit more disgusting than the black-and-white reproductions." The poster certainly "charted no new territory in the graphic arts," the paper concluded.

The radical young designers connected to Otl Aicher's shop, all much disgusted by the OC's choice for an official poster, were hoping all along to keep the Munich Games relatively free of the Germanic and Bavarian traditionalism dear to the hearts of more conservative elements in the planning process. Aicher and his staff of neo-Bauhaus artists stood rigorously for modernistic purism, envisioning an Olympic stage blessedly free of historicist allusions and tacky folkloric bric-a-brac. No cuckoo clocks, Bible-scene frescoes, Lederhosen, feathered Alpine hats, or yodeling mountain boys for them! (The OC radicals had support here from the similarly inclined head of Inter Nationes, an agency that promoted West German culture abroad, who saw the Munich Games as an excellent opportunity to move beyond the "one-sided folklore image" most foreigners seemed to have of Bavaria—an image whose "dark side" connoted "coarseness, anti-intellectualism, reactionary views, and just plain stupidity.") While the central aesthetic thrust of the '72 Games would indeed turn out to be largely futuristic and cosmopolitan—thus presenting a vivid contrast to the Berlin Games of 1936—Aicher and his staff proved unable in the long run to ban all elements of folksy Bavarianism, whether in the form of the dirndls worn by waitresses or the omnipresent oompah-pah bands that struck up polkas and classic drinking tunes at every opportunity.

Aicher's most significant defeat in the area of folk-kitsch came with the selection of an "official mascot" for the '72 Games. Olympic mascots had been introduced at the 1968 Winter Games in Grenoble, France, but Munich's addition to this dubious enterprise, which the IOC now hails as "a significant vehicle for the communication of the Olympic spirit to the general public," was the first to occasion much notice. It consisted, perhaps inevitably, of an archetypal piece of Bavarian kitsch—a cuddly little Dachshund stuffy named "Waldi." Waldi's defenders argued that this creature made perfect sense as a mascot for Munich '72 because Dachshunds not only were "very popular in Bavaria" but also possessed "qualities which are indispensible to an athlete: resistance, tenacity, and agility." In truth, most people probably do not think of Dachshunds as agile and tenacious, but at least they could never be confused with German shepherds, the favored breed of the Nazis. For Aicher, the only consolation in all this was a decision by Waldi's designers to color the toy in bands of blue, green, and orange pastels—to "express the gaiety and joy of the Olympic festival."

While Aicher and his colleagues in the design department strove to suggest a progressive new German consciousness in the '72 Games' look and aesthetic trappings, the subcommittee responsible for shaping the cultural and artistic program for Munich '72 hoped to build in to the athletic festival a veritable feast of cutting-edge artistic experimentation—the best that the "new Munich" and the "new Germany" had to offer. In addition, they were determined to document Munich's cosmopolitanism by opening the festival to artistic impulses from around the world. (In this ambition, as we noted above, they departed from explicit instructions from the IOC.) With some 21.8 million marks at its disposal, 8 million of that for freestanding artworks and artistic embellishment of the athletic structures, the arts subcommittee seemed to be in an excellent position to turn the 1972 Games into a true celebration of cultural creativity, just as Munich's application had promised to do. However, like Aicher and his staff, the planners dreaming of a "Kultur-Olympiade" (cultural Olympics) on a scale to match the athletic extravaganza on display at the Games soon found that they lacked the political backing and influence necessary to turn that dream into full reality.

The soaring aspirations surrounding Munich's "Cultural Olympics" came clearly to the fore in the planning and preparation for the Games' signature arts project: the so-called Spielstraße (literally, Play-Street). What could be more evocative of the "new Munich" than the idea of "art as play"? The Spielstraße was meant to combine serious culture with the mocking of serious culture in a kind of open-air art carnival in which spectators, strolling down a long arcade of interactive exhibitions, games, and impromptu street theater, would themselves become part of the art. Eventually, the Spielstraße did feature prominently in the cultural program for Munich '72, but characteristically, many of the arts subcommittee's more outré ideas for the project ended up on the cutting-room floor. The rejected ideas included a kind of industrial ghat where clunker automobiles were to be thrown on the flames; a shooting gallery in which patrons, rather than doing the shooting themselves, would be fired upon by their would-be targets; and a Dadaesque theatrical stunt involving actors hurling abuse at passersby from the sanctity of litterlike contraptions carried on the shoulders of other actors. According to Mayor Vogel, who witnessed the "difficult" brainstorming sessions regarding the Spielstraße, the OC was sometimes slow to shoot down the wilder ideas from the arts subcommittee for fear of seeming fuddy-duddy. Lamely, the officials tended to fall back on "financial considerations" as grounds for retaining a measure of sobriety.

The putative "financial constraints" deployed to tame the Spielstraße were also put forth to nix a particularly adventurous foreign proposal for the art exhibition planned to accompany the Kultur-Olympiade. The American landscape sculptor Walter de Maria proposed to sink a 120-meter-deep shaft into the Schuttberg (a hill composed of wartime rubble—see below) and to cap this hole with a bronze tablet on which passersby would be invited to stand if they so chose. Both the invisible and visible parts of this sculpture, said the artist, were meant to change "the thinking and behavior of people vis-à-vis art"; instead of simply looking at an artwork, viewers would be called upon to "stand at a place of special tension" and to become part of that tension themselves by "observing their act of observing." Observing that this "Thinkhole," as local skeptics instantly labeled it, was priced at 1.5 million marks, the OC concluded that, life-transforming as the project might be, 1.5 million marks was a lot to pay for an artwork that was largely invisible. They rejected it.

Although cost was certainly a factor in shaping the content and scope of the arts program planned for Munich '72, a more important determinant was undoubtedly the socio-cultural mindset of the OC top brass. Their oft-proclaimed determination to show the world a "new Germany" notwithstanding, men like Daume, Vogel, and Munich police chief Manfred Schreiber had precious little use for one very prominent dimension of the new nation—namely, its vibrant youth culture. Economic modernizers these men might be, but they hated everything about the world of *soixante-huit*. For the Münchners Vogel and Schreiber, the fact that Munich, their city, had become known as the "hippie capital" of West Germany was a source of genuine horror. How shameful it was that decent folk could not walk across the Englischer Garten without having to see legions of long-haired kids lying around—or even dancing around—in the nude!

It is not surprising, then, that among the proposals for Munich's Kultur-Olympiade that did not make the final cut was an audacious scheme for a monster week-long rock festival to take place during the Games on the slopes of the rubble-filled mound originally known as the Schuttberg and now redubbed "Olympic Mountain." The promoter of this so-called Rock Olympics hoped to bring in that era's rock-music equivalents of Mark Spitz: acts like Led Zeppelin, the Rolling Stones, and Frank Zappa's Mothers of Invention. If this idea came off as planned, Munich '72 would definitely not be just about sports—it would be "Woodstock on the Isar," an Olympics of Sex, Drugs, and Rock 'n Roll. But of course, it was just this prospect that alarmed law-and-order conservatives like Manfred Schreiber, the OC's chief security official. He envisaged Munich's respectable Olympic party being crashed by a rag-tag army of crazed hippie freaks, slamming down drugs, urinating in the streets, and openly fornicating on the sacred slopes of the Olympic Mountain. Using his authority as security chief, Schreiber, with backing from Daume and the Bavarian Ministry of Interior, not only squelched the possibility of a "Woodstock" at Munich '72 but also ensured that no such festival would transpire anywhere in Bavaria during the Games. (True, the British group The Who was allowed to perform their rock opera, *Tommy*, at the Deutsches Museum during the Games, but this was a one-evening, indoor affair that catered to well-heeled types who paid good money to get in. Not surprisingly, that concert came off without incident.)

In the planning for Munich '72's cultural program, it was not just ideas and proposals (especially radical ones) that came under fire; the arts committee itself—that is, its personal makeup—also drew fire, largely from social and political conservatives. One particular committee member, Günter Grass, West Germany's preeminent contemporary novelist, took the brunt of these attacks. Grass had risen to fame with his fanciful yet searing explorations of postwar Germany's troubled relationship with its Nazi past. He had also made headlines as an advisor to Willy Brandt in his campaign for the chancellorship. The West German right despised him. The fact that a man like Grass was invited to help define the cultural program for the upcoming Munich Games was too much for an arch-conservative lobby group called the Deutsches Kulturwerk Europäischen Geistes (German Cultural Foundation for the European Spirit), which had appointed itself to defend traditional German culture and values against "destructive influences." In the eyes of this group, Grass had shown himself to be an arch-corruptor of morals with novels like *Die Blechtrommel* (*The Tin Drum*, 1959) and *Katz und Maus* (*Cat and Mouse*, 1963), which employed "obscene" language and tropes to mock and satirize honorable German institutions. In a letter to Federal president Heinrich Lübke, whose office had legal responsibility for all officially registered German associations, including the OC, the head of the Deutsches Kulturwerk demanded that Grass be taken off the arts-subcommittee on grounds that his corpus of work represented a "mockery of the Olympic Spirit." To back up this contention, the official cited a passage from *Blechtrommel* in which the protagonist, Oskar the dwarf, touches the "little watering can" on a statue of the baby Jesus, causing Oskar's own "little watering can" to twitch with pleasure. Another guardian of public morals wrote the president with a similar demand regarding Grass, citing passages in the latter's *Katz und Maus* that were "dangerous to youth." "It is simply unacceptable that Herr Grass should be allowed to extend his destructive influence to the Olympics, thereby opening the FRG to derision across the entire world," huffed this critic. President Lübke, not known to be much of a cultural connoisseur, probably never read these earnest letters (much less the works of Günter Grass). In any event, a presidential aide advised the concerned citizens that the head of state was not in a position to "to register objections to the participation of Herr Grass on the Cultural Committee for the Olympic Games." Grass stayed on board.

By the summer of 1971, roughly one year before the opening of the Games, the dimensions of the planned "Cultural Olympics" for Munich '72 were clearly discernable. Those hoping for daring innovation, an exploration of new artistic frontiers, were disappointed by the rather staid and conventional program of offerings. According to the official plan, there would be juried competitions (but no medals given out) in the disciplines of painting, sculpture, architecture, music, and literature. There would also be weighty scholarly symposia exploring connections between the Olympic Games and medicine, technology, and society; exhibitions on such topics as "100 Years of German Excavation at Olympia," "Bavarian Art and Culture," and "Bavaria in the World and the World in Bavaria"; operatic and symphonic productions of the works of Richard Strauss, Mozart, Beethoven, Wagner, Carl Orff, and Werner Egk; evenings of folk music and folk dancing; guest performances by such renowned foreign ensembles as the New York Philharmonic, the Orchestra of the USSR, and the Vienna

Philharmonic; showings of "the most important sport films of the century"; and finally, "international jazz concerts featuring the most famous soloists and ensembles from around the world." While this program was laudable in its embrace of internationalism and less traditional art forms like jazz, it certainly did not promise a walk on the artistic wild side, which of course is what the more adventurous spirits on the arts subcommittee had been hoping for.

The situation with regard to free-standing sculpture works on the Olympic grounds was yet more problematical in the eyes of those hoping for a major "Art Happening" in connection with the Games. Walter de Maria's "Thinkhole" was not the only grand project to be denied funding. A competition for a large-scale "Artistic Enrichment of the [Olympic Complex] Entryway" was cancelled—so was an installation of several forty-five-meter-high concrete "prisms." In the end, it turned out that the Olympia Bau-Gesellschaft, which had the final say on major plastic-arts commissions for the Games, was uninterested in funding any grand pieces of sculpture or conceptual art. In this domain, what ultimately passed muster in the planning process was a series of small-scale pieces to be sprinkled here and there around Munich and the Olympic grounds. In the view of one influential critic, these approved works amounted to nothing but Kleckerkunst (literally, "dribble art").

Money Matters

It has now become standard for the modern Olympic Games to experience substantial cost overruns, especially in their construction budgets. This had not been the case with the earlier festivals, however. Berlin '36 was the first modern Olympics to go way over budget, largely because Hitler insisted that money must not be an object when it came to building an Olympic stage worthy of his "Thousand Year Reich." The first post–World War II Summer Games, the "Austerity Olympics" of London '48, amounted to a triumph of frugality in every respect.* The 1952 Helsinki Games also

---

* Operating on a bare-bones budget, the London organizers housed Olympic athletes in Royal Air Force (RAF) camps and local schools, and, with wartime rationing still in effect, encouraged foreign teams to bring their own food. The Americans, of course, brought more food than anybody else but still had to depend in part on local fare, which made them very unhappy. "I don't mind eating horse steaks but I do object to having the saddle put in too," complained one U.S. runner. Taking some pity on their own competitors, British authorities allotted them the same rations as heavy industrial workers and allowed them to receive food parcels from private donors. Lady Nancy Astor sent over bountiful hampers from Clivedon.

represented a model of fiscal modesty. But after that, a bloating process had set in, each national organizing committee trying to outdo its immediate predecessor in terms of facilities and amenities. Munich '72 was supposed to arrest this process. But in the end, especially with regard to the physical plant, the Munich organizers outdid even Hitler in the scope of their ambition.

Not long into the planning process it became obvious that the original estimation of DM 520 million for all Olympic construction was hopelessly unrealistic. Of course, some insiders had pointed this out from the very outset. To these skeptics, the only issues requiring resolution were how large the impending deficits would be, and how they might be covered.

In addition to perhaps consciously underestimating the projected costs of Olympic building in Munich's bid to the IOC, Daume and his chief financial advisor, former Bavarian finance minister Rudolf Eberhard, repeatedly gave assurances to financial watchdogs at the federal and state levels that the OC would be able to cover its own expenses out of existing revenue streams. This turned out to be an illusion, even though those revenue sources grew to become quite substantial.

Apart from the promised subsidies from state and federal coffers, the OC's revenue base quickly expanded to include a special nationwide TV Lottery administered by the individual states. Launched in the summer of 1967, this Olympic "Glückspirale" (Spiral of Fortune), which included guest appearances by such high-octane celebrities as soccer star Franz Beckenbauer, enriched the OC treasury to the tune of DM 288 million.

The sale in the same year of television rights to broadcasting companies around the world brought in another DM 170 million. (According to an income distribution scheme set up by the IOC in Rome in 1966, a little less than two-thirds of the total sale of TV rights would go to the national organizing committees.) ABC Television paid a then-record $13,500,000 for the exclusive American rights, easily beating out NBC. CBS, having lost its shirt on the Tokyo Games, passed on Munich. Initially, ABC had offered only about half its winning bid, but OC general secretary Herbert Kunze had studied the U.S. television market and well understood how much ABC stood to earn from advertisers. For his part, Roone Arledge, the hard-hitting head of ABC Sports, calculated that his network could afford to pay such a high price for the Munich rights because, by expanding coverage to sixty hours, taking over all of prime time for a full two weeks, and charging an average of $48,000 per minute to advertisers, ABC would generate $24 million in total revenue—"enough to cover the cost of rights, facilities, and production, with a healthy profit left over." Moreover, realizing that the size of viewership for the Games would depend greatly on the USA-USSR rivalry, ABC had a clause inserted into its contract that allowed it to withdraw should either superpower boycott Munich.

Despite promises to curtail commercialization at the Games, Munich organizers emulated their predecessors going back to the 1928 Amsterdam Games by selling off rights to various vendors to flog their products at the Games and to use the official Olympic emblem. In all, some two hundred companies signed up as official Olympic sponsors in 1972, paying the OC some DM 12.2 million for this privilege.

To manage the welter of financial and material contributions to the OC from corporations, foundations, and the general populace, the committee drew on crucial assistance from the Verein zur Förderung der Olympischen Spiele 1972 in München (Association for Support of the Olympic Games 1972 in Munich). Originally set up to raise funds for a municipal sports stadium, the "Förderverein" now focused on securing private contributions for the Olympic cause. By June 1969, the agency had managed to raise DM 3.5 million in coin contributions via an Aktion Sparschwein (Project Piggy Bank). A manufacturer of traditional Bavarian clothing donated dirndl dresses for the Olympic hostesses. A candy manufacturer promised to provide nightly chocolate bonbons for the bedside tables of every athlete and journalist at the '72 Games. But the Förderverein's task was not always an easy one, as it often involved tricky mediation between eager corporate sponsors, the OC, and the IOC.

The correspondence in a voluminous file on the Förderverein in Munich's municipal archive is full of interesting and amusing details on the corporate sponsorship behind Munich '72. In its planning sessions for an opulent Press Center at the Games, for example, the OC wanted to supply the center as much as possible with equipment and amenities donated free of charge by major corporations, which would be then allowed to put their corporate logos on those products. The OC turned to the Förderverein for help in locating corporate donors of everything from coffeemakers and ashtrays to the toiletry kits for journalists' bathrooms. Of course, no Press Center worth its salt would be complete without plenty of booze—this being an essential requirement for journalistic productivity (especially if one wished that output to be favorable). Thus, in June 1972, the Förderverein, worried that there might not be enough alcohol on hand for the fourth estate, dispatched a letter to the George Ballantine company in Scotland, distillers of fine scotch. Noting that only seventy-four days remained before the start of the '72 Games, the Förderverein's spokesman announced, "We are beginning our last major drive, namely to solicit alcoholic beverages."

Although the Munich organizers did "not want to give prominence to the connection between alcohol and the Olympics," alcoholic beverages were "nonetheless necessary to ensure the smooth functioning of the Games." Above all, the thousands of journalists who would be covering the Games expected "to be provided with an excellent assortment of alcoholic beverages by the host." Could Ballantine, "as a world-famous producer of Scotch whiskey," help out here? Fortunately for the OC (and the journalists), it turned out that Ballantine could help—with a timely delivery of over a hundred cases of Canadian Club. Helpful also in this domain was the Jim Beam distillery in the United States, which promised to outfit the Press Center bar with 120 bottles of Jim Beam bourbon. In exchange, the Förderverein arranged for six tickets to the opening ceremony to be earmarked for Jim Beam executives.

Of course, the Munich planners did not confine their search for alcoholic contributions to foreign suppliers. They made deals with German brewers, vintners, and distillers. For example, thinking ahead to the big Olympic reception to be hosted by President Gustav Heinemann, the Förderverein solicited (and received) three hundred bottles of fine Rhine wine from a distributer in Mainz.

When it came to non-alcoholic beverages at the Games, Coca-Cola had been a major supplier and sponsor since the Amsterdam Games in 1928. The Atlanta-based company had also been on board in Berlin in 1936, where Hermann Goering (for a price) had posed swigging from a bottle of Coke. The Munich OC was anxious to have Coke around again in 1972, though on Munich's own terms. The committee invited four companies— Coca-Cola, Pepsi-Cola, Sinalco, and Afri-Cola—to apply for the right to be the "Official Soft Drink of the Munich Games." Coke and Pepsi made it into the second round of negotiations, and although both firms offered similar deals, Coke got the nod because of its "relevant experience" in previous Games. According to the terms of its arrangement with the OC, Coke had to put up a guarantee of one million marks regardless of sales; the company also had to pay for all the sales personnel and for the installation of the latest dispensing machines. In the view of the company, the "prestige" inherent in having a major place at the forthcoming Games was well worth the price.

Coke and Jim Beam may have made good sense as sponsors for the Olympics, but what about tea? One of the odder sponsors at Munich '72 was a West German tea importer that hoped to make its beverage a big seller in Germany by promoting it at the Games, where it was to be dispensed in kiosks around the Olympic grounds and at the Olympic Village. "Not many people here in Germany drink tea," conceded a company spokesman, "but when Germans see so many others enjoying our tea [at the Games], they will try it themselves."

While a tea company was certainly an unexpected commercial booster for the beer-besotted Munich festival, the famed German car makers Mercedes and BMW were obvious choices for corporate sponsorship. Stuttgart-based Daimler-Benz paid a goodly sum to the OC for the right to print the Mercedes Star and the catchy slogan "Fair in Sports—Fair on the Road" on the back of every Olympic ticket. The company also gained itself considerable Olympic exposure by loaning the OC 1,700 passenger cars, busses, and trucks; for IOC brass and other VIPs, Benz provided top-of-the-line Mercedes 600s, complete with chauffeurs. Munich-based BMW, meanwhile, came strangely late to the corporate-sponsorship table and might have been shut out entirely on its own turf had not Vogel intervened at the last minute to ensure that the local company joined Mercedes, Audi, Opel, Ford, and Fiat in the Olympic motor pool.

Perhaps the most important corporate sponsor at Munich was the German sporting goods manufacturer Adidas. The company was run by (and named after) Adolf "Adi" Dassler, who in 1936 had scored his first athletic endorsement when he persuaded Jesse Owens to wear a pair of his spikes. Adi Dassler had initially worked closely with his brother Rudolf in the family firm, Gebrüder Dassler, and both brothers became active members of the Nazi Party. Shortly after World War II, however, the men had a bitter falling out, prompting Rudi to found a rival firm he eventually called Puma. The two companies, both located in the small Bavarian town of Herzogenaurach, carried on a fierce battle for market share that peaked in the Munich Games, where each Dassler brother expected to be the dominant player. Adi's Adidas, however, proved much more adept at currying influence with the OC than Puma, primarily because Adi was willing to spread more cash around than Rudi. The Munich organizers even allowed Adi's son Horst to set up a tent in the Olympic Village, where athletes could get free pairs of spikes. Seeing in the impending Games an advertising opportunity of a lifetime, Adidas hastened to outfit over twenty-five of the teams scheduled to appear at Munich with everything from shoes and sweat suits to athletic bags.

Yet, in its effort to make its three-bar trademark omnipresent at Munich, Adidas ran into opposition from the IOC, especially Avery Brundage. The crusty IOC president was determined to limit the display of corporate logos by entrepreneurial athletes, a practice that had been growing steadily over the years. "We will not tolerate Olympic athletes becoming walking

Litfaß pillars [billboards]," he announced. In the end, the IOC imposed a "compromise" on the OC and Adidas whereby athletes would be allowed to compete in trademarked Adidas shoes at the Munich Games but not otherwise display them in public, nor would they be permitted to parade about in logo-covered sweat suits or openly show off sports bags bearing the Adidas trademark. Adidas officials were infuriated with this arrangement, accusing Willi Daume of not doing enough to protect their company's interests vis-à-vis the IOC. By accepting the restrictions on displaying the Adidas logo, claimed the men from Herzogenaurach, Daume was crippling the global competitiveness of an important Bavarian company and a loyal Olympic sponsor. In response, Daume protested that he was "not a flack for the Bavarian sporting goods industry." But in reality, Daume and the OC were more than willing to allow corporate interests to exploit the upcoming Munich Games, provided those interests promised to play by the rules and (more importantly) helped to further the Games through their financial generosity.

While corporate sponsorships, the sale of TV rights, and the Olympic lottery constituted the most important infusions of cash into OC coffers during the run-up to the '72 Games, these were by no means the only significant sources of revenue. Another money spinner for the OC was the sale of souvenir Olympic medals in gold and silver. These handsome keepsakes looked very much like the medals awarded to the victorious athletes, which was undoubtedly the point. "The sale of these medals furthers a worthy and important goal," said Daume at the outset of the medals promotion. "Whoever buys one of these medals makes a significant contribution to the financing of the Games." Daume estimated that the medals' sale would bring in "a minimum of ten million marks." In fact, the project ended up raking in more than twice that.

Additionally, in an especially creative move, the OC induced the Federal Post Office to issue special Olympic postage stamps, a percentage of whose sales went to funding the Games. The first series of the Olympic stamps appeared on June 1, 1968.

Willing though the OC obviously was to put the Olympic emblem up for sale, it did in the end show some restraint in this area. All told, the committee refused to grant licensing permits to some thirty products—all deemed "unsuitable" to carry the Olympic logo. Among the rejected items were lingerie articles and virility pills. (Considering what was soon to become common in this domain—famous athletes modeling skimpy underpants and aging politicians flogging Viagra—the '72 Games do seem somewhat "innocent.")

All this energetic huckstering notwithstanding, by early 1969 a deficit had opened up to the tune of approximately DM 175 million. This shortfall would have been even higher had not the OC managed to tap into a municipal kitty set up by the city of Munich back in 1955 to fund the construction of an all-purpose stadium on the Oberwiesenfeld. Mayor Vogel pleaded with the stadium-fund administrators (the original Förderverein) to shift the focus of their ongoing money-raising activities to the projected Olympic Stadium and to turn their existing treasury over to the OC. Seeing the chance for a much bigger and better facility, the stadium officials duly complied.

While income from the earlier stadium fund-raising operation, along with the above-mentioned new income streams, helped keep the Olympic building budget deficit from getting completely out of hand, what finally brought this problem under control (at least temporarily) was an especially creative fund-raising measure that required an act of parliament to inaugurate. In April 1969, the Bundestag passed a measure allowing the West German Treasury to mint a new ten-mark Olympic coin bearing the Games' official emblem, along with an inscription reading "Olympische Spiele 1972 in Deutschland" ("Olympic Games 1972 in Germany"). The coins could be purchased at banks and post offices for thirteen marks, the markup going entirely to the OC.

The coin innovation proved much more successful than anyone had imagined. People stood in long lines to buy the coins, which they hoarded as souvenirs instead of immediately blowing on beer or Wurst. To cope with the rising demand, the treasury ended up minting some one hundred million Olympic coins, the revenue from which climbed to an astounding DM 700 million. Considering this windfall, Vogel quipped that whoever had come up with the idea for an Olympic coin should have a monument built in his honor at the Olympic complex.

Yet, as financially successful as the Olympic coin project undoubtedly was, it proved also to be the most controversial and problematic of all the OC's fund-raising gambits. The controversy stemmed not from the fact that West Germany's most hallowed object of worship, its sacred D-Mark, was being hawked around the country as a fund-raising gimmick; no, the problem derived from the above-mentioned inscription, "Olympic Games 1972 in Germany." This wording ignited a firestorm of protest in the GDR and across Eastern Europe because it seemed to underscore, once again, the FRG's claim to be the sole representative of "Germany." Moreover, as the USSR's delegate to the IOC pointed out, the inscription constituted a violation of the IOC's dictum that the Games were awarded to cities, not to nations.

Readily agreeing with this criticism, the IOC itself demanded that the OC immediately discontinue the coins or at the very least alter the inscription to conform to IOC standards. Given the Olympic coin program's huge financial success, the OC understandably chose the latter option and ordered a new coin series with an amended inscription reading "Olympische Spiele 1972 in München" ("Olympic Games 1972 in Munich"). All subsequent reissues of the coins carried this wording.

The East Germans and their allies celebrated this OC concession as a triumph over FRG imperialism, but a more solid triumph was enjoyed by all those collectors who had hoarded the original coins, which, due to their relative rarity, became quite valuable on the international coin-collecting market.

As the saga of the Olympic coin program suggested, the West German public—or at least a good part of that public—was beginning to catch "Olympic fever." A public opinion poll launched by a major West German polling agency roughly one year before the Games showed that 79 percent of the respondents planned to watch the Games on TV, 9 percent had no intention of following the affair, and 12 percent were unsure about their interest. To the question "Do you think it is a good thing that the Olympic Games are being carried out in the FRG?" some 63 percent answered "yes," 7 percent said "no," and 30 percent were undecided. Perhaps more revealingly, hundreds of private citizens, completely unsolicited, sent in suggestions to the OC regarding the financing and organization of the upcoming Games. Predictably, many of these suggestions were a bit on the bizarre side. A Berliner proposed that every non-native participant or spectator coming to Munich for the Games should bring along a little bag of earth from his or her homeland; the dirt could be piled up into a "World Mountain" (a sure commercial attraction) and the empty bags sold off as souvenirs. A resident of the Rhineland proposed that every German citizen be offered the chance to pay twenty marks for one minute of speaking time on the radio, fifty marks for equivalent TV time (topics for said bloviating were to be up to the speakers). The broadcasts would continue for one hour each day until the entire budget for the Games was covered. Yet another proposal involved putting fast-breeding rabbits to work for the Olympics. Starting with a "base capital" of just ten rabbits, in no time one would have a "World Rabbit Farm" whose offspring could be sold off to the tune of 1.5 million marks, all for Munich '72! In a way, it's too bad that the OC's ability to raise money in more conventional ways obviated the need to resort to such highly creative solutions.

"The Chance of a Century": Building Munich's Olympic Park

The success of the OC's fund-raising schemes for Munich '72 was another factor that emboldened the Olympic builders. The dream of making a major architectural and technological statement at the Oberwiesenfeld now seemed realizable from a fiscal standpoint—whatever the small-minded bean counters might say. In time, this "no expenses barred" attitude would generate a new budget crisis, but by then the die had been cast for an Olympics complex more ambitious in scope and design than any of its predecessors (and, indeed, more ambitious than any physical complex in Olympic history until Beijing 2008).

By far the most expensive part of the '72 building project was the so-called Olympic Park—the assemblage of competition sites, athletic housing, and press facilities that arose on the relandscaped Oberwiesenfeld, situated some four kilometers north of the city center. Apart from the original concept of concentration—"an Olympics of short distances"—just about everything else that ultimately materialized at the Oberwiesenfeld diverged significantly from the vision put forth in Munich's Olympic bid.

Even the primary location for the Games might have changed had not the original site proved to be so ideal, and so easy for the organizers to secure. The fact that a large, relatively undeveloped plot of land close to the city center was available to the Olympic planners as late as the mid-1960s was largely a matter of luck. As mentioned before, part of this area had served as Munich's first airport—the one used by foreign participants flying in for the Munich Conference of 1938. In 1936, the Nazis had begun construction on a new airport in the suburb of Riem, but that facility did not open until 1939. The Nazi authorities in Munich had intended to turn the old airport into a marketplace and slaughterhouse (for animals), but World War II forced them to put those plans on hold. The area was thus free at the end of the war to be used as a giant dumping ground for the thousands of acre feet of rubble removed from the heavily bombed-out inner city. Earlier, unidentified corpses from the bombing had also been taken out to this site, where they lay jumbled together in mass graves. Gradually, the masses of rubble and bones were piled up in low hills, the highest, at sixty-six meters, dubbed the Schuttberg (Rubble Mountain). Not long after the war, another section of this forlorn region was taken over by the U.S. Army, which built some barracks there along with a central administration building. Radio Liberty moved into the former airport's shabby operations center in 1952. Four years later, the U.S. Army barracks, having since been abandoned, were used to house refugees from the 1956 Hungarian Revolt. Yet another part of the area was taken over by a group of Kleingärtner (allotment gardeners)—enterprising folks who colonized plots of unused land for tiny vegetable and flower gardens, replete with cozy shacks and cheerful ceramic gnomes.

What had kept this land free from major urban development over the years had nothing to do with its multiple present uses or any piety regarding what lay under the surface. It turns out that the acreage in question belonged to three different owners—the federal government, the Bavarian state, and the municipality of Munich—and these three "partners" could never agree on a common plan of exploitation. The city, which had long hoped to build a municipal sports stadium and indoor ice-skating rink on its parcel of land, was able in 1965 to convince the state and federal governments to add their parcels to the mix, thereby making up the unusually large piece of property that Munich could propose to the IOC as its primary Olympic site. At this time, the city's ice-skating rink was already under construction, as was a 291-meter-high Television Tower. (Hastily rechristened "Olympia-Turm," this tower, which featured a revolving restaurant near its summit, was completed in time for the Games and became a major attraction at the festival.)

While it had proven relatively easy to determine where to build Munich's Olympic complex, questions about what should be built, how the structures should look, and who should have the primary responsibility for the construction turned out to be considerably more difficult to resolve.

The initial expectation was that the city alone would guide the construction process, since it was the city's building department that had come up with the scheme included in Munich's bid to the IOC. However, Mayor Vogel himself vehemently opposed this option, believing that municipal bureaucrats, acting on their own, would be overburdened by a task of this magnitude. He proposed instead that the responsibility be divided among federal, state, and municipal officials, working together under the aegis of a building agency established by the OC. His proposal, despite being a perfect recipe for bureaucratic infighting, became reality.

No sooner had the above-mentioned Olympia Bau-Gesellschaft been established than the various ministers appointed to it began to argue long-windedly over the list of items to be built. They also argued over what was going to happen when the building budget was exceeded, which everyone expected to occur sooner or later. These issues could not be resolved in even a preliminary fashion until a smaller Board of Directors was created to oversee the unwieldy Bau-Gesellschaft. Once Franz Josef Strauß agreed to chair this board, in August 1967, planning activities could begin in earnest. In a matter of a few weeks, the Bau-Gesellschaft approved an initial list of construction projects, including a main stadium, multi-purpose athletic hall, swim center, Olympic Village, and Olympic Press Center. With respect to the expected cost overruns, federal representatives on the Board of Directors, including Strauß himself, agreed that the Bund would assume 50 percent of the added costs.

Even before the Bau-Gesellschaft held its first planning meeting, Daume, Vogel, and other Olympic officials took aim at the existing overall concept for Munich's Olympic complex, the one drawn up by the city's building department and submitted with the bid to the IOC. Vogel himself now complained that the original scheme lacked flair and aesthetic power. It failed, he said, to come across as a Wagnerian Gesamtkunstwerk (total work of art)—an architectural counterpart to the great Munich buildings of the previous century. Perhaps under normal circumstances such aesthetic modesty might have been acceptable, he added, but the current moment, Munich's Olympic moment, represented "the chance of a century" to do something great. Therefore, he went on, what was needed was an international design competition from which a new conception could emerge that might be more in keeping with this unprecedented opportunity. Of course, he admitted, a more ambitious conception would undoubtedly not lend itself to the budgetary constraints contained in the original bid. Yet, this was no time to think small.

Amazingly, Vogel and Daume managed to convince the normally cost-conscious Munich City Council to embrace this new line of thinking and to sanction a juried competition for Munich's projected "Olympic Park." The council's only caveat was that the competition must be national, not international (with the council, cosmopolitanism only went so far). Shortly thereafter, Bavaria and the Bund signed off on this plan as well, and on February 1, 1967, design firms from across West Germany were invited to submit ideas on how to turn the spacious graveyard of old Munich into new Munich's putative architectural statement of the century.

In the five-month period allotted for the Oberwiesenfeld design competition, some 101 entries came in—making this the largest FRG architectural competition to date. Three cavernous exhibition halls were needed to display all the models and drawings. The jury, consisting of noted architects and designers as well as politicians and Olympic officials, had little difficulty making their first cut among the entries. It turned out that many of the submissions evoked, in the words of one jury member, "the atmosphere of the Reichssportfeld," the Olympic complex built for the 1936 Berlin Games. In fact, one of the rejected submissions came from none other than Werner March, the architect chiefly responsible for the neoclassical Olympic Stadium in Berlin. As it happened, March's design for Munich, in stark contrast to his work in Berlin, was quite bold and modernistic, but there was just no way that the man who had designed "Hitler's stadium" was going to win a similar assignment for Munich in 1972.

In assessing the various entries, the jury was interested in how the projected buildings worked together, how the structures harmonized with the hilly Oberwiesenfeld landscape, and how the landscape itself might contribute to the ideal of an Olympic Gesamtkunstwerk. Although most of the jury members spoke of a need for aesthetic "unity," they also worried about *too much* unity—an oppressive uniformity that would belie the playful heterogeneity said to animate the new Munich.

From the outset, the jury focused most of its attention on the main stadium. This is not surprising. Over the years, Olympic host cities had made their aesthetic statements chiefly through their central stadia and other key athletic facilities. One thinks of the 1932 Los Angeles Games' Neronic Coliseum; Berlin '36's neo-Dorian Olympia-Stadion; the bombastic Stadio Olympico in Rome, part of the Foro Italico built by Mussolini to attract the (cancelled) 1940 Games and then finally put to use for the 1960 Summer Games; and Kenzo Tange's swooping, suspension-roofed swimming and diving center for the Tokyo Games of 1964. The Olympic Park jury quickly became caught up in the old game of architectural one-upmanship—the "game behind the Games."

After eliminating the many obvious non-starters in the competition with relative ease, the jury fell into furious argument over the remaining twenty-three entries. The design that eventually won—an innovative glass-roofed affair proposed by the Stuttgart firm of Günter Behnisch and Associates—initially generated considerable opposition within the jury. Some said it was technically unbuildable, a "conceptual fantasy." Others prophetically noted that, even if it could be built, such a thing would be wildly expensive. (These reservations about the Behnisch design, incidentally, are highly reminiscent of the fears once expressed for that other pioneering glass house built over a century earlier in London's Hyde Park: Joseph Paxton's "Crystal Palace.")

Vogel himself belonged early on to the circle of doubters, but the more he studied Behnisch's design, the more fascinated he became with its potential. Daume, too, became a convert. Both men were impressed by the way Behnisch's scheme fit in to the hilly Oberwiesenfeld landscape, managing a "unity of technology and nature." This unifying quality in the Behnisch proposal reminded Vogel of Kenzo Tange's swim center for the Tokyo Games (which is not surprising, since Behnisch was directly inspired by this earlier work). In Vogel's view, Behnisch's glass-roofed complex not only would be the equal of Tange's great design but might also "help [Munich] give architectural expression to our own time, to all its tensions, aspirations, and sensibilities." Of course, Vogel knew such greatness would not come cheaply. But artistic brilliance had always been expensive, even in Bavaria: think of the great buildings endowed by the Wittelsbach kings, Ludwig I and ("mad") Ludwig II, which at the moment of their construction had seemed wildly profligate but over time had proven to be worth every Groschen. Given the high probability that the tented glass roof would "join the ranks of important contributions to the human spirit," penny-pinching considerations were "totally inappropriate." (Vogel was no doubt blissfully unaware that in talking this way he sounded exactly like Adolf Hitler justifying the extravagant spending for the Berlin Games of 1936.)

With backing from Daume and all the political representatives from the state and federal governments serving on the Olympic Park jury, the final vote fell seventeen to two in favor of the Behnisch design. Significantly, the only opposition came from professional architects.

The Behnisch firm's comprehensive design for the Olympic Park won because, in the end, it seemed best able to capture that elusive collection of ideals and images that Munich's planners hoped the '72 Games would convey to the world. As Behnisch himself explained in his firm's proposal, the Olympic Park and its edifices, above all the main stadium, must reflect "Munich's unique atmosphere as a city of the muses and the arts, thereby [also] returning the Olympic Games to their original purpose and content." Further, the various buildings at the Olympic Park must "reinforce each other in a fascinating 'architectural landscape' in which the athletic youth of the world, visiting Olympic guests, and the population of Munich could all come together in an atmosphere of openness and freedom." The main stadium would lie on the west side of an artificially sculpted valley, with the earth itself providing the foundation wall for two-thirds of the structure. Spectators would enter the stadium along its top rim and thus be able to see the whole complex spreading out below them, the site's reassuring "human dimensions" profoundly in evidence. By incorporating the hillside, with its grass and trees, into the built environment, and by offering a gently sloping seating area colored in a "fresh green," the stadium would give spectators the impression of lingering in an idyllic valley. Stretching above the seating area of the stadium, a swooping glass roof would provide a "transparent" cover that would simultaneously mirror the nearby Alps and suggest the openness and inclusiveness of the democratic system under whose beneficent aegis these Games were taking place.

Of course, as with just about everything else associated with Munich's would-be "care-free" Games, it proved one thing to propose such a grand scheme, quite another to bring it to fruition.

"Towers of Babylon"

On July 14, 1969, some four hundred Olympic officials, along with thousands of ordinary citizens of Munich, witnessed the ceremonial laying of the foundation stone for the sports installations at the Oberwiesenfeld. This moment marked the formal translation of abstract plans into steel, glass, and concrete realities. In his capacity as chairman of the Executive Board of the Olympia Bau-Gesellschaft, Franz Josef Strauß opined that the facilities about to rise up on the graveyard of Old Munich would both brilliantly serve the Olympic Games and contribute to the ongoing redevelopment of New Munich. Aware that the construction now beginning was going to be much costlier than originally projected, he declared, "We wish to receive the athletes, the officials, the journalists and visitors from all over the world with generosity and an open heart as friends. We believe in the Olympic Idea and its effectiveness; [this idea] justifies the ambitious efforts and expenditures of the host country."

Three months later, in October 1969, the OC allowed the general public to get its first look at building operations on the Oberwiesenfeld site. On this Tag der offenen Tür (open house), thousands of gawkers, mostly Münchners, traipsed around in the mud amidst a thicket of construction cranes. According to a local paper, the visitors expressed amazement over how much the area had been transformed in the short time since work had commenced—and some also expressed their concern about the growing cost of all this. The most prominent visitor on this occasion was the director of the USSR's office of tourism; he assured the locals that interest in the upcoming Games was high in his country, and that Munich '72 could expect "a great many" guests from Eastern Europe.

For all his earlier complaints about the escalating costs of the Games, Avery Brundage, who had gotten a private tour of the construction site and a close look at the building plans, had nothing but praise for what Munich intended to do at the Oberwiesenfeld. As he wrote Mayor Vogel, his visit to

Munich left him "with complete confidence in the organization that has been assembled to carry out your plans."

But the optimism evident during the early phase of Olympic building quickly gave way to doubts and internal feuding as a plethora of highly complicated technical problems arose—and along with them even greater than expected cost overruns. The biggest and most expensive problem turned out to be the emblematic glass roof, whose swooping tent-like surface was to cover part of the main stadium along with adjacent facilities such as the swimming hall and indoor sports center. The final design and construction work for this ambitious project was subcontracted by Behnisch to a noted industrial designer, Frei Otto, whose firm had recently built a transparent glass roof for the German Pavilion at the Montreal World's Fair.

Over five years later, Frei Otto, when interviewed about "his" Olympic roof, still bristled with anger, along with lingering regret over what might have been done instead. Otto revealed that he had never really wanted to "build for Olympia" in the first place because he believed the modern Games had become a "colossal theater," a new version of Roman Empire-style "gladiatorial combat" that had "little to do with [ancient] Olympia or true sport." As for the Olympic buildings of the modern era, they were in his view nothing but latter-day "Towers of Babylon," which either "fell into ruin themselves or drove their builders to ruin." In retrospect, he considered the iconic roof for Munich '72 to have been a kind of "veil" deployed by the Games' organizers to obscure the "giganticism of their project and to make this whole enterprise more palatable to the general public."

In Otto's opinion, it would have made more sense, and of course, been much less expensive, to erect some temporary structures for the Games that could then be taken down once the Olympic circus left town. But in the modern era, Olympic hosts had become obsessed with making permanent architectural statements, lasting monuments to their own ego. Yet—not surprising in an architect—Otto had a pretty healthy ego of his own, and when Behnisch called on him to disprove early contentions that his glass-roof concept was unbuildable, Frei Otto could not resist coming on board.

His initial idea was to build a somewhat larger version of his roof for the German Pavilion at the Montreal Fair, which had featured thin, lightweight panes of glass held together by a web of aluminum stitching. But because the Munich organizers saw in their Olympic roof design a long-lasting architectural symbol for their city, not just a temporary fairgrounds attraction, Otto soon found himself exploring terra incognita in the realm of suspension glass-roof construction, plotting out an undulat-ing surface of thick acrylic glass covering a massive space of about seventy-five thousand square meters. A thick glass surface like this was bound to intensify solar rays passing through it, potentially baking everything and everyone below it, rather like those magnifying lenses deployed by little boys to fry ants in the heat of the noonday sun. Therefore, Otto had to darken his glass panes, thus compromising to some degree their promised translucence. At the same time, he could not darken the glass too much, lest the resulting gloom ruin the prospects for high-quality color television pictures. The compromise he came up with managed to bathe the stadium in a slightly opaque brown—certainly not the color the organizers would have wished for.

Also problematic was the support system for the roof. Because the thick acrylic panes and the iron webbing that knitted them together proved extremely heavy, huge tubular steel pillars were needed to hold the thing up. And because these pillars would have to be grounded in unusu-ally weak firmament consisting largely of rubble, they had to be affixed to large "injection anchors" buried deep below the surface.

The demands of the stadium construction proved so daunting that, midway through the process, some members of the Bau-Gesellschaft wanted to throw in the towel, proposing that the sunken-field, glass-roof, and tubular steel design be scrapped in favor of a more conventional ap-proach—say, an above-ground bowl made of good old concrete. But of course, a roofless cement bowl would hardly have put Munich on the architectural map, and this idea went nowhere. Sticking to the glass-roof design, but obliged perforce to make constant adjustments and improvisa-tions, Otto's team quickly burned through the DM 40 million originally budgeted for the roof and had to request supplemental funds to keep their project on track. Word of Otto's expenditures reached the press, and soon papers across West Germany, and even some foreign journals, carried alarming stories about the huge cost overruns at the Oberwiesenfeld.

Smelling blood, a group of CSU politicians—the same ones who had earlier attacked Munich's Olympic bid—lambasted Mayor Vogel and the Bau-Gesellschaft for losing control over expenditures. But, as Vogel noted, the criticism from this quarter would have been even harsher had not Franz Josef Strauß, the CSU party boss, been chairman of the Board of Directors of the Building Corporation. Typically, Strauß tried to place the blame for escalating costs entirely on "incompetent experts from the city," but Vogel quickly shut him up by reminding him that experts from Strauß's own office had signed off on all the design decisions. Moreover, Strauß himself

might well have personally added to the problem of ballooning construc-
tions costs. An article in *Der Spiegel* magazine later reported that he had
channeled the primary construction contract for the Olympic Village to
a firm advised by his close friend, the lawyer Franz Dannecker. Strauß's
friend, it seems, had not been obliged to go through the normal bidding
process, and the final price tag for the Village was staggeringly high.

For its part, the OC responded to the criticism regarding Olympic
expenditures by establishing special "Savings Commissions" charged
with finding places to cut costs. These commissions proved ineffective.
Finally, in November 1969, following a heated protest from the National
Federation of Taxpayers to the Bundestag about Olympic spending, the
OC shuffled the leadership of the Bau-Gesellschaft, bringing in Carl
Mertz, the head of the German Federal Railways, to reorganize Olympic
contracting and construction financing. Mertz gave Behnisch, Otto, and
other Oberwiesenfeld builders new budget lines and set up a reserve of DM
200 million for additional cost overruns. Meanwhile, the federal Finance
Ministry, recently vacated by Strauß, agreed to rearrange the distribution
of financial responsibility, whereby the Bund now took over 50 percent of
total construction costs, leaving 25 percent each for Bavaria and Munich.

While the troublesome glass roof proved to be the most expensive
single item on the construction agenda for Munich '72, it was not the only
source of financial hemorrhaging. The Games' scull-rowing course, which
involved digging a long artificial canal, was scheduled for construction on
some 850,000 square meters of agricultural land near the small towns of
Feldmoching/Oberschleissheim, a few kilometers north of Munich. But
when it came time to start building the canal, owners of the designated
property, a group of opportunistic farmers, increased their asking price
"astronomically." Lacking the authority to requisition the land, the OC announced it would search for alternative sites. Soon it had a lower bid from
the village of Königsdorf, a place that was considerably farther away from
central Munich than Feldmoching/Oberschleissheim and in other ways
less attractive as a rowing site. Faced with the prospect of losing their land
sale to the lower bidders from Königsdorf, the Feldmoching farmers came
back with a more reasonable asking price, which the OC duly accepted.
However, the total cost of building the canal, which required the removal
of 2,300,000 cubic meters of earth, still came out to be seven times more
than the original estimate. And in the bargaining process, the organizers
got an object lesson in local greed, as they would time and time again during the run-up to the Games.

Another costly problem arose over the equestrian facilities, which, according to the original plan, were to be built on the Oberwiesenfeld at the foot of the Schuttberg. In the end, however, the facility had to be moved to a newly purchased property in the suburb of Riem, out near the airport, and the final tab for the whole enterprise ended up being ten times that of the original estimate.

Why did they make this costly move? It turns out that an aged Russian religious hermit calling himself "Father Timofej" had been squatting for sixteen years in the middle of the property chosen for the riding facility. He had built a small church out of pieces of rubble and had christened his little sect "The Community of the Founder of the Churchly Estate of the Holy Trinity East-West." Although he had no legal claim to the land on which he was squatting, he refused point blank to make way for the Olympic equestrians. Cleverly, he made his plight known to sympathizers in town, who threatened physically to block his expulsion. Realizing it faced a public relations debacle if it tried to remove Father Tim and bulldoze his quaint little church, the OC decided to leave him in place and to decamp for Riem. In announcing this concession, Daume tried to put a positive gloss on the situation: "We have after all promised to put on humane Games. I think [Father Tim] fits well into this conception." And in a way, Daume turned out to be correct: Father Timofej's tin-walled church became a must-see attraction for visitors to the Oberwiesenfeld during the Games.

If, as OC press secretary Johnny Klein assured, "Father Timofej can sleep in peace," there remained the much larger challenge of providing adequate sleeping (and eating) arrangements for the thousands of Olympic athletes, coaches, and team officials who would descend on Munich for the Games. Munich's planners, of course, had always intended to build a special "Olympic Village" for the '72 Games—something that had been done at most of the festivals since the 1932 Los Angeles Olympics (and which in fact had been added to the IOC rulebook for host cities in 1949). The Angelinos had set a high bar in 1932 with their inaugural village, quartering the male athletes in "garden cottages" sprinkled over a hilltop overlooking the Pacific Ocean. (The female athletes were relegated to a hotel downtown.) Berlin '36 outdid L.A. with a sprawling men's village containing virtually everything the athletes might need or want, including a dining hall serving meals suited to national taste, a full-size gymnasium, a running track, a soccer field, a swimming pool, a cinema, shops, and a rustic Finnish sauna. The Berlin Village's chief drawback from the athletes' point of view was its location on a military base some fourteen kilometers west of the main athletic complex.

Beginning in the early 1960s, the Olympic Games involved far too many athletes and officials for this army of Olympians to be housed in quaint cottages of the kind provided in Los Angeles and Berlin. The Munich organizers knew from the outset that their "village" would have to be more like a small city. Nonetheless, their original plan was to make the athletic housing in 1972 as modest and utilitarian as possible—in keeping with their overall scheme of low-cost, low-key Games. But like the early master plan in general, this initial impetus for Spartan housing soon gave way to something much more ambitious. In the end, about the only aspect of the original housing plan to remain in place was the notion of locating the Village close to the competition sites. Unlike at Los Angeles, Berlin, and indeed most of the other post–World War II Olympic festivals, athletes participating in Munich '72 would not have to travel long distances to compete in their events—or, for that matter, to get to the bars and brothels downtown.

The Olympic housing plan that eventually passed muster with the Bau-Gesellschaft called for some 3,000 apartments in the men's village and 1,800 in the women's village. While the architectural style at both villages was intended to be sleek and modern, the accommodations themselves would be quite varied: in the men's village, a mixture of two-story bungalows, one- to three-story row houses, three- to five-story terraced compounds, and a twenty-story apartment tower; and for the women, a small collection of row houses and two sixteen-story towers. For the men's village, the building plan promised "optimal views and a careful segregation of pedestrian and motor traffic." In addition to its varied housing options, the men's village would harbor several restaurants, a gymnasium, shops, a medical center, a post office, a bank, a book store, cinemas, a library, a dance hall, nine saunas, and "over five hundred massage cabins." There would also be a theater for such attractions as Bavarian yodeling exhibitions. Chess fans would be able to pursue their passion at a giant outdoor chess board whose pieces were so big they had to be carried individually to their positions. ("You felt as if you were in a giant war game," recalled America's Vince Matthews about playing chess in the Village.) Like the restaurant at Berlin's Olympic Village in 1936, Munich's eatery would feature foods from all over the world, but unlike in Berlin, no alcoholic beverages would be available in the '72 athletic quarters.

To justify the high cost of building such an elaborate complex, the planners promised after the Games to sell most of the apartment units in the men's village to private buyers and to turn the women's village (and a small part of the men's village) over to the University of Munich for student housing.

The post-Games inheritors of Munich '72's various athletic housing units would, of course, not be segregated by gender and would be free to move freely from what had been the men's village to the nearby towers previously set aside for the female athletes. During the Games, however, no such unfettered and indiscriminant mingling would be possible because the construction plan included a two-meter-high fence to encircle the female quarters in a kind of chain-link chastity belt. Female athletes were free to visit the men's village, but not the other way around.

This plan to fence off the ladies generated a spirited protest from the only female member of the OC, Frau Dr. Liselott Diem, the sixty-two-year-old widow of Carl Diem, chief organizer of the 1936 Berlin Games. A major figure in German sports circles in her own right, Diem had been a professor at the Deutsche Hochschule für Leibesübungen in Berlin before being dismissed in 1933 because she was Jewish. In 1947, she took up a similar position at the newly founded Deutsche Sporthochschule in Cologne. Diem was in some ways a modern woman, and she bristled at the idea that today's young females, especially athletic young females, needed protection of this "outmoded" sort. "I know there will be some strong men at the Games," she said, "but there will also be some strong women, particularly among the discus throwers. These days it is perhaps the men who will have to be protected from the sexual aggressiveness of the women!" If her OC colleagues insisted on putting a fence around the women's camp, she declared, she would demand a similar barrier around the men's.

In response to the protest campaign launched by Frau Diem, Walther Tröger, the OC official tapped to act as informal "mayor" of the Olympic Village, responded, "I'll defend the separation of the male and female villages to the death." Tröger eventually prevailed in this war of wills: the projected fence around the women's village was built as planned—though in the end, it did not prove very effective in protecting female chastity.* Yet, however effective this barrier turned out to be, in light of what was to happen in "his" Village on day 11 of the Games, Walther Tröger, one imagines, might well have wished that he had worried less about protecting feminine virtue than about ensuring the physical safety of all the athletes living under his care.

---

* Lawrence "Monk" Terry, who lived in the Munich Village as a member of the U.S. rowing team, recalls that there was "a lot of fence jumping" during the Games. Tröger's vaunted barrier proved to be little more than a speed bump for the male athletes.

At the Munich Games, not just the athletes and coaches would have a "village" of their own but also the army of journalists covering the festival. Munich's planners were very mindful of the crucial role that the press, radio, and television had come to play in the modern Olympics. Commenting on the significance of journalistic coverage for the '72 Games, Johnny Klein wrote in a report to the IOC on June 6, 1969,

> The image which the world receives of the Games, of the host city and the whole country will depend largely on the mass media. The organizers are also convinced that for the journalists the coverage of the Olympic Games is one of the toughest events on the program. This is one of the reasons why no trouble will be spared to offer journalists the best possible living and working conditions when they come to Munich in 1972.

To properly prepare the opinion-makers for their "tough" assignment, the Munich organizers announced the construction of a Press Village on the west side of the Oberwiesenfeld, less than a mile from the main competition sites. (The thinking here was that even sportswriters could walk a mile.) The approximately four thousand journalists expected to cover the Games would have the unprecedented luxury of "well-appointed single rooms equipped with television and telephones." The Press Village would also boast its own "swimming pool with a sauna and massage rooms attached"—for relaxation after a hard day of reporting. In the hope of influencing the nature of that reporting, a large and fully staffed bar would be open around the clock.* Also scheduled for the Village were an assortment of shops, airline offices, a travel agency, a post office, and a laundry service—"all for the sole use of members of the press."

A Press Center adjacent to the Press Village would, according to the planners, provide the journalists with everything they could possibly need to do their jobs quickly and efficiently. There would be an accrediting bureau; modern, well-equipped reporting rooms; a telex room with fifty teleprinters; delivery boxes; telephone rooms with 120 booths; a telegram counter; a special printing press providing up-to-date bulletins from the

---

* Commenting after the Games on the importance of the Press Center bar, one American journalist wrote, "At any given moment for 17 days, a visitor could count on seeing at least half of the press corps becalmed there. . . . The news hawks sat stuporous on squashy black Naugahyde sofas, with plastic half-liter containers of Löwenbräu at hand, and watched the Olympics by staring at the banks of color-television sets. A man could cover four events at a time by this method, think well of himself and never move more than 20 feet from the bar."

field; premises for international news agencies; a central laboratory for photographers; a large self-service restaurant; a snack bar; television and reading rooms; and the offices of the Olympic Press Center. (One is struck, in reading this list of amenities for the journalists, that the only item missing was an on-site brothel. Since Munich's planners intended to declare the entire Olympic Park a "prostitute-free zone," journalists in search of commercial sex, as opposed to impromptu trysts with their colleagues, would have to go into town, where some ten thousand prostitutes were expected to report for duty.)

Munich's planners were well aware that, among the various forms of journalistic coverage of the Games, radio and television (especially the latter) were by far the most important. By the 1960s and 1970s, Olympic festivals lived and died by the pictures flickering across TV sets around the globe. Munich planned to acknowledge this reality by providing a state-of-the-art broadcasting center, one considerably more advanced than anything in the past. The broadcasting center was to be built and maintained by a newly founded German Olympic Center Radio and Television Consortium made up of the main West German broadcasting networks. This agency was charged with "providing the very latest technical facilities for the reporting work of some 60 foreign television corporations and about 110 radio systems."

All this high-tech gear was absolutely necessary because the Munich '72 Games would be the first Olympics in history to be televised (at least by the German networks) in color and *in their entirety*—the broadcasting equivalent of the marathon but a lot more expensive. The German consortium alone invested some DM 100 million in the broadcasting facilities for 1972.

Another first in this domain involved those color TV transmissions. Eastern Europeans, including East Germans, had lived behind a "color curtain" since 1967 when it came to the reception of color TV signals from West Germany and Britain because these two countries had adopted the PAL (Phase Alternation Line) system, while the Soviet Bloc, for political reasons, had bought into France's SECAM (Systeme en Coleurs a Memoire). Receivers tuned to SECAM could not get PAL transmissions (and vice versa) without a special converter. However, the Soviets decided to lift this "color curtain" for the Munich Games by deploying a conversion process that would allow the West Germans to transmit fifteen hours of color TV to the East daily. Moscow took this step because it anticipated a raft of gold medals for its side—and it would be much more glorious if the comrades at home were able to see the actual golden luster on all those prizes.

Although home viewers everywhere were going to be able to see the '72 Games in color, the TV audience dependent on West German transmissions was in for an intriguing—and revealing—limitation on its coverage. Robert Lembke, the coordinator of the FRG's TV production, made clear early on his intention to direct his cameras only at the top performers in any given competition. In a race, for example, the cameras would focus exclusively on the first three runners. "If someone's running fourth—even if he's a German—then tough luck for him!" decreed Lembke. So much, one might add, for Baron Pierre de Coubertin's famous dictum that, in the modern Olympics, "being there" was all that counted.

The escalating costs of all this frantic Olympic building did not go unnoticed in Bonn. By April 1971, the total construction cost had reached a staggering DM 1.9 billion. At this point, the Bundestag held an emergency session on Olympic spending. What galled the parliamentarians was not only the high total cost but also various expenditures on special facilities for sporting events with relatively little public resonance, such as judo, wrestling, and whitewater canoeing. The reports about excessive spending at the Oberwiesenfeld generated (in the words of one paper) "a wave of parliamentary anger rolling toward Munich." Willi Daume, Herbert Kunze, and Carl Mertz were all called to Bonn, where they were told that under no circumstances would the Bundestag support paying for any additional sports facilities, nor would it countenance any more increases to the overall spending commitment on the part of the Bund. Enough was enough!

Fortunately for Munich '72's builders, by spring 1971 the facilities at the Oberwiesenfeld were well on their way to completion, and the grounds surrounding the buildings were, in the words of one enthusiastic commentator, fast being transformed into "the park-like setting" promised in Munich's Olympic bid. A team headed by a Munich landscaping expert had reshaped the contours of the Olympic Park by scooping out artificial "valleys" and by increasing the height of some of the rubble hills. The team also created a new artificial lake with a surface area of eighty thousand square meters. The edges of this lake were planted with reeds and willows to mimic the vegetation on the banks of the Isar River, the beloved waterway that flows through central Munich. Aside from its aesthetic function, this lake could also serve as a reservoir to hold all the rainwater expected to drain off the vast tent roof covering the main athletic complex.

After a quick visit in April to the Oberwiesenfeld complex, Chancellor Willy Brandt, who served as chairman of the OC's advisory board, declared optimistically, "With this [Olympic stage], we will be able to show ourselves off to the world!" A few months later, the construction site witnessed a visit from Japanese emperor Hirohito, who, accompanied by Carl Mertz, circled above the area for two minutes in a private jet.

The dozens of private companies working on Munich's vast Olympic complex managed to stay on schedule only by constantly adding to their labor force, which constituted yet another factor in the ballooning costs. At the height of the construction process, in 1969–1971, some three thousand laborers worked at the Oberwiesenfeld site. Tellingly, about 60 percent of these workers were Gastarbeiter (foreign laborers), imported for the job mainly from Yugoslavia, Turkey, and Italy. They earned DM 350 weekly, about one-third less than what a unionized German worker would have received. Not surprisingly, this reliance on relatively cheap foreign labor inspired bitter resentment among native German construction workers, who lobbied unsuccessfully for a "native-only" employment policy. These native workers pointed out that the construction of Germany's previous Olympic complex, the Reichssportfeld, in 1936, had relied exclusively on domestic labor.

Remaking Munich as "Olympia-City"

The athletic complex on the Oberwiesenfeld amounted to only one part of Munich's ambitious building program for the '72 Games. The city itself underwent substantial infrastructural and cosmetic alterations in preparation for the big show. The pre-Olympic makeover can be seen as a significant chapter in the larger story of Munich's reconstruction in the decades after World War II.

From the outset, Munich's resurrection from the ashes of defeat had been informed by competing urban-design ambitions: put simply, one school wished to strike out in bold new directions, while another pushed to reconnect quite literally with the city's architectural past. Both aesthetic schools, however, shared a desire to obliterate, as much as possible, physical reminders of the city's most recent past—the Nazi era.

After 1945, Munich was faced with a monumental task of rebuilding because much of the city's historic core, its fabled Altstadt, had been destroyed or badly damaged. In early postwar debates among urban planners over the nature and direction of reconstruction, the preservationist/historicist tendency gradually won out, largely because it enjoyed widespread support among the local populace. Tellingly, the earliest major inner-city reconstruction focused on the Residenz, the sprawling city-palace that had long been home to Bavaria's ruling dynasty, the Wittelsbachs. Costing over

DM 60 million, the Residenz was the largest historic restoration project in the Federal Republic in the early postwar period.

Facing the adjacent Marienplatz, Munich's monumental Neues Rathaus (New City Hall), which had been built in neo-Gothic style in the late nineteenth and early twentieth centuries, was painstakingly restored with financial support from municipal funds and local citizens' groups. Subscriptions from the citizenry also allowed other prominent landmarks such as the twin-towered Frauenkirche and medieval Peterskirche to rise again in all their former glory. The heavily damaged Siegestor (Victory Gate), commissioned by King Ludwig I to celebrate Bavaria's role in the defeat of Napoleon, was also restored but with a modern embellishment. A new inscription, "Dem Sieg geweiht. Vom Krieg zerstört. Zum Frieden mahnend" ("Dedicated to Victory. Destroyed by War. Admonishing for Peace") was etched above the south-facing archway to remind the world that the new Bavaria, and the new Munich, harbored a very different attitude toward war.

Not surprisingly, Munich's citizens were considerably less anxious to preserve surviving physical reminders of that recent twelve-year period when the city had served as "Capital of the [Nazi] Movement." As it happened, quite a few structures connected to the Third Reich—either built by the Nazis or closely associated with their rule—still stood when the Americans overran the city in May 1945. Fortunately for the many Münchners who hoped to move on with their lives as if the Nazi regime had never existed, the American occupiers of postwar Bavaria proved equally determined to purge the city of its Nazi associations.

Even as the Americans rolled into Munich's rubble-strewn Altstadt, they found citizens busily dismantling the Nazi shrine at the Feldherrnhalle, where sixteen storm troopers had been "martyred" in Hitler's ill-fated Beer Hall Putsch of November 1923. A little later, the U.S. military authorities themselves ordered the demolition of two "Honor Temples" built by the Nazis to house the martyrs' remains; these structures stood on the edge of the Königsplatz, Nazi Munich's administrative center. (The structures' pedestals, by the way, still stand today.)

Yet, it was these same Americans who, facing a chronic shortage of usable office space, ended up saving some prominent Nazi buildings for their own purposes. Thus it was that Hitler's Führerbau, site of the 1938 Munich Conference, became for a time Munich's Amerika Haus, advertising the American way of life to a (hopefully) chastened local population. Later on, the building assumed its present role as Munich University's Hochschule für Musik und Theater. A neighboring building on the Königsplatz, the National Socialist Verwaltungsbau, became a warehouse for recaptured European art that had been looted by the Nazis. The Haus der deutschen Kunst, the Hitler-commissioned art museum on the Englischer Garten that had anchored Nazi Munich's claim to be the "Art-capital of the Third Reich," became for several years an American military recreation center. (After the building was later converted back to a museum by the Bavarians, the colored lines marking the Americans' basketball court remained visible on the parquet floor for many years.) After making substantial repairs to the historic Bürgerbräukeller—the upscale beer hall that had served as the starting point for Hitler's abortive 1923 putsch, only to be severely damaged in Georg Elser's futile attempt to blow up the Führer in 1939*—the Americans used the place for a canteen. (Returned many years later to Bavarian ownership, this infamous edifice stayed out of the news until May 2, 1970, when a rally there sponsored by supporters of the Greek military junta inspired a counterdemonstration that left fifteen people injured. In the late 1980s, the structure was finally torn down.) The above-mentioned Munich Airport in Riem, though built by the Nazis in the 1930s, was seen by both the Americans and the Bavarians as far too valuable to demolish. Cleansed of its Nazi iconography, it remained Munich's central airport until 1992, when it was replaced by a new facility named in honor of Franz Josef Strauß.

Postwar Münchners were so anxious to forget the Nazi past that, in addition to wiping away physical traces of their erstwhile beloved masters, they also resisted an early effort to memorialize the millions of victims of Nazi rule. In 1946, Karl Scharnagl, Munich's first postwar mayor, proposed that sizeable monuments to the victims of Nazism be erected in heavily trafficked sites in the central city—including in that old heart of Nazi power, the Königsplatz, where local Nazis had burned "un-German" books in May 1933. The city council promptly vetoed Scharnagl's plan, citing a lack of funds. This excuse was trotted out again some fifty years later when a group of local historians proposed that informative signs be placed at the square to instruct passersby on the site's former function in the Third Reich. (It was not until 2008 that such markers were finally erected.) On

---

* On November 9, 1939, Johann Georg Elser, a carpenter and former Communist, planted a time bomb in the podium from which Hitler would give a speech commemorating the Beer Hall Putsch—a ritual he performed every year on the anniversary of the ill-starred coup attempt. The bomb went off as scheduled, but Hitler had cut short his speech and left the hall earlier than expected. Elser was murdered by the Nazis at Dachau on April 9, 1945, twenty days before the liberation of the camp.

the other hand, money was easily found in the early 1970s to beautify the Königsplatz in preparation for a mass celebration scheduled to be held there in August 1972 to welcome the Olympic Torch to Munich following the now-traditional relay run from ancient Olympia to the host city. And still later, in 1988, money was made available to tear up the Nazi-installed flagstone parade-round surface and to plant it over with grass.

When it came time to consider possible infrastructural improvements to the city of Munich in preparation for the 1972 Olympics, the related tasks of blotting out physical reminders of the Nazis' presence and reconnecting architecturally to happier times were largely complete. The resurrection of southern Germany's greatest city could be joyfully proclaimed in 1958 during year-long celebrations marking the eight-hundredth anniversary of Munich's founding. The central theme of the celebrations was "Munich Is Munich Again."

In contrast to the initial makeover of Munich during the first postwar decades, the improvements for the '72 Games were informed largely by a desire to modernize the city and to make it more user-friendly for visitors and locals alike. This enterprise harmonized well with Munich's new self-image as an up-to-date cosmopolitan metropolis that happened also to have a good bit of "heart" and traditional rustic charm. Yet, as the American historian Gavriel Rosenfeld has shrewdly noted, this modernizing impulse, much like the earlier restorationist one, could have a memory-repressing function with regard to the recent Nazi past. In the modernizing campaign, people's attention would be resolutely focused on the present and future—on Munich's new roles as "Olympia-City" and "Secret Capital of Germany"—thus effectively marginalizing any lingering memories of the not-so-long-ago days when the city fathers had proudly added a swastika to the municipal coat of arms.

One of the chief hallmarks of modern cities is an up-to-date public transport system, and Munich had begun working on a new underground railway (U-Bahn) and surface commuter line (S-Bahn) well before winning the right to host the 1972 Olympic Games. But, as noted above, Mayor Vogel had promised in Munich's Olympic bid to speed up completion of the city's public transport system and to add a brand new line connecting the downtown with the envisaged Olympic Park. (Vogel, we might add, was absolutely obsessed with moving Munich away from a dependence on the automobile, the dire consequences of which in his view were most evident in Los Angeles, a place he considered a "catastrophic" dystopia.)

Construction began on the new Olympic subway line on May 10, 1967, and was completed by May 1972, three months before the opening of the

Games. Along with the Olympic subway line itself, a new "Olympia-Park" U-Bahn station was opened on the edge of the Oberwiesenfeld, across the road from the BMW headquarters. Shortly before the U-Bahn station came on line, the German Federal Railways finished an extension of an S-Bahn line that had a terminus on the other side of the Olympic complex. Thanks to these train connections, the vast majority of visitors to the '72 Games could avail themselves of rail-based public transport instead of private automobiles, thus obviating the need for mammoth parking lots at the Olympic Park. Munich '72 would also be able to avoid the massive traffic jams that had blighted the Mexico City Games of 1968.

Despite their sensible plan to rely primarily on urban rail transportation for access to the '72 Games, Munich's planners also saw the Olympics as an opportunity to accelerate the expansion of the surface road network around the city. In addition to building several new "Olympic" streets around and across the main athletic complex, the city rushed its Middle Ring Road to completion with a final section near the Oberwiesenfeld. Now those Olympic visitors, mainly bigwigs, who chose not to mix with the hoi polloi on the commuter trains could drive relatively quickly to the Olympic Park and claim one of the severely limited (7,300) parking spaces available there.

Apart from the accelerated improvements to its transportation network, the most important infrastructural benefit that Munich reaped from its selection as host city for the '72 Games was the creation of a new Fußgängerzone (pedestrian mall) in the inner city. Such an innovation had been mooted by city officials for some time before the IOC's decision in 1966, but the prospect of hosting the world in a few short years suddenly made this project appear both necessary and urgent. And so, just in time for the Olympic opening, a sizable downtown area from the Marienplatz to the Karlsplatz (Stachus) became a pedestrian-only zone (with the exception of delivery vans, emergency vehicles, and autos registered to neighborhood residents).

Some merchants initially worried about a potential loss of trade due to the Fußgängerzone, but in fact the initiative proved to be a great boon to commerce in the area, which now attracted far more shoppers than before. Although this innovation harmonized with a progressive trend in contemporary European cities to free their most congested districts from the suffocating stranglehold of auto traffic, it was also inspired by a desire to turn the clock back—back to a time when people could actually enjoy a stroll through the narrow streets and lanes of their historic neighborhoods. Thousands of Olympic visitors would soon join the locals in taking advantage of this luxury.

Visitors would also find a city that had done much to spruce itself up. Shop owners were encouraged to refurbish their premises, with cash prizes offered to those that best achieved a "representative" look. Most of the cosmetic work focused on the Altstadt, and especially on the historic Marienplatz, which had always been a magnet for tourists. In the initial postwar restoration of the square's signature building, the Neues Rathaus, that gaudy neo-Gothic edifice had not been completely returned to its original look. In 1970, the Munich City Council voted to spend about one million marks to fully restore the structure's façade with its famous two-tiered Glockenspiel, whose life-size revolving figures depict a sixteenth-century ducal marriage and a coopers' dance celebrating Munich's deliverance from the plague. When one City Council member protested against this expensive face-lift, the body's chairman replied that the city "owed" it to the thousands of visitors who would be attending the upcoming Games to show off its "prettiest" face.

A pretty face may be a fine thing, but it was too bad, some critics pointed out, that, in all their preoccupation with tarting Munich up, the city fathers were not also taking more energetic steps to address some of the deeper problems afflicting the town, one of which was an exceptionally high cost of living. As the *Times* (London) noted in a June 1971 report on Munich's preparations for the Games, "Rocketing prices and rents" were "starting to lengthen over paradise." A recent study had shown that Munich had the highest retail rents in West Germany and that rents for private dwellings were such that (in the paper's words) "keeping a more modest roof over one's head than that of the Olympic colossus [had] grown prohibitive." Alas, bringing the Games to town was likely to make existential issues like affordability even tougher for the ordinary inhabitants of West Germany's most popular metropolis. No wonder, three years into the city's frantic six-year makeover for the Games, with whole sections of the city looking like they had just been bombed, many Münchners were wondering whether at the end of this process "their" Munich would still exist.

CHAPTER **Three**

On the Eve of the Games

Now, on the eve of the 1972 Olympics, Munich is emerging
as an international city, fairly singing with youthful ebullience,
steaming with new industry, energized with new citizens,
gleaming with new chrome, athrob with old culture and
new learning, and not unwilling to become, as it is often already
called, the unofficial capital of a democratized Germany.

—Horace Sutton, "Munich: Joie de vivre with an Umlaut," March 1972

A s Munich was busy building its grand Olympic stage for 1972, the
wider world whose athletes would strut and fret their stuff upon
that platform was changing rapidly. Indeed, so much changed in
Germany, in Europe, and in the world at large between the moment Munich was awarded the Games in April 1966 and opening day on August 26,
1972, that one can speak of a new era. Many of the seminal developments
around the globe may have seemed far removed from Munich and its
impending Olympiad, but of course, when the Olympic organizers issued
their invitation to "the youth of the world" to convene in summer '72, they
opened their doors to much more than mere fun and games: like it or not,
they really did get the world, in all its bewildering and sometimes menacing complexity.

In the Middle East, seedbed of the terror attack that would so darken
the '72 Games, the Six-Day War of June 1967 proved to be a turning point
in the protracted Arab-Israeli conflict. Crucially, it resulted in Israeli occupation of what was left of Arab Palestine—East Jerusalem, Gaza, and

the West Bank—which in turn put over a million more Palestinians under Israel's control and triggered a new flood of refugees into other parts of the Middle East. Unquestionably, the war and consequent shift in the regional power balance contributed to a further strengthening of the Palestinians' sense of victimization, while hardening their conviction that they could depend only on themselves.

At the same time, Israel's chief Western ally, the United States, was beginning to chart a momentous new direction in its relations with the Soviet Union. The years between 1968 and 1972 saw the beginning of détente between the two superpowers, an easing of tensions that continued apace despite Washington's escalation of the Vietnam War and Moscow's suppression of the "Prague Spring" in 1968 and continued backing of anti-American regimes in Africa, Cuba, and South Asia. Washington also launched new overtures toward China, beginning with "ping-pong diplomacy" in 1971 and cresting with President Richard Nixon's historic trip to China to meet with Chairman Mao in February 1972. China's tentative "opening" to the West fueled vague hopes in distant Bavaria that Beijing might even abandon its previous opposition to Olympic participation and join in Munich's joyous festival. For a brief time, Willi Daume worked back channels to Beijing with the hope of luring the elusive People's Republic of China (PRC) to Munich. The effort foundered on "the Taiwan problem," as Avery Brundage had warned it probably would.

Momentous diplomatic changes were also transpiring in West Germany itself, as post-Adenauer governments, above all the Social Democratic Party (SPD)-dominated government led from 1969 on by Willy Brandt, inaugurated its historic policy of Ostpolitik (Eastern Policy) aimed at improving relations with the USSR and other Eastern European nations, including the German Democratic Republic (GDR). The advent of a new, more "East-friendly" regime in Bonn had a huge impact on the Munich Olympics, effectively putting an end to any possibility of a boycott by the Eastern European nations. Yet, precisely because Ostpolitik implied a softening of boundaries between East and West—including the boundary between the two Germanys—it encouraged East Berlin to sharpen its separate identity as a socialist nation, a tendency that would become visible at the Munich Games.

Interestingly enough, the same period that saw a reduction of tensions between the two superpowers and their respective allies also witnessed vast domestic turmoil across the democratic West and even in some Communist states. This, after all, was the "Era of '68"—that epoch of great political, social, sexual, and cultural upheaval that was no more confined to one year than it was to one place. ('68 certainly lived on musically in '72, the year that the Grateful Dead toured Europe and the Rolling Stones graced America with their "giant inflatable cock" tour.) Among the many manifestations of the socio-political turbulence of the late sixties and early seventies was home-grown terrorism: violent attacks on "the system" by radical groups like the Weathermen, the Black Panthers, the Red Brigades, and the Baader-Meinhof group. In West Germany, the actions of the Baader-Meinhof band and other leftist radicals certainly did attract the attention of the Olympic organizers—and for good reason: Munich, having been relatively placid until the mid-sixties, suddenly found itself pulled into the vortex of violence. Some of the violent protests focused on the Vietnam War, while others grew out of grievances closer to home, such as a shortage of study places at the local universities and a new set of emergency laws (Notstandsgesetze) that enabled the authorities to circumvent civil rights in their fight against domestic terrorism. In April 1967, the near-fatal shooting of student radical leader Rudi Dutschke by a deranged right-winger in West Berlin sparked a particularly violent response in Munich. In that same month, leftist radicals in Munich anticipated the Baader-Meinhof group's tactics by fire-bombing a major downtown department store. And in early June 1967, Munich witnessed a bloody protest against a visit to the city by the Shah of Iran.

Significantly, in response to potentially violent demonstrations, Munich chief of police Manfred Schreiber devised the "Munich Line," which entailed, whenever possible, preventing mass protests or other unruly actions from occurring in the first place and, if that didn't work, deploying psychological suasion and dialogue with the rowdies instead of brute force. The new procedure was tested at a Rolling Stones concert in 1967, where the police appeared in white shirts rather than uniforms, joked with the crowd, and as an extra precaution, persuaded the band not to play its most raucous numbers at the end of the performance, which tended to put young concert-goers in a riotous frame of mind as they headed out into the night. The Munich Line became standard operating procedure for local and state authorities throughout the chaos of '68 and, as we shall see, during the summer of '72.

Of course, 1968 was an Olympic year in addition to everything else, and the '68 Summer Games in Mexico City turned out to be both an inspiration and a cautionary tale for the Munich Olympic organizers—actually, considerably more the latter. Representatives from the Munich Organizing Committee (OC), including Willi Daume and Mayor Hans-Jochen Vogel, were impressed by the vibrancy and energy of the Mexican festival. But they were also privately appalled by inadequacies in the organization, massive congestion, vast distances between venues, and, above all, the brutal gunning down of over one hundred anti-government protestors by government troops on the eve of the Games. Daume and Vogel also took great umbrage at the "un-Olympic" behavior of American sprinters John Carlos and Tommie Smith, who each raised a black-gloved fist on the victory podium during the playing of "The Star-Spangled Banner." The German Olympic officials came away from Mexico City determined that their Games would not be blighted by similar organizational inadequacies or by any "incidents" that might reflect badly on the host city.

But could the Munich organizers be certain that this would be the case? In fact, they knew well that they could not be completely certain, and for this reason the security planners for Munich '72 spent a great deal of time and energy scrutinizing the global political landscape for potential trouble spots. A big problem was that there were just so damn many places around the globe from which threats might arise, so damn many festering antagonisms and age-old animosities that might, willy nilly, spill over into Munich's impending festival of peaceful play and international good cheer.

"Does '36 + '36 = '72?" The USSR and GDR at the Gates of Munich

During the run-up to Munich's selection by the International Olympic Committee (IOC) to host the 1972 Summer Games, the GDR had repeatedly protested the Bavarian city's unsuitability for this honor and continued to do so after the decision was announced. At a reception for the GDR Olympic team upon its return home from Mexico City in 1968, Willi Stoph, chairman of the Council of Ministers, predicted that the next Olympics in Munich would amount to "a new edition of the Games of fascist Germany." The chief party journal, *Neues Deutschland*, helpfully expanded on this theme with a series of articles on Munich's impending Olympiad entitled "Does '36 + '36 = '72?" The prevalence of "neo-fascist tendencies" in the Bavarian city, said the paper, "provides almost a solid guarantee that 2 times 36 does indeed make 72 not only in mathematics but in Olympic sport. The Olympic Games of 1972 promises to double what the Games of 1936 offered."

Although the GDR's chief foreign patron, the USSR, had not gone so far as to sabotage Munich's bid to host the Games (as it might well have done), the Soviets joined the East Germans in a concerted campaign to force Bonn to treat East Berlin as a fully sovereign entity in the upcoming Munich Olympics. The IOC, caught in the middle of this East-West confrontation, worried that the Eastern Europeans might actually boycott Munich unless the West Germans found a way to placate their critics.

When Munich was named host city for 1972, Bonn's protocol for handling a visit from a separate and potentially sovereign GDR team on Federal Republic of Germany (FRG) soil was still up in the air. In October 1968, following the Mexico City Games, the IOC made its position clear by mandating that all teams be accorded exactly the same treatment at the Games. This meant of course that the GDR participants, for the first time in Olympic competition, would be allowed to fly their own national flag and hear their own national anthem played in the Olympic sites.

For their part, the Munich organizers would have been happy enough to go along with this arrangement, but the government in Bonn—which between December 1, 1966, and October 21, 1969, consisted of a "Grand Coalition" (Christian Democratic Union [CDU]/Christian Social Union [CSU]-SPD) led by a silver-tongued conservative (and former Nazi) named Kurt Georg Kiesinger—remained for some time steadfastly opposed to any steps that might have signaled diplomatic recognition of the GDR. Bonn's position, dating back to a 1962 decision by its Interior Ministry, was that any display of the GDR flag on the territory of the FRG constituted a "breach of public order" to be handled by the police.

For West Germany's Foreign Office, the Olympic symbolism issue could not have been more momentous. Its experts argued in a series of memos to the chancellor that, if Bonn agreed that the symbols of the "so-called GDR" could appear on FRG territory during the Games (which is what the federal Interior Ministry wanted to do), Bonn's "policy of non-acceptance of two sovereign states on German soil would lose all credibility." By giving in to the IOC on this issue, Bonn would in effect be allowing an outside agency to determine a core dimension of its foreign policy. Moreover, a concession on symbols would smack of political "opportunism"—a craven retreat instituted solely to protect the Munich Games. The Foreign Office advised therefore that Bonn do "everything possible"—short of formally giving up the Games—to ensure that the symbolism protocol for the two German teams that had been used in Mexico City also apply to Munich.

Believing, with some justice, that the very existence of the Munich Games might be jeopardized by this contretemps over symbols, the Bavarian government pleaded with Bonn to change its policy, at least for the 1972 festival. The SPD, whose leader Willy Brandt had become foreign minister in the Grand Coalition, likewise pressed for an accommodation that would satisfy East Berlin and the IOC, thereby allowing the Munich

Games to "contribute to harmonious sporting relations among the peoples of the world." The conservative newspaper *Die Welt*, on the other hand, urged Bonn in October 1968 not to backslide in this matter. Allowing the GDR's "splitter flag" to fly in Munich would only embolden East Berlin to push for full-scale recognition from the FRG, the paper warned. Better to give up the Games entirely, editorialized *Die Welt*, than to let East Berlin "misuse the Munich Olympics for its own nefarious political purposes."

Another figure who worried that the '72 Games might slip through Munich's fingers because of the dispute over national symbols was OC chairman Willi Daume. Caught between the rock of Bonn's intransigence and the hard place of GDR/IOC demands, Daume desperately searched for a compromise that might satisfy all parties. In late 1968, he thought he might have come up with a solution to the flag problem: He suggested that at the '72 Games each participating nation might display one banner at the main stadium but that no national flags be hoisted—and no national anthems be sung—at the awards ceremonies following each event. On those occasions, only the five-ringed Olympic flag should be visible, he argued. Furthermore, proposed Daume, the opening and closing ceremonies should be entirely bereft of national banners, though athletes might march around the stadium in characteristic national costumes, if they so chose. In Daume's view, such a dramatic and (in Olympics history) revolutionary reduction in nationalistic display would be particularly appropriate for the Munich Games, whose underlying theme after all was the joyful unity of all peoples.

No sooner had Daume and the Munich OC floated this idea than Avery Brundage enthusiastically embraced it as if it were his own. Although the IOC president was himself something of an American chauvinist, he had never been comfortable with the heavy emphasis on nationalism at the Olympics. Intense nationalistic display undercut his chimerical vision of Olympic sport triumphing over politics. To him, Daume's compromise offered not only a solution to the imbroglio over the East German flag at Munich but also a route to reduced national pathos at all Olympic festivals in the future. The dark cloud hanging over Munich might thus turn out to have a true and lasting silver lining: an emphasis at all Olympics henceforth on individual competition between amateur sportsmen—just as had been the case (at least in Brundage's imagination) at the original Games in ancient Olympia. (In reality, the ancient Games typically involved mercenary athletes competing for money and prizes put up by the city-states these men—no women—represented.)

In June 1969, Brundage began talking up this idea at every opportunity. As was increasingly the case when this imperious old man went on the stump, however, his crusade turned out to be a lonely one. Apart from the Munich Olympic officials, no one showed much interest in this just-say-no-to-nationalism gambit. Brundage couldn't even get his colleagues in the IOC to sign off on it.

Although the Daume-Brundage "compromise" on symbolism was dead on arrival, the very fact that the IOC president and the Munich OC had put forth such a plan in the first place threw the GDR authorities into near apoplexy. Again tossing the West German Olympic committee and the West German government into the same black pot, the GDR government (in fact, Walter Ulbricht himself) accused "the Kiesinger/Strauß/Brandt regime and its Daume-clique" of seeking "to assert [Bonn's] sole-sovereignty pretention . . . in the upcoming Munich Olympics by discontinuing the traditional [national] victory ceremonies, which have been part of Olympic ritual since 1896." Following Ulbricht's lead, *Neues Deutschland* launched a full-throated crusade against any possible reduction in national display, insisting that other nations around the world, fully aware that Daume's plan was "but a ploy to shore up Bonn's tattered and illegitimate sole-sovereignty claim," would also cry foul.

Indeed, many other nations *did* cry out against the notion of curbing nationalistic symbolism at the Games, but they did not do this out of solidarity with the GDR. The protesters were motivated by a desire to protect their own sovereign rights, their own opportunity to be noticed and celebrated on the world's grandest athletic stage. This was even true—in fact, especially true—of those GDR "brother states" in Eastern Europe, for whom the open expression of national identity and national pride could not be taken for granted. Concerning those states' insistence on displaying their national symbols at Olympic festivals, one West German commentator aptly noted, "The national consciousness of the Poles, Czechs, Hungarians, and Romanians has long been proverbial. After those nations fell under Russian control their nationalistic feelings only grew. [Olympic] sport offered them an opportunity to put on displays of national prowess and identity that were ordinarily circumscribed by [Moscow's] oppression."

Similar motives underlay the resistance to a reduction in national display at the Games on the part of various "developing nations" from the Third World. Having in many cases only recently attained independence, these countries saw the Olympics as a grand coming-out party, a chance to make the world acquainted with the symbols of their new national status. The last thing they wanted was internationalist homogeneity.

The Daume-Brundage proposal regarding national symbolism for the Munich Games was hardly the only grievance harbored by the GDR, other East Bloc nations, and indeed Moscow itself. As they had done in the period preceding Munich's victory in the 1972 host-city sweepstakes, East Berlin and Moscow harped on Munich's centrality in the West's "crusade" against the "socialist system" prevailing in Eastern Europe. But now those attacks on Munich as the European headquarters of "revanchist imperialism and neo-fascism" became even sharper and more insistent. In 1969–1970, Moscow and East Berlin worked double-time to whip up anti-Munich sentiment around the globe, especially in Africa and Asia. Olympic officials from Moscow and East Berlin also repeatedly called upon the IOC to pressure the Munich organizers to comply with Olympic regulations prohibiting discrimination against any participants based on political, ideological, or racial principles.

Shortly before Munich had been awarded the '72 Summer Games, an internal GDR report on the city had included the presence there of Radio Free Europe (RFE) and Radio Liberty among the reasons the Bavarian capital was "unacceptable" as an Olympic host. Starting in 1969, East Berlin went public with its concern about the Washington-subsidized "propaganda stations" in Munich. Eliciting no response from Bonn, Washington, or the Munich Organizing Committee, the East Germans ratcheted up the pressure in early 1971, when, ominously, they were joined by Soviet protestors. On February 28, 1971, the (London) *Sunday Times*, under a headline "Olympic Boycott?" could report that, "with 545 days [to go] before the Olympic flame is lit in Munich," Soviet and East German newspapers were "threatening an Olympic boycott unless two Munich-based radio stations [stopped] operating what East German newspapers were calling 'heirlooms of the Cold War . . . and lie factories.'" Pressures from the East, said the *Sunday Times*, had resulted in a pledge from the two stations not to "molest, contact, interfere with, or otherwise inconvenience visitors from the Communist countries to the Games." But the Russians in particular, added the British report, would "not be satisfied until the 20-year-old stations [were] closed down altogether." The Soviets were worried, concluded the paper, that "a wave of defections to the West will take place from the largest team of athletes the Soviet Union has ever sent abroad."

Had it been up to Avery Brundage, Moscow's goal of muzzling the broadcasters would have been achieved. Horrified by the thought that Moscow and its allies might boycott the Munich Games unless the American-sponsored radio stations changed their tune, Brundage appealed directly to the heads of both stations to observe an "Olympic truce" during the '72 festival. His letter to Radio Liberty headquarters in New York City warrants extensive quotation:

You have a transmitter we understand in the Munich area. It would be appreciated by the Organizing Committee of the Games, by the International Olympic Committee and perhaps by the general public as well, if, during the period of the Games when all the foreign visitors are there, all political and controversial subjects would be eliminated from your program. In the ancient Games, 2,500 years ago during the Golden Age of Greece, an armistice was declared and all hostilities, even open warfare, were stopped at that time. The modern Olympic movement has not been able so far to accomplish this—but, it does set a good example in its success in developing international cooperation and bringing the people of the world together.

Brundage's heavy-handed pressure on Radio Liberty and Radio Free Europe to hold their fire during the '72 Games did not sit well with the broadcasters. After pointing out that Radio Liberty had a studio in Munich, but no transmitter, the head of that agency said it would continue broadcasting as usual during the Games, as always emphasizing "the principles of peace, international brotherhood, human rights and freedom of information." Under no circumstances would the broadcaster suspend its efforts to influence the peoples of Eastern Europe and the Soviet Union: "The concept of an 'Olympic Peace,' devised as a worthy means of suspending hostilities between warring nations, can hardly have application to the constructive and non-violent activities of Radio Liberty." General Lucius Clay, formerly commander of America's occupation zone in Western Germany and now chairman of Radio Free Europe, answered in a similar fashion for his agency, insisting that the station "will devote considerable broadcast time to reporting the Olympic Games of 1972 as well as the social and cultural manifestations in Munich which will be part of the Olympic scene." There would certainly be no letup in RFE's usual political programming during the Games, though this reporting would "be fully in the Olympic spirit." To this, Brundage could but lamely reply that he was sure that RFE was at one with the Olympic movement "in endeavoring to develop international amity." But he reminded General Clay (as if Clay needed it) that the European political situation in advance of the Games was "particularly sticky" and therefore the broadcaster's "cooperation in helping us keep the peace [would] be appreciated."

From Moscow's and East Berlin's perspective, one of the "stickier" aspects of the political situation on the eve of the '72 Games involved all those associations of refugees from the former German-controlled areas of Eastern Europe that had set up shop in Munich. The GDR government, along with Moscow, saw these groups as "revanchists of the worst sort." According to *Neues Deutschland*, Munich harbored no fewer than eighty-four of these associations, whose "only goal [was] to agitate against the Socialist lands." Moscow was equally up in arms about the refugee groups. In a public statement, the Soviet Olympic Committee complained bitterly of "neo-Nazi" associations whose activities presented "a clear danger to the safety and security of teams from the Socialist nations." The Munich OC's recent proposal for a "politics-free zone" at the Olympic grounds was not satisfactory, said the Soviets, since by Olympic rules host cities had to be free in their entirety of political threats to the participants. "We therefore turn to the Executive Committee of the IOC with the demand that it revisit the question of whether the [Munich organizers] have established the preconditions for the conduct of the Summer Games of 1972 according to the Olympic traditions of peace and [international] friendship."

In spring 1971, delegations from the GDR Olympic Committee visited the Bavarian capital to meet with the Munich OC and give vent to their grievances regarding "un-Olympic activities" on the part of Bonn and the host city. According to a confidential report on one of the meetings by the head of the GDR delegation, the East Germans made clear their concerns on a host of pressing issues, starting with the matter of protocol for the GDR team at the '72 Games. East Berlin would not accept any modification of traditional Olympic practices (including a last-minute suggestion from Willi Daume that the playing of national anthems at victory ceremonies be reduced to half a minute). The delegation also insisted that the GDR be referred to by its official name, Deutsche Demokratische Republik (DDR), on all occasions. (Bonn typically referred to the East German state as "Ostdeutschland," or even, in some cases, as the "Soviet Occupation Zone.") This had implications for the opening ceremony, where, per Olympic tradition, teams entered the stadium in alphabetical order, using the host country's spelling. Thus, the GDR's team, as "DDR," must be allowed to enter with the nations starting in "D." Of course, the team would carry its own national flag—and that banner, like all the others in the stadium, must be protected from possible "vandalism or abuse." Similarly, the organizers must do something about the various "revanchist organizations," that is, exile groups, whose activities constituted a "serious threat" to Olympic visitors from Socialist Eastern Europe.

The GDR officials were also much exercised about a special publication on the Olympics that Daume had commissioned for use in West German schools and as a gift for visiting dignitaries. Entitled *Deutsches Mosaik: Ein Lesebuch für Zeitgenossen* (German Mosaic: A Contemporary Reader), the anthology contained contributions on the Olympics from figures as diverse as Baron Pierre de Coubertin, Jean Giraudoux, Roger Bannister, and Pope Pius XII. In GDR eyes, this rather anodyne volume was nothing short of "a nasty power-political work designed to stir up West German youth against sporting people from other lands and to spread untruths about the athletic programs in [socialist] nations." In this book, "the disgraceful deeds of the German imperialists," including "their constant misuse of the Olympic Games," were whitewashed or ignored.

A final grievance raised by the GDR delegation concerned the Munich OC's plan to award a prize for Olympic service named in honor of Carl Diem, the chief organizer of the 1936 Berlin Games. Because (in GDR eyes) Diem had been an "arch proponent of militaristic and fascistic ideas in sport," his honoring via a prize in his name was clearly designed to "popularize" his fascist legacy and thus constituted yet another "mockery and abuse of Olympic ideals." In conclusion, the East Germans warned that, if the Munich organizers did not immediately remedy all these "injuries to the Olympic charter," the National Olympic Committee of the GDR would "alert world opinion [as to these infractions] and step up its own efforts to prevent any such political misuse of the Olympic Games."

What is especially interesting about the GDR's ongoing offensive against Munich '72 is that it did not contain an explicit threat of boycott. The GDR did not threaten to stay away from Munich barring full compliance with its demands because it did not wish to get boxed into a corner should its adversaries remain recalcitrant. In fact, GDR officials seem not to have expected total compliance with their wishes—and were prepared, even anxious, to carry a political chip on their shoulder into Munich. But most importantly, staying away from the Games would have deprived East Berlin of a goal it had harbored from the outset and continued to nurture: that of humiliating their German rival by thoroughly thrashing the West German team in Olympic play on the FRG's own soil. Soon enough, this ambition was provocatively encapsulated in a taunt by a prominent GDR journalist: "The band leader in Munch had better study our national hymn carefully; he's going to have to play it often enough!" (Painfully aware of East German intentions to turn Munich into "a political triumph" for the GDR, an official in the FRG Interior Ministry warned that "Soviet-zone" officials were doing absolutely everything to ensure victories for their side, including subjecting potential Olympic judges to "political schooling.")

The IOC seems not to have been cognizant of East Berlin's determination to send a team to Munich, come what may. Still deeply worried that East Germany might stay home in '72, the committee did everything it could to placate the malcontented Easterners. At its annual congress in 1971, held in Luxemburg, the IOC affirmed that all traditional practices in regard to ceremony and protocol would be followed in Munich. The committee insisted that Willi Daume formally agree to this arrangement on behalf of the Munich OC.

Daume was finally able to make this commitment in late 1969 because the Bonn government, just before Chancellor Kiesinger left office in October of that year, announced that henceforth it would "tolerate" an appearance of the GDR flag on FRG soil under special circumstances, including international sporting events.

In the wake of the IOC's Luxemburg declarations, the Central Committee of the East German Communist Party (SED) issued a public statement declaring that, while the GDR would continue to do "all in its power" to ensure that the Munich Games took place "under acceptable [political] conditions," it would not be deterred from participating in the Games if this or that feature were not to its liking. On the contrary, GDR athletes would see to it that, especially in Munich, "Socialist sport and the Socialist Fatherland [were] actively and worthily represented."

Moscow, despite its similar bluster over the American-sponsored Munich radio stations and right-wing émigré groups, had been committed for some time to making its presence felt in Munich. For the Soviets, though, this commitment was considerably eased by the momentous political seachange in Bonn, whereby, as of October 1969, Willy Brandt became the new West German chancellor and embarked on his groundbreaking policy of Ostpolitik.

Brandt's Ostpolitik campaign scored its first significant success with the Soviets, in large part because Moscow was anxious to expand trade with the economically robust Federal Republic. Moreover, realizing that their recent invasion of Czechoslovakia to crush the "Prague Spring" had not exactly heightened their popularity among the peoples of Eastern Europe, the Soviets were all the more anxious to have the West, especially West Germany, formally recognize the legitimacy of Eastern Europe's postwar borders. The Brandt government proved accommodating on both scores, and in July 1970, the FRG and USSR signed the historic Treaty of Moscow, by which each government renounced the use of force and any claims to each other's territory or that of other states. Crucially, they formally recognized as "inviolable" the postwar boundaries, including the border between the two Germanys and that between the GDR and Poland (Oder-Neisse Line). Later, in spring 1971, Moscow and Bonn signed a new trade agreement that helped tie these two states closer together economically.

Among the first to feel the warmth from the thaw in relations between Moscow and Bonn was Willi Daume. He had done his own bit to improve German-Soviet relations by promising to back Moscow in its bid for the 1976 Summer Olympics (a promise he later extended to Moscow's successful bid for 1980). Daume's own "Ostpolitik," when massively reinforced by that of Willy Brandt, was enough to bring the Russians around. In spring 1971, the Soviet sports leader Nikolai Pavlov showed up in Munich with a case of vodka for Daume. Pointing to his present, he declared that these bottles of booze represented "Russia's position" on the Munich Games. A few months later, on a goodwill visit to Moscow, members of the Munich OC basked in USSR-FRG "friendship," and Daume spoke approvingly of the Soviets' "self-image as a great sports nation."

Willy Brandt also made good progress in bettering Bonn's relations with Poland, the country that had suffered most from German aggression in World War II. As part of this process—and, indeed, as a prerequisite for Ostpolitik in general—Bonn finally abandoned the Hallstein Doctrine, that Cold War relic that since 1955 had impeded normal relations between the FRG and Communist countries around the world. In December 1970, following long and complicated discussions, West Germany and Poland signed the Treaty of Warsaw, by which Bonn came close to accepting the Oder-Neisse border (the wording fell slightly short of full legal recognition). Warsaw, for its part, agreed to allow ethnic Germans residing in Poland to emigrate to one of the German states (not surprisingly, the overwhelming majority of Polish Volksdeutsche chose the FRG). Brandt himself traveled to Warsaw to sign the treaty. While there, he visited the area once occupied by the Warsaw Ghetto, where in 1943 some seventy thousand Jews had been massacred by the German occupation forces. At a monument near the former ghetto, Brandt suddenly fell to his knees. This spontaneous gesture occasioned scorn among conservatives at home but went down well with most Poles, who—lingering anti-Semitism in their own nation notwithstanding—had been waiting a long time for any sign of contrition on the part of the Germans.

Following Brandt's historic trip to Warsaw, the Polish press cut back noticeably in its attacks on Bonn and, not uncoincidentally, also in its criticism of the upcoming Munich Games. Now the Poles let it be known that they expected to find a warm welcome in the city where Nazism had been born and from which the "worst evil" in the twentieth century had spread to engulf their own nation.

Brandt's effort to improve relations with the GDR, a critical part of his Ostpolitik, proved much more difficult. Among the chief impediments was the status of divided Berlin. For years, Bonn took the position that West Berlin was an integral part of the FRG. The West German constitution (Basic Law) even stipulated that the former capital of united Germany should again assume that role once Germany was reunited under democratic rule. The GDR, meanwhile, claimed "Berlin" as its national capital and did not recognize West Berlin as a legitimate separate entity, much less an integral part of the Federal Republic. In reality, and by international law, the entire city was legally still a ward of the four former Allied partners, whose consent was required for any significant changes in Berlin's status or administration. Brandt, realizing that Bonn could not productively negotiate with the GDR on the relationship between the two Germanys until the Berlin problem had been adjudicated by the Allied Powers, pressed for a four-power meeting on Berlin.

Amazingly, the powers agreed to conduct negotiations on the city and, even more amazingly, came up with a new arrangement for the old Reich capital in September 1971. In the Berlin Accord, the three Western powers affirmed that West Berlin was not a full-fledged state of the Federal Republic and therefore could not host plenary meetings of the federal parliament; the Soviets, for their part, abandoned their long-held position that, because West Berlin lay inside GDR territory, it technically fell under East Berlin's authority. Instead, Moscow agreed that henceforth Bonn could legally represent West Berliners internationally and include them under its consular and diplomatic protection. The accord also gave West Berliners the right to enter GDR territory, including East Berlin, a privilege that had been denied them (except on rare occasions) ever since the construction of the Berlin Wall.

Another impediment to productive negotiations between the two Germanys was the continued presence of Walter Ulbricht at the helm in East Berlin. However, in May 1971, the old Stalinist was elbowed aside by his former top aide, Erich Honecker, who, though also a Stalinist ideologue, believed he could strengthen the GDR regime by working out a favorable new deal with Bonn.

With East Berlin ready to talk, Brandt could press ahead with the final phase of his Ostpolitik program, though before the negotiations with East Berlin could even begin Brandt barely escaped an effort to unseat him by conservatives at home who regarded his entire opening to the East as little short of treason. Shortly after the signing of the Berlin Accord, when Brandt was in Munich inspecting work on the Olympic Stadium, a young right-winger clobbered him in the face, shouting, "That's for betraying Germany to Moscow!" As fate would have it, the beginning of the talks between Bonn and East Berlin on the future of their tortuous relationship coincided with the final countdown to the Munich Games, as well as with the run-up to the fall 1972 Bundestag elections, which would decide whether Brandt retained the chancellorship for another term. Brandt did manage to win these elections, which, largely because of the Olympics, were put off until November. This victory was a great personal triumph for the chancellor and a historic breakthrough for the SPD, which for the first time in West German history won a majority of seats in the Bundestag. Because the German-German negotiations proved extremely arduous, no agreement between the parties could be achieved until after the Munich Games were over. With the historic Basic Treaty, signed in December 1972, the two German states finally acknowledged each other's sovereign existence, without however extending each other full diplomatic recognition (instead of embassies, they established "permanent missions" in each other's capitals).

Although the Basic Treaty came too late for the Munich Games, one might have thought that the very process of working toward it might have somewhat moderated East Berlin's hostility toward Bonn and, as a corollary, softened the GDR's denunciation of the Munich Games. No such thing happened. On the contrary, Brandt's policies awakened fears in East Berlin that a kinder and gentler Bonn might undermine the GDR's status as an independent, sustainable German entity with its own unique identity and political system. In East German eyes, Willy Brandt's West Germany was doubly dangerous precisely because it was more accommodationist vis-à-vis the East.

With respect to the upcoming Olympics, this view was evident in a secret GDR report on the "political-ideological situation" prevailing in Munich and the FRG on the eve of the Games. The report acknowledged that Bonn had been obliged to make key concessions on protocol and ceremony, especially regarding the display of national flags. Also, by establishing a no-go zone at the Olympic sites for political demonstrations, the Munich OC was clearly trying to clip the wings of the "revanchist" émigré organizations. With regard to Radio Liberty and Radio Free Europe, Daume was making a legitimate effort to secure a Burgfrieden (cease fire) for the duration of the Games. But these measures were all mere "tactical moves" designed to "avoid an open confrontation with the Socialist lands" and to weaken the GDR's campaign against political misuse of the Games by fostering "divisions within the Socialist camp." In reality, Bonn and Munich continued to harbor "the same old goals." Indeed, their recent efforts amounted to little more than a last-ditch effort to protect their precious Games by throwing "a cover of peaceful demagogy" over their "ongoing nationalistic and militaristic policies." This ploy, resembling as it did various belated concessions to the IOC by the Nazis in advance of the Berlin Games, made "the parallels between '36 and '72 more apparent than ever." In consequence, the GDR's main task on the eve of the Munich Games must be to expose and combat these more "refined" tactics. Above all, it must be shown that the new West German slogan declaring a "Unity of the German Nation" was not only "false" but also "dangerous" in light of Bonn's continuing "imperialist" agenda. Any attempts by the West Germans "to cozy up" to the GDR's Olympic officials or athletes with the hope of "transforming their enemy image [of the West] into a mushy amity must be clearly rejected." (So much for Daume's expressed hope that the Munich Games would be able "to fulfill a certain humanitarian mission, especially between us Germans from both sides of the Fatherland.")

Counterattack: Getting Out the Good Word on Munich '72

The organizers of the '72 Games believed that they could not let all the bad-mouthing of Munich by the GDR and other East Bloc states go unanswered. They were especially concerned about Munich's image in Africa, Asia, and the Soviet Union. Daume and company were also mindful of the crucial importance of generating excitement about the Games in the United States, since they harbored high hopes of attracting a large American audience. The OC therefore launched vigorous publicity campaigns focused on those regions, replete with personal visits and much glad-handing on part of committee leaders and other Munich boosters.

In November/December 1971, a delegation from the Munich OC led by Bavarian cultural minister Ludwig Huber, who was also one of the committee's vice presidents, visited capital cities across East Africa. Huber personally delivered official invitations to the Munich Games to the Olympic committees of Ethiopia, Kenya, Somalia, Uganda, Malawi, and Egypt. In Addis Ababa, Ethiopian emperor Hailie Selassie hosted a reception for the German visitors, assuring them that "many athletes from Ethiopia and other African lands would participate in the Munich Games." "I know," he added, "that these Games will be especially successful, because we've long been close friends with the Germans." For his part, Huber declared that the Munich Games promised to afford "an outstanding opportunity for African self-promotion."

At various press conferences during their visit, Huber and his colleagues reminded the Africans of the FRG's "generous technical assistance to African sport" (see more below). The Africans were reportedly very excited by Bonn's promise to deliver state-of-the-art artificial running tracks to sports clubs throughout East and West Africa. The Africans responded with generosity of their own. At a reception at Zaire's embassy in Addis Ababa, Jean-Claude Ganga of Cameroon presented Huber with a six-month-old lioness. On the same occasion, a Masai chieftain appointed Huber an "Honorary Chief" of the Masai tribe. But most importantly, once again, the heads of the African Olympic committees assured the German visitors of "their absolute determination to send strong athletic delegations" to Munich, with the hope of achieving "the greatest possible sporting success." As if to buttress this prospect, the Germans promised to accommodate Kenya's desire that the 1,500- and 5,000-meter races would be staged with a sufficient interval between them so Kenyan star Kip Keino could compete effectively in both.

Willi Daume did not leave this kind of publicity junketing to the likes of Huber and OC press secretary Johnny Klein. He tirelessly took to the skies and seas on behalf of Munich '72—not, he was careful to insist, to "sell tickets" for the Games but to enlighten the world regarding "our hopes for Munich and our guiding principle that these Games will not be deadly earnest but easy-going and happy, an affair where alongside hard battles in the athletic arena there will be lots of time for laughter and important human interaction."

In December 1970, Daume attended the Asian Games in Bangkok in order personally to deliver official invitations to the heads of the Asian Olympic committees. A week later, he was off to Moscow to give the Soviets their invitation and to hoist a glass of vodka or two with his "Russian friends." Next up was a sailing exposition in Barcelona, where he passed Munich's calling card to the Spaniards. He then flew to New York City, where in addition to delivering Munich's invitation to the United States Olympic Committee (USOC), he previewed Munich's "beautiful" Olympic posters at a soirée involving local art dealers. Later, he sailed on the *Hamburg* to Dakar, Senegal, where he hosted a shipboard reception for West and Central African Olympic officials, to whom he once again personally delivered the requisite invitations.

In a timely effort to help the OC combat anti-Munich publicity coming out of the East Bloc, and to ward off a possible African boycott of '72 over Rhodesia, the West German Foreign Office significantly increased its foreign aid to African and other "Developing World" countries in advance of the Games. Understandably, much of this financial and technical support was directed towards sports. A November 1970 Foreign Office memorandum on "Sports Development Measures in Support of the 1972 Games in Munich" outlined the diverse scope of this aid operation. Among the projects already completed or planned for the near future were an amateur boxing tournament in West Germany featuring young fighters from Burma, Kenya, Ghana, and Tunisia; a training camp in West Berlin for boxers from Singapore, Korea, and Thailand; another training camp for "top boxers and judges" in Lagos, Nigeria, conducted by ex-European boxing champion Wilhelm Hoepner; "continuing developmental" assistance for Mohammed Junus, a middle-distance runner from Pakistan; hosting a visit to Bundesliga teams by Naby Camora, head trainer for Guinea's national football team; dispatching West German trainers to track and field programs in Peru; channeling sports-development grants to "a number of countries in Africa, Asia, and Latin America"; and providing a DM 10,000 subsidy for the publication of a handbook entitled "Sport in Africa."

In addition to spreading money and German technical expertise around the Third World, the Munich organizers and their backers in Bonn resorted to the time-tested promotional strategy of recruiting celebrities to push their product. Perhaps the most noteworthy big names to take on this project were Jesse Owens and Max Schmeling. Owens, for whom Berlin '36 remained the great shining moment of his life, signed on for a hefty fee and ended up not doing very much. Schmeling, by contrast, asked for no stipend (after retiring from the ring he had become wealthy as the owner of West Germany's largest Coca-Cola franchise) and actually put in a lot of effort on behalf of Munich.

This kind of work was nothing new for the ex-boxer. In December 1935, Schmeling had paid a visit to Avery Brundage, then head of the American Olympic Committee, to reassure him that American athletes, especially blacks and Jews, would encounter no hostility or discrimination at the upcoming Berlin Olympics. In his memoirs, Schmeling claims to have single-handedly warded off a possible American boycott of Berlin, though in fact his intervention had little influence, Brundage not needing Schmeling to convince him that the Yanks must go to Berlin. After the fall of the Third Reich, Schmeling always downplayed his association with the Hitler regime, suppressing the fact that he had allowed Joseph Goebbels to exploit his fame for Nazi purposes. Schmeling's effectively air-brushed past presented no problem for Daume and Klein, who counted on his (hopefully lingering) star power to light up various Munich '72 promotions around the world. In 1971, the former pugilist and Jesse Owens were the chief attractions at a gala dinner party on board the German liner *Bremen*, docked in New York Harbor. Whether Schmeling's diligent shilling for Munich did any more for the '72 Games than it had done for Berlin '36 is, however, open to question.

Although the OC's campaign to put out the good word on Munich—in part to compensate for all that trash talk coming out of East Berlin—understandably focused on foreign targets, the domestic scene was hardly ignored. As a member in good standing of West Germany's Fourth Estate, Johnny Klein paid a lot of attention to his journalistic colleagues, who he hoped would do their part to promote the upcoming Olympic show. In mid-September 1971, roughly one year in advance of the Munich Games, Klein invited over a hundred West German journalists, print and broadcast, to travel to Munich to inspect the Olympic sites and to sample some down-home Bavarian hospitality. (Klein hinted at the opulence of the impending junket by informing the invitees that the event in question was being jointly sponsored by the OC, the Olympia Bau-Gesellschaft, the Bavarian state government, the municipality of Munich, and Wienerwald restaurants.) In his letter of invitation, Klein noted that all guests would be transported to Munich from Bonn on a special private train, served en route by "Olympic hostesses." After being welcomed by Bavarian minister-president Alfons Goppel, the visitors would be treated to a private guided tour of the Oberwiesenfeld. In the evening, there'd be a gala banquet with Olympic officials, who would explain the Games' accrediting procedures for German journalists. Following the dinner, guests could either attend a late performance at Munich's Werkraum Theater or undertake a walking tour (Bummel) through Schwabing. Accommodations for the junketeers would be at one of the "First-Class hotels" recently constructed for the upcoming Games. On the following morning, Mayor Vogel planned to host a breakfast "mit Weißwürsten und allem bayerischen Drum und Drang" (with white sausages and all the traditional Bavarian trimmings). For the return trip to Bonn, Klein promised kegs of freshly tapped Weißbier.

As we noted above, Willi Daume planned on his travels to pitch the OC's vision of the Munich Games as a not-so-earnest affair—a gathering where everyone (save perhaps the athletes) could just take it easy. But as the Munich organizers' arduous and painstaking publicity campaign showed, there was nothing lackadaisical or laid-back about the OC's effort to convince the world that—voices from that "other Germany" notwithstanding—Munich intended to put on the friendliest and most convivial Olympic party ever.

"The Games Will Proceed Normally": Security Planning for Munich '72

On the eve of the '72 Games, Munich's Olympic planners could breathe a sigh of relief in regard to the FRG's Eastern European neighbors; there might be continuing criticism of the host city, especially from the GDR, but these nations' participation in the Games seemed guaranteed. The expected presence of the Eastern Europeans, however, raised problems on another front: security. Might there be attacks on the Eastern European Olympic delegations from refugee associations or domestic neo-fascist groups, just as East Berlin and Moscow feared? Possible threats from this quarter were hardly the only ones to plague Munich's Olympic organizers during the two years of security planning that preceded the '72 Games. Olympic officials and police authorities across West Germany were flooded with threats from all sorts of political factions and assorted malcontents. Just as the prospect of an Olympiad in Munich proved to be an attractive sounding board for ongoing Cold War animosities and the German-German rivalry, the impending festival also promised to be an irresistible stage for (among other dissident voices) anti–Vietnam War activists; opponents to the Shah of Iran; Black Power advocates; Yippies and hippies; various "New Left" factions; anarchists; Rote Armee Fraktion (RAF) terrorists; Maoists; Uruguayan Tupamaros; disaffected Italian Gastarbeiter; the Irish Republican Army (IRA); and, yes, Palestinians and other Arab factions.

Moreover, beyond the horrifying threat of politically motivated terrorism loomed the prospect of vastly heightened common criminality: security planners expected the Games to be inundated by pick-pockets, auto thieves, hotel "cat burglars," aggressive prostitutes, vandals, drug dealers, and other assorted hooligans.

The Bavarian authorities planned to keep a watchful eye on every group that might pose a threat to the security of the Games, though, as a memorandum from Bavarian interior minister Bruno Merk warned, "an absolute prevention of any and every kind of disruption, especially of the sort carried out by radical single-actors, can probably not be achieved given the vast number of visitors and the polarized relations between states with differing political outlooks." Moreover, in the face of the complicated challenge confronting them, the Olympic security planners remained determined not to lose sight of their fundamental goal of putting on a jovial and laid-back festival. The various safety measures that would have to be taken must not detract from that ideal.

The tension between abiding worries over possible threats to the Games and the determination to cope with those threats as unobtrusively as possible informed the nature of the security regime that was ultimately put in place for the '72 Olympics. The Munich OC worked with federal and Bavarian officials to fashion the security arrangements by which the Games would be kept safe. The federal government in Bonn played a secondary role here because under the West German constitution internal security matters devolved primarily to the individual states. This was yet another aspect of Bonn's determination to erect a counter-model to the Nazi state, which had featured a highly centralized security apparatus. On the other hand, Bonn could not be left entirely out of security planning for the Games because, as a representative from the federal Interior Ministry explained, "a disruption-free [Olympic festival] is not only of interest to Bavaria, but, due to the Games' world-wide resonance, to the Federal Government as well."

On July 1, 1970, the Executive Board of the OC held a meeting to establish an Ordnungsdienst (literally, "Order Service") for the Munich Games. The basic purpose of this order-keeping agency (later affectionately dubbed the "Olys") was to provide all the essential first-line security services on the Olympic grounds during the Games.

A planning document prepared by the Bavarian government's "Olympic Security Commissioner," Dr. Heinrich Martin, proposed a set of guiding principles for this Ordnungsdienst; for the most part, these suggestions eventually found acceptance by the Executive Board of the OC and thus became the basic blueprint for the "Olys." In a preamble to his proposed guidelines, the commissioner pointed out that Munich's unique vision for its Olympics—an "open" festival with most of the athletic events and much of the ancillary entertainment concentrated in one area—brought with it certain risk factors. "The decision to provide entertainment for everyone all day long and into the night at the Olympic grounds will mean large crowds of people [at the site] and consequently plenty of chances for trouble," warned the commissioner. "The short distances between competition venues will push participants and spectators alike into close proximity and thus heighten threats to safety and [the Games'] vulnerability to mass disruptions." Moreover, Munich's design scheme for its Olympic buildings and grounds presented problems of their own. All those glass walls would present natural targets for rock throwers, while the projected Spielstraße was an open invitation to "willful disturbances." These challenges, concluded the commissioner, demanded the establishment of a highly qualified and exceptionally adroit security force—one that would be able to ensure that the Games remained as "orderly and disruption-free as possible."

Normally, of course, such security services would have been provided by the regular police, backed up perhaps by state troopers or federal military units. But the Munich Games did not constitute a "normal" occasion. As the security commissioner noted, during the Olympics, "the eyes of the entire world would be directed at Munich." And he went on: "For political reasons, our state must avoid even the outward appearance of being dependent exclusively on the deployment of uniformed police forces."

It followed therefore that the principal order-keeping agency at the Munich Games had to be an unarmed, purely civilian body functioning under the auspices and legal sanction of the Olympic Organizing Committee. Echoing the "Munich Line," the Olys's primary tool for keeping the peace would be "psychological suasion," not strong-arm tactics. Above all, the Olympic security personnel must avoid "provocations" that could lead to "an escalation of violence requiring the intervention of armed police." In keeping with its non-provocative modus operandi and civilian status, the security personnel must be dressed in "sporty" attire lacking "any military cut." (Clearly, the security commissioner was on the same page here as Otl Aicher, the OC's chief Olympic designer, whose leisure suit–like outfits eventually won approval as the official "uniforms" of the Olys.)

From which sources might the personnel for the Olympic security force be drawn? The commissioner proposed that the agency be made up primarily of members of state police forces and Bundesgrenzschutz (Federal Border Guard) units placed on paid leave from their regular duties. Another major recruitment pool should consist of the nation's sports clubs, since for "optical reasons" it would be advisable to have well-honed athletes on the force. All the recruits, whatever their origin or prior occupation, must receive extended special training in non-coercive crowd control, anger management, stress reduction, community relations—and a cram course in the English language.

Of course, there was always the danger that the proposed Olympic Ordnungsdienst, carefully selected and trained as it might be, would find itself confronted by challenges that simply could not be contained by the latest techniques in stress management. More traditional order-keeping measures might be required. The commissioner therefore recommended that regular units of both the Bavarian State Police and the Bundesgrenzschutz be kept on standby. However, in the interest of presenting a "convivial image" to the world, these uniformed forces must be stationed well away from the Olympic grounds, preferably in police or military barracks in the suburbs of Munich. Moreover, the "threshold" for their deployment should be as "high" as possible—though the commissioner refrained from speculating on just how high that threshold might be.

All the state and federal experts brought in to work on the security framework for the Munich Games agreed that predicting precisely what safety problems might actually materialize during the Olympic festival was a major challenge. Nonetheless, a group of security analysts from the Bavarian Cultural Ministry did their level best to examine all the political hot spots around the world from which some kind of messy fallout might possibly descend on Munich, rather like the ash from a distant volcano. They defined "danger" to the Games in the broadest sense—not just physical attacks or violent disruptions but also political campaigns designed to discredit Munich and Bonn and thereby discourage participation in the '72 festival. The ruminations of these security experts are worth examining in some detail, for they constitute a fascinating *tour d'horizon* of the world's troubled political landscape in 1970–1972. The sheer clutter of potential dangers also helps us to understand why it might have been difficult for the relevant authorities in Bavaria to identify where the "real" threat (obvious only in retrospect) might have resided.

In the first of two reports on "Foreign Political Danger Zones in Regard to the Olympic Games," Bavarian Cultural Ministry experts noted that the twelve-month period between June 1970 and June 1971 betrayed heightened tensions in many parts of the world. Not surprisingly, from their perspective, the most worrisome complex of dangers derived from the FRG's "geopolitical hot-seat" in the ongoing Cold War. Although Moscow's anti-Munich sentiment had "noticeably moderated," and the prospects for a wholesale East Bloc boycott were virtually zero, East Berlin was continuing to attack the Games, and its propaganda apparently was having some impact on leftist circles in France and Italy—not to mention on similar groups in the FRG itself. In short, East Berlin's continued hostility to Munich remained a major source of danger.

Much farther afield, the PRC also emerged as a source of worry in the eyes of the Bavarian analysts even though Beijing, in protest against Taiwan's presence at the Games, had since 1958 entirely turned its back on the Olympic movement. The problem with the PRC derived from Beijing's efforts over the years to encourage various Third World nations to follow its example and reject the Olympics as a bourgeois/capitalist/imperialist travesty. China was now taking the same line with respect to the Munich Games. However, recent trends in Chinese foreign policy—"ping pong diplomacy," and so forth—suggested that Beijing might be developing a greater interest in the Games. Perhaps what was keeping China away from Olympic competition these days was not just the Taiwan issue but also matters of prestige—the fear of performing badly and thus "losing face." A high Romanian official, with strong ties to China, had recently suggested that Beijing would not participate in the Games until it was confident that it would be able to steal some gold medals not only from the Americans but also from the "hated Soviets." Until that day arrived, however, China meant trouble. In the immediate future, it was therefore imperative for the Munich OC to lobby hard in the Third World to counter the negative Chinese influence.

Turning to Africa, the Bavarian report noted that a generally positive view of Munich and its upcoming Games might be endangered because of a growing rift over Rhodesia. At the goading of East Germany and Beijing, some Black African states were threatening to boycott Munich if Rhodesia, governed autocratically by the apartheid regime of Ian Smith, were allowed to participate. Munich was caught in a bind here because, while the UN had called for a ban on Rhodesian athletes (black and white) from competing in the territory of member states, the IOC was insisting that the white-ruled country, having recently added blacks to its team, must be admitted to Olympic play. If Munich followed the IOC lead and admitted Rhodesia, it risked a large-scale African boycott; moreover, it would thereby play into the hands of those, like the Chinese, who claimed that the Olympics were merely a plaything of the "bosses and imperialists."

While the African situation was complicated because of the potential boycott implications, other parts of the Third World offered prospects for genuine terror. The Uruguayan Tupamaros, for example, were openly threatening to extend their patented kidnapping and terror tactics to the Bavarian capital during the Games. Perhaps this was mere bravado, but given this group's recent actions, a slew of murderous attacks in Montevideo, "the seriousness of this threat [could not] be discounted."

With respect to the Middle East, said the report, the threat of terror was bound up with the lamentable reality that the major Arab states and the mainstream political organizations in those countries often lacked control over smaller splinter groups, which tended to follow their own lights. For this reason, one could "not discount as mere self-serving recent Israeli warnings that, despite the pro-Olympic and cosmopolitan posture of the Arab governments, a splinter group of the so-called 'Liberation Front for Palestine' could be in a position to undertake airline hijackings or other actions during the Olympic Games." In general, the Israelis had warned, the situation in the Middle East posed "particular dangers for participants and visitors from those states which today [were] directly involved in the fight against guerillas and partisans belonging to Arab extremist groups."

Finally, the first installment of the Cultural Ministry's political assessment concluded with a look at the Black Power movement in the United States, which of course had made its presence felt in prominent fashion at the Mexico City Games. Although a Black Panther–sponsored campaign for separate "Black Olympic Games" had petered out due to lack of interest, the will to stage "attention-getting demonstrations" at the Games remained very much alive, according to newspaper reports from the United States. Indeed, a growing disengagement on the part of American blacks from anti–Vietnam War demonstrations at home would leave them free for other activist campaigns, which were likely to intensify in the coming year and might well peak in the "hot summer" of 1972. For the Munich Games, this danger was intensified by the fact that black GIs stationed in West Germany had shown considerable sympathy for radical politics and had even forged ties to extreme left groups in the Munich area. "The problem of [radicalized American blacks]," concluded the report, "may well be the most worrisome in the entire political picture."

In their second report, covering the rest of 1971, the Bavarian observers saw no difference in the overall threat level, though there had been shifts in the degree of menace from one danger zone to another. In the case of the East Bloc, Moscow and its Warsaw Pact allies (with the notable exception of the GDR) had continued to moderate their criticism of Munich—obviously a good sign. The GDR's persistent "virulent" hostility to Munich '72 signaled a larger split between East Berlin and Moscow regarding attitudes toward Bonn and the West. This divergence tended to make the GDR, in its growing isolation, all the more determined to denigrate the FRG on every front, including that of sport. More specifically, East Berlin continued to leave no stone unturned in its efforts to mobilize Third World countries against Munich. Its latest salvo in this direction was a propaganda film entitled *Gefahr für Olympia* (Danger for Olympia), which, among other alleged horrors, warned of the FRG's attempt to "exploit" its host function in the Games in order to "extend its commercial and political influence in the developing world." Thus, while the GDR itself was undoubtedly not a candidate for a boycott in '72, its endless agitation against Munich was clearly designed to turn other nations, especially in the Third World, against the Bavarian capital and its impending Olympic festival.

Within the Third World the greatest source of danger to the Games remained Black Africa, where in recent months the situation had become even more threatening due to "serious complications" in the Rhodesia problem. This development was especially frustrating because the impasse over Rhodesia, which threatened to produce a large-scale boycott of Munich by African nations, had seemed to have been resolved through a compromise worked out by the IOC at its Luxemburg meeting: Rhodesia would be allowed to participate in Munich but only under the British Commonwealth flag and with the anthem "God Save the Queen." Indeed, many Black African sports leaders had welcomed this concession as a "great victory for African sport." But alas, this view was not shared by the most influential African political figures. The general secretary of the Organization of African States (OAS), an Ethiopian named Diallo Telli, rejected the compromise as a typical product of the politically retrograde IOC, an agency that (in Telli's words) was "dictatorially controlled by its American president and a few aging European racists." Emperor Hailie Selassie of Ethiopia, originally inclined toward compromise on Rhodesia, had moved to a position of intransigence because Chinese foreign minister Chou En-lai had apparently advised him that his "role as one of the greatest African leaders" was contingent on his joining the effort "to rid the African continent of the remains of colonialism and neo-colonialism." Beijing had also helped to convince Ethiopia's Telli to take the Rhodesian question before the United Nations' "Anti-Colonial Committee," which on October 10, 1971, had put out a statement demanding Rhodesia's expulsion from the '72 Games and threatening (undisclosed) sanctions against Bonn and the IOC if this were not done. For the moment, therefore, the division over Rhodesia looked "very difficult to bridge," though the OAS was not likely to take a final position on this issue until its upcoming meeting in February 1972, when it would throw the ball one last time into the IOC's court.

In the eyes of the Bavarian analysts, Beijing's problematical role in the Rhodesian affair showed that the PRC was a force to be reckoned with in the modern world. But exactly what kind of force China would turn out to be in the long run was quite hard to say: the tea leaves presented a very "confused" picture. Perhaps Beijing itself was not fully sure how to proceed along its newly opening avenue to the West, though Nixon's upcoming meeting with Chairman Mao in February 1972 might help sort that out. In the meantime, with respect to Bavaria's own upcoming meeting, the Munich Games, China had recently made indirect contact with the OC through a Bundestag representative, expressing "serious" interest in rejoining the IOC. But the Bavarian analysts were not terribly impressed by this demarche, which had not been corroborated at the official level. Indeed, no top political figures in China had shown any "real interest" as yet in bringing Beijing into the Olympic fold, much less participating in the Munich Games. There remained, after all, that intractable problem of Taiwan, which showed no sign of going away soon. On the other hand, Chinese sporting officials were clearly developing an interest in international athletic competitions, possibly even in hosting an event themselves down the line. This interest apparently extended to the Olympics. One could be sure, then, that athletic officials in the PRC were quietly trying to accumulate as much information as they could about the Munich Olympics. Moreover, efforts were now vigorously under way to make China more athletically competitive at the international level. All of this suggested that the PRC might one day make a positive contribution to the Olympic movement. For now, however, at least with respect to the Munich Games, Beijing remained another source of worry and "danger" because of its unsavory agitation in the Third World.

Yet another source of worry from the Far East, though from a different corner of it, had to do with Japan. This concern had its roots not in any direct antagonism toward Bonn, much less toward Munich; rather, it stemmed from Japan's increasingly strained relations with the United States. Of late, the Bavarian report noted, Tokyo had been turning away from Washington, a move accompanied by a very strong upsurge in anti-American sentiment on the popular level. What made this development relevant to the Munich Games was that Japan's popular anti-Americanism was finding an outlet at the Olympic level. Recently, anti-American groups in Japan had urged America's exclusion from the upcoming Sapporo Winter Games and threatened disruptions if the Yanks were allowed to compete there. According to the Bavarian analysts, Japanese security officials, pointing to the existence of an "Anti-US Sapporo Committee," took this threat very seriously. Unless the Sato government in Tokyo found ways to cool down Japanese emotions, concluded the Bavarian report, "the pent-up anti-American energy could not only disrupt the Winter Games in Sapporo but also spill over to the [Summer] Games in Munich." The report did not spell out what form this spill-over effect might take, but presumably the analysts worried that Japanese agitators might urge their nation's athletes not to compete in the same arena as the hated Americans—or try to persuade Japanese visitors to the Munich Games to use them as an occasion to demonstrate their opposition to a continued U.S. military presence in Japan.

And what about the ever-volatile Middle East? Anti-Israel sentiment continued to run high across the region, observed the Bavarian report. The analysts noted with alarm that, having failed to successfully hijack flights belonging to Sabena and Air France in early 1971, "Arab terror organizations" had taken the occasion of the anniversary of the [1967 Six-Day War] in June to threaten renewed actions against civilian aircraft. More specifically, the groups Black September and People's Front for the Liberation of Palestine had threatened hijackings of Lufthansa, Sabena, Air France, and German charter airlines. The Arab groups had reportedly recruited German, Japanese, Greek, and Turkish terrorists to assist them.

It was not only the Bavarian state experts who scanned the global political landscape for looming dangers to the upcoming Munich Games. Manfred Schreiber, the OC's point man for security at the Games, charged a thirty-nine-year-old police psychologist named Georg Sieber with the task of plotting out yet another risk analysis. Despite working for a municipal authority rather than the federal or state sleuths, Sieber was a serious student of global terrorist activity, and he accordingly worked up a list of some twenty-six worst-case scenarios, most of them involving foreign-based terror networks. Among his sketches were bombing attacks by the IRA and the Basque separatist group ETA (Euskadi Ta Askatasuna or "Basque Homeland and Liberty"), kidnappings by the Tupamaros and the Italian mafia, and a suicide airliner crash into the packed Olympic stadium engineered by Swedish neo-fascists. He also found a place for the Palestinians in his catalogue of potential catastrophes—one that turned out to be eerily prescient. Threat scenario number 21 involved twelve armed Palestinian commandos scaling the perimeter of the Olympic Village, invading the Israeli team compound, taking a number of hostages, and threatening to kill those hostages unless Arab political prisoners were freed from Israeli jails and the Palestinian commandos flown to safety in some friendly Arab capital. Even if the Palestinians failed in their primary mission, warned Sieber, they would undoubtedly make a bloody mess of the Munich Games and on no account would they surrender alive.

Manfred Schreiber was not entirely pleased with Sieber's work. In the Munich police chief's view, Sieber's scenarios seemed too far-fetched and unrealistic. Couldn't the expert come back to the committee with a revised set of possible threats that were more likely to materialize and against which the authorities could take practical measures in keeping with the kind of festival they intended to put on?

The dangers to the Games that Manfred Schreiber considered most realistic derived from the troubled national and local scenes. As it turned out, however, the experts who studied this side of the security question proved hardly more sanguine than Sieber and the Bavarian state security officials. Certainly, many of the threats that came in from West German sources were scary enough, and they were hardly of the sort that could be effectively countered with kid-glove tactics.

A major concern was West Germany's domestic radical Left, which most Bavarian authorities considered a more likely source of actual physical attacks on the Games than the GDR (though the GDR was also seen as a possible outside sponsor of home-grown leftist terror).

The domestic radical Left was not a monolith, of course. Like a hydra-headed beast, it had multitudinous faces and forms. The German Communist Party (DKP) was again active in Bavaria after having been banned in the late fifties and early sixties; it had participated in municipal elections in Bavaria in early 1972 for the first time since 1956. The DKP had proven to be a flop at the ballot box, but its very weakness in this domain made it seem, in the eyes of the Bavarian authorities, a more likely source of subversive activities against the state—and possibly against the Olympic Games. A report prepared by Bavaria's Office of Constitutional Protection (BLVS) on domestic security threats to the Games noted ominously that the DKP leadership had ordered rank-and-file members to take their annual vacations right before or just after the Olympics, so they could "be available to the party during the Games." The report did not speculate on exactly what the Communists might do during the Games, but presumably their intent was not to contribute to the festival's peaceful and harmonious atmosphere.

A more explicit threat to public order, and to the Games, was posed by the Baader-Meinhof group, also known as the Rote Armee Fraktion (RAF). The group had gone on a bombing and killing spree across Germany in early 1970. Andreas Baader was arrested in April 1970, only to be freed a month later in a bloody rescue raid led by Ulrike Meinhof, a radical journalist. Another campaign of bombings and killings quickly ensued; among the targets were U.S. Army bases (where three GIs were blown to bits) and the Axel-Springer publishing company, which published the *Bild Zeitung*, a populist tabloid. On May 12, 1972, the group descended on Bavaria, bombing the police headquarters in Augsburg and the Bavarian State Criminal Investigations Agency in Munich. A nationwide manhunt resulted in the capture and incarceration of both Baader and Meinhof in June 1972, but other elements of the band remained on the loose, while new "copy-cat" terror groups sprang up like mushrooms on a dung heap. A letter possibly written by Baader and smuggled out of his prison cell warned that the gang members who had not been caught would "never give up" and that the armed struggle "had just begun." Shortly after Baader and Meinhof's incarceration, a self-described offshoot of the RAF sent a letter to the Bavarian police faulting the original band for holding too closely to "bourgeois morality" and threatening to "turn the Olympic Protzspiele [show games] into a bloody disaster" with multiple bombings if the jailed RAF members were not immediately freed and flown to Algeria, along with a payment of DM 30 million.

While underground terrorist groups like the RAF and its imitators clearly constituted the most frightening face of the radical Left in West Germany, a host of other leftist groups, operating more or less in the open, also took aim at institutions of the state, largely because they saw local and national authorities as complicit in the "crimes of Western imperialism," most notably the Vietnam War. A new wave of anti-war demonstrations swept across West Germany in 1970–1971 in the wake of America's escalation of bombing in North Vietnam and its invasion of Cambodia. Although the war in Indo-China remained the focus of most of the West German demonstrations, some of the more radical groups, such as the Communist Youth Organization of Germany, threatened explicitly to include the Munich Games in their attacks against the "criminal establishment." This group announced that it regarded the Games as an especially inviting target because of the expected presence there of a host of foreign dignitaries, including the Shah of Iran and perhaps President Richard Nixon himself. Another anti-war group, the Vietnam Committee of the Aachen-based League against Imperialism, distributed fliers around West Germany calling for a mass demonstration against the Games on the opening day of the festival. This group chose to target the Olympics because, as one of its fliers put it, the "imperialist states" hoped with the Games "to once again distract the peoples of the world from [these states'] criminal aggression." Yet another anti-war faction, the National Vietnam Committee, a Maoist outfit based in West Berlin, called for a violent demonstration of its own on opening day. West Berlin security officials warned that some Technical University students affiliated with this group planned to charter a special train to travel to Munich for the Olympic opening. Meanwhile, as if to make opening day more scary still, a group calling itself the Anti-Olympia Committee was distributing fliers in major cities across Europe calling on the "residents of Woodstock-World" to attend a "Hippie Gathering" in Munich's Englischer Garten, where revelers could experience a "counter-program" to the big opening celebration going on in the Olympic Stadium. During the competitions this group hoped to stage such "anti-Olympic events" as sand-castle construction, high-jumping over a two-centimeter bar, and "long-distance spitting."

Compared to the threat from the radical Left, that emanating from neo-Nazis and other far-right circles seemed to be less pressing, in large part because the radical Right had lost ground in West Germany since the mid-sixties and was particularly weak in Munich. To the delight of Mayor Vogel, the SPD man, an election rally staged by the far-rightist National Democratic Party (NPD) in Munich in 1969 had ended in a "fiasco," with more counter-demonstrators than demonstrators. More recently, however, the radical Right had been somewhat energized by fervent opposition among nationalists across West Germany to Brandt's Ostpolitik, which, as we have seen, right-wingers took to be a sellout of the former German lands in the East. In January 1972, the NPD had held a "Day of German Unity" rally at a Munich beer hall that attracted some three hundred people. In that same month, an anti-rightist watchdog group called Democratic Action warned Bavarian authorities that the NPD planned to disrupt the Munich Olympics with a "Resistance Action" aimed at the participation of the Communist-ruled Eastern European states. The NPD also allegedly planned to host during the Games a "Congress of Nationalist European Youth," a giant radical rightist rally. The Bavarian authorities, however, discounted this threat. The Bavarian Interior Ministry, which closely monitored both rightist and leftist activities, reported that as of January 1972 it had "no concrete evidence" of planned neo-fascist attacks on the Games. Nonetheless, some eight months later, right on the eve of the Games, the Soviet Embassy in Bonn urged the authorities in Munich to be prepared for "provocative actions by Eastern European neo-fascist émigré groups against members of the Soviet delegation" to the Olympics. The Soviets, however, provided no specific information that might have given credence to this warning.

In addition to possible attacks or disruptive actions emanating from identifiable leftist and rightist groups in Germany, the security planners had to contend with, or at least think about, an array of threats from single actors or obscure grouplets that had never been on their radar screens before—and which might not exist at all. Among the many threats received by the Bavarian authorities was a letter written in broken German promising "explosion destroying Olympic Village" if "Rhodesia not play." Two Iranian students belonging to separate anti-Shah groups in West Germany and Austria were reported to have traveled to Munich with the intention "of politically influencing" members of the Iranian Olympic team or possibly attacking the Shah himself. Italian "guest-workers" in Munich had recently established a Comitato difesa dei diritti dei lavoratori italiani all'estero (Defensive Committee for the Rights of Italian Workers Abroad), which had distributed fliers calling for "a day of war" to coincide with Olympic opening day. A Bundeswehr soldier reported meeting a Palestinian in an Avignon youth hostel who confided that on opening day a bomb was going to go off "in the fully packed Olympic Stadium." A rambling missive under the letterhead

"General Consulate of the United Arab Republic, Hamburg" promised a veritable orgy of violent actions in Munich and around the world at the time of the Games unless "world Jewry" did not immediately withdraw "from all occupied Arab regions" and pay fifty million dollars "as compensation for the crimes committed on our bodies and property by Jewish napalm bombs." Among the threatened actions was the poisoning of Munich's water supply with "bacteriological agents developed by the world's leading scientists," along with the lethal contamination of mailboxes in Jewish neighborhoods everywhere—"so that the world Jewish population [would be] completely exterminated." The Bavarian Office for Constitutional Protection took this whacky threat seriously enough to check on the possible past or present existence of a "General Consulate of the United Arab Republic, Hamburg" but could find no trace of any such animal.

Politically motivated threats to the Games—however serious or believable—were not the only dangers the security planners faced. Officials worried about a huge spike in common criminality during the Games. In fact, in the years just prior to the Games, Munich had already seen a notable increase in criminal activity—a development that local police blamed on rapid population growth, a higher percentage of foreign immigration, and economic dynamism. "We can estimate that among the 40,000 people who are magically drawn here every year, 400 will be criminals," insisted one exasperated police official. A bad situation was expected to get considerably worse around the time of the Olympics because these festivals were known to be a magnet for "criminals of all types." One criminal specialty, pick-pocketing, was already making its presence felt in Munich during the weeks leading up to the Games. According to a police report from July 1972, "well trained" gangs of pick-pockets from Portugal and Yugoslavia were busy practicing their skills on the locals in order to be ready for the bigger game to come. Yet another criminal activity enjoying a pre-Olympic boom was Autoknacken—stealing valuables from parked automobiles. Munich police reported an average of fifty such thefts daily in the month immediately preceding the Games. Thefts from hotel rooms were also on the rise and were expected to become epidemic during the Games due to the wealth and naïve carelessness of Olympic guests.

To deal with the present spike in criminality—and to be ready for the veritable crime wave expected during the Games—Munich's police force imported some twelve thousand additional officers from other Bavarian cities. It also established a special unit to combat pick-pocketing and tripled the number of beat patrols in the downtown area. (On the very eve of the Games, three dark-skinned Italians were arrested for pick-pocketing, but the culprits were initially categorized by the Munich police as *Egyptians*, a mistake that did not go down well in Egypt.) The beat patrols were ordered to focus their vigilance on immigrants—that social category considered by the police to be "especially prone to commit punishable offenses during the Games." Having instituted measures like these, Munich's police authorities were reasonably confident that they were ready for the challenges to come. "We look with some optimism toward the Games," the chief of the Criminal Division said, "because we feel ourselves to be strong."

It was one thing to prepare for the sort of garden variety criminality that any large international event was likely to attract—quite another to do what was necessary to get ready for politically motivated disruptions or downright terror. As mentioned before, part of the problem was the sheer volume and diversity of the threats. How could one keep track of them all, let alone institute exactly the appropriate procedures to prevent or counter them? And crucially adding to the security challenge, once again, was the difficulty of taking adequate defensive measures without, to put it bluntly, looking like 1936 all over again. As Manfred Schreiber himself later stated,

> Open displays of armed force and coils of barbwire would not have been consistent with the OC's determination to create an atmosphere conducive to peaceful international encounters, nor would they have conveyed an accurate picture of today's Germany, which precisely in this respect [its lack of militarism and intimidating force] differentiates itself so clearly from the Germany that hosted the Games in 1936.

So what special Olympic security measures *did* the Munich authorities undertake? Apart from the establishment of the "Olys" and the above-mentioned augmentation of the Munich municipal police (which was designed primarily to deal with regular criminality), the Bavarian State Police brought in six thousand additional officers from other states; four thousand of them were to be stationed in the newly renovated Werner Kaserne in Munich, while the rest would be dispatched to rural regions near the Bavarian capital. The federal Interior Ministry in Bonn agreed to send two units of the Bundesgrenzschutz to Bavaria for the duration of the Games. Due to the necessity of preserving state control in the security realm, however, these federal units would be "fully integrated" into existing Bavarian forces and serve under the exclusive command of the Bavarian authorities. Bonn's Office of Constitutional Protection also agreed to augment Bavaria's equivalent agency with a temporary loan of agents from the central office and other regional branches. A special VIP Division was set up to protect visiting heads of state, such as Britain's Queen Elizabeth II, whose announced intention to attend the Games was expected to spur other world notables to come as well.

Just prior to the Games, security officials from Bremen, Bonn, Hamburg, and West Berlin sent Munich a list of forty-six named individuals, all of them foreign immigrants residing in the FRG, who were "suspected of planning actions against public figures, domestic and foreign, during the Games." Moreover, the Munich Police requested that officials at all FRG points of entry be on the lookout for specified "foreign individuals" with known radical backgrounds and credentials, who might have Olympic terror on their minds. For example, Munich asked to be notified immediately if one Gregg Kennet, a "right-wing radical" from the United States, tried to enter the Federal Republic at any time during the Games.

Protecting the Olympic grounds and Village was seen to be an especially delicate task. Bavarian authorities wanted to keep these areas free of all political activities and unwelcome intruders, but also absent of "militaristic excess" on the part of the security forces. The entire Olympic complex was to be a no-go zone, not just for political demonstrations, but also for political proselytizing of any kind, including the distribution of posters and the delivery of speeches augmented by loudspeakers. Furthermore, all visitors would have to leave the grounds by ten o'clock every evening during the Games. There would be no semi-permanent campgrounds, no rowdy, drug-besotted midnight parties next to the Olympic Lake.

As for the Olympic Village, that part of the complex was to be surrounded by a two-meter-high chain-link fence, though of course, said fence would not be topped with barbwire. At night, but only at night, the perimeter was to be patrolled by police vehicles. Perhaps surprisingly, given the above-mentioned threats to the Israeli delegation, no special precautions were planned for the Israeli compound, save for a decision not to house the Egyptians directly next door. (Instead, Israel's immediate neighbor in the Village would be the team from Hong Kong.) According to testimony by OC members subsequent to the terror attack, security officials from Israel had inspected the Village two weeks before the Games and found the safety measures there fully adequate; they hadn't requested any special precautions for Israel's delegation. (As we shall see, however, this claim would later be hotly disputed by the Israelis.)

On August 23, three days prior to opening day, Bavarian interior minister Bruno Merk reviewed the various security preparations before a group of Munich police officials and pronounced himself satisfied with all that had been done. One had to expect "disturbances here and there," he said, but he didn't foresee any "serious disruptions." With respect to security and safety, then, the Munich Olympic Games would "proceed normally."

"A Gift of the Germans to Themselves"

The Bavarian police and Munich OC may have been confident that they had the security situation well in hand on the eve of the '72 Games, but in the final run-up to opening day local officials and the IOC could not help but be reminded that the impending Olympic festival remained a treacherous political minefield through which they had to tread very carefully indeed.

Just as the Games were about to begin, one of those mines—the long-simmering Rhodesia problem—finally exploded messily, claiming as victims not only the Rhodesian team but also Munich's hope of overcoming old animosities through inclusive diplomacy and bountiful good cheer. As we have seen, Bavarian political analysts had identified the African scene early on as a "danger zone" for the Games because several Black African states were threatening a boycott of Munich if Rhodesia were admitted to the Games. By this time, the boycott movement had expanded to include nine African states: Cameroon, Ethiopia, Egypt, Ghana, Kenya, Somalia, Tanzania, Uganda, and Zambia. The Rhodesian Olympic Committee sought to counter the boycott movement by putting together a mixed team and agreeing to compete under the British Commonwealth flag. In the eyes of the IOC and Munich OC, Rhodesia had thereby done enough to comply with Olympic rules. "The situation is resolved," declared Willi Daume, who had sent Rhodesia an invitation as early as March 1971. Avery Brundage, too, was convinced that the Black African nations would now come to their senses and cease their talk of a boycott. If they did not do so, and actually followed through on a boycott, Brundage issued a threat of his own: to expel the Olympic committees of the boycotting nations from the Olympic movement. They would merit such treatment, he thundered, because by yielding to the "political" demands of their governments they would have demonstrated their lack of independence from those regimes.

But the African states were not intimidated. With the support of the OAS, they renewed their boycott threat and sharpened their attacks on Rhodesia. A spokesman for the aggrieved nations denounced the seven blacks on Rhodesia's forty-four-person Olympic team as "collaborators," akin to the Moroccan athletes who in the colonial era had competed in the Olympics for France. Such "turncoats," they said, only buttressed the racist regime of Ian Smith. Smelling blood, Haiti and Cuba declared their "solidarity" with the Black African states.

To complicate matters even further, a rumor made the rounds to the effect that Britain's Queen Elizabeth and Prime Minister Edward Heath might not attend the Games if Rhodesia, which had fallen afoul of London through its apartheid policies, were allowed to participate. This rumor turned out to be unfounded, but that did not prevent a junior official in West Germany's Foreign Office from citing this "danger" to justify a proposal of his to the Brandt cabinet that the FRG close its borders to the Rhodesians should they try to come to Munich for the Games.

As this incident indicated, Bonn's Foreign Office was extremely worried about the Rhodesian matter, especially the ongoing threat of a large-scale boycott. Noting that West Germany's relations with the Black African states would be "severely burdened" by a Rhodesian presence at the Munich Games, the Foreign Office proposed in July 1972 that Bonn should forbid the OC from issuing any of its special Olympic visas to the Rhodesians. The government could cite as legal grounds for this action the UN sanctions against Rhodesia and its own promise to the IOC in 1966 to guarantee "harmonious conduct of the Olympic Games." As further ammunition for a possible ban, the Foreign Office cited a British government aide-mémoire declaring that the use by the Rhodesian team of the Commonwealth flag and British anthem "would not alter the illegal status" of Smith's breakaway regime.

On August 18, 1972, Willy Brandt personally wrote Brundage to ask him, in effect, to back down on the Rhodesian issue so as to spare Germany the huge embarrassment of an African boycott:

> The Federal Government respects the decisions of the IOC, but I ask you, Mr. President, to understand my worry that the absence of many friendly nations [from the Munich Games] could do irreparable harm to the unifying ideals of the Olympics. The Federal Government would therefore be grateful if the IOC could find a solution that allowed our African friends to participate in the Games.

Matters came to a head during meetings of the Executive Board of the IOC in Munich on August 21–22, followed by a plenary session on August 22. By this time, the Rhodesian team was already in Munich, settling in to the Olympic Village—so were the Black African teams, but they insisted they would promptly leave if Rhodesia were allowed to stay. During the August 21 Executive Board meeting, Daume told Brundage and the Board he "was sure that all the African NOC's [National Olympic Committees] would withdraw [from the Games], as well as the Black Americans and some South American teams." Perhaps the Pakistani and Indian teams would also pull out. At the tension-filled plenary session on August 22, IOC members listened for two hours to arguments put forth by the African delegates, headed by Abraham Ordia of Nigeria and Jean-Claude Ganga of Cameroon, president of the Supreme Council for Sports in Africa. Rhodesian delegates, for their part, protested that they had complied with all IOC requirements. Brundage fully agreed with them, but in this instance he could not prevail. By a vote of thirty-six to twenty-one, with three abstentions, the committee decided to exclude Rhodesia.

Brundage was apoplectic with anger, as were many conservative editorialists and pundits in West Germany and elsewhere. "Sport has to dance to the pipes of politics," sputtered the *Frankfurter Allgemeine Zeitung*. "Kicking out a nation's athletes because of the country's government is contrary to the spirit of the Games. . . . It is enough to blow out the Olympic Torch," declared the *Los Angeles Herald Examiner* (a Hearst paper). Letters poured into the IOC complaining of the committee's "violation" of its own statutes. A Canadian gentleman opined that the IOC would have done better to ban all black athletes, because, as everyone knew, "their bodies are built somewhat differently than Caucasians." No blacks "had participated in [ancient] Greece," he added, as if that were the clincher. Echoing Nazi sentiments about Jesse Owens and other victorious African Americans in 1936, a man from Naples, Florida, weighed in with the observation that "a member of the Negro race is not far from being an animal. Therefore, I feel that it is unfair to place a member of the Caucasian race in direct competition with a Negro anymore than I'd ask him to compete with a cheetah. I do hope that some thought can be given to this aspect of the Games before the 1976 Olympiad." Yet another correspondent reminded the IOC that "Jesus was betrayed for 30 pieces of silver." What "financial gains" had prompted the committee "to betray a country which [it] had invited to take part in the Games, and which had met every requirement?" Brundage himself was spared some of this enlightened criticism, for his opposition to the decision on Rhodesia had been well publicized. As one American writer wrote to the IOC president, "Angry as I am this evening, I can still pause to tell you that I appreciate and respect the attitude with which you have served international sports for so many years. . . . Every true sportsman has to be most grateful to you—as I am."

One imagines that such praise was small consolation for the veteran IOC president, who hated to be crossed by anybody. On the day after the crucial vote by the IOC's full body, Brundage announced that the IOC Executive Board would begin inquiries to determine whether the national committees of the countries demanding Rhodesia's exclusion had acted on orders from their governments; if this turned out to be the case, declared Brundage, the offending committees would be expelled from the IOC. (In the end, no African National Olympic Committees were expelled because of their stance on Rhodesia.)

Brundage delivered his threat to the Africans at the end of the IOC's plenary session, which would be the last one he would preside over, for he planned to step down from the IOC presidency at the end of the Munich Games. As for the Rhodesian team, they vacated the Village for secret quarters near Munich provided by the West German Defense Ministry. The team was given tickets for all the events in which its members would have participated had they not been expelled.

With the Black African nations finally on board, there was no danger that black American athletes might stay away from Munich, as some had threatened to do if their African brothers walked out over Rhodesia. (While admitting that "a few black athletes representing the U.S." had indicated "their sympathy" for the Black African nations, the USOC denied there was any talk of a boycott of Munich. However, Vince Matthews states in his memoirs that, if Rhodesia had not been excluded, he was "prepared to pack up and leave," as were his black teammates John Smith, Wayne Collett, and Chuck Smith.) In any event, given all the tension over Rhodesia, Brundage for one remained very worried that at the Munich Games there might be a repeat, or even an escalation, of the Black Power protests that had, in his view, so deeply marred the 1968 Mexico City Olympics. In an effort to preempt any similar incidents at Munich, the IOC, backed by the Amateur Athletic Union (AAU) in the United States, announced that any "political demonstrations" by athletes during the Games would be punished by the immediate expulsion of the offending competitors.

The IOC/AAU action did not sit well with a number of top athletes in the United States, white as well as black. In advance of the U.S. Olympic track and field trials, to be held in Eugene, Oregon, in July 1972, over one hundred Olympic hopefuls founded a group called United Amateur Athletes (UAA) as a counterweight to the establishmentarian AAU. The founders of this group included Jack Scott, a former Stanford sprinter and leading sports activist in the San Francisco Bay Area*; Phil Shinnick,

---

* In 1970, Jack Scott founded the Institute for the Study of Sport and Society, based in Oakland, California. Scott and his institute were influential in a growing movement that was highly critical of authoritarianism and commercialism in high-level sport in America. From 1972 to 1974, Scott was athletic director at Oberlin College, where he appointed Tommie Smith to his staff.

an Olympic long-jumper; and Harold Connolly, winner of the hammer-throw competition at the Melbourne Games (and participant in three other Olympics).

One of the UAA's purposes was to provide support—strength in numbers—for any athlete who might choose to demonstrate his or her political views at the Munich Games. The UAA founders hoped that the mere existence of their new group would deter Olympic authorities from censuring anyone at Munich for doing something similar to what Carlos and Smith had done in Mexico City. "We want to control our own lives, and we don't want other people telling us what to do or what not to do," explained Shinnick, the long-jumper.

Another part of the UAA's raison d'être was to stand up against the growing influence of nationalism in the Olympics, a goal that was not inconsistent with Brundage's own posture, or indeed with that of the Munich organizers. But some of the gestures being mulled over by the UAA athletes as possible means to this end were certain to cause trouble in Munich if actually implemented. Clearly, this was true of a proposal that all UAA athletes wear generic Olympic uniforms rather than the official red, white, and blue outfits prescribed by the USOC; equally provocative was a proposal that UAA members insist on having the Olympic anthem played after their victories instead of "The Star-Spangled Banner." While still undecided about exactly what they might do in Munich to counter chauvinistic excess, the UAA athletes were determined not to be "pimped out by the USOC" as enthusiastic icons of the American way of life. "The Games are supposed to be competitions between athletes and not nations against nations or one particular way of life against another," pronounced Scott.

Not surprisingly, the stance of the UAA aroused patriotic hackles in America. Vice President Spiro Agnew denounced the group as "un-American," singling out Scott in particular as a "Berkeley guru" and "perma-critic coming before the American people behind misleading facades." President Nixon himself said nothing publicly about this latest un-American activity in the world of sport, but the White House announced in July that, contrary to earlier reports that the president intended to attend the '72 Summer Games, he would not be going to Munich after all.

Meanwhile, although the AAU showed little concern about the UAA malcontents, suggesting the whole thing would soon "blow over," Stan Wright, the African American assistant coach for the U.S. men's track team for the '68 Games and again for '72, wasn't so sanguine. He warned the IOC and the Munich OC that "something more drastic" than a clenched-fist salute might transpire at Munich. Asked what that might be, Wright said he didn't know. "But they [the discontented athletes] are a hell of a lot wiser than they were in 1968, and they'll be organized as a highly knit group. And they'll use this to get some of the things pertinent to their needs."

While the pronouncements of the dissident American athletes hinted at possible "political" trouble during the upcoming competitions, the festival's signature preliminary event, the Olympic torch relay from ancient Olympia to the host city, had been caught up in political acrimony for months during the planning period. In a way, the controversy was only fitting: after all, the ritualistic torch relay had been introduced by the Nazis in 1936, when it had occasioned pro- and anti-German demonstrations all along the route from Greece to Berlin.

In summer '72, Munich's version of this invented Olympic tradition would involve a 5,538-kilometer, 29-day trek by some 5,976 torch-bearing runners and bicyclists. If the Berlin organizers in 1936 had insisted (at least for the German parts of the relay) on deploying perfect examples of Nordic manhood, Munich's event would include women and, for the first time, disabled athletes. On the other hand, Munich emulated Berlin in assigning the design and manufacture of the high-tech torches to the Essen-based industrial giant Krupp, which desperately wanted its high-grade steel to be identified with the Games. In the end, Krupp supplied torches that were not only exceptionally heavy but also so poorly designed that one in ten proved faulty. The '72 relay would traverse some of the same territory as in 1936, though of course the political landscape along the route had substantially changed. It was this changed political landscape that provided for most of the headaches and controversy in the planning for the '72 torch relay.

From the start, Willi Daume and the Munich OC had hoped to include as many Eastern European nations as possible in the relay itinerary so as to promote Ostpolitik on the Olympic level. Daume had in mind six Eastern states: Bulgaria, Romania, Yugoslavia, Hungary, Czechoslovakia, and East Germany. Rather more ambitiously, some members of a special Torch Relay Subcommittee of the OC favored a much-expanded itinerary that would accommodate a request from several African nations to be included on the route. Another, even more adventurous, proposal involved sending the torch into space via an American rocket and having it circle the globe a few times before returning it to earth in time for the festival. Frau Liselott Diem, whose husband Carl had been largely responsible for the '36 relay, proposed that the '72 relay touch every city that had ever hosted the Games—and that furthermore during this epic trek the sacred Olympic flame should be allowed to burn again in the ornamental braziers at all the former Olympic stadia, provided such facilities still existed. One of Frau Diem's colleagues gently reminded her that the old Olympic stadium in Berlin still boasted such a cauldron, where the sacred flame had burned merrily during "Hitler's Games." For "political reasons," he suggested, it might be best to leave Berlin off the route for '72.

As it happened, neither the political problems posed by Berlin nor the logistical nightmare of a global trek (let alone a space voyage) remained relevant for long; after additional deliberations, the Torch Relay Subcommittee opted for a limited land route—albeit not a perfectly direct one— between Olympia and Munich. Still, however, there remained the question of the Eastern European nations' willingness to join in Daume's envisaged Olympic Ostpolitik. To the OC chief's frustration, Bulgaria, whose Olympic committee had initially welcomed the idea of the torch passing though its territory, declared in January 1971 that it would not participate, offering "unavoidable circumstances" as its reason. Asked by a reporter if "political issues" were behind this decision, Daume said he didn't know, but he would "hold the door open" to Sofia should it reconsider. About one year later, in fact, Sofia did reconsider, declaring it would participate in the relay after all. No explanations for the switch were given, but pressure from the USSR, which as we know had come to embrace the Munich Games, undoubtedly played a role here. (Moscow's support for the torch relay deeply frustrated the GDR, which had hoped for a full-scale East European boycott of the project.)

A similar story played out with Romania, which also opted out of the relay, citing the FRG's "misuse" of the Games as the reason. However, a mere five weeks later Bucharest reversed that position, this time without an explanation. No doubt the Bavarian security commissioner, Heinrich Martin, was correct in detecting another "intervention by Moscow" behind this welcome development.

Czechoslovakia and the GDR, however, refused Daume's invitation to participate in the relay from the beginning and held to that refusal throughout their negotiations with the Munich OC. Czechoslovakia's position was predictable, given that this country was run by one of the most hard-line and parochial Communist governments in Eastern Europe. But Daume had harbored high hopes for East Germany, despite its constant sniping at the Munich Games—and he was sorely disappointed by East Berlin's intransigence because he saw mending fences with the GDR as central to his Olympic diplomacy. His "partners" in the East, of course, did not share this goal. In East Berlin's view, a torch relay through its territory, especially if it included a direct crossing of the German-German border, would, at least symbolically, have suggested rather more cordiality between the two Germanys than Erich Honecker thought permissible or desirable. At this point, East Berlin remained determined to pursue its policy of Abgrenzung (demarcation) vis-à-vis Bonn even in—in fact especially in—a supposedly "people-uniting" enterprise like the Olympic torch relay.

Fortunately for the OC, the '72 torch relay, once it finally took its course through eight countries—Greece, Turkey, Bulgaria, Romania, Yugoslavia, Hungary, Austria, and the FRG—from July 28 to August 26, managed to escape the kind of political quarreling that had bedeviled its planning. True, there were a few snafus—the misdesigned torches went out twice in Greece and had to be relit from a replacement flame conveniently carried in a following car; and the flame car's driver had his passport stolen in Romania. Moreover, a rather embarrassing incident occurred in the heart of Bavaria on August 23 when a young man stopped a torchbearer in the village of Ruhpolding to get a light from the traveling torch for his cigarette. The fellow then lit a candle from his cigarette and promptly transferred said lit candle to some young men waiting in a nearby car, who then sped away in the direction of Munich. Once in Munich, the men used the "sacred flame" to light a bonfire outside the Turnvater Jahn Gymnastics Club. Thus, at least unofficially, the Olympic flame reached Munich some three days ahead of schedule.

On the other hand, and more importantly, none of the torchbearers in the '72 relay was physically threatened or assaulted by bystanders, which had happened in eastern Czechoslovakia in 1936 (and would happen again in 2008 in places like London and Paris as the torch wound its way painfully from Olympia to Beijing). At a ceremony for the sacred flame in Athens, soldiers carrying the flags of all the nations that had thus far hosted the Games discreetly substituted a City of Berlin banner for the national swastika flag that had flown all over Germany in 1936. Similarly, when the torch arrived in Munich's Königsplatz for a major celebration before moving on to its final destination in the Olympic Stadium, no one mentioned that this particular square had constituted the heart of Nazi Munich during the Third Reich, with Hitler's local office a mere stone's throw from the stage on which a similar torch-welcoming ceremony in 1936 had taken place.

Mention of Germany's dark past could not be avoided at a different, certainly less cheery, ceremony on August 25 at Dachau, just north of Munich. On the site of the former concentration camp, about 1,500 people, including Olympic dignitaries and members of the Bavarian and West German federal governments, gathered to commemorate the millions of victims of Nazi criminality during the Third Reich. The event was sponsored by the International Dachau Committee, the Protestant and Catholic churches of West Germany, and the FRG's Jewish community.* Archbishop Adam Kozlowiecki from Zambia, of Polish origin and himself once an inmate of Dachau, appealed to the dignitaries not to forget the suffering of their fellow men now that the Munich Games were starting. Because of "international indifference," he warned, a situation similar to that in the 1930s could arise again. He concluded his homily with his best wishes for a peaceful Olympiad.

In the final week before the Games' opening day, athletes from around the world settled into the Olympic Village. Not surprisingly, given all the work that had gone into the planning and building of this elaborate complex, and the effort by the Village "mayor" Walther Tröger to anticipate every possible need, most of the athletes expressed satisfaction with their quarters. Some of the Americans, however, found the efficiency and all-encompassing meticulousness of their hosts a little hard to take. "There's too much organization," complained marathoner Frank Shorter. "I mean, there's a pinball machine here, a milk bar there, a miniature golf course across the sidewalk. You can't even say, 'Let's go out for such and such,' because you turn around and it's already there." Another American, the quarter-miler John Smith, contrasted the dull hyper-efficiency of the Munich Village with the stimulating chaos of the ramshackle athletic housing at the recent Pan-American Games in Cali, Colombia. "There you had some excitement. You had people jumping from buildings, assassinations, fights, drugs, all kinds of things. It got the adrenalin going. Here, you just slide comfortably along." (Smith, of course, would soon have to eat those words.)

In the view of some of the foreign athletes and officials, the efficiency and precision governing life in the Village did not extend to the realm of security. Vince Matthews noted that just about anyone could get into the complex without much trouble. Reporters who lacked the special Press Pass "would slip by guards flashing something that resembled it." Athletes loaned out their own passes to friends and relatives. Village guards, "eager to create a non-military image, turned their backs or, in the case of some women athletes, turned on some charm in hopes of lining up a date for

* Members of Israel's recently arrived Olympic team were supposed to have been present at this ceremony as well, but they decided to skip it in order to train. Indignant protests from home regarding their "insult" to the memory of the Holocaust prompted the athletes to go to Dachau the following day for a private makeup ceremony.

after-duty hours," added Matthews. This view was echoed by Matthews's coach, Bill Bowerman. A legendary mentor at the University of Oregon (and a co-founder of Nike), Bowerman was appalled by what he discovered during an advance reconnaissance of the Village on August 19: "I walked around the Olympic Village and saw there was [no security]. As guards they had boys and girls dressed in pastels, not one with a weapon. The back fence was nothing. Six feet, chain link, no barbed wire." Bowerman promptly wrote a letter of complaint to USOC chief Clifford Buck. "We should at least be able to keep out thieves, harlots, and newspapermen," he wrote. Buck passed Bowerman's letter on to Tröger, who according to Bowerman "took strong umbrage" at the complaint, suggesting that the American simply didn't understand the Germans' larger political concerns, their pressing need to minimize a police and military presence.

While the athletes were making themselves familiar with the Olympic Village's many amenities (including a robust selection of porno magazines in the bookstore), thousands of Olympic guests from abroad and other parts of Germany were starting to descend on Munich. The difficult situation they found there—inadequate accommodations, price-gouging at every turn, and aggressive whores of antiquated vintage—presented the organizers with a new set of headaches, these more PR than political, but still.

Actually, the problems with accommodations had shown up well in advance of opening day, and even the price-gouging could be felt during the run-up to the Games, not just during the Games themselves. The OC officials in charge of advance booking for hotels and Olympic events had put together a scheme seemingly calculated to infuriate foreign Olympic fans who harbored fond hopes of a blissful stay in West Germany's capital of hospitality. In early 1971, angry articles started appearing in British and American newspapers decrying a system whereby potential Olympic visitors from those countries (but this applied to other foreign countries as well) would have to book their stays in Munich at least one year in advance and do so through a single approved travel agency. They would also have to pay for a minimum of twenty-five days in Munich (though the Games lasted only sixteen days); buy event tickets and hotel accommodations in one package (even if they owned a villa in the Bavarian capital); and, the kicker, purchase the whole package without any guarantee of which events might be included or where their lodgings might be—the only promise being that the hotels would be in a *seventy-five-mile radius* of Munich. The application process was also extremely complicated, involving all kinds of forms and official stamps. (Having been inundated with complaints from Americans about the advance reservation setup, Avery Brundage looked into the matter and concluded that it "would take a Philadelphia lawyer" to figure it out. He warned Daume that, because of the intimidating and injurious booking system, many Americans had "dropped their idea to attend the Games.") In addition to all their other faults, the Olympic tourist packages were also extremely expensive, the tariff amounting to "highway robbery" in the words of one British paper. The outcry over this system was such that the Olympic officials eventually reduced the obligatory stay from twenty-five days to twenty, but the other onerous features remained in place, including the requirement to "buy blind."

Why in the world, one wonders, would the Olympic hosts have put together such a loathsome system? In fact, the organizers were in a considerable pinch, albeit one of their own making. With respect to lodging, the problem was that, far in advance of the Games, the vast majority of beds in Munich itself had already been reserved for officials, dignitaries, and high-profile West Germans. Contrary to its promise to build plenty of fine housing for visitors to the Games, Munich had erected relatively few new hotels of substantial size in the past five years. (Two exceptions to this rule were new Munich additions to the U.S.-based Sheraton and Hilton hotel chains, a development that caused the Munich Hotel Owners' Association to complain that the big American hostelries might in the long term endanger the livelihoods of local innkeepers.) Foreigners insisting on staying in Munich proper had better be prepared to fetch up "in a phone-booth," reported the *New York Times*.

As for Olympic tickets (at least to the choice events), they too were scarce. As the Manchester *Guardian* complained, Britain had been allocated only ninety-five thousand tickets for the 196 events in twenty-one sporting categories over the course of the entire festival, which was "nothing more than crumbs from a total of nearly 4.5 million tickets." But as with hotel beds, most of the tickets had already been allocated elsewhere, and tickets for the particularly choice events were being held back for "special guests." Americans felt similarly disadvantaged. *Sports Illustrated* complained that less than 2 percent of the 115,000 tickets allocated to the United States were for the "glamorous" events. Moreover, "even if you should win one of those prizes," said the magazine, odds were high that you would have to stand up rather than sit down: the Olympic Stadium had a capacity of eighty thousand, but only forty-five thousand actual seats.

But it wasn't just foreigners who feared being deprived of the chance of getting good Olympic tickets—or indeed any tickets at all. Münchners and residents of nearby towns worried that they would not be able to secure tickets for visiting relatives and friends because the latter would not have signed up for the Olympic Booking Agency's lodging/ticket packages. It was a hell of a note, the locals complained, when fellow Bavarians had to fear being shut out of their own party.

Widespread complaints about overpriced housing and tickets, along with other forms of price-gouging in advance of the Games, prompted *Sports Illustrated* to observe that the Germans were "intent on making their marks." Indeed they were, as I can attest from personal experience. I happened to be in Munich during the final run-up to the Games, though my presence there had nothing to do with the impending Olympics. I was conducting research on my doctoral dissertation at one of the local archives, all the while trying doggedly to ignore the frantic last-minute buildup to the big happy festival. But I couldn't escape the price-gouging that accompanied that buildup. Even two months before the Games began, modest accommodations—say, simple Pension rooms near the center of town—were going for about three times the price for equivalent lodgings elsewhere in West Germany. As a consequence, I ended up residing in a tiny basement room out by the Riem Airport, for which I paid a small fortune. I would have liked to drown my sorrows in Löwenbräu, but that was far too expensive.

Of course, I had plenty of company. Once the Games drew nigh and more visitors arrived, Munich housing authorities were flooded with complaints about "swindles" perpetrated by "clip-joint owners." A bad situation was made worse by the high value of the mark relative to most foreign currencies. Foreign visitors naturally bristled when they discovered that their hotels were way out in the sticks, somewhere near the Austrian border. Few rental cars were to be had, and for the price of "shuttle service" into Munich guests could have *bought* the cabs or busses that conveyed them, even though these vehicles were generally made by Mercedes.

The Munich authorities responded to the visitor outrage with warnings to landlords and nightclub owners about swindling, but the officials' major concern seemed to be the city's supposed image as a "wholesome" place. The City Council tried to induce cinemas showing porno films to switch to "clean screens," but the Bavarian Cinema Owners' Association refused to comply. Police Chief Schreiber declared the inner city and Olympic grounds to be off limits to prostitutes. "Girls violating the off-limits rule may find themselves in jail during the Games," he warned. (At least these women would have a place to stay!)

In the week before the Games were set to open, Hamburg's *Der Spiegel*, not always a friendly voice when it came to Munich, summed up a grim situation for the Munich Olympic officials. "Protests, boycott threats, cancellations [by prospective visitors]—one piece of bad news after another has hit the Olympic organizers. . . . No one is speaking anymore of a 'radiant Olympia.'" The situation in Munich made one wonder, continued the magazine, whether the huge organizational effort and the ballooning price tag for the Games (already estimated at over two billion marks) could be rationalized or justified. After all, whom did the Olympic Games actually serve, in the end? *Der Spiegel*'s answer, in the case of Munich, was that the '72 festival seemed to consist of little more than "A Gift of the Germans to Themselves." But which Germans got this gift? No one, noted the magazine, had ever held a referendum to ask the German people if they actually wanted the Games in the first place. On the other hand, now that Munich's putatively "modest" Olympic proposal had mushroomed into the bloated spectacle it promised to be, the fat-cat Germans who had campaigned for the Olympics might just be getting "exactly the kind of Games they deserved."

CHAPTER Four

Let the Games Begin

> It seems to me that next to *Homo Faber*, and perhaps
> on the same level as *Homo Sapiens*, Homo Ludens,
> Man the Player, deserves a place in our nomenclature.
> —Johan Huizinga, *Homo Ludens* (1950)

Rumor has it that the quadrennial wandering athletic circus known as the modern Olympic Games actually involves some athletics. This rumor turns out to be true enough, though the sporting contests in question often seem to get hopelessly lost in all the surrounding controversy over venue selection, roster of participating nations, TV rights, physical plant, escalating costs, commercialization, amateurism, symbolism—and, increasingly, doping. In the case of Munich '72 the run-up to the Games had been even more acrimonious than usual, as we have seen. It would be comforting to think that, once the big affair had actually commenced, the festival might finally have managed to break free of all the preceding acrimony. But this was not quite the case. In the early days of competition, there were plenty of examples of truly brilliant athleticism— but also numerous reminders that, even on the field of play, this "joyful" party in laid-back Munich remained intensely political and fractious.

Munich Gleamed

On the opening day of the Twentieth Olympic Summer Games, Munich's weather, following a stretch of cloudy skies and rain, was warm and clear. "Is [this] a meteorological conspiracy, an augury of happiness?" wondered

Richard D. Mandell in the diary he kept during his visit to the Munich Games. After all the stress, disappointments, and grim forebodings during the run-up to the Games, a palpable sense of relief hung in the air now that the festival was finally getting under way.

From the outset, the Munich Organizing Committee (OC) had hoped to set the tone for the entire enterprise with a revolutionary new kind of opening ceremony. At a brainstorming session back in 1969, members of a subcommittee on the opening and closing ceremonies agreed that there should be as little military and nationalistic display as possible—no cannon salutes, hoisting of flags by soldiers, armed forces parades, or flyovers by military aircraft. Aesthetics guru Otl Aicher proposed that the Olympic hymn be substituted for national anthems and that the Olympic flag be carried into the stadium by a delegation of Nobel Peace Prize winners. He also suggested that the tradition whereby athletes marched around the stadium track grouped by national teams and dressed in identical outfits be scrapped on grounds that this was too militaristic. Why not, he asked, allow the athletes to stroll about dressed in whatever they wanted and in whichever order they pleased? Summing up their aspirations for the opening ceremony, one committee member declared, "The ceremony must be simple, colorful, joyous, playful, and loose—and all of it executed with a light hand."

Such a spectacle obviously called for a talented choreographer, someone who knew how to put on a good show. The committee's first choice for this role was the famed Italian film director and opera designer Franco Zeffirelli. He initially accepted the job, only to withdraw at the last minute in protest against Rhodesia's exclusion from the Games. A local TV producer, Uly Wolters, took his place.

The loss of Zeffirelli was not the only disappointment for the Munich planners. The International Olympic Committee (IOC), which had established specific rules for opening ceremony protocol, refused to let the Munich OC completely revamp the show. Willi Daume got an inkling of this problem when an IOC official, responding to a Swiss newspaper account of the OC's plan for a "demilitarized" ceremony, sharply reminded him that *Lausanne* set the basic parameters for Olympic opening ceremonies. Thus, there could be no total elimination of national banners or anthems, no higgledy-piggledy athlete march-in sans identical team outfits. The planners were obliged to go back to the drawing board and come up with a compromise between their adventurous aspirations and articles 57–59 in the IOC rulebook, which governed opening ceremonies. Nonetheless, what eventually emerged in the revised plan was refreshingly different, certainly a significant departure from the nationalistic and militaristic bravura that had typically characterized Olympic opening ceremonies over the years.

Given the rumors about exciting innovations in the opening show, the eighty thousand ticket-holders crammed into the Olympic Stadium—along with a sizeable mob of freeloaders perched atop the neighboring Schuttberg—did not know exactly what to expect on that sunny afternoon in late August. The first thing that happened was predicable enough: West German president Gustav Heinemann, the official patron of the Munich Games, entered the stadium through the "marathon tunnel" and took his seat in the Honor Tribune alongside Avery Brundage and other top IOC brass. Nearby in the VIP section were Bavarian minister-president Alfons Goppel, ex-Munich mayor Hans-Jochen Vogel, chancellor Willy Brandt, foreign minister Walter Scheel, federal interior minister Hans-Dietrich Genscher, and UN secretary-general Kurt Waldheim (who would later be elected president of Austria despite revelations that he had been a member of the Nazi Party). Also present were Jesse Owens, hero of the Berlin Games of 1936, and Emil Zátopek, the great middle-distance runner from Czechoslovakia. As soon as Heinemann reached his seat, a Bundeswehr orchestra struck up the West German national anthem, which was traditional protocol, but then came something a little different: an Olympic fanfare played on ten-feet-long Alpenhorns by eight Lederhosen-clad Bavarian mountain men.

The main attraction of the opening ceremony is always the march-in by athletes, coaches, and team officials. In 1972, this involved more athletes (7,131) and more teams (121) than ever before. Per tradition, the team from Greece entered the stadium first. But the music to which they entered was a huge surprise. Rather than a typical Olympic march, strains of wild bouzouki music, replete with zither and cymbals, erupted from the loudspeaker system. This seemed to be a kind of ethnic joke, but one that did not at all trouble the Greek athletes, who literally danced their way on to the Olympic track. For the entrance of the next national team, Egypt (Ägypten in German—the order of entry followed the host country's alphabet), the soundtrack segued into a belly-dance number straight out of the bazaar. This verged on central-casting "Orientalism," but it was apparently no insult to the Egyptians, who laughed and danced like the Greeks. And so it went down the alphabet: Argentina got a tango; Brazil, a samba; Mexico, "The Mexican Hat Dance"; Spain, a bullfight fanfare; the USSR, a balalaika; and the United States, "When the Saints Go Marching In." Tellingly, for East Germany, the soundtrack's composer, a Cologne-based jazzman named Kurt Edelhagen, came up with a brand new pop tune devoid of historical associations so as "not to embarrass anybody."

The costumes, too, were generally colorful and sometimes wonderfully exotic. The East German men wore fashionably cut suits in two tones of blue, while the German Democratic Republic (GDR) women sported pants-suits in *five* different colors: orange, yellow, green, lilac, and hot pink. A bare-breasted contingent of Mongolians (alas, all men) favored high-topped boots, arm wrappings, braided loin cloths, peaked caps, and capes. Indian heads were covered in huge black turbans, while the Cubans chose red berets. The American men wore snappy red blazers and white pants (thankfully, no cowboy hats). Sprinkled among the American delegation were some mushroom-like Afros and (for the white males) the requisite seventies look of longish hair and bushy sideburns.

The Israeli delegation, dressed rather conventionally in blue blazers and white hats, did not clown around like some of the other teams. As one member of their group recalled, "Now we were marching on German soil, the proud, strong representatives of the independent sovereign state of Israel, and any Nazis still around would have living proof of our indestructibility." Apparently not many Nazis were still around, at least in the audience. According to Jim McKay, the small Israeli team got a very respectful reception indeed. He reported at the time, "There was a great applause when the nation of Israel walked in here, and of course, you couldn't be in Germany and not remember. We're just about fifteen miles here from the concentration camp of Dachau. But it is perhaps a measure of the fact that peoples and times do change that Israel is here. The Germans are cheering the Jewish athletes."

The Americans in the audience wondered how the 584-person-strong U.S. delegation would be received, given the ongoing castigation of America as a land of aggressive militarists. The team members themselves were worried about their image, and in an effort to defuse possible hostility they selected Czech-born Olga Connolly to be their flag-bearer. Connolly, who in her previous incarnation as Olga Fikotová had won a gold medal in the discus in Melbourne in 1956, and then married America's great Olympic hammer-throw champion Harold Connolly, was a well-known opponent of the Vietnam War. The first thing she did upon arriving at the Olympic Village was to distribute peace buttons and anti-war pamphlets from the Olympic Project for Peace. The fact that this violated IOC and United States Olympic Committee (USOC) policy bothered her no more than did the complaints from conservative commentators and officials at home that a woman with her beliefs had no business carrying the Stars and Stripes. When she took her place in line for the march-in, holding the flag, she "thought of Thomas Jefferson, Dr. Martin Luther King, the

Kennedys, and all the people nowadays who were striking out on the path of peace."

Whether the strapping thirty-nine-year-old Connolly's prominent place at the head of the American delegation had any effect on Team USA's reception is hard to know, but it turned out that the welcome was almost uniformly warm, with only the odd catcall. True to a Yankee custom dating back to the 1908 London Games, when Irish Americans on the team had refused to dip the flag to Britain's King Edward VII ("This flag dips to no earthly king"), Connolly did not lower the Stars and Stripes when she passed the Honor Tribune. The only other team in 1972 to take this stance was East Germany.

For what it was worth, the applause the Americans received was certainly louder than that for the Soviets. There was nothing surprising in the coolness of the welcome for the USSR squad. The largely West German crowd could hardly have been expected to be enthusiastic about the mighty "Ivans," who, of course, were widely associated in the German mind with the rape and pillage practiced by the Red Army in its invasion and occupation of the Reich in 1945.

As for the chief German victims of Soviet occupation, the East Germans, their 324-member team, appearing for the first time under its own flag (carried proudly by a welterweight boxer, Manfred Wolke), apparently reaped the benefit of the Western crowd's sympathy for the Easterners' plight. According to the local press, the GDR team received "hearty applause" and a "demonstratively warm" greeting. With respect to the huge contingent of West German fans in the crowd, that warm welcome for their Eastern "brothers and sisters" no doubt reflected underlying feelings of national community, along with lingering aspirations for an eventual end to the "unnatural" division of the former Reich. Yet, it should also be noted that there was no sign of similar sentiments among the *East* German fans, who all sat together in one section of the stadium. Each of the GDR supporters came equipped with a small hammer and compass banner (as if to make up for the previous ban on their national symbol in West Germany), and according to West German reports they clapped exclusively for their own team and for those of the other socialist nations.

The East German applause was not terribly noticeable, however, because there were relatively few GDR fans on hand for the opening ceremony and subsequent events. In a gesture of goodwill, the Munich OC had offered the GDR one hundred thousand tickets for the Games, an allocation far out of proportion to the country's size. The GDR government, however, had accepted only nineteen thousand event tickets, to be distributed among a mere one thousand Olympic visitors. Obviously, East Berlin wanted to keep the number of Munich visitors small in order to be able to monitor them more effectively while they were in the West. The majority of those allowed to make the trip were functionaries of various factory sports clubs and other state-run athletic institutions: middle-aged or elderly men who had distinguished themselves through their contributions to East German sport. But apparently not even these proven loyalists could be fully trusted to return home when the Games were over. None of them was allowed to take along a spouse or any other family member.

In addition to drastically restricting the size of the East German fan contingent at Munich, the GDR government also insisted that all these supporters lodge together in two small rural villages, Kiefersfeldern and Oberaudorf, each about one hundred kilometers away from the bright lights and seductive temptations of downtown Munich. The GDR encampments lay dangerously close to the Austrian border, but to cross into that neutral state, East German visitors would have needed a visa, which of course none of them had.

And how did these Easterners—the first official "tourists" from the GDR to visit the Federal Republic of Germany (FRG)—behave vis-à-vis their anxious West German hosts? In general, they behaved very guardedly, as if any display of enthusiasm or friendliness would be misinterpreted as a sign of discontent with present political realities. When a delegation of well-wishers from the Bavarian Communist Party came out to Kiefersfeldern to greet their comrades from the East, the comrades showed a marked reluctance to let their hair down, if they had any. They retained a stiff and formal demeanor throughout the encounter, insisting that their only purpose in coming to West Germany was "to cheer on our own Olympic athletes." Rather than drink the local Bavarian beer, about whose "thinness" they complained, they fell back on supplies of East German brew they had brought along from home. The Western leftists were naturally disappointed by their colleagues' coolness, but they wrote this off to insecurity. The local Bavarian farmers, on the other hand, were downright appalled by the standoffish behavior of these Eastern guests, who, in their view, had precious little to be standoffish about. In the words of one indignant Bavarian, the Easterners acted "as if they had carried their damn Wall along with them."

The GDR athletes displayed a similar aloofness toward their Western counterparts in the Olympic Village. East German officials accompanying the team did their best to minimize impromptu encounters between their charges and Western athletes by discouraging unchaperoned excursions around the Village or the city of Munich. Under the watchful eye of their political nannies, East German Olympians understandably minded their step wherever they went, careful to maintain that reticence and cool demeanor their government clearly expected of them. But it may not have been just prudence that produced this behavior. West Germany's Heidi Schüler was surprised to discover that her Eastern colleagues cold-shouldered her even when she encountered them on their own, unaccompanied by their minders. "It can't be easy for them," she surmised, "they simply don't know how they should behave over here." Whether out of insecurity, fear, or arrogance, the Eastern athletes made a point of fraternizing only with athletes from the other socialist nations. When Willy Brandt joined a table of Olympic officials in the Village cafeteria, a group of GDR athletes sitting at a neighboring table ostentatiously got up and moved to a distant corner of the room. West Germany's President Heinemann got no reply at all when, again in the Village cafeteria, he asked some GDR athletes how they liked the food. "They suffer from complexes that we have imposed on them," Heinemann charitably concluded. In retrospect, what is interesting about this "failure to connect" between the citizens of the two Germanys at the Munich Games is how much it anticipated the difficulties of mutual acculturation that would attend the German reunification some twenty years hence.

If the East German athletes who paraded into the stadium on opening day could—and apparently did—take pride in finally being able to march behind their own national colors, the West German Olympians that day had the satisfaction of taking the track as the home team in this greatest of all athletic spectacles. They were very mindful that their host role represented a signal honor for the FRG, suggesting that at least *their* part of Germany not only had been readmitted to the community of civilized nations but was also seen as a major political and economic player, solid enough to take on the challenge of mounting a successful Olympic show. At the same time, though, these young Germans knew that they must not appear to be *too* proud and puffed up. They had best come across as model new Germans: cheerful, easy-going, unassuming, even playful. Accordingly, their entrance was accompanied by *three* different jaunty pop songs.

West Germans in the audience also seemed to be mindful of the historic significance of this moment. When their own team entered the stadium (by custom, the last to do so), the huge German crowd stood and cheered enthusiastically, many of them waving little FRG flags. This behavior itself was historically significant. In the early postwar years, there had been a kind of informal taboo against displaying too much patriotic enthusiasm—both because nationalism had been deeply tainted by the Nazis and also because specific FRG patriotism might have suggested an acceptance of Germany's division. (When West German fans had celebrated the FRG's surprising victory in the 1954 football World Cup—the "Miracle of Bern"—by singing the *verboten* first stanza of the "Deutschlandlied," a Danish newspaper commented that "only cries of '*Sieg Heil*' would have been needed to give the impression of being back at the Berlin Olympics of 1936.")

Now, as the West German fans watched their own team enter the stadium, some of them must have given thought as to how they would, or should, respond to victories in the Games by those other Germans, the East Germans, either over their own athletes or over those from other nations. They had been told by an influential pro-unification lobby group in Bonn, the Kuratorium unteilbares Deutschland, that victories by German athletes from *either* team should be seen as a victory for *all* of Germany—that "*their* victories are also *our* victories." But it was very doubtful that this dictum would be followed. In reality, the West Germans were just as anxious to show up the Easterners as vice versa. After the debacle in Mexico City, where the GDR had won almost twice as many gold medals as the FRG, the West German Olympic Association had brought in Josef Neckermann, a travel agency tycoon and active Olympian (dressage), to beef up the West German Olympic program. To do so he raised money privately from companies like Mercedes and Lufthansa. His friend Herbert von Karajan was induced to conduct a benefit performance by the Berlin Philharmonic. Neckermann also demanded significantly higher budgets from the state—all in the hope that West German Olympians could win "twice as many" medals in Munich as they had in Mexico City.

Once the athletes had all marched into the stadium and assembled on the infield, 2,800 Munich school children greeted the Olympians with a "Salute to Youth" written especially for the occasion by Munich's most celebrated composer, Carl Orff. While singing Orff's modern setting of the Middle English ballad "Sumer is icumen in," with repeated refrains of "sing coo-coo, sing coo-coo," the kids, dressed in bright blue and orange outfits, danced about waving hoops braided with multicolored crepe paper. Of course, there was nothing new here—Olympic openings almost always include synchronized dances by school children—but the audience appeared to delight in this tour de force of kitschy cliché.

There followed another piece of opening ceremony boiler-plate, a speech by the president of the host Olympic Committee, Willi Daume. Daume's address was mercifully short. After that, Avery Brundage invited President Heinemann to open the Munich Games, which he duly did, intoning "I hereby declare the Games celebrating the Twentieth Olympiad of the modern era opened." Continuing to follow prescribed ritual, the mayor of the previous host city, Mexico City's Octavio Sentiés, presented an Olympic banner to Munich's new mayor, Georg Kronawitter. Then the vast three-hundred-member Bundeswehr orchestra played the "Olympic Hymn" (Daume elected to go with the hymn composed for the first Games in 1896), while the eight oarsmen from the FRG's gold medal–winning crew in '68 carried out a huge Olympic flag. For Avery Brundage, all these ritual procedures must have seemed bitter-sweet, for he knew this was the last opening ceremony he would witness as IOC president.

Brundage was a great lover of things Bavarian—he would die while vacationing in Garmisch-Partenkirchen in April 1975—so he undoubtedly took pleasure in the next event on the program: an appearance by Lederhosen-clad folk-dancers, who demonstrated Munich's joy in receiving the Olympic banner by performing traditional Schuhplattler and Goaßlschnalzern dances, replete with much heel-slapping and cracking of whips. (Interestingly enough, these rustic dance numbers, along with a brief performance by traditional folksingers and the above-mentioned Alpenhorn fanfare, constituted the only "Bavarianism" present in the opening ceremony; Daume and even Vogel seem to have thought that too much of this sort of thing would make the host city look backward and provincial—the German equivalent of redneck.)

Another tradition in the opening ceremony was the release of doves. In 1936, the doves had belonged to the German army, and they flew off in proper military order, strafing the VIP section with droppings as they gained altitude. In 1972, the five thousand doves were all civilians, and they flew helter-skelter around the stadium until finally coalescing into a swirl that (thankfully) spiraled safely past the glass overhang and into the bright blue Bavarian Himmel. One poor bird, however, mistook the glass roof for the open sky and, after glancing off the surface, fell lifeless into the front row of the horrified Brazilian team.

The audience was still contemplating the possible symbolic significance of this broken bird of peace when the sound of three shots, fired from antique miniature mortars, announced the arrival into the stadium of the Olympic flame, now completing the final leg of its 5,538-kilometer trek from ancient Olympia. The last torchbearer was an eighteen-year-old West German middle-distance runner named Günther Zahn. To symbolize the five continents represented in the Games, Zahn was flanked in a V-formation by four other runners from Africa, Asia, Oceania/Australia, and the Americas. Zahn himself looked much like his counterpart from

1936, fair haired and lanky, but unlike in the Berlin Games, where all the men who bore the torch through Germany were perfect Nordic specimens, the German torchbearers in '72 were a United Benetton of color, gender, and shape, some of them even handicapped. To the sound of drum rolls and some New Age "Music of the Spheres," Zahn and his retinue made a half-round of the stadium track before the German runner peeled off and climbed 116 stone steps to the top of the stadium and put his torch to a brazier fueled by clean-burning natural gas. (Fortunately for Zahn and all those seated near the brazier, the size of this contraption had been significantly reduced after tests of the original version showed that its heat would have thoroughly cooked anyone within two meters.)

Next up was the swearing of the Olympic Oath by the athletes and the referees. As was now customary, a single athlete and single referee performed this function on behalf of all the participants. In 1972, West German hurdler Heidi Schüler took the athletes' oath to compete "in the true spirit of Olympic sportsmanship" (she was the first woman to be so honored), while another West German, Heinz Polley, promised that the referees and judges would do their work fairly, without national bias or ideological prejudice—a vow that would be honored, as we shall see, almost as much in the breach as in the observance.

Before the athletes finally got the opportunity to flee the heat of the stadium infield for the comfort of their Village quarters, they, and the audience, had to endure one last bit of inspirational hoopla: a pre-recorded choral number entitled "Oracle of the God Apollo," written for the occasion by the avant-garde Polish composer Krzysztof Penderecki. To a crescendo of discordant electronic bleeping, ghostly voices sang out "Keep up your old traditions / Take loving care of your country / Stay aloof from war / And give to the world a signal of brotherly friendship / Until the time of the next Olympiad returns."

The tedium of some aspects of the opening ceremony did not, apparently, detract from the pageant's overall success. Press accounts of the occasion suggest genuine enthusiasm on the part of the large crowd. Arthur Daley of the *New York Times* was full of praise, writing, "This was pomp and circumstance at its glamorous and eye-catching best. . . . German efficiency was operating overtime and everything went off so precisely that not one detail was out of place." Daley's fellow *Times* columnist, Red Smith, was equally impressed:

> The weather was brilliant, the color exuberant, the great crowd obviously enchanted and the whole splendiferous occasion free—

outwardly, at least—of political, racial and social overtones. When the two and one-half hours of pageantry ended, the feeling seemed to be general that perhaps the next two weeks would help heal some of the wounds of the past—slurring the memory of the 1936 Olympics in Berlin, which Adolf Hitler's propagandists made into a Nazi carnival, and giving a happier meaning to the name of this city, which for 34 years has been synonymous with appeasement.

Not surprisingly, West German luminaries and journalists were fully in accord with these glowing assessments. After witnessing the ceremony, Willy Brandt opined, "We couldn't have chosen a more beautiful German city than Munich to put on this festival for the sporting youth of the world." Former chancellor Ludwig Erhard declared, "I'm glad today that I said yes to Munich's application in 1965." "The most beautiful festival-day that our city has ever experienced," rhapsodized the *Münchner Zeitung*. Munich's influential *Süddeutsche Zeitung* was struck by the extent to which the Munich pageant subverted the semi-religious solemnity typical of Olympic opening ceremonies:

> With brass-band music, Schuhplattler, Trachtlern [native costumes], Böllerschützen [antique miniature mortars], and Goaßlschnalzern [folkloric whip-cracking dancers], the pathos of traditional Olympic fire-cult and flag-fetishism was skillfully undercut in classic touristy-Bavarian fashion. If tears nonetheless flowed, then not because of ceremonial bombast but in the spirit of the old Bavarian adage: "Schee war's, und viel Leut hamm gwoant." [It was beautiful, and many people cried.]

Of special interest among the evaluations of Munich's opening ceremony was the one supplied by Leni Riefenstahl, who, of course, knew her way around Olympic pageantry. She had made herself famous as "Hitler's filmmaker" and as the captivating beauty who had always managed to stay one step ahead of the randy little Joseph Goebbels when he chased her around the table trying vainly to get her into his bed (fortunately for Leni, the dwarfish propagandist was slowed by his clubfoot). After the collapse of the Third Reich and demise of her patron, Riefenstahl had been banned from making films in Germany, and she was certainly persona non grata with the Munich Olympic organizers, who would have preferred that she stay entirely out of town during the Games. Riefenstahl, however, wrangled an assignment from the *Sunday Times* (London) to cover the '72 Olympics.

Avery Brundage, who considered her film on the 1936 Games, *Olympia*, to be a "masterpiece," and at whose behest the IOC had awarded her its Olympic Diploma in 1939, went to bat for her again in 1972, urging Willi Daume to secure her press credentials for the Munich Games. Riefenstahl eagerly took up her correspondent duties despite receiving warnings from the Munich Police of threats against her life. Of course, she would rather have been *filming* the opening ceremony as opposed to merely writing about it. According to her memoir, she had been offered the opportunity to do just that by David Wolper, producer of the 1972 Olympic film *Visions of Eight*, but apparently representatives of the federal government pressured Wolper to withdraw the offer. Riefenstahl's regret over not having a camera in hand at the '72 Games was evident in her generous comment about the opening ceremony: "That [pageant] was so grandiose, that one could have made a great film on the opening ceremony alone. It was much more beautiful than [the opening ceremony] in 1936 in Berlin."

While the opening ceremony was still in progress in the Olympic Stadium, some ten kilometers away, on the margin of the city, another event was taking place whose purpose was to show that all the protestations of peace and brotherly love in the stadium that day constituted a hollow mockery of the brutal realities of world politics—especially the brutal realities of the Vietnam War. Most of the "counter-Olympic" activities that had been threatened for opening day did not materialize, but about three hundred young "Maoists," most of them apparently from West Berlin, did manage to stage a non-violent demonstration during which they reminded all who would listen that at the very moment when doves of peace were being released in the Olympic Stadium, "30,000 tons of American bombs" were falling on North Vietnam. Showing typical hyperbole, the self-proclaimed Maoists insisted that the Vietnam War was "the worst crime against humanity ever committed by a modern industrial nation." The demonstrators tried to engage passersby in a discussion about the imperative of expelling the "U.S. imperialists" from the Munich Games. According to local observers, it was hard to know what visiting foreigners might have made of all this, but some Münchners expressed their own view of the matter quite clearly. "Piss off to the GDR!" they shouted at the demonstrators.

On the evening of opening day, President Heinemann and his wife hosted a reception for one thousand special guests at the Residenz, the recently restored Wittelsbach royal palace in central Munich. As with the opening ceremony, an effort was made here to break away from stuffy tradition. No formal speeches were scheduled, and male guests were advised to wear business suits rather than black tie. Still, certain hierarchical distinctions prevailed. Only about two hundred VIPs had the privilege of being personally received by the president and his wife in the palace's former throne room. These lucky few included Prince Rainier and Princess Grace of Monaco; the Shah of Iran; King Constantine of Greece; President Franz Jonas of Austria, and Ugandan president Idi Amin, who had taken time off from butchering his people and filling his pockets with plundered national wealth to attend the Games.

In the crowded rooms of the Residenz that evening, politicians from all the major parties of the FRG babbled away at each other across sectarian lines, as if this gathering were one big happy family. But this was strictly a *West* German family; East Germans were conspicuously absent. At the very center of all this action was not the self-effacing Heinemann but charismatic Willy Brandt, who deftly handed out beers with one hand, shook hands with the other, all the while paying court to the beautiful young hurdler, Heidi Schüler. Her deeply low-cut little black dress also departed from stuffy tradition.

"Munich gleamed," wrote Thomas Mann in "Gladius Dei" (1902), a short story extolling the radiant beauties—but also the darker sub-currents—of his newly adopted home town.* Munich certainly gleamed again on that opening day of the 1972 Summer Olympic Games—at least on the surface. The town was awash in pastel-colored Olympic flags; bright sunlight bathed classical monuments and baroque churches in a golden glow. On every other corner, brass bands belted out Bavarian folk tunes, while buskers working the U-Bahn stations competed for the attention of passersby with everything from Bach to Bob Dylan. The city's official cultural program had now begun in earnest, with an orgy of museum expositions, art shows, theatrical performances, symphony concerts, and opera productions. Among the plethora of films showing in town were the latest James Bond movie, *Diamonds Are Forever*, and Leni Riefenstahl's *Olympia* (despite efforts by the OC to keep it out of local theaters).

The authorities had somewhat better luck banning street prostitution from the inner city, but the ban's main effect was to shift this tenacious

---

* In this story, a haggard young man dressed in a monk's robe demands that a reproduction of a modernist painting of the Madonna be removed from a shop window and burned forthwith. When the indignant shopkeeper has this latter-day Savonarola thrown into the street, the young zealot calls upon God to consume the beautiful but heathenish city in a cleansing inferno—a bonfire of the vanities. In a certain way, the Mann story anticipates what was to happen seventy years later against a similar backdrop of gaiety, beauty, and municipal pride.

trade to somewhat less central precincts. Over the objections of neighborhood housewives, a new "Puff" (whore house) opened on the seedy Dachauerstrasse near the building where Hitler had lived when he moved to Munich from Vienna in 1913. The ban on open solicitation in the inner city also spawned a new (for Munich) wrinkle in hustling: none-too-subtle advertisements in tabloid newspapers for "escort services," "hostesses," "photo-models," and "masseuses." Here is a small sampling of these ads: "Peggy massages with a tough or tender hand, depending on your wish"; "Two young cosmeticians seek small and intimate circle of clients"; and, fully in keeping with the Olympic spirit, "Get fit, screw more often!" As Hamburg's *Der Spiegel* noted condescendingly, this practice of peddling sex through newspaper ads, old hat in New York, Rome, Paris, Berlin, and Hamburg itself, was a revelation to Munich. Thanks to the Olympics, said the magazine, Bavaria's capital had finally made it into "the erotic world class."

Along with prostitution, another local business that prospered with the influx of Olympic tourists was the sale of folkloric kitsch. Never before had the city gotten so much commercial mileage out of "Mad King Ludwig," who, after having been removed from power back in 1886 for almost bankrupting the royal treasury with his manic castle-building, had gone on (posthumously) to become the state's single biggest source of tourist revenue. Special for the Olympics, tourists could buy gaudy beer steins with Ludwig's portrait on one side, the Olympic rings on the other. Also available were Mad Ludwig music boxes that played drinking songs.

Apart from prostitutes and kitsch purveyors, however, many Münchners were already beginning to tire of the foreigner influx even before the first Olympic medals were handed out. Ausländerfeindlichkeit (xenophobia) had always lurked under the surface of the city's officially touted Gemütlichkeit, with resentment focusing especially on "foreigners" from Northern Germany, generically castigated as "Sau-Preisn" (pig-Prussians). Not surprisingly, then, a popular bumper sticker on cars around town declared "I bite Prussians." In recent years, the city's rapid growth, almost all of it from in-migration, had added to the beleaguered sense harbored by many old-time residents. Thus, the invasion of Olympic tourists, who were often awkward and clueless in their dealings with locals, touched off a new wave of nativist grousing and nostalgia for quieter times. Another popular bumper sticker announced, "Shit on the Olympics in Munich. We want our peace and the return of our King Ludwig." A Japanese tourist who exactingly fondled the produce at the city's central fruit and vegetable market, and then walked off without buying anything, had the epithet "Sau-Japaner" hurled after her by a fruit seller. But nothing enraged the natives more than the penchant on the part of some foreign visitors to ask after the town's erstwhile leading citizen, Adolf Hitler. "Where had the Führer lived?" "Which was Hitler's favorite restaurant?" The mere mention of Hitler's name by a Sau-Amerikaner caused a balding accountant to leap up from his beer hall table and shout, "*We* have forgotten Hitler. Why can't *you*?"

Opening Rounds

The first day of competition got off with a bang, literally, since pistol shooting was on the schedule, along with the opening rounds of boxing, basketball, soccer (football), wrestling, gymnastics, the modern pentathlon, field hockey, diving, volleyball, and water polo. Of course, these disparate events elicited considerably varying degrees of interest among the fans, just as they do with me.

Like the just-concluded World Championship of Chess between the USSR's Boris Spassky and America's Bobby Fischer, which Fischer gracelessly won, the 1972 Summer Olympics proved in part to be an extension of the Cold War to the fields and courts of athletic play. This became evident on the very first day of competition, when America's premier heavyweight boxer Duane Bobick squared off against the Soviet Union's Yuri Nesterov. Having won all of his last sixty fights (including an Olympic trials victory over future world heavyweight champion Larry Holmes), Bobick was the clear favorite in this contest, a fact that the Soviet coaches hoped might make him over-confident and underprepared. Bobick indeed came off as the quintessential cocky American, but he fully grasped the political implications of this match and was determined to take nothing for granted. He won handily.

Bobick's opening victory over Nesterov set him up for an even more politically charged bout in the second round of the boxing competition: a rematch with Cuba's charismatic giant, Teófilo Stevenson, whom Bobick had defeated in the Pan American Games a year earlier. With that win under his belt, Bobick claimed not to be too worried about the six-foot-five Cuban, telling reporters that, although Stevenson was "tall and strong," his only good punch was a jab, and he "had no right hand." What Bobick did *not* know was that Stevenson had spent the last year correcting that very problem. Now, in his rematch with Bobick, the Cuban deployed a powerful right hook along with a stinging left jab to make a nasty mess of Bobick's face. Mercifully, the referee stopped the fight early in the third round.

Fidel Castro immediately dispatched a congratulatory telegram to Stevenson, who would go on to win the gold medal in his division in Munich. His final victim was West Germany's Peter Hussing, who fared even worse than Bobick. After the bout, Hussing's face looked, in the words of one commentator, as if "strawberry jam had been spread all over it." Hussing himself admitted that he'd never been hit so hard in any of his previous fights. "You just don't see [Stevenson's] right hand, all of a sudden it's there . . . and on your chin."

After striking gold in Munich, Stevenson, despite repeated offers from professional boxing promoters in America, refused to turn pro, declaring steadfastly, "Professional boxing treats fighters like a commodity to be bought and sold and discarded when they are no longer useful. I wouldn't exchange my piece of Cuba for all the money they could give me." (Stevenson, by the way, was not the only Cuban boxer to win in Munich. Cuba's three gold medals, one bronze medal, and one silver medal made it the top boxing squad in '72. The United States, with one gold medal and three bronzes, finished a lowly sixth.)

The Bobick-Stevenson fight, although a highlight of the early boxing competition in Munich, was just one of a staggering 346 bouts in total, which made Munich '72 by far the largest boxing show in Olympics history up to that time. Most of the boxers at Munich hailed from small Third World countries, since the training and equipment involved in this discipline were relatively inexpensive. All too many of these Third World fighters came to Munich with very little prior experience, especially against the quality of opponents they would encounter in the Olympics. For this reason, the referees were advised by the Federation of International Boxing Associations (which regulated Olympic competition) to stop bouts quickly if it became apparent that one of the contestants was seriously overmatched.

While the concern on the part of the referees to protect overmatched fighters was unobjectionable enough, the same cannot be said for the political mindset that some of the judges seem to have brought to their work. According to the West German press and a host of international observers, all too many judges were allowing their political or ideological sympathies to color their verdicts. For example, Eastern European judges often showed painfully obvious favoritism toward fighters from their own region. Thus, in a second-round light middleweight-class battle between Russia's Valeri Tregubov and America's Reginald Jones, a Yugoslav judge awarded the victory to the Russian even though Jones had nearly sent his opponent to the canvas three times, while hardly getting hit at all himself. ("Now we know how the Brink's people felt after that job in Boston," commented Red Smith.) The same Yugoslav judge helped Russia's Boris Kuznetsov earn a very controversial 3–2 second-round victory in the featherweight class over Venezuela's José Baptista. Some judges also tended to favor fighters from the Third World in bouts with First World opponents. West Germany's Werner Schäfer clearly out-boxed Ghana's Joe Destino in the second round of the bantamweight division, but the latter came away with a 3–2 decision courtesy of an African judge.

Decisions like these led the Olympic boxing officials to take a hard look at the judging. On the third day of competition, one boxing judge was dismissed outright and six more received warnings. Two days later, six more judges were dropped. This was small compensation for victims of discrimination like Reginald Jones, who swore he would never box again.

The boxing matches in Munich were well attended. Despite the Box-halle's small capacity of 7,200, tickets were relatively easy to come by. Richard Mandell secured a ticket for one series of bouts and watched an East German heavyweight quickly knock out an overmatched Bulgarian, who "dropped to the canvas, bounced an inch, and stayed there twitching" like the poor little squirrel Mandell had once run over with his bicycle. Of course, it was precisely this kind of vicious mayhem that the crowd craved, but they did not get to see much of it in Munich because the bouts were only three rounds long, the gloves were extra heavy, and, as mentioned, the referees were inclined to stop fights before they got too bloody.

Often the best action was not in the ring but out in the stands among the fans. America's "Sugar Ray" Seals put on such a dull performance in winning his light heavyweight final that many fans preferred watching Seals's mother enthusiastically shadow-box at ringside, putting up a much better fight than her son. Another source of diversion was the vigorous pummeling meted out to would-be pick-pockets in the stands by the enormous ushers, whose ranks included former West German boxing champions.

Perhaps the most intriguing story connected to the boxing in Munich had to do with a fighter who did not appear in the Olympic ring at all but did become involved in a pre-Games dustup between Willi Daume, Avery Brundage, and Clifford Buck of the USOC. The fighter in question was an African American flyweight named Bobby Lee Hunter, who as the Munich Games approached found himself serving an eighteen-year prison sentence for fatally stabbing a man in a snack-bar scuffle in South Carolina. A talented boxer, Hunter had been given temporary release from prison to represent the United States in the 1971 Pan American Games (where he won) and was also promised a release to compete in the U.S. Olympic boxing trials scheduled for July 1972. On the eve of the trials, however, Willi Daume weighed in with a declaration that Hunter, even if he were to qualify for the '72 Games, would not be welcome in Munich because "an Olympic athlete should be an example to youth" (this, of course, coming from a former Nazi!). If the USOC insisted on sending Hunter to Munich, warned Daume, the organizers might be forced to house him in a local prison rather than in the Olympic Village. This, however, would make him ineligible to compete because "all Olympic athletes must live in the Village." Quizzed by reporters on the Hunter issue, "Slavery Avery" Brundage seconded Daume's position.

News reports on Daume and Brundage's posture regarding Bobby Hunter generated cries of outraged protest in the United States. The *New York Times'* Red Smith denounced Daume and Brundage, stating that "But for the grace of God," these two Olympic bigwigs might be in Hunter's shoes. Wisconsin congressman Les Aspin wrote Brundage to urge him "to consider the great contribution that Mr. Hunter can make, instead of basing your decision on his past errors. It would be a very sad reflection on our system of crime and punishment if this man, who has shown evidence of rehabilitation and has proven his ability, was not given the opportunity to represent his country." Similarly citing Hunter's "rehabilitation," an irate citizen wrote Daume demanding that the German reconsider his position. "What better example of the Olympic ideal could there be than a man who had righted himself through sport? If you deny Bobby Lee Hunter the privilege of competing if he qualifies for the team, you deny the right of a man to rise above his environment (over which he has little control); you deny the possibility of change and progress." Most importantly, USOC president Clifford Buck promptly took Hunter's side, declaring, "We [the USOC] believe that it is our prerogative to decide who goes to the Games. If Hunter qualifies at the U.S. boxing trials next month, he will go to Munich and stay with the rest of the team at the Olympic Village."

It should be noted, however, that Daume and Brundage also received letters encouraging them to "stick to their guns" in the Hunter affair, as well as in the case of another imprisoned African American athlete, Gene White, who hoped to qualify for Munich in the high jump. A citizen of Cincinnati urged Brundage not to listen to "do-gooders" wailing about alleged social inequalities that had supposedly contributed to these men's crimes. Hunter and White, said this writer, were "criminals," pure and simple, and the fact that they were black was significant only insofar as blacks were apparently criminal by nature, committing "about 85% of the crime in the

Cincinnati area." Another letter writer asked why "good clean youths . . . should be forced to compete alongside convicted felons?"

Much to Daume and Brundage's relief, Hunter (and White) failed to qualify for the Games, thus obviating any need to bar them (or incarcerate them) once they landed in Munich. It is revealing, however, that while Brundage passionately favored including white-ruled Rhodesia in the Munich Games, he was just as determined to exclude two African Americans on grounds that their criminal records might stain the otherwise pristine vest of the Olympic movement.

Like boxing, the wrestling competition in 1972 sometimes amounted to a sporting extension of the Cold War. Both the USSR and the United States came into the Games with very powerful teams, fueling expectations of an epochal superpower duel on the mats of Munich.

And, in fact, that expectation was satisfied immediately—in an opening-round super heavyweight match between Russia's mighty Alexander Medved, a seven-time world champion and two-time Olympic gold medal winner, and America's Chris Taylor, a national collegiate champion from Iowa State University who, at 434 pounds, outweighed his opponent by 181 pounds. Richard Mandell, who happened to be present for this seminal contest, originally confused the two wrestlers because, in his patriotic prejudice, he thought that the smaller and more harmoniously built fellow must be the Iowan, while the towering six-foot-five behemoth with "overhanging, Cro-Magnon brows, brittle fair hair, and a face torn with adolescent pox" must hail from Russia. Embarrassed to learn that Medved was the classical beauty and Taylor the hulking pug-ugly beast, Mandell left the hall before the match ended.

He missed a major scandal. Although Taylor dominated the action and seemed to have waged a clean enough battle, the referee, a Turk, cautioned Taylor twice, once for fouling and once for passivity. The penalty points incurred by Taylor gave Medved the victory. The American coaches vigorously protested this decision, which the Olympic wrestling officials also found so egregiously flawed that they dismissed the Turkish referee for the rest of the Games, the only time this happened in the wrestling competition. Nonetheless, the controversial decision was allowed to stand, and Medved went on to win all the rest of his matches and the gold medal. Taylor ended up with the bronze—and a strong sense of having been cheated.

If Medved and Taylor could be seen to represent the political polarity between the United States and the USSR in the wrestling competition, there was another intriguing polarity *within* the American wrestling squad, one also tinged with socio-political implications. This was the stark dichotomy between two of the team's most celebrated grapplers: lightweight Dan Gable from Waterloo, Iowa, and bantamweight Rick Sanders from Portland, Oregon.

Even before he got to Munich and won the gold medal in his division, Dan Gable had become legendary for his athletic brilliance and fanatical commitment to his sport. In his entire college career he lost only one match, his last. As a teenage wrestler he kept his weight down by mowing lawns dressed in a wet suit with lead weights attached to his arms and legs. In preparation for the Munich Games he trained seven hours a day every day for three years straight. In winning his gold medal at Munich he did not surrender a single point, an unprecedented achievement. Eventually he went on to become an extremely successful wrestling coach at the University of Iowa, building a dynasty that won nine National Collegiate Athletic Association (NCAA) championships in a row. If American wrestling had a shining poster boy, Gable was it.

Rick Sanders was not such an icon; indeed, he might be considered an anti-poster boy. Although a domineering wrestler in his own right, having compiled a high school record in Oregon of 80–1 and winning five national freestyle championships in college, Sanders was famous for not training very hard and for having to go on crash diets to meet his weight before upcoming matches. Once, on his way to a dual meet in the Soviet Union, he got his weight down by jogging up and down the aisle of the plane. And then there was his physical appearance and personal style. Put simply, Sanders was a classic Oregon hippie, adorned in long hair, beard, sandals, and love beads. Of course, he smoked his share of weed and drank his share of Ripple. While working as a part-time bartender in Portland, Sanders took part in local anti–Vietnam War rallies. Like Olga Connolly, he refused to trim his beliefs—much less his beard and hair—to conform to the image of athletic Americanism that most USOC officials expected to see represented in Munich. And yet, probably all this would have been forgiven if he had only won a gold medal, as he was expected to do. Instead, he came away with a mere silver medal, and for that he was widely vilified in the U.S. press as a slacker whose dissolute lifestyle had contributed to his failure to bring home the gold.

The opening round of the soccer (football) competition in '72 saw an Olympic first: an appearance by a team from the United States. America had always fielded Olympic soccer teams, but until 1972 they had never made it into the actual Games. In the qualifying competition for Munich, the Yanks won just enough matches to grab one of the fourteen available slots (sixteen teams would play in the tournament, but the defending champion, Hungary, automatically qualified, as did the host, West Germany). The afternoon of August 27 found Team USA playing Morocco in Group A, which also included Malaysia and West Germany. The game was held not in Munich but in Augsburg, about eighty kilometers from the Bavarian capital. The Augsburg stadium could seat forty-four thousand people, but fewer than five thousand fans showed up. The small crowd was made up of mostly Americans and North Africans, since the locals were only vaguely aware that America even *had* a football team.

The U.S. team was sluggish at first, and it looked like the Yanks would go down in ignominy, just as expected. But America's goalie, Mike Ivanov, an ethnic Russian who grew up in the Bay Area and played soccer for the University of San Francisco, held off repeated Moroccan attacks. With their fans screaming "Get the lead out!" America's strikers finally mounted some attacks of their own, though never actually managing to get the ball into the net. But then, neither did the Moroccans, and the game ended in a scoreless tie.

Mike Ivanov's father was in the stands in Augsburg when his son's team pulled off this surprising "moral victory." Ivanov senior had dutifully applied for tickets through the official Munich Olympic Tourism Office, which informed him that, while there were plenty of tickets available for the opening football matches, the later rounds were already sold out. As if in consolation, the Munich authorities told Mr. Ivanov that the medal rounds would undoubtedly be of no concern to a supporter of the *American* team.

The West German fans, on the other hand, had reasonable hopes that their team might make it into the final rounds. If this happened, however, it would be another Olympic first. Of course, unlike America, West Germany had traditionally fielded superb national football teams, but the country's best players were almost all professionals and thus ineligible for Olympic football, which until 1984 remained heavily amateur—heavily amateur, that is, except for players from the communist nations, who, though financially supported by their governments, managed to avoid being classed as professionals. Thus, beginning in 1952, Olympic football tournaments were dominated by teams from communist Eastern Europe. Hungary won in 1952, 1964, and 1968; the USSR, in 1956; and Yugoslavia, in 1960. Bulgaria, Czechoslovakia, and the GDR had also medaled in these years. In fact, of the twenty-seven soccer medals awarded at the Olympics between 1948 and 1980, twenty-three were won by teams from Eastern Europe. By contrast, World Cup powers like Italy, Brazil, England, and West Germany did not figure at all in Olympic soccer in the period between 1952 and 1980.

The reason West German fans nonetheless had hopes for 1972—apart from home-field advantage—was that some fifty German players from the professional Bundesliga had eschewed signing club contracts in the "Olympic year" preceding the Munich Games, agreeing instead to subsist on the 350-mark monthly subsidies allowed them from West Germany's Olympia-Sporthilfe. (A new regulation for 1972 stated that Olympic teams could have up to twenty players on their rosters who had once played professional football, provided they earned no professional salaries in the Olympic year.) West Germany's 1972 Olympic team therefore bristled with Bundesliga veterans. Some of these players, moreover, had also played on the West German national eleven that had just won the European football championship.

In the early rounds of the Olympic football competition in '72, it looked as if the West German team might indeed be of championship fiber, while upstart Team USA, alas, showed that its opening credible performance against Morocco was a fluke and that it wasn't really ready yet for prime time. In the first round, West Germany coasted to 3-0 victories over Malaysia and Morocco and then pounded the United States 7-0 on August 31 in the Olympic Stadium in Munich. Thus, while West Germany advanced to the second round, the United States was out of the tournament, its players free to enjoy the rest of the competition as spectators.

In the second round, however, West Germany sputtered. Seeming to lose focus, the team managed only a 1-1 tie against Mexico. Then, horror of horrors, the FRG club exited the tournament via a 2-3 defeat to the *GDR*. The loss to rival East Germany came after a hard-fought match whose outcome "stood on a knife-edge" for most of the ninety minutes of regulation play, the two teams handing the lead back and forth until the eighty-second minute, when GDR striker Eberhard Vogel scored what turned out to be the winning goal with a headshot past West German goalie Hans-Jürgen Bradler. The real star for the GDR, however, was its goalie Jürgen Croy, who in the final minutes parried shot after shot by the desperate West Germans. As one might expect in such a bitter rivalry, there was a lot of nasty fouling on both sides, and star players for each club owed it to a "psychologically sensitive" referee from Scotland that they weren't ejected from the match. When it was all over, even highly partisan West German commentators had to concede that the GDR had fielded "the stronger eleven" despite the presence on the FRG side of numerous Bundesliga professionals, including the great Uli Hoeness of Bayern-München. Assessing West Germany's performance over the course of the tournament, local journalists mocked that, although their country's players "may not have been amateurs, they often played as if they were."

Once again, then, West Germany failed to make it into the medal round—doubly painful this time because it was the *other* Germany that eventually got to play for a place on the podium (about which more below). Not surprisingly, the West German fans were deeply disappointed in this result, showing no inclination whatsoever to regard the GDR's relative success in the tournament as a triumph for the German people as a whole.

If the Olympic football tournament proved in the end to be a bitter disappointment to the host nation, the basketball tournament would conclude in a virtual orgy of shock and indignation for the United States. (See chapter 7 for details.) As the competition commenced, though, the odds certainly favored the Americans, who had not only won the gold medal in every Olympic tourney since the inaugural one in 1936 but also never lost *a single game* in Olympic play. While in soccer the regulations on amateurism had been relaxed enough to allow a limited number of former professionals to play, Olympic basketball remained strictly amateur (until 1992). This restriction, however, had generally not endangered the U.S. domination because the level of play at the collegiate level in America remained so high.

Over the years, American teams continued to rely largely on college players, though not, as they had in 1936, exclusively on *white* college players. Since 1948, when Don Barksdale became the first black to play Olympic basketball for the United States, the Yank teams had drawn increasingly on African American talent (though UCLA's great Lou Alcindor—who took the name Kareem Abdul Jabbar—declined to try out for the U.S. team in 1968 in order to support a threatened black boycott of the Mexico City Olympics).

The American team for 1972, which included collegiate stars Tom McMillen of Maryland, Jim Brewer of Minnesota, and Dwight Jones of Houston on the front line, with playmakers Ed Ratleff of Long Beach State, Doug Collins of the University of Illinois, and Tom Henderson of San Jacinto Junior College in the backcourt, was considered reasonably strong, though no member on the '72 team had ever played in the Olympics and only a handful had any experience in the international game, which allowed a somewhat rougher style of play. Moreover, the best collegiate player that year, UCLA center Bill Walton, declined to play in Munich, probably because he feared an injury that could jeopardize his impending professional career. Yet another possible disadvantage for the U.S. squad was their very limited experience playing together as a team. They had been an ensemble only for about a month during the Olympic trials, whereas the teams from Cuba, the USSR, Yugoslavia, Czechoslovakia, and Brazil had been together for years. Cuba, in fact, had defeated a similar U.S. collegiate squad in the Pan American Games in 1971, the first time this had happened to the Yanks. Perhaps with that precedent in mind, Hank Iba, Team USA's head coach for the '72 Games, warned as the tourney opened, "People in the United States had better quit taking it for granted that we are going to win the gold medal in the Olympics year after year. It just isn't going to happen that way."

Prophetic words, of course, but in the opening rounds of the '72 tournament Team USA played with such dominating power that even Iba might have become pretty confident that the Americans' downfall would not come on his watch. The Yanks won seven straight games before the basketball tournament came to a temporary halt with the terrorist attack on September 5. Among the teams to go down to the United States were relatively powerful squads from Cuba, Brazil, and Czechoslovakia. Moreover, the margins of victory were so huge (an average of thirty-three points!) that the Americans were obviously not much affected by the slightly different Olympic rules or the rougher style of play. Especially gratifying for Team USA was their lopsided win over Cuba, 67–48, which gave them sweet revenge for the loss in the Pan American Games. The battle with Cuba in '72 was extremely physical, with forty fouls called in the first half and seventy overall, as the referees desperately struggled to keep the game from turning into an all-out brawl.

As the basketball tournament progressed, the Yanks' only reason for worry, perhaps, was that the dangerous Soviets, competing in a different group, were also winning by large margins. Among the teams the Soviets walloped in the early going was West Germany (87–63).

Rowing was another sport in which the United States had been the dominant Olympic power over the years, at least in the glamour event, the eight-oared shells with coxswain. Since Stockholm, American boats had won that event in every Olympics except Rome and Mexico City (where the West Germans had won with a high-tech shell that was seventy-five pounds lighter than the other boats). In hopes of regaining supremacy in the eights competition at Munich, the Americans had borrowed the latest German technology for their craft. In another innovation, instead of simply entering championship college or rowing-club crews, as they had in the past, they held Olympic trials to determine the makeup of their shells for '72. The result was collections of all-star oarsmen who were highly talented but not very experienced in working together as a unit (rather like the U.S. basketball team). In the American boat scheduled for the eights competition at Munich, moreover, only two of the oarsmen had previous Olympic experience. Nonetheless, in that particular discipline, the American boat had won a pre-Olympics race in Switzerland against the powerful New Zealanders, whom most pundits considered the best in the world at that time.

At Munich, as previously in Mexico City, the American rowers were coached by Harvard's Harry Parker, a legendary figure in the sport. Once his boys had arrived in the Bavarian capital, Parker was so determined to keep them focused on their impending competitions that he forbade them from marching in the opening day ceremony—nor did he allow his charges to sample the delights of the town. When not sleeping or eating in the Olympic Village, they were training out at the new rowing course in Oberschleissheim, which lay about thirteen kilometers north of central Munich. The 2,000-meter course was a state-of-the-art facility, which indeed it should have been given its enormous cost.

In the much-anticipated eights competition, the American boat advanced easily through the qualification heats, as did the New Zealanders and another powerful boat from East Germany. The East German crew was composed exclusively of very young policemen from a rowing club out of East Berlin. It seems that these fledgling cops spent a lot more time on the water than on the beat. They rowed an astounding nine thousand kilometers a year in twice-daily training sessions. While still teenagers they had won the junior world championships in 1968 and again in 1970. New Zealand's crew had similar extensive experience but was considerably older and physically bigger—indeed, they were the biggest boys in the competition. The Kiwis had profited from rowing through a film of ice on the River Avon near Christchurch during the months of April, May, and June—their winter—before moving on to Switzerland for additional pre-Munich training. To raise money for their trip to Europe they had organized bingo games and raffled off a $1,500 "dream kitchen."

The finals for the eight-oared sculls with coxswain included boats from West Germany, Poland, and the USSR along with the East Germans, New Zealanders, and Americans. At the start, the Kiwis predictably pushed out first, while the American boat, starting on the far left, got off poorly. Over the first five hundred meters, New Zealand developed a lead over the East Germans and the Americans, who managed to recover enough from their bad start to pull into third. Over the next seven hundred meters, New Zealand held its lead, with the Soviets, the Americans, and both German boats fighting for second. With five hundred meters left to go, New Zealand expanded its lead by over a boat length, while East Germany moved into what looked like a secure second place. Yet amazingly, in the last ten strokes the Americans managed to push their prow just inches ahead of the

GDR craft, taking the silver in a photo finish. This performance was not quite so spectacular as the gold medal victory by the U.S. eight in Berlin in 1936, when the University of Washington "Husky Clipper" went from last to first, but it certainly helped atone for the American eight's (an all-Harvard boat) last-place finish in Mexico City.

Sadly for the Americans, though, this silver medal in the eights was the *only* medal that the U.S. rowers would bring home from Munich. The competition in the other events was solidly dominated by the Soviets and East Germans, with Soviet rowers winning the single and double sculls, and GDR oarsmen taking the coxed pairs and the coxless fours. Apart from New Zealand's win in the eights, the only break in this string of East European victories at Oberschleissheim came in the coxed-four event, which, happily for the home crowd, was won by a West German scull.

While the rowing competition at Munich was still exclusively male (that would change in 1976), women had participated in Olympic gymnastics since 1928 (at the team level) and in various individual events starting in 1952. But 1972 was the real breakthrough year for women's gymnastics at the Olympics. This had much to do with one specific athlete, Olga Korbut of the USSR (Belarus). Before Korbut, female gymnastics attracted relatively little attention, but after her this hitherto neglected sport emerged as one of the most widely watched of all the Olympic events. And ever since Korbut came to the fore in '72, hardly an Olympiad has gone by without some other tiny woman-child tumbling forth into the international limelight.

While the seventeen-year-old Korbut had no more *global* resonance than any of the other female gymnasts when the Munich Games opened, she had been a rising figure in Soviet gymnastics since her early teens and, by the late 1960s, was considered one of the strongest competitors in a very strong national program. Typically, she had entered a government sports school even before her teens. A keen-eyed coach in Korbut's native Grodno (Belarus), Renald Knysh, who kept a card file detailing the physical attributes of all the child-bearing couples in Grodno, identified Korbut at age 11 as a promising prospect for the government sports program. Knysh took full control of little Olga's training himself as soon as it became evident that she possessed extraordinary talent.

Korbut, who at four foot eleven and eighty-five pounds, was one of the smallest competitors in a sport not exactly known for giganticism, attracted fan attention in the opening team competition at Munich when she executed a spectacular routine on the uneven parallel bars. She flung her tiny body around the apparatus with breathtaking boldness but also perfect discipline. With strong performances by the rest of her teammates, the USSR/Belarus women edged out a powerful team from the GDR for the gold medal.

Henceforth, however, all the fan attention was on a single member of that Soviet team, Olga Korbut. As she later recalled, "It was amazing. One day I was a nobody and the next day I was a star. It was almost more than I could take in." Indeed it was. When the final events for the All-Around individual championship began two days later, Korbut's mere presence in the arena generated cries of "Olga, Olga" from the crowd. Totally unaccustomed to all the attention, Korbut found herself exhilarated but also rattled. Rather than staring intently at whichever apparatus she had to conquer, she gazed up into the stands, smiling shyly.

Disaster struck in the very event she had mastered so brilliantly two days before: the uneven parallel bars. She had trouble even on her mount; then, unbelievably, she fell off the bars entirely after flubbing a fairly routine move; and finally, to cap off this tour de force of errors, she messed up the simple kip necessary to remount the apparatus. The judges gave her a miserable 7.5, the lowest score in the competition. Now, with absolutely no chance of becoming the All-Around champion, Korbut limped to the sidelines and began openly to sob. Oddly, or perhaps not so oddly, Korbut's open show of emotion endeared her even more to the fans. Her sobbing was obviously so much more *genuine* than the contrived stiff-upper-lip stoicism customarily displayed by the young female gymnasts after some mishap or other.

In the case of Korbut though, the Munich fans in the end were able to reconnect with her as an inspirational winner, not merely as a loveable loser. Twenty hours after her humiliation in the All-Around competition, she returned to the Munich arena to compete in the four individual events in which championships were awarded: Side-Horse Vault, Uneven Parallel Bars, Balance Beam, and Floor Exercises. Now fully back in the groove, Korbut won gold medals in both the Balance Beam and the Floor Exercises, plus a silver medal behind the GDR's brilliant Karin Janz in the Uneven Parallel Bars. She finished fifth in the Side-Horse Vault, never her specialty.

What could be more captivating than this bravura performance combining initial triumph, heartbreaking failure, and finally renewed success on a much greater scale? After her brilliant beginning, Korbut had had to adjust to the adulation of the fans in Munich; now she had to contend with adulation from the entire world. (Her global fame stemmed in part from the work of ABC Sports producer Roone Arledge, who, sensing a star in the making, had ordered his cameras to focus on her crying face and then on her every move.) Now Korbut's room in the Olympic Village overflowed with flowers, stuffed animals, telegrams, and love letters. The telegrams and mash notes were written in practically every language known to man. She could not walk around Munich without being mobbed by autograph seekers and people wanting to be photographed with her. When she tried to buy presents for friends and family back home, the shopkeepers refused to take her money—a first, probably, in the history of Munich retailing. Finally, desperate for a little peace and anonymity, she got herself a wig, dark glasses, and a big floppy hat, just like some Hollywood sex symbol trying to foil the paparazzi.

What no one realized about Korbut during this time of sudden glory and public adulation was that she was also living under a different—and considerably more painful—burden of stress. Some twenty-five years later, in the wake of widespread allegations by former Soviet athletes about abuses on the part of USSR coaches during the Cold War era, Korbut revealed that her own coach, Renald Knysh, had used her as a "sex slave" for years, beginning during her final preparations for the '72 Games. "My own training, in his opinion, was complete just before the Olympics of 1972," she wrote. "He came up to my room with a bottle of cognac and forced me to drink several glasses. What came next was a terrible memory that lasted several years."

"Spitz Is *Spitze*"

One of the big questions concerning the athletic competitions at Munich '72 was whether America's prodigiously gifted swimmer, twenty-two-year-old Mark Spitz, would win seven gold medals—a theoretical possibility if he were to triumph in every individual event he was scheduled to enter, as well as help the U.S. squad sweep the team relays. Arthur Daley of the *New York Times* speculated a few days before the swim competition began: "Preposterous though it must seem, it is still possible that this swiftest of water babies can come popping up from the waves like Poseidon, but with a gaggle of seven gold medals clutched in his fist. It's possible all right, but how probable is it?"

The note of skepticism in Daley's comment seemed warranted by Spitz's previous Olympic performance, in Mexico City, where he had rashly predicted he would win six gold medals but had not even come close, garnering only two team golds and one silver medal in the butterfly. Still, he seemed the one competitor in the '72 Games who might just surpass the record five gold medals in a single Olympiad won by Italian fencer Nedo

Nati in Antwerp in 1920. Even winning four gold medals in one tournament would put him in illustrious company with the likes of Jesse Owens and America's Don Schollander, who had dominated the swimming
competition in Tokyo in 1964. The West German hosts had some strong
competitors of their own in 1972, as did the GDR, but none who had any
reasonable hopes of doing what Spitz might do: put Munich '72 in the
record books for the largest gold medal haul by a single athlete in a single
Olympiad.

The young Californian in whom such high hopes were invested was
known to be a complicated and quirky figure—and sometimes, quite
frankly, a royal pain in the ass. Born into a Jewish American family in
Modesto, California, in 1950, Spitz moved with his parents to Honolulu
when he was two. There, while still a toddler, he began swimming in the
ocean, prodded on by his father, Arnold, who told him repeatedly, "Swimming isn't the only thing; winning is." Four years later, the Spitz family
moved back to California, this time to Sacramento, where Mark's father
enrolled him in a swim program at the local YMCA. By age eight, Mark was
in the water ninety minutes a day, receiving private instruction. When his
swimming routine interfered with his after-school Hebrew class, Arnold
told the rabbi, "Even God likes a winner."

Young Mark won nearly all his races at the YMCA, but this was not
enough for ambitious Arnold. Because the boy's rare losses came at the
hands of some older kids from the nearby Arden Hills Swim Club, Arnold
immediately transferred Mark to that institution, where he fell under the
tutelage of Sherman Chavoor, a brilliant swim coach (and Mark's mentor,
on and off, for the rest of his career). Under Chavoor, Mark improved so
rapidly that he established seventeen national age-group records and one
world record for his 9–10 age category.

Arnold Spitz was still not content with the instruction his son was receiving at Arden Hills, so he moved the family once again when Mark was
fourteen, this time to Santa Clara so that the young prodigy could train
with George F. Haines at the Santa Clara Swim Club, the most prestigious
swimming academy in the nation. During his four years with the Santa
Clara club and as a student at Santa Clara High School, Mark managed
to set high school records in every stroke and at every distance. By age seventeen, he was no longer a mere prep sensation, nor even just a national
figure, but a rising international star. In a single year, 1967, he set or tied
five American records and broke five world marks in international competition. He won five gold medals in the Pan American Games and was named
Swimmer of the Year by *Swimming World* magazine.

Perhaps not surprisingly, this huge success went to his head. Increasingly cocky and full of himself, he tried to associate only with older champions like Schollander. When they put him off, he withdrew into himself but became even more cocksure and swaggering, much to the disgust of his teammates. It was at this point, full of injured defiance, that he made his rash promise to win six gold medals at the Mexico City Games.

If ever failure was good for someone, it was good for Mark Spitz. By all accounts, including his own, his less-than-stellar performance in Mexico City—especially his failure to win a single individual gold medal and his loss in the 100-meter butterfly to a fellow American whom he had beaten in ten previous encounters—brought him off his high horse, at least to some degree. Following the Mexico City humiliation, he enrolled at the University of Indiana as a pre-dental student. He chose Indiana because it had a powerful swimming program run by the nation's preeminent college coach, James ("Doc") Councilman. "Doc" knew how to handle his prickly new charge much better than Haines, and under his patient supervision Mark prospered as a competitor (setting almost three dozen records) and also maturing as a person. He even joined a fraternity to improve his social skills. "He was a little boy before [coming to Indiana]," said Councilman. "Now he's a man."

The "man" Spitz still had his quirks, though. Unlike virtually all serious swimmers, he let his hair grow fashionably long and, even odder, grew a mustache. Asked why he had the trim black brush above his lip, he said it helped keep water out of his mouth. His training routine, too, was a little strange. Before every practice he'd put a toe in the pool and complain the water was too cold; then he'd make Coach Councilman chase him around the pool waving a leather belt before he would finally dive in. He defended "Bad Boy" Bobby Fischer's refusal to compete in chess matches without being paid, insisting Fischer's stance made perfect sense as a business strategy. At times, too, he could be tactlessly flippant during interviews. Queried after his arrival in Munich whether, as a Jew, he felt any discomfort about competing on German soil, he replied, while tapping a lampshade on a nearby table, "Actually, I've always liked this country, even though this lampshade here is probably made out of one of my aunts."

Still, Spitz had learned to become more circumspect before big meets. In advance of the Munich Games he was careful not to say how many medals he might win—though privately he was confident he would take in a sizeable haul. Upon arrival in Munich, he also went out of his way to fraternize with his teammates, a marked change from his loner behavior in Mexico City. With fellow swimmer Gary Hall, Spitz visited Munich's famed

Hofbräuhaus, scandalized to see the locals downing stein after stein of beer at ten o'clock in the morning. He was equally amazed by the city's plethora of sleazy sex shops, with their mammoth dildoes and inflatable Mädchen displayed prominently in the windows. "Do you believe this place?" he asked Hall. On the other hand, and more importantly, Spitz was greatly impressed by Munich's Olympic swimming facilities. They were the best in the world, he averred, and the pool in the Schwimmhalle was the fastest he had ever been in. If he did not do well in the '72 Games, he said, it would not be Munich's fault.

That he was going to do well in this very fast pool was evident in his first competition, the 200-meter butterfly, an event in which he had finished dead last in Mexico City. This time he not only won but won by a preposterously large margin and set a new world record of 2:00.70. When he hit the finish and saw his time, the usually phlegmatic Spitz threw his arms up in triumph, obviously hugely relieved to have a major monkey off his back.

Less than thirty minutes later, Spitz returned to the pool and anchored the U.S. team in the 400-meter freestyle relay to a world record victory in 3:26.42. On the following day, he won his third gold medal (and second individual) with another world record time in the 200-meter freestyle. This was an event in which the West German team had hoped to have a shot at Spitz in the person of Hans Fassnacht, who had spent the last three years training in America. Fassnacht had prepared even more tenaciously than Spitz, covering eighteen kilometers a day in killer practices. "Better die than lose," he said grimly. In fact, he practically died in the water at Munich, swimming, in the words of one saddened German observer, "like he had a lead-vest on." Spitz's closest competition came from another American, Steve Genter (who, unbelievably, was swimming with a collapsed lung), while West Germany's Werner Lampe finished third.

After receiving his third gold medal, Spitz took a kind of victory walk around the pool, stopping at one point to acknowledge cheers from the crowd by lifting up his left arm. In his hand he held up a pair of blue Adidas running shoes. TV cameras in the building beamed images of Spitz waving the distinctive German-made shoes above his head, looking as if he were making a pitch for Adidas.

The Russians immediately jumped on the incident, filing a grievance with the IOC that accused Spitz of violating an Olympic rule prohibiting any commercial engagement on the part of the athletes. Konstantin Andrianov, the USSR's man in the IOC, insisted that the American be immediately disqualified. Suddenly, Spitz was in dangerous water indeed.

Earlier that year, Avery Brundage, the high priest of Olympic amateurism, had stripped Austrian skier Karl Schranz of the medals he had won in the Sapporo Games on grounds that he had a consulting contract with a ski company. Spitz was duly called before the IOC's Eligibility Committee, on which Brundage himself sat. According to Spitz's authorized biography, the young swimmer pointed out that he had bought the shoes himself several months back and that he had no commercial connection with Adidas, which in any event would hardly choose a *swimmer* to promote its products. He was carrying the shoes rather than wearing them, he claimed, because he had been given no time to put them on before the awards ceremony. While seeming to accept Spitz's argument, Brundage reportedly told the swimmer that he was quite naïve to believe that he would have no value to Adidas: the company would have paid him $100,000 for his endorsement! Suddenly, as Spitz told his biographer, he was less concerned about possible wrongdoing on his part than about missed opportunities. "All I could think about was, 'Wow! A hundred grand? That's a lot of money. Maybe I'll make a deal. They can have their medals back.'"

All this sounds convincing enough, but it may not be the truth. In her book on the "sneaker wars" between Adidas and Puma, business historian Barbara Smit relates that on the eve of the Munich Games Adidas's Horst Dassler had implored Spitz to show up at an awards ceremony with Adidas shoes, and to *carry* them rather than wear them because the wide-bottomed sweat pants worn by the swimmers tended to obscure their footgear. When Spitz got into trouble with the IOC, writes Smit, it took "all of Horst Dassler's appeasement skills to settle the matter." The minutes of the IOC Executive Board meeting on the matter state that fear of a "public outcry" if Spitz were declared ineligible played a major role in the decision to let him skate free.

Whatever the real story behind the shoe incident, Spitz did not come away from it with his reputation unscathed. The Russians continued to scream foul, and the West German press had a field day with what it called the "stealth advertising" carried out by America's "Superman of Swimming."

Spitz won a fourth gold medal in the 100-meter butterfly, beating Canadian Bruce Robertson by more than a body length. East Germany's Roland Matthes, who had earlier won gold in the 100-meter backstroke, was expected to challenge Spitz for the victory in that event, but he got such a poor start that he could only finish fourth. Spitz himself was not surprised by this win, since the 100-meter butterfly was his favorite event. He was fortunate, however, to be able to compete in this particular race at the Munich Games, since it had only been added to Olympic competition four years earlier, in 1968. With his fourth victory, Spitz had equaled the achievement of his hero, Don Schollander, in 1964, and the Californian still had three events left that he could enter. No swimmer had won five gold medals in a single Olympiad, much less six or seven. But Spitz, as the Germans said, was *spitze* (slang for "the best"), and he now had a huge international fan base cheering him on.

However, it turned out that, in Spitz's next outing, the 4 × 200–meter freestyle relay, which transpired just forty minutes after the butterfly competition, the loudest cheering was not for Mark and the Americans but for the West Germans, who after the first two legs incredibly held the lead. The German fans went wild, sensing a possible upset of the Amerikaner. Richard Mandell scribbled in his diary, "I believe I see some mature [German] women, aged thirty or more, who are out of themselves, thoroughly insane. In their howls they seem to be biting the air. Their chaotic outpourings of emotion and desire are at the limits of life's possibilities." But the German ladies' cheering was to no avail. The Americans took away the lead in the third leg, and Spitz, swimming anchor, sealed the job. He now had gold medal number 5.

Spitz admitted to being reluctant to compete in his next scheduled event, the 100-meter freestyle, because he feared that he might turn in a less-than-gold-medal performance. Before the race he confessed to ABC Television's commentator Donna de Varona, "I know I say I don't want to swim before every event but this time I'm serious. If I swim six and win six I'll be a hero. If I swim seven and win six, I'll be a failure." Spitz was especially uncertain about winning the 100-meter freestyle because one of his teammates, Jerry Heidenreich, had been swimming this event very well of late and had to be considered a serious threat.

Hearing rumors of Spitz's reluctance to enter the race, Sherman Chavoor, his old mentor and now coach of the U.S. women's team, confronted his former charge and told him (according to Spitz) that he would be perceived as a "chicken" if he avoided a showdown with Heidenreich. Apparently in Spitz's world being thought a chicken was even worse than losing, so he stifled his doubts and entered the race. Going for broke from the outset, he pushed off faster than he ever had and built up a commanding lead. With fifteen meters to go, however, he suddenly fell off his rhythm and barely managed to hold off a surging Heidenreich. His winning time of 51:22 was another world record.

Mark Spitz's seventh and final chance at a gold medal came in the 4 × 100–meter medley relay. Most experts thought this was almost a sure thing because the U.S. relay team was very strong. But this time it was the East Germans, powered by Roland Matthes, now with two gold medals to his credit, who were determined to upset the Americans. Matthes, incidentally, was reported to possess a commercial cunning that belied his socialist credentials. Because East German swimmers received financial premiums from their sports clubs every time they set new records, Matthes had developed the habit of setting his records by small margins so they could be frequently surpassed, allowing him repeatedly to top the new times and earn more premiums. In the medley relay, Matthes charged out with a world record time in the first leg, the backstroke (his specialty), but after that the Americans took over. Swimming the butterfly leg, Spitz earned his seventh gold medal. Immediately thereafter, his teammates picked him up and carried him around the pool on their shoulders. "I'd gained their respect," he said later. For him, this peer respect was the most rewarding part of his historic accomplishment.

By the time Spitz managed this unprecedented feat, which would stand until Mark Phelps won eight gold medals in 2008 in Beijing, the young Californian's biggest problem was not getting from the starting blocks to the finish line in the Olympic pool but getting safely from the Schwimmhalle back to the sanctity of his room at the Olympic Village. Hundreds of fans, mostly teenage girls, crowded around the participants' exit at the Schwimmhalle to get a glimpse of—and perhaps a hand on—the studly American super-swimmer, who was said to be a spitting image of actor Omar Sharif. Cleverly, Spitz evaded his aggressive fans by taking a different exit and hopping immediately into a getaway car driven by U.S. men's coach Peter Daland. It would not be the last time that Spitz made a hasty bolt to safety during the Munich Games.

Mark Spitz's counterpart in the women's competition in Munich was Australia's Shane Gould. True, Gould's bag of bling was not quite as impressive, either in quality or quantity, as Spitz's, but her five individual medals—three golds, one silver, and one bronze—was more than any female swimmer had garnered in any previous single Olympiad and obviously made her the standout performer of the women's swimming competition in '72. Moreover, she achieved this prominence at age *fifteen*, an age when Spitz was still just a high school over-achiever.

Gould's medal haul in Munich constituted fully half the total pulled in by the rest of her teammates and represented a larger count than all but the first three female swimming squads in the tournament. She certainly was, as one commentator noted, "almost a one-woman Olympic team." (Overall, by the way, Australian women outperformed their male counterparts in '72, as they had in most previous Olympiads. At Munich, Australia was represented by 148 men and only 27 women, but the ladies took home ten of seventeen medals, including five of the eight golds. As one Australian Olympic official put the matter, "Women have been our greatest success story.") Gould came into the '72 Games with a record that rivaled Spitz's. She had set world records in all five of the internationally recognized freestyle distances: the 100, 200, 400, 800, and 1,500 meters. At Munich, she planned to compete in twelve races in eight days, an unbelievable test of stamina.

The young Australian girl won her first medal, a gold, in one of the few events she was not expected to enter, the 200-meter individual medley. America's Lynn Vidili led that race by over a second at 150 meters, but Gould used her great freestyle strength to catch her and an East German swimmer in the last leg and to take the gold medal in a world record time of 2:23.07.

Gould was approaching the podium for the medal ceremony when Dawn Fraser, Australia's reigning Queen of the Pool, winner of Olympic gold in Melbourne, Rome, and Tokyo, took her aside and thrust into her hands a stuffed Koala Bear that she herself had held while standing on the victory podium many times past. Gould tearfully clutched the bear while picking up her first gold medal—and for the rest of the Games this worn-out toy became her good luck charm. (Alas, due to the Spitz shoe incident, Gould's display of her beloved Koala Bear sparked accusations that she was advertising for the Australian Tourist Board!)

"She could go all the way now," said an American commentator of Gould after her victory in the medley. "Tonight's race can work two ways, for her or against her. But knowing Shane, she's going to be tough to beat now."

She was considered especially tough to beat in her next event, the 100-meter freestyle, in which she held the world record. And yet, whether her initial victory in fact worked against her, or perhaps her Koala Bear lucky charm had just taken the day off, she ended up finishing a disappointing third behind two Americans, Sandra Nelson and Shirley Babashoff. This was her first loss in two years. For the Americans, their one-two victory was a tonic for their confidence and a sign that perhaps the logo on their T-shirts was not all wet. It read, "All that glitters is not Gould."

But a lot of the glitter continued to go to the young girl from Australia. Gould came back from her loss in the 100-meter freestyle to win the 400-meter freestyle in 4:10.04, another world record. After that, she broke Shirley Babashoff's world record in the 200-meter freestyle with a time of 2:03.56. With her third gold medal dangling from her neck, and still hugging her Koala, she declared, "I reckon I'm fit enough to do another good one." Then she added, rather in pre-1972 Spitz fashion, that the two-minute barrier in the 200-meter freestyle would undoubtedly be broken by a woman in the 1976 Games in Montreal—and *she* would probably be that woman.

But Gould did not "do another good one" in Munich (for her, a silver medal in the 800-meter freestyle was not good), and she did not swim at all in Montreal. A year after Munich, at age 16, she announced her retirement from competitive swimming, explaining that she was tired of all the sacrifices required to stay on top. (Here she echoed Spitz, who once said, "The great thing about being a competitive swimmer is that you know it's going to end quickly. When you're 23, you quit.") Two years after retiring, Gould married a domineering man seven years her senior and disappeared to a sheep farm in the outback of Western Australia, where she raised four children. Now swimming only for fun, she confined her competitive activities to local horse shows and the Western Australian State Open Plowing Competition, which she won in 1994 and 1995. But local horse shows and regional plowing contests turned out not to be fully satisfying for this tough Sydney woman who had once been a world beater in the water, and one day she announced to her controlling husband that she wished to enter the Australian Masters' Swimming Championship. He responded by knocking her unconscious with a blow to the head. She eventually divorced her brutish husband, but she never returned to competition in the pool.

The historian Dennis Phillips has shown persuasively that, throughout the history of their participation in high-level sports, Australia's highly talented female athletes have had to struggle mightily to find any kind of acceptance in their country's male-dominated and deeply sexist society. Shane Gould's story suggests that, even for Australia's "Golden Girl," athletic acceptance was fleeting and certainly did not extend to the private sphere.

Olympic Injustice:
The Sad Case of Rick DeMont

The spectacular successes of Mark Spitz and Shane Gould tended to overshadow all the other stories connected to the swimming competition at Munich, but there was another '72 swimming drama that was much more revealing about the existing state of the Games, and also more meaningful for their future, than the achievements of Spitz and Gould. This was the sad case of a sixteen-year-old swimmer from San Rafael, California, named Richard DeMont, who won the 400-meter freestyle race only to have his gold medal stripped from him by the IOC three days later. The IOC explained that DeMont had failed a mandatory drug test administered shortly after his race.

Before going into more detail about the DeMont incident, it is necessary to say something about the broader issues of doping and drug testing in high-level sports and in the Olympics prior to the Munich Games.

Of course, the use of (supposedly) performance-enhancing substances is an old story in sport. According to Phylastratos and Galen, even participants in the Ancient Olympics used special herbs and secret potions to get a leg up on their competitors. But it was only in the second half of the nineteenth century that "doping" by athletes became unquestionably verified and a source of concern among athletic officials. In the famous Six-Day Cycle Races in the 1870s and 1880s, racers of various nationalities employed all sorts of "miracle" concoctions to enhance their performances: the French favored mixtures of caffeine and Calvados; the Belgians went in for sugar cubes coated in ether. The Tour de France, too, was from the outset a test of drug recipes as much as leg muscles and bicycle technology—indeed, a race "Not [Just] About the Bike." In the seedy world of professional boxing, trainers not only doped up their own boys with mixtures of brandy and cocaine but also slipped truly nasty concoctions to opposing fighters in order to improve the odds for their guys. Horse racing, of course, was even rifer with drugs—the poor horses having no choice in the matter at all.

The modern Olympic Games, supposedly an oasis of virtue in a sporting desert of corruption and vice, were also infected with dope use from the beginning, though not much notice of this was taken until the post–World War II era. Official brows furrowed deeply when a litter of broken ampoules and syringes turned up in the changing rooms of the speed skaters at the Oslo Winter Games in 1952. In the Helsinki Summer Games that same year, the *marathoners*, of all people, were subjected to random tests of their food for evidence of God knows what. In fact, at that time there were no rules on doping at the Games, no regulations on just what could or could not be consumed, so of course there were no punishment measures on hand either.

The Rome Olympics of 1960 inspired the first, very tentative, moves by the IOC and various international athletic federations to address the problem of doping. This occurred because in that festival a Danish cyclist, Knud Jensen, got his med protocol mixed up and died from an overdose of powerful amphetamines. In 1962, the IOC, at a meeting in Moscow, passed a resolution against doping, its first official acknowledgment that there was a problem. On the other hand, the committee was reluctant to adopt serious regulatory measures to address this issue because any such steps were expected to be costly and laden with potential legal ramifications. The men from Lausanne also insisted that any systematic policing of high-level international sport should be conducted by the various sports federations, which supposedly were in a better position to judge the gravity of the problem in their respective disciplines. There was some drug testing at the Mexico City Games in 1968, but it was very rudimentary and only one athlete, a Swedish pentathlete, was disqualified (too much booze).

Following those Games, in 1969, the IOC's Executive Board proposed that the committee's jurisdiction over drug use "should be limited to the period immediately preceding and following the Olympic Games." IOC president Avery Brundage was willing to empower the committee's Medical Commission to institute specific drug regulations for the upcoming 1972 Games, but he did not want to spend too much money on this project. Informed in 1971 by his information director that the expenses for IOC Medical Commission meetings on doping policy were likely to be "tremendous," he responded, "There is no use wasting a lot of money on these superfluous meetings if we can avoid it."

The IOC's Medical Commission developed a draft doping-control proposal in July 1971 that entrusted actual policing to the federations and put the onus of expelling any athletes found guilty of infractions also on those bodies. The federations, for their part, tried to pass the buck back to the IOC. Meanwhile, many national Olympic committees, realizing that doping was too serious and widespread for continued turf-passing and dithering, called for systematic regulation by *somebody*. U.S. superheavyweight weightlifter Ken Patra called attention to the issue in 1971 when, explaining his eagerness for a rematch at Munich with a Russian who had bested him the year before, he stated, "Last year, the only difference between him and me was that I couldn't afford his drug bill. Now I can. When I hit Munich next year, I'll weigh in at about 340, maybe 350. Then we'll see which are better—his steroids or mine."

Bucking to pressure from national Olympic committees and various governments, including that of the United States, the IOC finally came up with a set of rules and regulations on doping just in time for the 1972 Winter Olympics at Sapporo. But this program hardly seemed effective. Two hundred eleven athletes were tested, but only one instance of doping—a West German hockey player—was discovered. This appeared pretty paltry in light of the remarks by Patra and evidence in pre-Olympic national competitions that drug taking was quite widespread. There were already stories in circulation about extensive drug use and gender manipulation treatments by the East German Olympic teams ("Where men are men, and so are the women"), but it turned out that the *West* Germans hardly had a clean vest in the doping realm either. In the German Indoor Track Championships in 1971, the West German Athletic Federation found two athletes guilty of taking "illegal substances" and gave them brief suspensions.

By the time of the '72 Summer Games, the Munich OC claimed that it, along with the IOC and the international federations, had finally gotten together a rigorous control system with "uniform guidelines drawn up on a sound scientific basis," adding that "the entire question of doping control in Munich has been well thought out so that mistakes and protests are virtually impossible." For the first time ever, moreover, all female athletes were required to submit a piece of their hair for gender testing by Medical Commission scientists. Now back to Rick DeMont.

DeMont had been taking medications for allergies and asthma since age 4. His affliction did not prevent him from becoming a child prodigy in swimming. Upon qualifying for the U.S. swim team in the '72 Games, DeMont dutifully informed his coaches of all the medications he took. He also filled out the new IOC forms listing his medications. The U.S. team doctors should at that point have checked to see if DeMont's asthma drugs contained any of the ingredients that had been placed on the IOC's list of banned substances. One of those substances happened to be ephedrine, which was a basic component in Marax, DeMont's medication of choice. Of course, had the doctors taken this elementary step, DeMont could have switched to a permissible alternative drug. Compounding their ineptitude, the U.S. team physicians also failed to turn DeMont's drug forms over to the IOC Medical Commission.

With no reason to assume that his favored drug was a problem, DeMont took it with him to Munich. The night before he was scheduled to compete in his first event, the 400-meter freestyle, he suffered an asthma attack, so he swallowed a tablet of Marax. He took another tablet later the next day, between qualifying for the 400 and the actual race at 6:40 p.m.

Although starting out slowly in the race, DeMont picked up just enough speed in the last one hundred meters to defeat Australia's Bradford Cooper by one-hundredth of a second, the smallest possible margin of victory.

Directly after the race, DeMont and the other top finishers submitted to a drug test administered by the IOC Medical Commission. Then it was off to the awards ceremony, where the tall, young Californian basked in a moment of glory that proved very brief indeed.

Two days later, DeMont easily qualified for his second competition, the 1,500-meter freestyle, in which he held the world record. But on the following morning, he was informed that he would not be able to compete in the 1,500 final because he had failed his drug test. The officials also explained that he might be stripped of the gold medal he had won in the 400.

Over the course of the next two days, IOC officials conducted hearings on the DeMont case and collected testimony from the U.S. team physicians and coaches. Inspectors went to DeMont's room and confiscated his Marax, which of course he had not bothered to hide. The chairman of the IOC Medical Commission, Alexandre de Merode, initially recommended that DeMont be allowed to keep his medal but then reversed himself and proposed taking it away on grounds that the athlete was "co-responsible" with U.S. team officials for the infraction. The IOC Executive Board backed up Merode, stating that the Medical Commission "had to be consistent in its work."

DeMont immediately appealed this decision in a personal letter to de Merode. He based his appeal on his medical history of severe asthma and his individual compliance with all the Olympic rules regarding notification of medication consumption. He explained that he took Marax "not in order to improve my competitive performance, but in order to stay alive." He insisted that he had not been told by "anyone in the USOC medical staff to cease using Marax." DeMont's appeal was promptly rejected.

As soon as the IOC judgment was officially confirmed, Avery Brundage instructed USOC president Clifford Buck to confiscate DeMont's medal and return it to the IOC. Brundage, who had no use for Buck, added that, since "much of the responsibility for this incident rests on your team's medical authorities," the entire USOC leadership stood "severely reprimanded." But of course, Brundage's reprimand of Buck was nothing compared to the harsh punishment he meted out to DeMont, who now became only the second American in the history of the Olympics to be forced to return a medal. The first was Jim Thorpe in 1912.

In a statement to the press released on September 10, Clifford Buck gave DeMont his own personal endorsement (for what it was worth), while mentioning nothing about the USOC's principal role in this fiasco: "I want to state positively that DeMont has done nothing wrong and that he took the medicine solely to ease his asthmatic symptoms, as he had done for years. . . . The connotation of 'dope' in connection with this outstanding competitor is unthinkable and totally unwarranted." In defending the

Willi Daume and Hans-Jochen Vogel admiring a giant pastry displayed in support of Munich's Olympic candidacy. *Süeddeutsche Zeitung Photo 275951.*

Otl Aicher with his "pictograph" symbols for the 1972 Games. *Süeddeutsche Zeitung Photo 30735.*

Dirndl-clad Olympic hostesses. *Süeddeutsche Zeitung Photo 111990.*

Munich '72's iconic—and controversial— glass roof. *Süeddeutsche Zeitung Photo 552204.*

Athletes recreating in the Olympic Men's Village. *Bundesarchiv, Bild 183-L0826-0203. Photo: Ulrich Kohls.*

Israel's Olympic delegation entering the stadium at the opening ceremony. *Süeddeutsche Zeitung Photo 155339.*

The massive team from the USA. *Süeddeutsche Zeitung Photo 760150.*

The Olympic torch enters the stadium on opening day. *Süeddeutsche Zeitung Photo 760148.*

Anti–Vietnam War demonstration in Munich prior to the '72 Games. *Bundesarchiv, Bild 183-L0902-0212. Photo: o.Ang.*

A sobbing Olga Korbut.
Süeddeutsche Zeitung Photo 351113.

Mark Spitz on his way to one of his seven gold medals. *Süeddeutsche Zeitung Photo 155352.*

Valery Borzov—"The Fastest Man in the World Is a Commie." *Bundesarchiv, Bild 183-L0901-0230. Photo: o.Ang.*

America's Bob Seagren grudgingly accepting his silver medal while East Germany's Wolfgang Nordwig smiles on in victory. *Bundesarchiv, Bild 183-LO903-200. Photo: Ulrich Kohls.*

West Germany's "Golden Girl," Heidi Rosendahl, in action. *Süeddeutsche Zeitung Photo 499727.*

Ulrike Meyfarth jumping for gold with the "Fosbury Flop." *Bundesarchiv, Bild 183-L0904-0228. Photo: o.Ang.*

Finland's Lasse Virén breaking
the tape in the 10,000-meter race.
Bundesarchiv, Bild 183-LO903-0215.
Photo: o.Ang.

Israeli Olympians backstage
after *Fiddler on the Roof.*
Süeddeutsche Zeitung Photo
760311.

"Issa" confronted by policewoman Annaliese Graes. *Süeddeutsche Zeitung Photo 760145.*

The abortive "Operation Sunshine" rescue attempt. *Süeddeutsche Zeitung Photo 161264.*

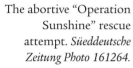

A burned-out helicopter at Fürstenfeldbruck. *Bundesarchiv, Bild 183-L0906-0213. Photo: o.Ang.*

Avery Brundage announcing, "The Games must go on." *Süeddeutsche Zeitung Photo 161265.*

Vince Matthews and Wayne Collett on the victory podium after the 400-meter race. *Bundesarchiv, Bild 183-L0907-0220. Photo: o.Ang.*

Frank Shorter on his way to victory in the marathon. *Bundesarchiv, Bild 183-L0910-0212. Photo: Friedrich Gahlbeck.*

The "Great Gold Heist." A scene from the USA-USSR basketball final. *Süeddeutsche Zeitung Photo 179597.*

A scene from the closing ceremony. *Bundesarchiv, Bild 183-L0911-0209. Photo: Friedrich Gahlbeck.*

Memorial plaque at Connollystrasse 31. *Süeddeutsche Zeitung Photo 760144.*

IOC's action against DeMont to outraged letter writers, Brundage admitted that the problem could have been avoided entirely if the USOC had properly performed its duties. "It is unfortunate that he [DeMont] was the victim of someone else's neglect," he declared.

Although it was undoubtedly no consolation to DeMont, he was not the only athlete in the '72 Games to be charged with drug infractions. Once again, however, the policing process was imperfect, to put it mildly. A Puerto Rican basketball player tested positive for banned substances, which according to the Olympic rules should have made both him and his team ineligible for further play; moreover, the team's victories should have been nullified. Confirmation of the test results in this case took so long, however, that the Puerto Rican team was allowed to continue playing throughout the tournament and its victories were upheld. Contradictorily, when a rider on the Dutch cycling team tested positive for Coromine (a banned substance), the entire Dutch team was stripped of its bronze medal. Coromine, it might be added, was prohibited by the IOC but not by the International Cycling Union. Then there was the revealing case of fourteen modern pentathlon athletes from six countries who tested positive for an illegal tranquilizer used to calm nerves before shooting. The IOC Medical Commission turned the names of the athletes over to the International Federation of the Modern Pentathlon for disciplinary action, but the federation's powerful president, Thor Thofelt (Sweden), argued that any action against the athletes would harm their sport because of the negative publicity. His argument prevailed despite vehement protests from West German and American pentathlon officials that such "evasive tactics" would in the end generate "an image of manipulation."

Inconsistency in the application of drug rules was not the only problem. Sloppy and superficial testing, including an inability to detect steroids, generally allowed modestly sophisticated dopers to evade identification. The East German Olympic program was by no means the only national program to encourage doping, but the GDR's reliance on pharmaceutical enhancement was especially egregious. Indeed, East Germany's major contribution to sports medicine at this time was the development of a new anabolic steroid called Oral-Turinabol.* And yet, although widespread speculation during the '72 Games regarding the use of steroids and

---

* Oral-Turinabol is an artificially produced male sex hormone that engenders extremely rapid muscular growth. Over the course of several decades of use in East Germany, it made some ten thousand athletes sick with cancer, heart disease, severe depression, and other afflictions.

other drugs by GDR athletes was confirmed by testing a few months after the competition, not a single East German Olympian was fingered for doping violations in connection with the Munich Olympics.

On to the Track

Like the swimming facilities at Munich, those for track and field, located in the grand Olympic Stadium, were first rate. The track itself, made of a new composite material, was extremely fast. Also new was a starting system for the races featuring blocks with miniature loud speakers telling runners when to go, and a micro-switch that would activate if a runner started too soon. Yet another novelty involved tiny electronic eyes spaced every ten meters along the track that beamed in on the metal spikes in the runners' shoes and dispatched real-time data on the race to powerful Siemens computers. All the placings in the races would be decided by photo-finish cameras on the edge of the grandstand. The timing and processing of results, and their near-instantaneous transmission around the world, were handled by the big Siemens machines. Yet, what amazed competitors and spectators most about the facilities was not the electronic wizardry but the revolutionary acrylic roof spanning the athletic complex. The main buzz about the roof remained its breathtaking cost, and many critics were already complaining that "the dropped handkerchief" (as some called the roof) was not worth the huge expense.

The track and field competition did not start until August 31, day 5 of the Munich Games. Munich promised exciting individual and team contests between the United States, USSR, and the surging East Germans. In the European Track Championships in the summer of 1971, the East Germans had bested everyone, including the previously sovereign Soviets.

The U.S. men had traditionally dominated track and field at the Olympics, especially the sprints. In Mexico City, the American men had won fifteen (out of twenty-four) track and field gold medals. Munich, however, looked much more challenging for the Yanks. One possible weakness lay precisely in the sprinting events—that traditional strong suit for the United States. Some of America's fastest sprinters—Jimmy Hines, Tommie Smith, and John Carlos—had elected to try out for professional football rather than compete in Munich. Russia's Valery Borzov had come out on top in two recent dual USA-USSR meets. On the other hand, the United States had legitimate medal contenders in the 100 meters in Rey Robinson and Eddie Hart, who had both equaled the world record time of 9.9. In some other track disciplines, including the middle-distance races, and in many of the field events, American performances at the recent Pan American Games at Cali, Colombia, had been weaker than the European showings at the European Track Championships in Helsinki. Moreover, the U.S. team as a whole was inexperienced at the Olympic level, with only fifteen men having participated in a previous festival. Looking toward Munich after the Olympic trials in Eugene in July, head coach Bill Bowerman warned, "We will be fighting for our lives, there's no question about it."

Although the U.S. trackmen posted some strong individual showings in the qualification rounds at Munich, the run-up to the medal competition suggested that the team was in considerable disarray. Confusion prevailed over which athletes would compete in which events, and who would run on the relay teams. Bowerman did not help matters by publicly chastising some of his athletes and by firing off salvoes of criticism over everything from mismanagement in the USOC to alleged screw-ups by the Munich organizers. Regarding the latter, he said undiplomatically, "I thought the Germans were supposed to be the most efficient people in the world, but they haven't been able to do anything they said they were going to do."

Bowerman was not the only grouser. U.S. female athletes made known their unhappiness with conditions in the Olympic Village, complaining that women competitors typically got only half of whatever the men got, whether it was equipment or passes for their friends and families to enter the Village. "When we are issued anything, we always seem to come up a few short," said Doris Brown, a 1,500-meter runner. "The men seem to get as much of anything *they* want."

However, if there were an Olympic medal awarded for incompetence in the handling and management of athletes, that prize certainly should have gone to the U.S. coaches and officials, not to the German organizers. As if challenged by the failings of the U.S. swimming bosses, whose egregious errors cost Rick DeMont his gold medal, U.S. sprint coach Stan Wright made a boneheaded mistake that prevented America's two best hopes in the 100-meter dash—Robinson and Hart—from even getting a shot at the medal event. Having easily won their first-round heats on the morning of August 31, Robinson and Hart failed to show up for their quarterfinal heat in the 100. The reason they were not on the starting blocks at the appointed time of 4:15 p.m. was that their coach, Wright, had told them the starting time was 7:00 p.m. Wright, it turned out, was using an eighteen-month-old schedule that was completely out of date by the time the Games opened. "I gave them the wrong time," Wright admitted. "It's my fault. But I don't want to talk about it." Robinson, on the other hand, was not so reluctant to talk. "I don't care, the man is a coach, he can say he's sorry," fumed Robinson. "What about three years [of training]? What about torn ligaments, pulled muscles, a broken leg? He can go on being a coach. What can I go on being?"

In the end, Stan Wright was not allowed to get off without discussing his mistake in public. ABC's pugnacious color man, Howard Cosell, saw fit to subject Wright to what a disgusted Roone Arledge called an "inquisition" on national television. "An American tragedy," Cosell piously intoned. In the view of sprinter Vince Matthews, Wright, an African American, should not have been subjected to Cosell's merciless grilling all alone, with no support from Bowerman and Buck. "It was a typical USOC copout," concluded Matthews.

Meanwhile, another American sprinter, Robert Taylor, *did* manage to make it to his qualifying heat for the 100, but only because he happened to wander over to the stadium in the afternoon to watch some of the other races. "The other guys missed their heats and I got there just in time for mine. I didn't have any time to warm up." Nonetheless, Taylor won his heat and thus became the only American to qualify for the finals.

On the same day that Robinson and Hart watched on TV in their rooms the heat that they were supposed to be competing in, two other American medal hopefuls, Richard Bruggeman in the 400-meter hurdles and Rick Wohlhutter in the 800-meter race, failed to qualify for their events. Looking for someone to blame for all this misery, Bowerman pounced again on the German organizers, accusing them of not accommodating the Americans' needs. In particular, he said, the organizers had failed to provide the U.S. team with enough vehicles. U.S. coaches also complained loudly when German officials did not immediately expel from the Village a group of American reporters who had crashed the place in hopes of interviewing Robinson and Hart. Needless to say, the Germans were not amused by all this American whining. Willi Daume sent an official letter of protest to Clifford Buck, the only such protest he issued during the Games. Bowerman, Daume said, was totally out of line and needed to be reined in. Another German official stated publicly, "The American delegation is the worst-led of any in Munich." He then went on to speak of the "loveable" character of the Soviet delegation, pointing out that while the Soviets had treated the German organizers to a caviar party all the Americans did was bitch and moan. Clearly, the Americans were not just screwing up on the field of play.

On that field of play, the glamour event of the track competition, the male 100-meter dash, took place on September 2 before a capacity crowd.

The event was won handily by Valery Borzov, a twenty-two-year-old Ukrainian who claimed after the race that he wasn't even going full throttle. America's only participant in the final, Robert Taylor, managed to edge out Jamaica's Lennox Miller for the silver medal.

By winning this prestigious event, Borzov became the first Soviet runner to win an Olympic gold medal in a race of less than five thousand meters in length. Borzov's victory was the product of a highly meticulous preparation program at the Kiev Institute of Physical Culture, where he was a graduate student. As his coach explained,

> We began with a search for the most up-to-date model of sprinting. We studied slow-motion films of leading world sprinters of past and present, figured out the push-off angle and the body incline at the breakaway and went deeply into a whole number of minor details. . . . For Borzov to be able to clock 10 seconds flat over 100 meters, a whole team of scientists conducted research resembling the work of, say, car or aircraft designers.

After his victory, Borzov himself paid due credit to "the people who helped me develop," but he also could not resist getting in a dig at his American rivals, who had rashly predicted that he'd "win nothin'" in Munich. "It seems that the American sprinters are suffering from stagnation, while the Europeans are making progress," Borzov declared. The Ukrainian's win was so important to the USSR, quipped Red Smith, that his gold medal would probably "be placed on public display in the Kremlin right alongside Lenin's well preserved cadaver."

But Team USA's African American sprinters were not about to deify Borzov. After spending a night drinking in downtown Munich, Larry Black, Lawrence Burton, and Chuck Smith came to the conclusion that the Russian had just been "lucky" in the 100 and that they "would wipe him up in the 200." There was just no way, they said, that "any white dude was going to pull any Olympic double on them."

Alas, two days later, Borzov did just that—won the 200-meter race and became thereby the first man in sixteen years to win both sprints in a single Olympiad. Now it was incontestable that—as Smith put it—"The fastest man in the world is a Commie." The second-fastest man in the 200 was Larry Black, who had held the lead until the last seventy meters, when, shifting into another gear, Borzov shot by him. Near the finish line, Borzov actually turned his head and looked back at the field, something that coaches always counsel strongly against, but in this case it made no difference: nobody was gaining on him. Borzov's "double" in the sprints—along with his good looks and possibly his race—made him such a poster boy for athletic prowess that a picture displaying his magnificent form in the 200 was selected for the Voyager Golden Record, launched into space in 1977 aboard the Voyager spacecraft.

The men's 800-meter final, held on September 2, also turned into a duel between Soviet and American talent. The USSR's Yevgeny Arzhanov, another Ukrainian product of the Kiev Institute of Physical Culture, came into the race as the world's top-ranked half-miler, having not lost an 800-meter final in four years. America's Dave Wottle had equaled the world record at the Olympic tryouts in Eugene, but because of a lack of international experience and a recent bout of tendinitis, he was not the favorite in Munich. Kenya's Mike Bolt and Robert Ouko were considered Arzhanov's greatest threats for the gold medal.

Once the race got under way, it looked indeed as if Bolt might be the man to defeat Arzhanov. The two Kenyans went out very fast, Bolt taking the lead, while Wottle wallowed in the back of the pack. But Bolt and Ouko began to fade just as Wottle found his stride. The American slipped methodically through the pack and surged into second place on the final leg. With some fifty meters still to go, however, he didn't think he would be able to catch the Soviet star. Nonetheless, even while Wottle's brain was conceding victory, his legs were propelling him ever closer to Arzhanov, whom he in fact managed to catch right before the finish. Wottle made a desperate lunge that put him across the line a mere inch or so ahead of Arzhanov, the closest finish in the 800 in Olympic history. (In fact, the two racers clocked exactly the same time, 1:45.9, leaving Munich's sophisticated photo-finish device to decide the winner.)

Dave Wottle's unexpected victory was the first gold medal for the beleaguered U.S. men's track team at the '72 Games—a deeply welcome moment in what so far had been a pretty dismal showing. For Wottle personally, this victory was welcome also as a rebuttal to Coach Bowerman, who had pointedly told him *not* to bring his brand new bride to Munich on grounds that she would be a distraction and that any sex with her would sap his strength. Wottle brought his bride anyway, though he admitted later that he had been so nervous about getting a medal that he couldn't have successful sex with his wife until his event was over. He didn't say what his new bride thought about his performance in Munich.

Wottle and Arzhanov showed no ill will toward each other either before or after their meeting in Munich, but the same cannot be said for another major East-West confrontation in the early rounds of the track and field competition: the pole-vault duel between America's Bob Seagren and East Germany's Wolfgang Nordwig. The two men had developed an active dislike for each other during the vaulting competition at Mexico City, where Seagren finished first and Nordwig third. Their mutual animosity intensified during the lead-up to the Munich Games because Nordwig and East German track officials were instrumental in a decision by the Technical Committee of the International Amateur Athletic Federation (IAAF) to ban so-called Cata-Poles, a new kind of pole used by Seagren and many other leading vaulters. The IAAF decision, which was handed down on July 25, 1972, just one month before the Games' opening, derived largely from a complaint by Nordwig (a precision engineer by trade) that Cata-Poles contained carbon fiber, making them exceptionally springy. Seagren and the other Cata-Pole users argued in an official protest against the ban that their new poles did *not* contain carbon and that the rules said nothing about pole composition anyway. The IAAF was not moved; it refused to withdraw the ban on grounds that the new poles had not been available to all the competitors for a full year before the Games. (This in fact was not true: Nordwig himself had tried the Cata-Pole in the months before Munich but found it not to his liking.)

The IAAF's belated Cata-Pole ban left Seagren very little time to train with the older model poles, so he was vastly relieved when, on August 27, four days before the pole-vault competition in Munich, the Technical Committee surprisingly ruled that the Cata-Poles would be legal after all. Now Nordwig and the East Germans cried foul, with the consequence that, three days later, the IAAF reversed itself yet again and reimposed the ban. To ensure compliance with this ruling, Olympic officials confiscated all the Cata-Poles and issued new (old) poles to the competitors.

When the battle over the poles finally segued into the battle *with* the poles on September 2, many of the vaulters seemed still to be affected by the confusion over equipment, and only ten managed to clear the qualifying height. Predictably enough, though, the event ultimately turned into a Seagren-Nordwig duel, with Seagren clearing 5.40 meters and Nordwig responding with a vault of 5.40.5. Seagren failed three times to clear this height, leaving Nordwig free to take a final vault with the bar at 5.50 meters. This he also managed to clear, setting a new Olympic record.

Seagren did not take his loss gallantly. He shunned giving his conqueror the customary handshake until well after the awards ceremony. Instead of congratulating Nordwig, he walked over to one of the IAAF officials and thrust his pole at the startled man, as if to suggest where the fellow might stick this loathsome piece of equipment. At a press conference later that day, a still embittered Seagren complained, "He [Nordwig] had six months to use the [approved] poles. I had six weeks."

The East Germans got another opportunity to crow when, in the women's 100-meter dash, the GDR's Renate Stecher prevented America's Iris Davis from continuing the recent U.S. dominance in this event established by Wilma Rudolph (1960) and Wyomia Tyus (1968). In fact, the best Davis could do was to finish fourth, while Stecher ran away from the field with a world record time of 11.07. Stecher's time seemed almost too good to be true, and sure enough, documents released a few months after the Games showed that she had been taking Oral-Turinabol for the previous two years.

Fortunately, most of the on-field battling in the early track competition at Munich did not involve contentious confrontations between "arrogant" Americans and their equally smug East-Bloc rivals. On September 2, the sixth day of the track competitions, West Germany's Heidi Rosendahl brought great joy to the home fans by winning the long jump—thereby bringing the FRG its first gold medal in the Munich Olympics. West Germany's "Goldmädchen" (golden girl) was, like her teammate Heidi Schüler, quite svelte, and the eye-glasses she wore even when competing added a hint of intellectuality. In the words of an admiring West German sportswriter, Rosendahl was "typical of a new class of female athlete whose ticket to sporting achievement did not have to be purchased with muscle-bound deformity" (a snide reference, perhaps, to the hulking East German women).

The big news on the following day, especially for the West German fans, was their country's garnering of *three* gold medals in track—the best single day in Olympic track ever for the FRG and, of course, doubly gratifying in this case because it came on home ground. In the javelin event, Klaus Woltermann out-threw the mighty Soviet star Janis Lusis with an Olympic-record toss of 90.48 meters, just one-half inch farther than Lusis's heave. Hildegard Falck outran the USSR's and GDR's best women to win the 800-meter race in 1:58.6, another Olympic record. Berndt Kannenburg took the 50-kilometer walk in yet another Olympic-record time.

While the home fans had plenty to cheer about on September 3, the next day's track competition presented them with yet more delights. Heidi Rosendahl, who two days earlier had gotten gold in the long jump, now won silver in the pentathlon, revealing thereby her extraordinary all-around talent. Amazingly, Rosendahl had been in fifth place and three hundred points behind leader Mary Peters of Great Britain after the first day of competition. But the second day featured her strongest events, the long jump and the 200-meter race, in which she performed so brilliantly that she almost caught Peters. Had the latter run just one-tenth of a second slower in the 200, Rosendahl, not Peters, would have won gold in the pentathlon. To their credit, the German fans cheered on Peters despite the fact that she was competing against their "golden girl."

An even greater delight for the home fans involved the greatest upset victory in the track and field competition thus far: Ulrike Meyfarth's astounding win in the women's high jump. The sixteen-year-old high school girl from Cologne, who had barely made the West German team, was certainly not expected to be a medal threat in Munich. Yet, using the revolutionary jump style pioneered by America's Dick Fosbury in 1968 (the "Fosbury Flop," where the jumper goes back first over the bar), Meyfarth managed on her final try to leap 1.92 meters, a height that equaled the standing world record. (Fortunately, Meyfarth cleared the bar without touching it with any part of her body. Although touching the bar was legal, the technical director of the Games, Karl von Schwanzbogen, had ordered the bar to be electrified to discourage competitors from holding it in place as they went over, a devious tactic rumored to have been perfected by the Americans.) Like Olga Korbut, Meyfarth instantly became a darling of the Munich fans. In part, this was because the leggy brunette was physically very fetching, but her extreme youth also played a role here: she was the youngest competitor of either sex ever to win an individual Olympic gold medal in track and field.

Unlike Meyfarth, Finland's Lasse Virén was expected to do well in his first Olympic competition, the 10,000-meter race, but he certainly was not expected to do what he in fact did: pull off one of the most amazing come-from-behind triumphs in the entire '72 festival.

Finland, of course, had a great tradition in distance running at the Games, having won twenty-four Olympic championships in these events from 1912 through 1936. The Finns had fallen off quite a bit following the Soviet invasion of Finland in 1939 and their country's ensuing smothering by Brother Russia, but now it seemed they might be back. Virén's teammate Juha Väätänen had taken first place in both the 5,000- and 10,000-meter races at the European Track Championships in Helsinki the year before. Virén himself had achieved very impressive results while training with the Kenyans in Thomson's Falls (Kenya) and had broken the two-mile world record in a meet in Helsinki earlier in 1972. Some track cognoscenti even thought Virén might turn out to be another Paavo Nurmi, the next "Flying Finn."

As the 10,000-meter race unfolded on a warm early September morning in Munich, however, Virén suffered a disaster that seemed to take him entirely out of contention for a medal, perhaps even out of the race entirely. On the twelfth lap, he got tangled up with Belgium's Emiel Puttemans and hit the deck hard, almost taking down America's Frank Shorter with him. By the time Virén could get back on his feet, the rest of the pack was some forty meters down the track. Undaunted, Virén embarked on a frantic chase, the Fallen Finn suddenly becoming the Flying Finn. In less than 150 meters, he had caught the pack and then began picking his way through it. He ran with an eerie smoothness, hardly showing strain. With six hundred meters to go, he "dropped the hammer" on his fellow front-runners, covering the last two laps in an unbelievable 60.0 and 56.4 seconds. He ended up winning by about two meters in a world record time of 27.38.4. This was impressive enough by itself but truly mind-boggling when one considers that he had essentially spotted the second-place finisher, Puttemans, about half a football field in distance.

Sitting in the stands as this amazing performance transpired was America's great middle-distance runner, Steve Prefontaine, who was scheduled to compete against Virén in the 5,000-meter race a few days hence. One of "Pre's" teammates turned to him and said, "Better hope that guy has shot his wad."

Kultur-Olympiade

However brilliant the athletic performances at these Twentieth Summer Games might have been, Munich's Olympic festival was hardly a mere sports show. True to its self-image as a world-class center of the arts, Munich offered its Olympic visitors a prodigious array of cultural attractions. All the city's vaunted cultural institutions—its opera, concert halls, theaters, and museums—were enlisted in this great enterprise. The lineup of performers, as had been the planners' intention, included plenty of foreign artists, above all from the USSR and GDR. (The GDR had agreed to participate in Munich's Kultur-Olympiade provided it would be able, as an internal SED memo put it, "to use the resources of culture to demonstrate the superiority of our socialist way of life.")

In addition to the more conventional artistic fare on offer in the city's theaters and concert halls, there was also the carnivalesque Spielstraße, that innovative jumble of interactive art exhibits and edgy street theater, running daily (and nightly until ten) on the Olympic grounds. On this avenue of playful experimentation, boasted the promoters, visitors could happily experience the essence of the laid-back and frolicsome new Munich. All told, the Munich OC spent some fifteen million marks on its wide-ranging "Kultur-Olympiade."

In the end, the organizers might have put *too much* emphasis on this pet project. It seems that they somewhat overestimated the interest in high culture on the part of ordinary Olympic fans. A great many seats at the opera and in the theaters went unfilled because all too many visitors apparently preferred hanging out at the Hofbräuhaus, or perhaps taking in the latest James Bond movie, to sitting through Wagner or Sophocles. Another problem was that the Munich Organizing Committee had held back fully 50 percent of the tickets for the most prestigious events, expecting to hand these passes out to VIPs and other special friends. When the visiting bigwigs took only a small percentage of their complimentary tickets, the OC returned them to the theaters, but by this time word had gotten out that tickets for the most sought-after productions were unavailable. Thus, despite a last-minute distribution of cut-rate tickets to student groups, a much-anticipated production of Wagner's *Tristan und Isolde* at the Nationaltheater played to a half-empty house. A little later, 466 tickets went unsold for Sophocles' tragedy *Oedipus Rex*, while performances of Alban Berg's demanding twelve-tone opera *Wozzeck* and Richard Strauss's *Die Schweigsame Frau* both had plenty of vacant seats.

With the exception of a few high-brow offerings—the Royal Shakespeare Company's production of *Midsummer Night's Dream*, the Negro Ensemble of New York's rendition of Schiller's *Wallenstein*, a new adaptation by Erwin Axer of Chekov's *Uncle Vanya*—the attractions that drew the greatest interest tended to be rather less challenging. Major hits included the Moscow Puppet Theater and an "International Folklore Festival" at the cavernous Circus-Krone building. An exhibit entitled "Vita Bavarica," devoted to historic traditions and customs in Bavaria, attracted disappointingly small crowds, as did a scholarly exhibition on "100 Years of German Excavation at Olympia." (Both these exhibitions were held in the Deutsches Museum, where the Nazis had mounted a show called "The Eternal Jew" in 1937.)

The Kultur-Olympiade's signature art exhibition, "Weltkulturen und Moderne Kunst" (World Cultures and Modern Art), held in the Nazi-built Haus der Kunst, suffered an embarrassing moment when, one week before it opened to the public, a special preview for VIPs took place. The embarrassment had nothing to do with the fact that the venue, originally called Haus der deutschen Kunst, had been commissioned by Hitler to showcase ideologically acceptable "German art." Rather, the problem was a lack of adequate security. Shortly after the preview got under way, as Bavarian minister-president Alfons Goppel was droning on about artistic "giving and taking" between disparate parts of the globe, one of the guests did some taking of his own: he furtively removed a small Degas painting from its hanging place, put the picture under his arm, and disappeared. Later, it turned out that the "thief" actually owned the painting and had lent it to the museum for the exhibition; seeing how lax the security was, the donor took his artwork back home.

When the Weltkulturen exhibition opened to the public a week later, security had been beefed up, but the anticipated huge crowds did not arrive. Throughout the festival, this ambitious art show attracted far fewer visitors than did the attractions at the abutting Englischer Garten, where throngs of young people sprawled nude on the meadows and beer drinkers clustered in their hundreds beneath the much-loved "Chinese Tower." The paucity of patronage at the Weltkulturen show was unfortunate, for this was the first comprehensive exploration of the influence of Asian, Middle Eastern, and African art on European modernism. To take but one example, the exhibition illustrated the impact of Persian miniatures on the "Oriental" drawings of Delacroix. In the realm of music, visitors could trace the influence of Indonesian Gamelan artistry on Debussy and Ravel.

Meanwhile, one part of the Kultur-Olympiade that was unquestionably thriving was the Spielstraße. This was the place to go if one wanted to visit the Olympic grounds without actually going to the Olympics. Ursula von Kardorff, a columnist for Munich's tabloid *Abendzeitung,* heartily recommended a visit to the Spielstraße to her readers, though she warned potential patrons to bring along their own food and drink since the sausages there were inedible and beer was unavailable, its sale having been banned. Properly equipped, though, a visitor could spend an entire day surrounded by "magicians, clowns, beautiful models, speechifying dreamers, Jesus-freaks, world-improvers, and artists anxious to put themselves on display." At times, she conceded, the scene there might be confusing, what with five different shows going on simultaneously, but all in all this was "the best street theater that [Munich] had ever seen." Even if one didn't understand everything that was going on, Kardorff concluded, this bit of "Munich-Olympia" could not fail to make any visitor very "happy" indeed.

CHAPTER Five

Invasion of the Sanctuary

We were completely unprepared for something like this.
—Hans-Jochen Vogel on the Olympic terror attack (2005)

The splendid athletic accomplishments during the first phase of the 1972 Olympic Games were putting Munich on the map in just the way that the Games' organizers had always wanted. It seemed certain that more Olympic and world records would be broken at these Games than ever before. The organizers also took heart from the fact that most foreign visitors seemed to be having a good time during their Olympic visit—the ongoing difficulties with lodging, price-gouging, and occasional outbursts of local xenophobia notwithstanding. The foreign press, too, was full of praise for this "new Munich" and "new Germany," which seemed so different in values and spirit from the threatening Germany of old.

Then, on September 5, day 10 of the competitions (and day 11 of the Games), came the horrific attack by Palestinian guerrillas on the Israeli compound at the Olympic Village. Overnight, as ABC commentator Jim McKay put it, the "Olympics of Joy" had turned into the "Olympics of Terror." The attack seemed all the more terrible because the modern Olympic Games, like those of the ancient world, were supposed to afford participants and spectators a kind of sanctuary—a place where, if nothing else, they would not be subject to the wars and strife afflicting the world outside those sacred precincts. Now, amidst the play in Munich, that "Olympic Truce" had been brutally violated.

For the Germans, the scenario that unfolded on September 5 could not have been worse: Jews, having been invited to the Federal Republic of Germany (FRG) and placed under the host country's protective care, once again faced political murder on German soil, and this during what was supposed to be the proudest moment so far in the history of the "new" Germany.

"Nothing Happens at Night"

With each passing day in the early phase of Munich's Olympic festival, the officials responsible for security at the Games breathed a little easier. Their relief did not derive from a complete absence of challenges to law and order in the host city. On September 2, a coalition of radical leftist groups from all over the Federal Republic violated the Olympics-period ban on political demonstrations in the inner city by staging a "Red Antiwar Day" rally near the Karlstor. Protesters carrying megaphones shouted "Streets free to the Communists!" The demonstration turned violent when police tried to disburse the protesters. In the course of a running battle between police and demonstrators, fifty-eight policemen were injured, four of them seriously. Fourteen protesters were arrested. Another leftist demonstration the following day remained non-violent, largely because police immediately confiscated the weapon-like implements carried by some of the demonstrators.

Apart from actual disturbances during the early days of the Games, the authorities were also confronted with additional intelligence information pointing to possible dangers from foreign sources, including the Middle East. In the evening of September 4, the day before the Black September terror attack, the Bavarian branch of the Federal Office for Constitutional Protection (BVS) received a tip from an operative in Lebanon that five "fedayeen terrorists" were apparently planning some kind of "operation" in West Germany. According to the report, the five Palestinians were still in Beirut, awaiting orders to fly to Cairo, where they would receive fake Yemeni passports. From Cairo, they would proceed to Athens, there to meet a Dane calling himself "Jim," who would fill them in on the operation in question. The terrorists had long hair and wore new clothing. The exact time of their intended departure from Beirut was not known.

Information like this was obviously troubling, but offered no conclusive proof of a planned attack against the Games, much less a target date or mode of operation. In any event, the BVS authorities had no clue that, while they were keeping their eyes peeled for a possible appearance by five long-haired Palestinians bent on who-knew-what mischief, the men who would actually attack the Games were already safely ensconced in Munich, making final preparations for their operation.

For Munich's security officials, the most important fact about the early days of the festival was not the accrual of additional vague and confusing warnings about possible trouble down the line but rather the lack so far of any actual attacks that could have threatened the continuation of play. Another important reality was that some foreign journalists, principally Americans, were complaining bitterly that the security around the Olympic Village was unnecessarily *tight*, impeding their access to the athletes. Indeed, the Americans were complaining of "Gestapo" tactics by Village officials, a charge to which the German authorities were, of course, hyper-sensitive.

In consequence, after an opening week of relative quiet, the Munich Organizing Committee (OC) decided to relax their rules on entry into the Village. Henceforth, journalists (or purported journalists) could gain access virtually without question. A French journalist was shocked that he and his colleagues were now able to get in without even showing their press credentials. Apparently, even tourists had no trouble gaining access. The same French reporter encountered a Belgian visitor driving around the Village in his private automobile, though personal vehicles were supposedly banned from the Village. "You see how easy it is for anybody to get into the Village," the Frenchman reported just before the attack. A few days earlier, Richard Mandell had jogged into the Olympic Village through a back gate, posing as a Peruvian marathoner; under the new security dispensation, he probably would not even have had to deploy any fakery.

Some of the athletes were apparently also troubled by the security situation in the Village. A secret Israeli investigation conducted after the September 5 attack, the so-called Kopel Report, stated,

> The testimony of athletes . . . makes clear that [many] talked among themselves about the obvious lack of security in the village, particularly regarding their housing. The uncomfortable feeling intensified as the alacrity of the security ushers abated. [For the Israeli athletes,] the proximity of the Sudanese team's dorms and the ubiquity of Palestinian workers in the village intensified the general discomfort. Many of the athletes feared they would be attacked during their events. No one considered the possibility of a hostage situation, however. The fears festering in the minds of the athletes didn't result in a call to bolster security. They didn't act, they said, because they assumed that the security forces must be working undercover.

But if some athletes, especially Israelis, were worried about a possible lack of security in the Village, many other athletes were bothered by precisely the opposite phenomenon: too much hassling by Village guards when they tried to get back to their dorms after curfew or to smuggle friends and relatives into their quarters. It was such whining by the athletes, along with the above-mentioned complaints by journalists, which led to a relaxation of the rules. The Olys got the word that they should not be too "Prussian" when it came to the enforcement of the regulations, especially during the evening hours. "Nothing happens at night," explained a police inspector by way of justifying a cutback in nighttime patrols.

Black September

Early in the evening of September 4, 1972, eight Palestinian *fedayeen* ("self-sacrificers") sat around a restaurant table in Munich's Central Train Station, discussing in whispered Arabic the details of an operation planned for the wee hours of the coming morning. Six of the men, whom we might call the operation's "foot soldiers," had arrived in the city five days earlier. Three had flown from the Libyan capital of Tripoli to Rome and then on to Munich. The other three had come by train from Belgrade. All carried forged Jordanian passports with crudely faked West German entry visas. Their names were Afif Ahmed Hamid, Khalid Jawad, Ahmed Chic Thaa, Mohammed Safady, Adnan Al-Gashey, and Jamal Al-Gashey (Adnan's nephew). In addition to their youth—all were in their late teens or early twenties—they had in common miserable childhoods spent in the sprawling Palestinian refugee camps in Lebanon.

Upon arriving in Munich, the six young men were met by two slightly older Palestinians who had been in and out of Munich since mid-summer, using their visits to reconnoiter the Olympic facilities, especially the Village. One of these men, a twenty-seven-year-old Palestinian named Luttif Afif, had been assigned the role of "tactical commander" by the operation's planners. His background was not what you would expect in an Arab guerilla. His father was a wealthy Christian businessman, and his mother was Jewish. Born in Nazareth, Afif chose the name "Issa" (Arabic for "Jesus") as his nom de guerre. Issa had studied engineering in West Germany for several years and spoke fluent German. As a cover for his reconnoitering activity in Munich, he got himself hired on as a civil engineer for the Olympics. The operation's second in command, a twenty-five-year-old named Yasuf Nazzal (a.k.a. "Tony"), had also studied in West Germany and learned the language. And again like Issa, Tony had taken a job with the Olympics, in his case as a cook in the Village. (There were, in fact, many Palestinians employed in the Village and at other Olympic sites.) Neither Tony nor Issa had been required to undergo any significant security checks to obtain their positions.

After establishing their six foot soldiers in the Eden-Wolff Hotel near the train station, Issa and Tony took delivery of eight AK 47 automatic rifles (the weapon of choice for terrorists and guerillas the world over), hundreds of cartridges, and ten hand grenades, all of which had been concealed in the luggage of a well-dressed Arab couple flying into Cologne Airport from Libya on August 23. A customs inspector at the airport duly went through the first of the couple's two suitcases, which turned out to contain piles of women's underwear. Berated by the case's owner for pawing through her panties, the inspector waved through the second bag—the one filled with weapons.

With their weapons safely stored in a locker at the train station and all the foot soldiers in situ, Issa and Tony were ready, at that September 4 dinner meeting, to explain to the six young guerillas why they were in Munich and exactly what they were expected to do. Up until that point, the men knew only that they faced an important mission for the cause of Palestine. Now they learned that they were to assault the Israeli compound in the Olympic Village and to take as many Israeli Olympians hostage as they could. The prisoners were to be held captive in the Village pending agreement by the government of Prime Minister Golda Meir to release Palestinian "prisoners of war" being held in Israeli jails. The Munich operation was code-named Iqrit and Biri'm, in memory of two ancient Arab villages in northern Israel that had been violently cleared by the Israeli army in 1948 to make room for Jews.

The fedayeen all belonged to a shadowy organization calling itself Black September. This outfit derived its name from a September 1970 massacre of Palestinian refugees in Jordan by the army of King Hussein, who feared that embittered Palestinians connected to Yasser Arafat's Palestine Liberation Organization (PLO) were bent on overthrowing the king's autocratic regime and taking control in Jordan. A new wave of Palestinians had settled in Jordan after being expelled from the West Bank in the wake of the 1967 Arab-Israeli War. From the outset, they had little use for King Hussein, who, with Washington's backing, had staged a coup against his own parliament in 1957 and taken secret subsidies from the CIA ever since. In Jordan, the Palestinians around Arafat had increasingly acted as if they owned the place, humiliating Hussein at every opportunity. Following their expulsion from Jordan, surviving Palestinians fled to Syria and then on to Beirut, where they joined other refugees from their native region who had been squatting in Lebanon since 1948. From their new post in Lebanon, Arafat and his followers were determined to wreak revenge on Hussein for the September massacre and subsequent expulsion, and it was to this end that Black September was established in the fall of 1971. Arafat put one of his most faithful lieutenants, Mohammed Daoud Oudeh (a.k.a. Abu Daoud), in charge of building up the group. Daoud, who had commanded forces belonging to the militant Fatah wing of the PLO in Jordan, was careful to avoid any traceable links between the mother organization and this new commando group: Fatah should be able to take credit for success internally, but not bear any responsibility externally, for Black September's dirty work.

Given the later evolution of Arab terrorism, it is important to stress that Black September had nothing to do with Islamic fundamentalism and was originally not even directed against Israel—its mission, at least initially, was to strike against the hated Hussein. And that is exactly what it did on November 27, 1971, when Black September killers gunned down Wasfi Al-Tell, the Jordanian prime minister, in a Cairo hotel. The killers had been stalking their prey for several weeks. Immediately after the assassination, one of the gunmen bent down and lapped up some blood from a gushing wound in Al-Tell's chest. "I am proud we have finally done it," the assassin told Egyptian police. "We wanted to have him for breakfast, but we had him for lunch instead." (Tellingly, Egypt never put these killers on trial; a few months after the Al-Tell murder, President Anwar Sadat saw to it that they quietly left for Damascus.)

By late 1971, the Black September organization had come under the immediate command of a Fatah operative named Salah Khalaf (Abu Iyad), with Abu Daoud remaining in the background. Under Abu Iyad, the group continued its revenge campaign against Hussein with grenade attacks against Jordanian targets in Geneva and Paris. In December 1971, Black September operatives tried to assassinate Jordan's ambassador to Great Britain in a London street; the attack failed.

Although these actions did not seriously threaten King Hussein's hold on power, they showed that the PLO was eminently capable of making him pay for his "betrayal" of the Arab cause. Having gotten their pound of Jordanian flesh, Black September might have disappeared from the scene had it not been for increasing pressure on Arafat from radicals within Fatah to show greater militancy vis-à-vis Israel, the original bête-noir of the Palestinian Arabs. Rather than fading away, therefore, Black September expanded its hit list to include Israeli targets along with Jordanian ones.

In February 1972, Abu Iyad's commandos murdered five Jordanians suspected of spying for Israel; the venue of the hit was Cologne, the first time Black September had struck in West Germany. Shortly thereafter, Black September operatives blew up a factory in Hamburg that manufactured machinery for Israel. More spectacularly, in early May 1972, four Black September commandos, two men and two women, took over a Sabena airliner en route from Brussels to Tel Aviv, threatening to blow up the plane with its eighty-seven passengers unless some two hundred Palestinians were released from Israeli jails. When the Sabena plane landed in Tel Aviv, Israeli officials "negotiated" with the hijackers for ten hours while the Sayeret Matkal antiterrorist unit prepared a rescue operation. As soon as all was ready, Israeli commandos stormed the plane and in a manner of seconds shot the two male terrorists dead and subdued the two females. One passenger was fatally injured in the assault, but all the rest came out unscathed.

Senior Black September leaders concluded after this fiasco that they would have to strike again soon to show that they meant business. They were not insistent, however, upon acting alone, as they had in the past. In mid-May 1972, two top Black September figures, Abu Iyad and Fuad Al-Shamali, traveled to the Baddawi refugee camp in Lebanon to attend a kind of terrorist convention hosted by Dr. George Habash, a charismatic Greek Orthodox medical doctor who had founded the Marxist-oriented Popular Front for the Liberation of Palestine (PFLP) just after the 1967 war. Also in attendance were representatives of the Irish Republican Army (IRA), the Japanese Red Army (JRA), and the West German Baader-Meinhof terrorist group. The guerilla leaders agreed to pool resources and to "represent" each other in specialized operations.

The first rotten fruit of this terrorist fraternalism was an act of grisly mayhem carried out by the Japanese Red Army on behalf of their "Palestinian brothers." On May 30, 1972, three JRA operatives took a flight from Rome to Tel Aviv, carrying in their checked baggage an arsenal of submachine guns and grenades. After retrieving their suitcases at Lod Airport, they extracted their weapons and calmly opened fire on their fellow passengers. In the ensuing carnage, twenty-four people died and seventy-eight suffered injuries. Most of the victims were Puerto Rican Catholics on a pilgrimage to the Holy Land. In his murderous zeal, one of the commandos accidently gunned down a colleague; then, upon running out of ammunition, the killer detonated a grenade next to his head. The third killer, Okamoto Kozo, having also exhausted his ammo supply, ran outside to the tarmac, hoping to blow up an airplane. Fortunately, he was tackled and subdued by an El Al employee before he reached his target. Unable to commit suicide, Kozo became a prisoner of the Israelis. (It should be noted that the JRA, unlike the Palestinian militant groups of that day, regarded suicide attacks as absolutely legitimate methods of operation. Indeed, self-willed "honorable death" was for these Japanese militants an expression of a unique cultural heritage. They saw the Lod attack as an emulation of the suicide-bombing kamikaze missions of World War II.)

Although Black September personnel were not directly involved in the Lod Airport massacre, they celebrated the strike as if it had been their own. The PFLP saw the action as just revenge for the Deir Yassin massacre of April 9, 1948, when militant Zionists connected to the Irgun and Stern Gang had gunned down over one hundred Palestinians, many of them women and children. Not surprisingly, then, Okamoto Kozo, the surviving JRA terrorist, became an instant hero in the Palestinian refugee camps in Lebanon.

It was against this backdrop of escalating terror that the attack against the Israeli delegation at the Munich Games took form. Perhaps fittingly, the plot was born in the same locale—Rome—that six years earlier had provided the stage for the International Olympic Committee's (IOC) award of the 1972 Summer Games to Munich. This congruence of sites, however, was purely fortuitous. It so happened that in mid-July 1972 Abu Daoud, Abu Iyad, and another Black September senior figure named Fakhri Al-Umari were in Rome in order to meet with Italian neo-Fascist leaders whom they hoped to recruit for their "anti-Zionist" terror network. On July 13, the three Palestinians were sitting at a café in the Piazza della Rotonda when they happened to notice a newspaper article about the upcoming Munich Games. The article reported that the IOC had decided definitively to reject a bid from the PLO's Youth Federation to enter a Palestinian team in the '72 Games. Although the IOC archive contains no record of such a move by Lausanne, the committee traditionally rejected bids from groups without national backing—and, of course, Palestine was not a nation in the traditional sense. In any event, to the Palestinians, the rejection meant that the supposedly non-political IOC was just another front for European and American imperialism. As Abu Iyad declared later, the IOC had in effect declared that "we [the Palestinians] didn't exist, or worse, didn't deserve to exist."*

* This IOC view of the Palestinians was shared by Golda Meir. In 1969, she famously said, "It was not as though there were a Palestinian people in Palestine . . . and we came [along] and threw them out and took their country away. They did not exist."

The IOC's apparent "snub" of the Palestinians apparently gave Fakhri Al-Umari an idea. Why not send a "team" to Munich after all but make that team a group of commandos who would assault the Israeli quarters at the Olympic village, take some Jews hostage, and then trade them for the release of those hundreds of Palestinians still rotting in Israeli jails? Abu Iyad was initially skeptical about this audacious scheme—surely security around the Israeli Olympians would be extremely high—but he (and also Abu Daoud) warmed to the bold idea the more they discussed it over their coffee on that sunny afternoon in Rome.

Although the prospect of "payback" to the IOC may have kicked off discussion of a possible Munich operation, a much more important consideration had to do with publicity value: An attack on the Olympic Games would clearly attract *huge* attention to the Palestinian cause; after all, the entire world media would be present in Munich. The fact that the Games were transpiring in West Germany was an added bonus because, in the view of the PLO, Bonn, next to Washington, was the most hateful defender of Israel in the world. Since the early 1950s, West Germany had pursued a "special relationship" with Israel in hopes that extensive economic, technical, and diplomatic support for the new Jewish state would foster some form of "moral legitimacy" for the fledgling German democracy headquartered in Bonn. In more recent years, Chancellor Willy Brandt's government had made itself obnoxious to the PLO in yet another way—by working behind the scenes with the mainstream Arab states (especially Egypt) for a solution to the Palestinian problem that did not include the PLO as an equal bargaining partner or legitimate government-in-waiting. An action aimed at Israelis at the Munich Games would undoubtedly not only test the newly forged bond between Jews and Germans but also drive a wedge between Bonn and the moderate Arab states, which, like it or not, would be obliged to come down on the side of the PLO. The city of Munich, otherwise of interest to the Palestinian people mainly as a place where some of their young men could find occasional employment, suddenly loomed as a strategic milepost on the march to liberation from Jewish control.

"Something Serious Is Going On in Munich"

Having finalized their plan of operation at their dinner meeting at the Munich Central Train Station on the evening of September 4, the eight Palestinian fedayeen retired to their hotel for a few hours of fitful rest. At 3:30 a.m., they packed their weapons (giving each a fond kiss) into sports bags and donned athletic warm-up suits bearing the names of Arab countries.

After ascertaining that they carried nothing that might have revealed their true identity, they went down to the street and hailed two taxis to take them to the Olympic Village. They reached their destination, the perimeter fence encircling the compound, about a half-hour later.

The six younger fedayeen had been extensively prepped on Olympic security (such as it was) and the layout of the Village by their two leaders, who of course had thoroughly reconnoitered the entire area. Although they expected the perimeter security to be virtually non-existent and the Israeli compound to be unguarded, they realized that something could always go wrong and that they might have to lay down their lives in this action. Jamal Al-Gashey, one of the three guerillas to survive Operation Iqrit and Biri'm, later claimed that he and his colleagues were prepared to suffer "martyrdom" for the Palestinian cause, should this prove necessary.

At the Village perimeter, the eight Palestinians divided into two groups of four. The section of Village fence that Issa had preselected for penetration by one of the groups ran next to Gate 25A, which he knew to be locked but unguarded after the 10:00 p.m. curfew. During his "engineering" work in the Village, Issa had also noticed that athletes often chose this part of the perimeter fence to scale upon returning to their lodgings after hours.

Sure enough, just as the first commando group approached Gate 25A, they encountered some American sportsmen, obviously quite drunk, preparing to make a shaky assault on the fence. Reasoning that these inebriated Americans would make excellent cover for his own crew's entry, Issa proposed that the men help each other over the barrier. The Americans, blearily eying the six-foot fence, were only too happy to oblige. Meanwhile, the second commando group chose another gate farther along the fence for their entry. It, too, was unguarded—and, to make matters easier, right next to it stood a stool, obviously left behind by one of the guards. Making use of this convenient prop, the Palestinians quickly climbed over the fence.

Once inside the Village, the fedayeen, still divided into two groups of four, set out separately for the Israeli quarters. Some postal workers saw one of the groups hurrying across the grounds and reported the sighting to security, but the police, assuming the men to be athletes, took no action. After a few minutes' walk, both groups of terrorists reached the row of buildings that included the Israeli lodgings at its far end. They paused briefly to don ski masks and to extract their weapons from their sports bags. Issa exchanged his track suit for a white linen safari outfit, which he topped off with an oversized white hat resembling a pith helmet. Eschewing a balaclava, he disguised his facial features with black shoe polish and large sun glasses. (This getup, which was soon to become familiar to millions of TV viewers, was certainly ridiculous, but in the end its effect was less comical than deeply sinister.) The men then proceeded on to Connollystrasse 31, a twenty-four-unit dormitory complex named for the great American Olympian Harold Connolly. The Israeli delegation occupied five of the two-story apartments; teams from Uruguay and Hong Kong lived in the other units. As Issa had expected, there was not a guard in sight.

Upon reaching their destination, the fedayeen passed through an unlocked outer door at street level and entered a foyer from which a number of apartments could be accessed. The men went immediately to Apartment 1, which housed seven Israeli coaches and referees. (On August 28, Issa, along with "Tony" and Abu Daoud, had been able to canvass this part of the compound by posing as Brazilian athletes keen to learn more about Jews in preparation for a visit to the Holy Land. Thus Issa knew that Apartment 1 had convenient exits and commanded access to the upper floors and the basement parking garage; it would serve as an ideal command post and gathering point for hostages.)

The door to Apartment 1 was locked, but the intruders carried a crudely made copy of the appropriate key, with which they managed to turn the lock, albeit only after repeated tries and with considerable noise. The commotion awakened a lightly sleeping wrestling coach named Yossef Gutfreund, who, immediately suspicious, rushed to the entrance. Seeing an armed masked man easing open the door, the 285-pound Gutfreund threw his bulk against the structure, yelling simultaneously, "Run guys, run!"

Gutfreund was able to buy enough time with his holding action for one of the residents of Apartment 1, weight-trainer Tuvia Skolsky, to jump out of bed and run to a back window. After a few seconds, the intruders, using a rifle butt as a crowbar, managed to push their way into the apartment. Seeing Skolsky leaping through the back window, they fired a few shots at him but failed to stop him. He was the only resident of Apartment 1 to escape.

Alerted by Gutfreund's cries and the sounds of gunfire, the other Israelis in the apartment arose to find themselves facing eight masked gunmen. Before they could flee or do anything to defend themselves, they were herded into the unit's living room. In addition to Gutfreund, the hostages included a forty-year-old track coach and father of four named Amitzur Shapira; marksman coach Kehat Shorr, aged fifty-three; Andrei Spitzer, a newly married fencing coach with a one-month-old daughter; a fifty-year-old veteran weightlifting referee named Yaakov Springer; and thirty-three-year-old wrestling coach Moshe Weinberg, father of a newborn son.

As the terrorists began to bind their captives with lengths of pre-cut rope they had brought with them, one of the hostages, Weinberg, took a flying leap at Issa, knocking him down. But before Weinberg could grab Issa's rifle, another terrorist shot him through the cheek, wounding him severely.

Leaving four of the Israeli hostages bound and under guard, "Tony," the operation's second in command, forced a profusely bleeding Weinberg to lead him and four other terrorists on a search for more hostages. No doubt aware that he could not simply lead his captors on a wild goose chase, Weinberg chose to take them to Apartment 3, which was home to the Israeli weightlifters and wrestlers: if anybody could give the terrorists a good fight, Weinberg must have reasoned, it was these guys.

Oddly, the denizens of Apartment 3 had slept through all the commotion over in Apartment 1. (Actually, perhaps not quite so oddly. They had gotten to bed very late after attending an evening performance of *Fiddler on the Roof* in town, then having a few drinks while talking over the exhilarating peculiarity of their situation: Jews back again in a German-guarded "camp," but this time free to come and go as they pleased. Thus, the Israeli athletes were caught totally by surprise when Tony and his men burst through their front door.) The five fedayeen were able in short order to add six more hostages to their haul. The new captives were Eliezer Halfin, a Soviet-born lightweight wrestler; Mark Slavin, another Soviet-born wrestler who at age 18 was the youngest member of the Israeli team; Yossef Romano, a thirty-two-year-old Libyan-born weightlifter and the father of three young girls; Ze'ev Friedman, a twenty-eight-year-old weightlifter of Polish extraction; Gad Tsabari, a diminutive but very tough light flyweight wrestler; and David Berger, a Cleveland-born dual citizen weightlifter with a law degree from Columbia who had emigrated from America to Israel in 1970 in order to pursue his dream of competing in the Olympics.

Prodding their captives with their weapons, the terrorists promptly marched the six Israeli athletes back in the direction of Apartment 1. In the foyer outside that apartment, little Gad Tsabari suddenly slapped aside the rifle held by the guard closest to him and deftly sprinted down a stairway leading to the underground parking garage. As they had with the fleeing Skolsky, the Palestinians tried to gun Tsabari down, but the wrestler, dodging between concrete pillars in the garage, managed to elude the fire. Alas, he was the only one among the twelve Israeli Olympians originally captured by Black September to escape and survive.

The distraction caused by Tsabari's flight prompted Moshe Weinberg, still bleeding from his wound, to attempt a second assault on his captors.

But as he leapt for the gun held by one of the terrorists, another fedayeen opened fire, this time tearing open his chest and killing him instantly. Leaving Weinberg's corpse in the corridor, the fedayeen shoved the other five hostages into Apartment 1.

Meanwhile, a Village cleaning lady, alerted by the gunfire, put in an alarm call to the Olympic security office. Officials there sent a blue-shirted Oly, armed solely with a walkie-talkie, to check out the situation at Connollystrasse 31. He arrived at 4:50 a.m. to find a masked gunman guarding the street door. "What is the meaning of this?" the Oly asked. Getting no response, he radioed headquarters with a description of the scene and promptly left.

No sooner had the Oly departed than another hostage, wrestler Yossef Romano, took matters into his own hands. Although he was on crutches because of torn knee ligaments, Romano emulated Weinberg in making a grab for one of the terrorists' guns. He managed to knock a fedayeen flat on his back but, like Weinberg, was unable to secure the man's weapon before another terrorist shot him dead. Issa ordered that Romano's body be left as it was, slowly leaking blood in the middle of the room, as a grisly admonition to the remaining nine hostages.

The Palestinians' hostage haul might have been considerably larger had not the sound of their gunfire prompted Israelis in other parts of the complex to scamper for safety through back windows and other exits. Among the first to get out was Dr. Shaul Ladany, a Belgrade-born race-walker and engineering professor at Ben-Gurion University who as an eight-year-old child had spent six harrowing months in the Bergen-Belsen concentration camp. Calling instinctively on the residual wariness that came with this background, Ladany bolted from his bed and sprang through a window at the first sound of shots. Running in his underwear to a nearby dorm complex, he knocked on the first apartment door he saw. As chance would have it, the apartment belonged to Bill Bowerman, the U.S. track coach who until that fateful morning had undoubtedly been the Munich organizers' principal pain in the ass. No more.

Bowerman groggily opened the door to find a terrified and half-naked Ladany, demanding to be let in. "What for?" demanded Bowerman, ever the diplomat. "The Arabs are in our building," reported Ladany. "Well, throw the bastards out," barked the American. "They've shot some of our people. I got out through a window," explained Ladany. "Oh, that does change things," conceded Bowerman, and pulled the Israeli into the apartment.

Bowerman then put a call through to the U.S. Consulate in Munich. Explaining that there was "a problem in the Olympic Village," he asked for some extra security for the American complex. "What for?" asked the consul, who, of course, had been pulled out of bed to take the call. Bowerman replied, "Across the street from us, armed Arabs have moved into the Israeli quarters and we've got Jewish kids in our building, one the swimmer Mark Spitz and another the javelin-thrower Bill Schmidt." "You've got it!" exclaimed the consul instantly. Thirty minutes later, two U.S. Marines stationed themselves at the entrance to the Americans' building. It was the only dormitory in the entire Village to receive any special protection.

Not long thereafter, Bowerman got an irate call from an official of the IOC, who had been alerted by Walther Tröger about the coach's action. "You've done it again, Bowerman," said the caller, "bringing Marines [into the Village], a gross violation of security." The IOC official demanded that Bowerman report to the committee that very morning to explain himself.

The American coach did just that a couple hours later. Accompanied by Jesse Owens, whose presence he knew would impress the IOC bureaucrats, Bowerman described Ladany's panicked arrival at the U.S. building, adding, "If it's trouble to secure a building where people might be killed, then I guess I'm in trouble."

At roughly the same time that Bowerman was calling in extra security for the Americans, Olympic officials were finally springing into action themselves. A security officer based at the Olympic administration building near the Village called Munich police chief Manfred Schreiber at home, telling him about the scene at Connollystrasse 31. Schreiber immediately ordered all available guards at the Olympic complex to cordon off the Israeli compound and to lock down the Village. Before racing off for the Oberwiesenfeld, he also placed a called to Bavarian interior minister Bruno Merk, the chief of law enforcement in that state. Merk in turn telephoned his federal counterpart, Hans-Dietrich Genscher, who for the duration of the Games was staying with his wife at Munich's Intercontinental Hotel. Genscher said later that the news "hit me like a blow," for it "meant Jews in Germany were again in danger." The rattled minister immediately threw on some clothes, awakened his driver, and sped to the Olympic administration building, arriving there just before Schreiber. They were joined shortly thereafter by Tröger, Willi Daume, and Avery Brundage (the latter extremely irritated to have been pulled out of his comfortable bed at the Hotel Vier Jahreszeiten).

Sensing the gravity of the situation, Genscher put in calls to Chancellor Willy Brandt and Foreign Minister Walter Scheel in Bonn. Scheel contacted Eliashiv Ben-Horin, Israel's ambassador to West Germany, who in turn immediately got on the line with Golda Meir.

Although the movers and shakers of Munich '72 were obviously horri-fied by the apparent hostile takeover of the Israeli compound, and deeply worried about what might transpire next, they were equally concerned to prevent knowledge about this startling development from reaching the outside world until the crisis could be contained. After locking down the Village, Manfred Schreiber's next move was to order an "absolute black-out" on information from the scene; no reporters or TV crews would be allowed access to the Village, nor would the Olympic Press Center have anything to say on the matter, at least for the time being.

The ban on regular news dissemination from the Village succeeded only in generating a host of confusing and inaccurate reports in the early hours of the crisis—a problem that would persist throughout the entire ordeal. Of course, there was no preventing *some* coverage of what was going on—or thought to be going on; a small army of journalists rushed to the Village as soon as a stringer for West German Radio (WDR) alerted his col-leagues at 6:00 a.m. that "an Arab" had apparently broken into the Israeli compound and perhaps killed an athlete. "Something serious seems to be going on in Munich," reported WDR in a news flash.

This comment at least was accurate. Other bulletins emanating from Munich a little later spoke of sixteen or perhaps seventeen hostages. Re-ports on the number of intruders ranged from one or two to twenty-five. But it wasn't just the journalists who were in the dark. None of the officials assembled at the Olympic administration building had any clear idea of who the attackers were, much less how many of them were involved or how many hostages they might have taken. In fact, vital details about the Black September operation that day would elude the relevant officials until the terrible drama was almost over.

Negotiations

At 5:10 a.m., a Munich police officer cautiously approached Connollys-trasse 31 holding his arms out from his sides to show that he carried no weapons. He had been sent to the Israeli compound by Manfred Schreiber to find out just what in hell was going on there. When the police officer reached the building, a masked figure at a second floor window threw out two pieces of paper, which drifted to the street. Picking them up, the cop hurried back to Schreiber.

The papers, containing a typewritten message and a long list of names, clarified at least who the intruders were and what they wanted. Revealing themselves as "Black September," the men who had seized Connollystrasse

31 demanded the release of 236 "political prisoners," whose names were listed on one of the papers. Most of those on the list were Palestinians held in Israeli jails, among them the two women involved in the recent Sabena Airlines hijacking. Another Israeli-held prisoner on the list was Okamoto Kozo, the Japanese Red Army operative captured after the Lod Airport massacre.* Black September also demanded the release of Andreas Baader and Ulrike Meinhof, who were currently being held in a maximum-security prison near Stuttgart. If all these prisoners were not released by 9:00 a.m. on that very day into the custody of a friendly Arab country, warned the Black Septembrists, they would start killing off their hostages—one for every hour their demands were not met. The message did not state how many hostages were involved, nor did it say anything about the killings of Weinberg and Romano. Any effort by the Germans to "interfere" with the operation, added the communiqué ominously, would lead to "the liquidation of all the Israeli prisoners, with the Federal Republic being held responsible."

Schreiber and the other top German officials assembled in the administration building next to the Village were staggered by the Black September ultimatum. Having become confident that their Games would proceed tranquilly despite earlier warnings of possible trouble, they were caught completely off guard by this brazen violation of the "Olympic truce." They simply could not believe that this was happening to *them*, and to *their* Games. Their primary concern was to clean up this mess as quickly as possible so as to avoid any significant embarrassment to, or disruption of, the Munich Games. But they were uncertain about how to proceed. The only thing they knew for sure was that they had to persuade these Black September people to put off their 9:00 a.m. deadline for the release and transfer of the Israeli-held prisoners. The Israeli government would obviously have to agree to the prisoner release and then arrange a turnover to Arab control—momentous matters that could hardly be taken care of within a couple hours. The immediate necessity, then, was to buy some time—time to talk with the Israelis and time to plan further moves should Golda Meir's government prove unwilling to bargain, which the Germans feared would be the case.

Before attempting to deal with the "terrorists" (as the Black September attackers were now being called), the Germans put together an informal Krisenstab (crisis team) to manage the situation on the ground. Because

* Kozo would be released from Israeli custody in May 1985 as part of a prisoner exchange between Israel and the PFLP.

West Germany's constitution accorded the individual states primary jurisdiction in all matters of domestic security, Bavarian officials would assume control over management of the present crisis, just as they had over security planning for the Games. Given his central role in establishing Munich '72's security setup, Manfred Schreiber was the natural choice to head the Krisenstab. Other team members included Merk, Genscher, and Tröger. Knowing that Israel's cooperation would be necessary in any prisoner-hostage swap deal—and mindful of the extreme political sensitivity of this particular crisis—the Germans decided to bring Ambassador Ben-Horin into their loop. Flown in immediately from Bonn on a Bundeswehr jet, Ben-Horin was given his own room in the Olympic administration building from which he could stay abreast of the situation and maintain contact with his government. As Genscher—defensively and not entirely accurately—explained later, "Aware as we were that Israel had considerably more experience in situations like this than we did, we undertook nothing without informing him [Ben-Horin] and soliciting his advice."

Ben-Horin was not yet present in Munich when, at 5:25 a.m., Schreiber sent another police officer to Connollystrasse 31. His purpose was to make contact with the intruders and find out as much as he could about their intentions. The officer was met at the outer door by Issa, decked out in his soon-to-be-familiar safari suit and oversized white hat. A masked figure poked a gun out one of the second-story windows and trained it on the cop. Issa said nothing to the policeman to amplify Black September's written ultimatum or to explain its rude crashing of Munich's Olympic party. Rather, he did something considerably more dramatic to underscore the seriousness of this business: he signaled over his shoulder to have Moshe Weinberg's bloody corpse dragged out the door and dumped onto the sidewalk at the policeman's feet.

The Munich policeman was not the only witness to this new horror. Looking out the window of Apartment 5, a few yards up the street from Apartment 1, Shmuel Lalkin, chief of Israel's delegation to the '72 Games, observed Weinberg's body being shoved onto the pavement. Lalkin had earlier been awakened by the sound of gunfire but had not understood its import. Now he did. He immediately ran downstairs to a telephone, the only one in the entire Israeli compound. He called the Sheraton Hotel in downtown Munich, where Israeli journalists and other members of the country's Olympic delegation were staying. "Call Israel," he barked, "Arab terrorists have taken part of our delegation hostage."

Meanwhile, the Munich policeman had reported back to Schreiber's crisis team on the grisly scene he had witnessed at Connollystrasse 31.

News that at least one Israeli hostage had already been murdered further alarmed the Germans, without enlightening them on the extent of the terror operation or the possibility of negotiating their way to a solution.

Schreiber therefore sent a new emissary to the terrorists in the person of Annaliese Graes, a forty-two-year-old policewoman from the gritty Ruhr Valley town of Essen, who had signed on as an Oly to see the Games. Now Graes bravely volunteered to go alone and unarmed to the Israeli compound with the goal of parlaying with the Palestinians and possibly arranging a meeting between them and top German officials. That Schreiber selected a woman for this delicate mission might seem odd, given that Arab culture was not exactly renowned for its acceptance of women in prominent roles, but Graes possessed a mature, calming manner that might, Schreiber hoped, remind the terrorists of their mothers and thereby put them at their ease.

As it happened, though, not even Graes was able to get much information out of Issa. Confronting the head commando at the outer door, she asked, in her down-to-earth Ruhr District fashion, "What kind of rubbish is this?" Startled, Issa mumbled, "This has nothing to do with you, or with Germany." Deciding to wing it, Graes pointed out that the Munich officials and even Bonn had no authority to authorize a release of the Israeli-held prisoners, so why not put forth some conditions that the Germans *could* act upon? To this, Issa said simply, "Free all those prisoners, or the hostages will die." On the other hand, before disappearing back inside the building, Issa at least agreed to a meeting with Graes's superiors.

Shortly thereafter, a three-person delegation gingerly approached the Israeli compound. Led by Schreiber, the group also included Tröger and A. D. Touny, an Egyptian member of the IOC whom Schreiber had recruited to deal with the Palestinians, Arab to Arab. However, if the Germans hoped via Touny to be able to work out an amicable deal with the terrorists, they were quickly disabused of that illusion. Arriving at Connollystrasse 31, they discovered two gunmen at the upstairs windows pointing their AK 47s *directly at them*. Issa appeared at the threshold with his hands behind his back, his safari jacket pockets bulging with hand grenades. The Germans politely asked what they might do to resolve the situation, but Issa contented himself with repeating his organization's original demands and terms, like a mantra. At one point, Tröger, showing considerable tone deafness, offered Issa "an unlimited sum of money" and safe passage out of Germany if he and his men would immediately release the hostages. Shaking his head in disgust, Issa grumbled, "This is not about money."

His financial offer rejected, Schreiber briefly considered grabbing Issa and holding him as a counter-hostage, but he must have entertained this notion too demonstrably, for Issa suddenly brought his hands in front of him to reveal that he was holding another grenade, with his finger on the pin. "If you lay a hand on me," he growled, "I'll blow us both up." In the end, the only concession Schreiber's group got from Issa was an agreement to extend the deadline on hostage execution until noon.

While Schreiber's crisis team was struggling in vain to deal with the Palestinian commandos in the Olympic Village, the federal government in Bonn was busy working the telephone lines with the Israeli government, hoping to work out some kind of arrangement. The Olympic crisis came at a very delicate moment for Chancellor Willy Brandt, who faced an election in early November that would determine whether he remained in office. Brandt feared that, if the Munich hostage crisis were mismanaged in any way, even if he were not personally to blame, his chances for reelection would be severely jeopardized. (Oh, how the Christian Democratic Union [CDU] opposition would feast on a well-publicized line from Genscher: "Out of the [Olympic] Stadium and into the election campaign!") Oddly enough for a politician, however, Brandt's own political fate did not seem uppermost in his mind at this particular moment. Like Genscher, he was supremely aware of the special horror of the Munich situation—one in which Jews once again faced political murder on German soil. The fact that German citizens were not the culprits this time offered little comfort for Brandt, since that reality only underscored the limits of his own power to resolve the matter peacefully. Knowing that only Israel could engineer a rapid and non-violent end to this crisis, Brandt ordered Bonn's Foreign Ministry to try to find out how Prime Minister Meir's government intended to respond to the Black September ultimatum. Although no one in Brandt's circle would say so publicly, they all fervently hoped that the Israelis would cave in. That would not only avert further loss of life but also ensure that the Munich Games could continue without any embarrassing interruptions.

Israel's response, however, turned out to be just what the Germans feared: a resolute "no" to any release of prisoners. Golda Meir, who had learned of the hostage crisis via a 5:30 a.m. phone call from Ambassador Ben-Horin, offered this negative response even before her cabinet confirmed it some three hours later. Explaining her position at an emergency meeting, she said, "If we should give in, then no Israeli anywhere in the world can feel that his life is safe." After the emergency cabinet meeting, she called Ben-Horin and instructed him to present the following operating principles to the Germans: (1) Israel would not bargain with the terrorists; (2) West Germany was responsible for the safety of the Israeli hostages and must use whatever means necessary to secure their release; and (3) Israel would countenance a promise of freedom to the terrorists only if that brought the immediate release of the hostages.

The Israeli government also had a message for the IOC: for God's sake, halt the Olympic competitions until the hostage crisis could be resolved! But Avery Brundage was not about to let this contretemps in the Village disrupt the progress of the Games. In the entire history of the modern Olympics, he noted, play had never been interrupted once the show had gotten under way. Thus, competition resumed as scheduled that very morning with a volleyball match between West Germany and Japan. Thirty-five hundred fans cheered wildly for the home team as if the outcome of this game were the most important thing in the world.

The scene in the Village itself was even more surreal. Athletes did exercises, played ping-pong, canoodled on benches, and sunned themselves on the grass—all within spitting distance of the building where fellow Olympians were being held hostage at gunpoint. Many athletes reported later that in the opening phase of the hostage crisis they had only the vaguest notion of what was going on in the Israeli compound. "Somebody's broken in with the Jews" was the word on the Village Street.

The Munich Games' most famous Jew, Mark Spitz, remained unaware of the hostage situation until well into the crisis. He learned about the terror attack during a mid-morning press conference at the Olympic Press Center— a conference that he assumed was going to be about *him*. When he heard about what was happening to the Israeli Olympians, Spitz immediately felt very vulnerable. The United States Olympic Committee (USOC) also considered him a possible terrorist target and therefore assigned him a U.S. Marine bodyguard of his own. Such precautions were not enough for the German organizers. The last thing they wanted was for another Jewish athlete—and the world's most prominent one at that—to come to grief on their watch. They thus put him on an airplane for London that very afternoon.

In hindsight, one might argue that the special care for Spitz was probably not necessary, since American Jews were of little interest to Black September. But at the time of the attack, no one knew whether or not other terrorists might be lurking around Munich, waiting to pounce. Certainly the Americans considered themselves likely targets. And in any event, the easy-going insouciance that had defined the mood in Munich up until the assault on the Village now gave way to extreme caution, at least on the part of the organizers.

As for the rest of the athletes in the Village, when word came through that Israeli Olympians were being held for ransom by Arabs who would give them up only in exchange for prisoners held by Israel, at least one of the sportsmen registered more concern about the fate of the Games than about that of the captured Israelis. "Golda Meir, holding the fucking world to ransom once again," grunted an Irish athlete. A weightlifter from New Zealand who had taken a Polaroid snapshot of an Arab guerilla on the balcony of the Israeli compound made the rounds among his colleagues trying to sell the photo. However, the vast majority of the athletes seem to have been gripped by genuine horror as the true gravity of the situation—and news of Weinberg's murder—gradually filtered through the Village.

Certainly this was true of the U.S. squad. Having been awakened by Shmuel Lalkin's arrival at their building, a number of American track athletes—Kenny Moore, Frank Shorter, Mike Manley, Jon Anderson, Steve Savage, and Dave Wottle—kept an anxious lookout on the Israeli compound from the vantage point of their third-floor balcony. "Imagine how it must be for them," mused Shorter. "Some maniac with a machine gun saying, 'Let's kill them now,' and another one saying, 'No, let's wait a while.' How long could you stand that?"

West Germany's Ulrike Meyfarth, for her part, was so devastated by the crisis that she could take no pleasure in all the congratulatory telegrams pouring into her room at the Village. Numb with despair, she was fully content to abide by a directive from her coaches to make no public comment about the terrible crisis unfolding at the Israeli compound.

At 10:45 a.m., Police Chief Schreiber suddenly called journalists to the Olympic Press Center in order to read to them a prepared statement on the evolving hostage crisis. His statement, which turned out to be a tour de force of misinformation, set the standard for further official communications on this topic down the line. According to Schreiber's communiqué, one Israeli hostage had been killed and between nine and sixteen hostages were still being held, one of whom was known to have been wounded. The *Egyptian* terrorists numbered as few as six, or as many as twenty-one. (Why Schreiber identified the terrorists as Egyptians, when he must have known that they were Palestinians, is anyone's guess.) Pressed by the journalists for further details on the situation, Schreiber simply left the room.

Many journalists tried to secure better information on the crisis by sneaking into the Village. Among them was Richard Mandell. He failed in this effort, since all the gates were now not only locked but also heavily guarded by armed police—a classic case of closing the barn door after the horse had run out or, in this case, run in. In addition to the guards around the Village fence, tanks and armored personnel carriers took up positions down the street from the Israeli compound. Meanwhile, a massive crowd had assembled just outside the Village, armed with portable radios, cameras, telescopes, picnic lunches, and collapsible chairs. Some older men among the gawkers, Mandell imagined, might well have been former "Jew-killers" themselves. One thing was certain: "Politics and terror [had] become spectator sports."

Indeed they had, and not just for the spectators at the Village fence. One of the more bizarre dimensions of the hostage crisis was that it was being broadcast live on television around the world—giving the Munich incident the dubious distinction of being history's first globally televised act of terrorism. At 1:00 p.m., ABC Television, which for hefty fees was covering the Games for many other foreign networks, began what turned out to be non-stop coverage of the Munich tragedy from a studio just one hundred yards from Connollystrasse 31. Anchoring the coverage was Jim McKay, who had been scheduled to have that day off. To film the scene, ABC had use of only one camera mounted atop a knoll outside the studio. The network also had access to two reporters who had managed to sneak inside the Village and establish shaky communications links. One of these was Canadian-born ace reporter Peter Jennings, who had been lured to Munich from his usual Middle East beat with the promise of a nice vacation-like assignment. Now, holed up on the sixth floor of the Italian team headquarters, some fifty yards from Connollystrasse 31, Jennings found himself, as McKay later put it, "closer to danger than he would have been in Lebanon."

From his post inside the studio, McKay could see on his monitors that the competitions were still being held in the early afternoon despite the menacing standoff in the Village. The broadcaster was appalled that Olympic athletes were calmly going on with their play while in the immediate vicinity fellow Olympians huddled together under terrorists' guns, their lives hanging by a thread.

Meanwhile, as the terrorists' latest deadline of 3:00 p.m. loomed, the crisis team decided to send yet another delegation to Connollystrasse 31, this one truly heavyweight, in hopes of working out a deal, or at the very least securing a new deadline extension. Federal interior minister Genscher himself, accompanied by Merk and Schreiber, undertook this new mission to Issa. Genscher did most of the talking for the Germans. He appealed to Issa, who as usual fondled a grenade with one hand while chain-smoking with the other, to back away from his terrible threats. Killing innocent people could only harm the Palestinian cause, Genscher said. Issa scoffed at this quaint piety. "I am a soldier," he responded. "I have my orders, and I will follow them." Switching gears, Genscher asked if Issa had any idea of how painful this situation was for *the Germans*—if he realized what it meant for them to have "Jews facing danger once again on German soil?" Getting no response, and, as he wrote later, feeling "the full weight of our entire history vis-à-vis the Jews" on his shoulders, Genscher now offered *himself* as a hostage to take the place of the Israelis. The self-important federal interior minister undoubtedly considered this noble gesture to be a potentially game-saving move, but in fact it was vainglorious and silly: How could having a *German* official like Genscher in their clutches help the fedayeen achieve their principal goal? Unsurprisingly, Issa replied that he had no use for German hostages, only Israelis. (Nonetheless, not to be outdone by their colleague, Tröger and Vogel later called Issa on the phone with offers similar to Genscher's and got the same predictably negative results. Even Willy Brandt's son Peter tried to stand in for the Jews.)

If the on-the-ground efforts by Genscher and company to negotiate a solution to the crisis proved fruitless, so too did ongoing efforts by Chancellor Brandt to resolve the imbroglio on the diplomatic level. The chancellor's personal role in this evolving crisis proved rather less central than what one might have expected from such an activist leader. Although in the early afternoon Brandt flew from Bonn to Munich in order to monitor the situation more closely, he did not take charge of the crisis team at the Olympic center. He gave no commands about how this grave matter should be handled. His reticence undoubtedly derived from a respect for Bavaria's sovereign prerogatives in security affairs on its own territory. And yet, this was clearly a crisis affecting the entire nation, one that cried out for firm and resolute leadership from the very top. Brandt simply did not provide that leadership. Instead, he asked his chief of staff, Horst Ehmke, to coordinate hour-to-hour crisis management in Bonn, while ordering Foreign Office officials to contact Arab governments to see what they might do to secure a release of the hostages. During the afternoon of September 5, Brandt also directed a personal appeal to the leaders of the Arab states, admonishing them that "the whole world expects you to bring your influence to bear immediately [in this crisis]." But with no significant arm-twisting from Brandt, the Arab governments made only half-hearted efforts to mediate.

Brandt seems also to have failed to grasp a helping hand from another source: Israel. By the late afternoon of September 5, Israeli security experts had concluded that the situation for the hostages in the Village was becoming increasingly precarious and that it would be necessary to free them by force, the sooner the better. Israeli authorities were not sure if West Germany had a special counterterrorism unit of its own that might be deployed in this instance (it did not), but in any event they reasoned that the Germans could use some help from Israel's famed Sayeret Matkal, an elite outfit founded in the 1960s that was specially trained to intervene in hostage-rescue situations. It was, in fact, Sayeret Matkal, commanded by future Israeli prime minister Ehud Barak, that had freed the Sabena Airlines hostages from the clutches of Black September a few months earlier. At 5:00 p.m. Israeli time, Golda Meir put this unit on alert for an order to fly to Munich. That order never came. The reason, claimed the Israelis, is that Willy Brandt politely but firmly rejected Meir's offer to send the team. The Germans could handle the matter themselves, Brandt reportedly said.

Not so, insisted Hans-Dietrich Genscher in his memoirs. (Brandt himself never denied nor confirmed Israel's claim.) Genscher claimed that he personally discussed the hostage crisis with two top Israeli security experts, Mossad chief Zvi Zamir and Victor Cohen, a member of Sayeret Matkal, who had flown from Tel Aviv to Munich in mid-afternoon. Zamir allegedly replied in the negative when Genscher asked him if Israel wished to deploy "its own forces" in a hostage-rescue operation. Moreover, added Genscher, the two Israelis offered no criticism whatsoever of the way the Germans were handling the hostage crisis.

Lacking documentary evidence of an Israeli commando offer or a German rejection of said offer, it is impossible to know which version of this story is true. But it seems quite plausible that the Israelis would have offered assistance and that the Germans would have been reluctant to take it. For the Israelis, this was a life and death matter, one calling for the kind of quick-action rescue measures they knew how to deploy. For the Germans, accepting outside aid would have been tantamount to admitting that they were incapable of handling the situation themselves. That the aid in question would have come from *Israel*, of all places, would only have added to the sense of humiliation. Moreover, any such intervention would have had to be cleared with the Bavarians, who were extremely prickly in matters of state sovereignty in general and control over the Munich Games in particular. (Brandt was well aware that the politically conservative Bavarian government was anxious to keep his own role in the Games to a bare minimum, so that the chancellor and his Social Democratic Party could not extract political profit from Munich '72.) Unwilling as ever to step on Bavarian toes, Brandt did not even seek to deploy the resources of the Bundeskriminalamt (Federal Criminal Office) or the Bundesgrenzschutz (Federal Border Guard) to deal with the hostage crisis.

Operation Sunshine

West German lack of experience in counterterrorism operations was painfully evident in the various attempts by Bavarian authorities to resolve the crisis in the Village by means other than negotiation. On one occasion, Schreiber's team dressed up two armed policemen as cooks in the hope that they might gain access to the Israeli compound under the pretext of delivering several cartons of food. But Issa immediately saw through this ruse and carried the cartons into the complex himself. He also ordered his own men not to eat any of the food, fearing it might be doctored in some way.

The Bavarians also tried briefly to follow up on a suggestion by Avery Brundage to neutralize the terrorists by pumping a "knockout gas" into the compound, a tactic used by the Chicago police in the 1920s to overpower gangsters. Brundage claimed that the Windy City authorities were experts in this tactic and could be counted upon to ship over quantities of their miracle weapon immediately. But Bavarian officials had no luck locating any such knockout agent in Chicago—Brundage, in his zeal to end the standoff quickly, seems to have led the Germans astray. In any event, the deployment of gas by German authorities, even in a noble cause, might not have been the keenest idea.

The Germans' most pathetic and wrong-footed attempt to penetrate Connollystrasse 31 and rescue the hostages by armed force came in the late afternoon, when fears were mounting that the terrorists, possibly running out of patience, might start shooting their captives. Examining the blueprints of the complex for ways to enter it by surprise, Bavarian security officials concluded that air-conditioning ducts with openings on the roof afforded the best possibility. Thirteen Munich policemen were recruited for this operation, code-named "Sunshine." The only qualification for appointment to this "Special Search Group" was experience in having fired a gun at one time or another. Group members were given plans to the duct system but would have to go in with no knowledge of exactly where the hostages were located—nor, of course, did they know how many terrorists might be involved. Although fearing that their mission could be "suicidal," the volunteers donned track suits covered by bulky bullet-proof vests and clamored atop the roof of Connollystrasse 31. After removing the mesh coverings on the duct openings, they listened on their radio for the code word "Sunshine," their signal to drop down into the building.

The order never came—and for good reason. The whole operation was being broadcast live from a TV camera mounted atop the East German team headquarters across the street. Along with millions of global TV viewers, Issa and his crew followed the assault preparations on a television set of their own. They were, to put it mildly, dumbfounded. Issa, a red streak of rage showing through his black-face, rushed out the door screaming at nearby officials that if the cops were not immediately withdrawn from the roof he personally would start executing the hostages. To the huge relief of the would-be rescuers, Operation Sunshine was abandoned.

All the while that Bavaria's finest were floundering in their various efforts to free the hostages, members of the West German public were helpfully offering advice about procedures and, in some instances, proposing to take over the job themselves. A World War II veteran volunteered to take the Israeli compound single-handedly in a surprise attack; another fellow offered to wade in with some of his buddies and bring out the Jews; and yet another citizen promised to "overwhelm" the fedayeen with one hundred thousand peace demonstrators.

Apart from the Israeli hostages and their relatives back home, no one was more anxious to see how the West German authorities handled this crisis than those East Germans inhabiting the complex across the street from the Israeli compound. Naturally, East German secret police personnel were embedded with the German Democratic Republic (GDR) delegation, and those "Stasi" agents, their professional interest thoroughly piqued, kept a blow-by-blow chronicle of what transpired during the standoff in the Village. They were not at all impressed by the prowess of their Munich colleagues. The Bavarian security forces, they reported back to East Berlin, "appear more hysterical than in control." (Left unsaid in the Stasi report was the assumption that, if the *East* Germans had been in charge of this operation, the whole thing would have been handled in a rather more orderly fashion.)

The East German critique of West Germany's rescue attempt at the Village in fact raises an interesting question: might operatives from some *other* nation have been able to pull those hostages safely out of Connollystrasse 31? It has recently been argued that "no other country in the world, with the exception of Israel itself, could have freed the hostages with confidence." After all, the terrorists were dug into a secure position, and it would have been extremely difficult to get at them in a manner that didn't leave them ample opportunity to kill their hostages first. This assessment may well be correct, though it is intriguing to contemplate how other then-existing foreign commando outfits, such as Britain's Special Air Service (SAS) or America's Navy SEALs (commissioned in 1962), might have handled the problem. But in the end, the question of alternative operatives or scenarios is beside the point. As the Israeli government made clear, securing the safety of the hostages was a *German* responsibility. The fact that the West Germans proved incapable of doing this—and apparently were unwilling even to ask for help from a party that *might* have been able to do the job—cannot be rationalized away by pointing up the severe difficulty of the challenge.

The hapless Operation Sunshine episode was watched intently not only by the Stasi and the terrorists but also by most of the athletes, who at this point had plenty of time to sit in front of their TV sets. At 3:51 p.m., Willi Daume, after consulting with Brundage and the IOC, announced that the rest of the afternoon's events would be postponed. He also announced that a memorial service (for Moshe Weinberg) would take place in the Olympic Stadium at ten o'clock the next morning. He said nothing about any further interruption of normal Olympic activity—and, in fact, the IOC, along with the West German government, strongly opposed any long-term suspension of the Games, not to mention their complete cancellation.

It is safe to say that most of the athletes, while perhaps relieved by the temporary stoppage of play, fervently hoped that the Games would not be halted for good. For those who had not yet competed in their scheduled events, a cancellation would have meant the end of their "Olympic dream" before they had gotten the chance to experience it. The very contemplation of such a prospect plunged American marathoner Kenny Moore into gloom; not being allowed to run, he said, would have rendered all his years of preparation "useless." According to Moore, his teammate Steve Prefontaine was filled with rage over the terrorists' temerity in attacking the Olympics. "These are *our* Games," Pre fumed. "Anyone who would murder us for some demented cause just proves he can't understand what *we* do."

Shortly before Daume put the Games on temporary hold, Schreiber and Merk met again with Issa, hoping to persuade him to extend his deadline for a few more hours. This time, the Germans solicited assistance from Tunisia's ambassador to Bonn, Mahmoud Mestiri, and also Mohammed Khadif, the Arab League representative in the West German capital. The two Arabs prevailed upon Issa to extend the deadline to five o'clock, but they got the distinct impression that the Black September leader was now thoroughly fed up with the protracted "negotiations," which he (rightly) took to be a stalling tactic. Issa told the Arabs that he knew the Germans were lying to him about trying to secure some agreement from Israel.

But if Issa was sure he was being conned, what could he do about it? He was reluctant to follow up on his threat to start killing the hostages, for he knew that this would provoke a full-scale assault by the Germans. Of course, if he simply slaughtered all the hostages in one fell swoop, he'd have no bargaining leverage left, and he and his men would probably be slaughtered in turn. (Again, we must remember that the Black September-brists, for all their brutality, were not Al-Qaida-like suicidal religious fanatics seeking mayhem and "martyrdom" as their *primary* goals: had that been the case, they would simply have blown up the Israeli complex—and themselves along with it.)

A possible way out of the dilemma came from one of the hostages, who suggested that the fedayeen and their captives might fly together to Cairo, with the aim of resolving the deadlock from there. To Issa, this idea had merit; it would shift the action to friendlier turf, away from the threat of more assault attempts by the Germans—or, much scarier, perhaps by the Israelis. As the 5:00 p.m. deadline approached and a new delegation of Germans returned with their usual pleas for more time, Issa abruptly cut them off and announced a change of plans: the fedayeen now wished to fly to Cairo immediately with their captives and to this end the Germans must prepare two aircraft to leave within an hour. West Germany must also, added Issa, persuade Israel to release their Arab prisoners and fly them to Cairo for a rendezvous with Black September. Otherwise, the hostages would be executed.

This proposal caught the Germans by surprise, and they demanded some time to discuss it among themselves. As they did so, they saw that, while the plan had the merit of shifting the whole ordeal away from German soil, and thus away from the site of the precious Munich Games, it would not go down at all well with the Meir government, which would understandably oppose having its citizens removed from West Germany to a hostile state—from the frying pan to the fire, so to speak. Israel had always insisted, rightfully, that it was the *Germans'* responsibility to protect its Israeli guests.

Nonetheless, Willy Brandt, acting on his own, decided to play the Cairo card in one last desperate gamble at a peaceful resolution to the crisis. Hoping to broker a deal whereby the Egyptians would separate the terrorists from their hostages and secure the safety of the latter, Brandt put a call through to President Anwar Sadat, with whom he thought he had some influence. (In June 1972, Brandt had agreed to send no more weapons to Israel, and Bonn and Cairo had resumed the diplomatic ties broken off in the wake of the 1967 war.) But Sadat, who was under pressure from anti-Zionist militants at home to be tougher vis-à-vis Israel, refused even to come to the phone when he learned who was calling. Brandt was left to make his pitch to Prime Minister Ariz Sidky, who, Brandt claimed later, flatly refused to be of any help. "We do not wish to be involved," the Egyptian allegedly said. Sidky, by contrast, later claimed to have offered to allow the fedayeen and their hostages to land in Cairo and to do what he could to protect the latter—though he could not accommodate Brandt's demand to *guarantee* a peaceful outcome. (The Egyptians later explained that, without a signed agreement between the Germans and the fedayeen regarding the fate of the hostages, Cairo could not take responsibility for the Israelis' safety.)

In the view of Brandt and the other German officials, this lack of an ironclad guarantee of safety for the hostages effectively killed the Cairo option. If the West Germans allowed the hostages to fly to Cairo without assurance from Egypt that they would be unharmed, and then they were in fact harmed, Bonn would not be able to unload the responsibility for the tragedy on to the Egyptians. That was simply unacceptable.

Still, Issa's demand for safe passage to Cairo gave the German negotiators an idea: they could *promise* to fly the terrorists and their captives out of Germany from a local airport, but once the fedayeen arrived at that airport, rather than letting anyone fly out, the Germans could launch a surprise assault on the terrorists and (one hoped) free the hostages in the process. Initially, the crisis team contemplated using Munich's main civilian airport at Riem for this purpose, but, at Tröger's insistence, they switched to Fürstenfeldbruck, a small and lightly used NATO air field some twelve miles outside of Munich. Staging the assault at Fürstenfeldbruck would reduce the risk of collateral casualties and would also remove this embarrassing mess from the purview of those damn TV cameras and civilian gawkers. At Fürstenfeldbruck, Bavarian authorities could do what they had to do without the whole world watching.

Before they "agreed" to Issa's Cairo proposal, however, the Germans made clear that they could provide only one aircraft for the flight to Egypt. They also insisted upon seeing the hostages personally to ascertain that they were indeed alive, in decent condition, and willing to travel.

Issa reluctantly allowed Genscher and Tröger to proceed under guard to Apartment 1. The two Germans entered the hostage room and saw Yossef Romano lying dead in a pool of blood on the floor. Gutfreund was bound to a chair, while the other eight Israelis huddled together on a bed with their hands and feet tied. Genscher admitted later that the "mental picture of these men, sitting on the bed and staring hopefully at me," would "stay with me forever." The interior minister assured the Israelis that Germany would do all in its power to secure their release. But in truth he had little confidence in the rescue plan. Tröger, for his part, was even less optimistic. "We were 99% sure that we wouldn't be able to achieve our objective," he admitted later. "We felt like doctors trying to bring the dead back to life."

CHAPTER **Six**

Battlefield Fürstenfeldbruck

How dumb do these morons have to be to think they're going
to get a plane? I don't mean him. *Any* hostage taker. Those rag-heads
at the Munich Olympics. Who the fuck ever got a plane? Shit, and
these days? Those guys don't even know that.
—Captain John Darius (Willem Dafoe) in Spike Lee's *Inside Man* (2006)

Swept with confused alarms of struggle and flight /
Where ignorant armies clash by night.
—Matthew Arnold, "Dover Beach"

I f the Germans' handling of the hostage crisis in the Olympic Village
showed signs of confusion and inadequacy, their management of the
envisaged rescue effort at Fürstenfeldbruck turned out to be a masterpiece of incompetence, a veritable textbook demonstration of how *not* to
conduct operations of this sort. In fact, what happened at that out-of-the-
way airbase on the night of September 5/6 called into question not only
the effectiveness of security preparations for the Munich Games but also
the whole mystique of German "efficiency" and organizational competence.
The German authorities' reaction to this (admittedly unprecedented) challenge betrayed a host of systematic inadequacies, including a glaring paucity
of resources and tools, failures to share intelligence information across governmental agencies, infighting over responsibility, deep political mistrust
between state and federal officials, and a fundamental lack of leadership
from the top. (The fact that a more seasoned Western democracy, namely

the United States, would display quite similar inadequacies in responding to a terror attack on its soil some thirty years later does not make the West German case any less problematical—though it does perhaps argue for some temperance in passing judgment.) We should also note that it wasn't just the Germans who proved incompetent at their work on that fateful night. The Palestinian hostage takers allowed themselves to be lured into a trap, with ugly consequences for all concerned. As the Willem Dafoe character in Spike Lee's *Inside Man* asks incredulously, "Who the fuck ever got a plane?"

"They're All Gone"

Although the hastily improvised German rescue scheme focused on Fürstenfeldbruck as the principal site of operations, the crisis team, still under the authority of Manfred Schreiber, entertained a slight hope of ending the drama even before the envisaged transfer via helicopters to the airfield. The idea was to have the Palestinians and their hostages walk from Connollystrasse 31 to a helicopter pad behind the Olympic administration building. During the beginning part of that walk, which would take place in the underground parking garage, hidden sharpshooters might have an opportunity to pick off the terrorists in one coordinated volley of fire. Schreiber duly ordered several sharpshooters into the garage. Alas, Luttif Afif ("Issa") insisted upon checking out the area in advance, and when he spotted armed men flitting about between parked cars and support pillars, he immediately vetoed the walk and demanded to travel to the copter pad by bus.

The requested bus, carrying the eight heavily armed terrorists and their nine captives, all blindfolded and bound at the waist, arrived at the helicopter pad at 10:10 p.m. Shmuel Lalkin and the two Israeli security agents, Zvi Zamir and Victor Cohen, stood on the roof of the administration building and watched the *fedayeen* and their hostages board two waiting Iroquois helicopters. Four of the hostages got on one machine under the guard of Yasuf Nazzal ("Tony") (wearing a cowboy hat) and three of his men. Issa and the three other terrorists loaded five more Israelis into the second chopper. "It was a terrible scene," Zamir recalled. "We had a hard time watching shackled Jews being taken to the helicopters."

Zamir's deep fears for his countrymen were hardly eased when a portly Bavarian standing near him, Franz Josef Strauß, suddenly exclaimed to another German, Hans-Dietrich Genscher, "Hey, they've got the number of terrorists wrong!" The Bavarian authorities, it seems, had come to believe during the crisis in the Village that the number of terrorists they were contending with was *five*, and this was the figure they had sent on to Fürsten-feldbruck. Amazingly, even when the true count became evident, this new and very critical piece of information was not relayed to the airbase.

The original rescue plan called for two separate ambushes carried out by different police units. Assuming that the two fedayeen leaders, Issa and Tony, would demand to inspect the Lufthansa 727 getaway aircraft before bringing their hostages on board, the first police team, disguised as Luf-thansa pilots and stewards and stationed within the plane, would pounce on the terrorists as soon as they boarded. A second squad of sharpshooters would pick off the other commandos as they stood near the helicopters awaiting the all-clear signal from their leaders. Even the Bavarian plan-ners must have known that the success of this scheme depended to a great degree on the cooperation of their intended victims—but that flaw, as it turned out, was hardly the only problem.

While the helicopters were still en route to Fürstenfeldbruck, the Ger-mans' plan began to fall apart. A team of seventeen policemen under the command of a rookie officer named Reinhold Reich had been assembled to carry out the assault aboard the plane. The cops' attempt to disguise them-selves as Lufthansa personnel went partly astray because only airline *jackets*, no trousers or shoes, could be located. The police pulled the jackets on over bulky bullet-proof vests while continuing to wear their distinctive uniform trousers and Doc Marten boots—a rather unconvincing ensemble. As they took their places in the aircraft, they caught a strong whiff of kerosene: the Boeing, despite having no destination apart from the Munich tarmac, had been pumped full of jet fuel. It was not long before the policemen began to question the wisdom of their mission. The heavily armed terror-ists, the cops reasoned, would immediately smell a rat (not just kerosene) upon seeing *seventeen* "airline crew" dressed in bulky mismatched outfits. A single stray bullet, not to mention a grenade, could turn the plane into a giant fireball. When his men pointed out to him the "suicidal" nature of their enterprise, Reich allowed them to vote on whether to continue with the operation or to abort it. ABORT, they voted unanimously, and scurried off the airplane.

A few minutes later, the two helicopters bearing the terrorists and hostages arrived, followed shortly thereafter by another chopper packed with German officials, along with the two Israeli security agents, Zamir and Cohen.

Discovering that the first phase of their plan had to be scrapped, the Bavarian commanders decided there was nothing for it but to fall back entirely on the second part of their operation—the sharpshooter offensive.

But this part of the plan was full of flaws as well. Still unaware of the actual number of terrorists they faced, the on-the-ground personnel at Fürsten-feldbruck, led by an assistant to Schreiber named Georg Wolf, assembled a team of only *five* police sharpshooters—one shooter, Wolf imagined, for each of the terrorists. (Actually, even if there had been only five terrorists this arrangement would not have been satisfactory, for the general rule in such scenarios is to have two snipers for each target.) Moreover, none of the snipers in question had been specially trained for this duty, nor did any of them have precision high-powered rifles, sniper scopes, bullet-proof vests, two-way radios, or even night-vision goggles, despite the fact that the two hastily erected light stanchions brought in to illuminate the scene left vast tracts of the field in darkness. Finally, the snipers were positioned in such a way that they might well hit each other rather than their intended targets.

The terrorists, for their part, failed to follow the ambush planners' script. Upon arriving at the airfield, only six of them left the helicopters, leaving the two others to guard their nine hostages. Issa and Tony went as predicted to the waiting plane; however, finding it empty and dark they im-mediately exited the craft and headed back toward the helicopters, yelling about a "trap." "What's happening?" whispered one of the Bavarian offi-cials while peering out from a window on the second floor of the darkened airfield administration building. No one seemed to have a clue.

At this point, Georg Wolf, surveying the scene from building's roof, gave instructions to two snipers stationed near him to open fire. He could not convey similar orders to the other three snipers because of a lack of radios. The sniper shots from the roof felled two of the terrorists standing outside the helicopters, although only one of them was killed outright.

Now all hell broke loose. The chopper pilots leaped from their craft and ran for cover (an option unavailable to the hostages, who were bound together inside the two machines). The other fedayeen stationed with the helicopters dove into pools of darkness under the craft and immediately started returning fire in the direction of the administration building and airport tower. They raked the buildings up and down with their AK 47s, smashing windows and also putting out some of the stanchion lights. Hans-Dietrich Genscher, who had been standing at one of the windows, thought better of it and dove under a nearby desk. Meanwhile, a third po-lice sniper opened fire on the moving figures of Issa and Tony. The sniper managed to put Tony on the tarmac with a shot to the leg, but Issa, after also being downed, managed to pick himself up and reach the relative safety of the copters.

With much of the field bathed in darkness, the German snipers fired wildly, shooting in the general direction of muzzle flashes and whatever seemed to be moving. Unaware that there were hostages locked inside the helicopters, the snipers shot at these targets as well. As one of the ambush organizers later admitted, "Nobody had an overview. There were shots and nobody knew where from or towards whom." Even Schreiber had to concede that there was no effective leadership from the German side during the chaotic gun battle. "We were all but paralyzed," he stated.

While the German officials stood by in numbed paralysis (save for Strauß, who reportedly ran around screaming obscenities at his colleagues and demanding beer), the Israeli security experts who had come along to the airfield sought desperately to find someone to coordinate the operation. They also tried to get a rescue squad to go to the hostages. None of the German policemen, however, would agree to approach the helicopters without the security of armored personnel carriers.

Astonishingly, there were no such vehicles at the scene. The armored cars the crisis team had ordered to the Village during the hostage standoff should have been dispatched to Fürstenfeldbruck as soon as the ambush plot was concocted. Instead, the order to move out came only after the firefight at the airfield had begun. The vehicles' arrival was further delayed by a huge traffic jam near the field because the authorities had neglected to close the incoming road to rubberneckers.

At a loss of what else to do, Zamir and Cohen ran to the administration building roof and, with a megaphone, shouted in Arabic at the terrorists, "Stop firing! If you carry on you'll be hurt or killed. STOP FIRING!" The terrorists responded by directing another salvo at the roof.

Sporadic firing continued for several more minutes, both sides now thoroughly battened down behind barricades, like troops on the stalemated Western Front in World War I. Finally, a little before midnight, five armored vehicles rolled onto the tarmac. Realizing that the balance had suddenly shifted decisively in favor of the police, the terrorists made the cruel decision to kill their hostages in cold blood, as they sat immobilized in the helicopters. It was a decision that spoke volumes about the desperate character and murderous nature of Black September. Tony ordered one of the fedayeen under his immediate command to throw a fragmentation grenade directly under helicopter number 1. When the grenade exploded, the copter's fuel tanks ignited, turning the machine into a flaming oven. Four hostages, Friedman, Halfin, Springer, and Berger were trapped inside the inferno. Almost immediately thereafter, one of Issa's men jumped into the second helicopter—where Gutfreund, Shorr, Slavin, Shapira, and Spitzer sat manacled in terror—and sprayed the captives at point blank range with automatic fire from his Kalashnikov. He did not stop until his magazine was empty.

Not being death-seeking religious zealots in the now-familiar radical Islamic mold, the terrorists did not follow their brutal execution of the hostages with acts of self-destruction. Instead, those that were still mobile took off running toward a darkened field on the other side of the airport runway. A police sniper managed to kill Issa, whose earlier leg injury hampered his progress, before he could clear the tarmac. Three other terrorists—Jamal Al-Gashey, Adnan Al-Gashey, and Mohammed Safady—made it to the field but were soon run to ground by policemen on foot and in vehicles. The terrorists surrendered without further fighting.

While all this was transpiring, the helicopter hit by the fragmentation grenade continued to burn. Firemen refused to approach it to put out the flames for fear that other terrorists might be lurking nearby (in fact, all the other fedayeen were now dead). When the firefighters finally did douse the flames, they discovered that David Berger's body was surprisingly intact, with only two or three bullet wounds in the thigh and calf. An autopsy would later reveal that Berger had died of smoke inhalation.

The Israeli security experts at Fürstenfeldbruck were amazed that the Bavarian authorities could have so thoroughly bungled an operation of this magnitude. After all, these were *Germans*—they were supposed to be good at things military and paramilitary. But in fact, the security culture of West Germany in the 1960s and 1970s was a far cry from what it had been under earlier Prussian-dominated German political systems. Long gone was the reverence for all things martial, the obsession with military craftsmanship, and the lust for battle. West Germany's new army, the Bundeswehr, which had come into being in 1955–1956 after much internal debate and popular resistance, touted itself as a thoroughly "democratic" institution—a force of "civilians in uniform" blessedly free of the old Kadavergehorsamkeit (corpse-like obedience) and spit-and-polish regimentation. The troops were unionized and enjoyed the right—indeed, the duty—to resist orders they considered unethical or needlessly sacrificial. (American military officers were often shocked by the liberalizing reforms in the Bundeswehr and worried, as one general complained privately, that "the quality of the soldiers in the new German army would not be as high as those of the Second and Third Reich.") The various provincial and local security forces, too, liked to think of themselves as kinder and gentler versions of their former incarnations. As we have noted, the Munich police in particular had recently adopted Schreiber's "Munich Line," which urged avoiding strong-arm tactics as much as possible in contending with civil disturbances. Moreover, the advisability of taking a cautious approach in dealing with hostage situations had been brought home to the local authorities exactly one year earlier. In responding to a robbery attempt at a Deutsche Bank affiliate in Munich's Prinzregentenstraße, police "sharpshooters" firing into the building had killed one robber and (so it was believed) also one of the robbers' hostages. Even the bellicose Franz Josef Strauß had criticized the order to fire into the bank.

Crucially, West Germany had avoided creating a federal counterterrorism force on the model of Israel's Sayeret Matkal on the grounds that this would both trespass on the authority of the separate states and seem too reminiscent of Nazi Germany's Gestapo or SS. (How ironic, by the way, for Germans to avoid emulating Israelis for fear of looking like Nazis!) One might argue, then, that the horribly botched rescue operation at Fürstenfeldbruck grew at least in part out of the well-intentioned reformist ideals that underlay the making of the "Bonn Republic" and its various security institutions.

As if to put an exclamation point on the horror of what transpired at Fürstenfeldbruck, the transmission of news about the developing disaster was also badly bungled by the German authorities. Instead of allowing any accredited journalists access to sources inside the base, the Organizing Committee (OC) imposed a lockdown on all news coverage, just as it had in the Village earlier. And, just as in that instance, the dearth of accurate reporting allowed rumor to hold sway for hours on end. At about 10:30 p.m., the main wire services, whose reporters were obliged to set up camp outside the entrance to the airfield, reported that shooting had broken out on the premises. According to one report, a single Arab had committed suicide, three others had been killed by police, and several more had escaped on foot into nearby fields.

At 11:00 p.m., while the firefight was raging on the airfield tarmac, a figure wearing an official Olympic hat (later identified as a local pub owner by the name of Ludwig Pollack), appeared at the main gate and announced that everything was fine, all the hostages had been rescued. Taking this man to be a bona fide authority, reporters on the scene rushed to call in the good news to their superiors. At 11:30, Reuters issued a bulletin saying, "All Israeli hostages have been freed."

Unable to check this report with officials on the scene—the regular phone system seemed to have gone down—Chancellor Willy Brandt rejected a proposal from his press secretary, Conrad Ahlers, to issue a celebratory statement on national television. However, Brandt did allow Ahlers to go on ABC Television and assure Jim McKay and the world that the situation at Fürstenfeldbruck had apparently turned out for the good. "I am very glad that as far as we can now see this police action was successful," said Ahlers. "Of course, it's an unfortunate interruption of the Olympic Games, but if all comes out as we hope it will come out. . . . I think it will be forgotten after a few weeks." In signing off, Ahlers added, "For us Germans, it was a tragic situation that all this happened to the Jewish people. . . . Thank goodness [it's all over], otherwise some of the old memories might have come back."

With this apparent confirmation from Ahlers, the news of the hostage rescue took on gold-standard quality. Joyous celebrations erupted around the world, above all in Israel, where, after their long ordeal, relatives of the hostages experienced a huge sense of relief. Even dour Golda Meir broke out the champagne.

But as the night wore on, Jim McKay started getting sketchy new reports indicating that all was *not* well at Fürstenfeldbruck. At 1:30 a.m., a very disturbing report came in from someone at the airfield saying, "All hell is breaking loose out here! A helicopter is burning!" An ABC reporter who rushed out to the scene called in to say that he'd heard an explosion and much gunfire.

At the Olympic Press Center, ABC's vice president in charge of Olympic planning, Marvin Bader, kept pressing the Olympics press chief, Johnny Klein, for details on what was happening at Fürstenfeldbruck, but the normally loquacious Klein replied that he was not authorized to say anything. He promised, however, that Bavarian interior minister Bruno Merk would soon hold a news conference at which he would report on the latest developments.

As more agonizing hours ticked by, McKay and Bader grew increasingly impatient for an update on the situation at the airfield because they knew that, at 11:00 p.m. New York time, ABC headquarters would insist on closing down reporting from Munich in order to allow affiliates across the United States to switch over to local and regional news. At 4:45 a.m. Munich time (10:45 p.m. New York time), they still had no statement from Merk.

As ABC was waiting for Merk's news conference, Roone Arledge, who was directing the network's coverage of the unfolding hostage drama, had to fend off frantic demands from Howard Cosell to take over the microphone from McKay. "I want to go on," he shouted. "Put me on, Arledge, I'm the only one who can tell it." "Telling it," in the view of Cosell, seemed to involve heaping abuse on the Germans. "Dirty bastards," he yelled. "They already killed six million of us. What's a few more?" Arledge told Cosell firmly that there was no place for him in the broadcast, adding, "Trust me, Howard, you'll be the first to thank me in the morning."

Merk's press conference finally began at 4:50 a.m. But instead of commenting on what everyone wanted to know—the condition of the hostages—the minister droned on ponderously about the entire course of the hostage crisis, starting at the very beginning. ABC's Bader located another German official with whom he'd worked closely, telling him that his network was about to go off the air and he needed to leave its millions of anxious viewers with a definitive word on the fate of the hostages. Finally, after a few more minutes of prevarication, the official said, "They're all dead, Marvin." Who was dead? asked Bader. "The Israelis."

The terrible news was immediately flashed to McKay, whose duty it now was to pass this information on to the waiting world. Struggling to hold his composure but looking as if he were about to break out in tears, McKay began his announcement with a personal comment. "When I was a boy, my father told me that in life, our greatest ambitions and our worst fears are seldom realized. Tonight, our worst fears have been realized." A pregnant pause. "Two of the Israeli hostages were killed in their rooms this morning—excuse me, that's yesterday morning. Nine others were killed at the airport tonight." Another pause. *"They're all gone."*

Some eight hours after the crisis, at 8:00 a.m. Munich time, Merk and Genscher held a public news conference at which they finally provided official confirmation of the grim news. Merk added that one Bavarian policeman, Anton Fliegerbauer, had also died, along with five of the terrorists. Three others were in custody. Merk spent the rest of his time defending and justifying the actions of the Bavarian officials. He emphasized that the Israeli government had been unwilling from the start to negotiate on the fedayeens' demand for a hostage-prisoner swap—leaving open the suggestion that the blame for this tragedy resided, at least partly, with Israel.

"The Worst Night for the Federal Republic": Reactions to the Munich Terror Attack

As might be expected, the murder of the Israeli Olympians sparked outrage and anger in many parts of the world. A widespread tendency was to hold Arabs in general responsible for the atrocity. There were protest demonstrations outside the embassies of Arab nations across Europe. At London's Heathrow Airport, unionized workers refused to process passengers or baggage for Arab-owned airlines. In the United States, the Jewish Defense League, made up of venomously anti-Arab American Jews, called for the murder of Arab diplomats around the world. In Israel itself, several newspapers demanded an immediate military retaliation against the Palestine Liberation Organization (PLO) as well as against Arab states that harbored Palestinian terrorists.

But of course, Black September was not without allies and apologists—and some of these were not hesitant to celebrate the Munich action as a great triumph for Palestine, or at least to offer reasons to justify it. Ulrike Meinhof, whose terrorist group had briefly trained in Jordan with Black September, hailed the Munich attack from her prison cell as the kind of "revolutionary action through which the West German Left can rediscover its identity." French philosopher Jean-Paul Sartre wrote that "the state of war" between Israelis and Palestinians left the latter with no viable option but terror, the "poor man's weapon." *Der Spiegel* publisher Rudolf Augstein, while deploring the killings, saw no difference between the Black September operatives in Munich and the U.S. "aerial killers" in Vietnam, save for the fact that the Palestinians believed they were acting for "a higher purpose," while "only the most obtuse American pilot" could see any genuine sense in his "murderous actions."

Apart from the polarization running through the opening commentary on the Munich attack, another feature of the early response bears noting: although much of the outrage was directed at the Palestinian terrorists, considerable criticism was also directed at the German authorities for badly mishandling the crisis (and this even before extensive information about the botched rescue effort was available).

From the German side, Bruno Merk's opening defensive comments turned into a full-blown apologia as his brothers in arms—Genscher, Schreiber, and Walther Tröger—all went on record to explain and justify the behavior of the various officials involved, from themselves on down. The gist of their position was that they and the police officers on the scene had done everything possible under the circumstances to rescue the hostages. They said nothing (at least early on) about possible flaws in the planning, preparation, or execution of the rescue operation.

Naturally, West Germany's political leadership was quick to express condolences to Israel. On the morning of September 6, Willy Brandt himself telephoned Golda Meir, relating his horror over the "tragic death of so many young people who in Munich had sought nothing but peaceful competition. . . . We bow before the victims of senseless, hate-filled action." Privately, however, Brandt and his ministers felt victimized by Meir's unwillingness to bargain with the terrorists, a posture that in their view so limited their "freedom of action" that it "practically guaranteed" the tragic outcome. To the degree that there might have been some German culpability in this sad affair, Brandt was inclined to load that on the broad shoulders of the Bavarians. Apparently with an eye on domestic opinion and the upcoming elections, the chancellor reminded his countrymen that the principal responsibility for the rescue operation belonged to the Christian Social Union (CSU)–governed state of Bavaria. Before a group of journalists, he spoke bitterly of "the bottomless difference between what was planned and what actually transpired." Just as predictably, Brandt's criticism sparked outrage from the conservative opposition, whose leaders upbraided the chancellor for trying "to evade political and moral responsibility for the Munich tragedy by dumping all the blame on the Free State of Bavaria." This was a time for Germans to pull together, said the Bavarian CSU, not to point fingers at each other.

The self-exonerating comments by Brandt, Merk, Tröger, and other leading figures notwithstanding, West Germany's feisty press and chattering class found plenty of reasons to be critical of, and deeply ashamed over, the behavior of German officialdom in this entire wretched affair. Many newspapers wondered aloud why security for the Israeli delegation had been so lax. They were clearly not impressed by the claim (advanced by a spokesman for the Bavarian Ministry of Justice) that to truly secure the Olympic Village "one would have had to build a Sing-Sing." Seeing obvious signs of incompetence on the part of the Bavarian authorities in the final stage of the drama at Fürstenfeldbruck, *Der Spiegel* spoke of "the worst night [in the history of] the Federal Republic." Günter Grass, West Germany's most celebrated novelist and normally a cheerleader for Willy Brandt, dashed off a letter to the chancellor complaining that Bonn's mishandling of the Munich crisis threatened to undermine the prestige and trust that the Federal Republic of Germany (FRG) had painstakingly built up around the world. Grass worried, too, that the "weakness of leadership" displayed in this fiasco would be exploited by Brandt's domestic opponents for political gain. He proposed that Brandt counter this gambit by giving expression as soon as possible to the "shame and helplessness" that most Germans felt in the aftermath of the Olympic tragedy.

In a virtuoso display of selective myopia, Munich OC press chief Johnny Klein reported to Conrad Ahlers shortly after the Munich massacre that foreign journalists, having witnessed the Olympic terror attack "at close quarters" while covering the Games, and having also enjoyed a full measure of Munich hospitality, were showing "understanding" for the "decisions and measures" undertaken by German officials in the hostage crisis. "Without exception," Klein wrote, "our guests expressed their agreement with what we tried to do by way of saving the hostages, and they also agreed with the decision to continue the Games despite the tragic events. This [favorable view] derived in no small part from the [foreign observers'] positive experiences in Munich."

The real picture was rather less rosy. Foreign opinion was often strongly critical of the German response to the terror attack, even while admitting the difficulties under which the authorities had had to operate. The intense scrutiny directed at German lapses during the hostage crisis brought with it broader criticism of the entire security regime for the '72 Olympics. Not surprisingly, foreign journalists were also extremely critical of the blackout of regular news coverage from the scenes of action, as well as of the German press authorities' unseemly haste to report (inaccurate) good news.

Thus, the *Chicago Tribune* could reflect that the murder of the Israeli athletes was "the most serious of a long series [of incidents] that has plagued this year's Games." In the *New York Times*, columnist David Binder commented critically on "the confusion created in the public mind by contradictory reports from German and Olympic officials after gunfire erupted at the airport." The French press was filled with stories about "superficial" controls at the Village and "un-German-like" casualness in matters of law and order. Britain's *Evening Standard* and *Evening News* both commented on how security restrictions had been "extensively loosened" after the early days of the festival. The *Economist* made note of "the ease with which Arab terrorists seem to be able to get in and out of [West Germany]"—a function of the FRG's "very liberal approach to the entry of foreigners." Noting that the "black" night of September 5/6 had been as black for Willy Brandt as for Munich, this same magazine observed that the conservative opposition in Germany would undoubtedly soon be asking "whether a government that could not even control a sporting jamboree [was] fit to control a country." Germany's dark past was not left out of the foreign critique either. A Swedish paper observed that the Munich catastrophe had special resonance because it had occurred in the former "Capital of the Nazi Movement," whose "first and last law [had been] the extermination of the Jews." "Among the terrorists of today," concluded this paper, "are mixed the ghosts of Munich's past."

Not surprisingly, some of the sharpest criticism of West German officialdom came from the German Democratic Republic (GDR), whose media and political pundits could not disguise a certain degree of Schadenfreude (gloating) in their commentary on the events of September 5/6 in

Munich. While dutifully registering their disapproval of "all acts of terrorism," East German radio and TV commentators were quick to add that the tragedy at the Games "confirmed suspicions abroad that FRG officials had not done all they could to protect foreign sportspeople in Munich." The party newspaper *Neues Deutschland*, while condemning a "terror attack" that would undoubtedly set back the Palestinian cause, argued that the West German organizers were fully at fault for the tragedy, since they had ignored "repeated warnings" that the Israeli delegation might be in danger. In general, concluded *Neues Deutschland*, the '72 Games had cast a "dark shadow over Munich."

Joining in the fray, GDR political leaders saw an opportunity here to score political points in the Third World. The FRG, said a spokesman for the ruling Socialist Unity Party in East Berlin, had no right whatsoever to criticize the Palestinians given its own dismal record of human rights abuses and its ritual defense of the "mass murder committed by Israeli air-pirates against [the inhabitants of] Arab villages and refugee camps" across the Middle East.

What GDR officials did not divulge, of course, was that their own secret police, while apparently having no role in the planning or execution of the Munich attack, had in the past cultivated ties to Black September. Moreover, one of the Munich operatives, Ali Hassan Salameh, maintained a forward command post in East Berlin during the Games. The Stasi may not have been aware of what Salameh was up to, but once the Games were over GDR operatives facilitated his flight to Beirut. He returned to a hero's welcome and a personal message of congratulation from Yasser Arafat.

Interestingly enough, Prime Minister Meir was careful not to cast stones at the West Germans in the immediate aftermath of the Munich tragedy. She gracefully accepted Willy Brandt's message of sympathy and offered no public criticism of the German authorities' behavior during the crisis. On the contrary, she thanked the Germans for their "decision to take action for the liberation of the Israeli hostages and to employ force to that end."

But not everyone in her government was so forgiving of the German bungling. Interior Minister Josef Burg declared, "Until today, we always said that Dachau lay close to Munich. Now we have to say that Munich sits close to Dachau." The Israeli press and public, moreover, showed no hesitation whatsoever to lambaste the Germans for what they saw as inadequate security arrangements at the Games and the Bavarian authorities' unbelievably mismanaged response to the Black September attack. The liberal newspaper *Ha'aretz*, for example, stated that "Our team went to

Munich under the condition that the host country would provide for its security. . . . This expectation was not fulfilled. Responsibility for this failure lies exclusively with West German officials." *Ha'aretz* quoted an Israeli military officer's comment that the rescue operation would have come out very differently had the Germans allowed General Moshe Dayan, Israel's defense minister, to deal with the problem.* Israeli newspapers recorded many similar expressions of outrage against the Germans among ordinary citizens. A hundred school children marched around outside West Germany's Embassy in Tel Aviv to protest the German authorities' handling of the hostage crisis. A bus driver told a reporter that "the Germans should have left the rescue operation to us; the way they went about it was lame and useless." A newspaper peddler who had survived Auschwitz exclaimed, "We Jews simply have no luck. First the Germans tried to get rid of us, then the Arabs tried, and now both of them are trying together."

The fact that, for the most part, Israel's top leadership chose not to jump on the West Germans for what happened on September 5/6, while popular opinion showed no such hesitation, requires a little elucidation. Over the years, the "special relationship" between Bonn and Tel Aviv had evolved from arm's length wariness—marked by West Germany's grudging willingness to pay economic compensation to Israel for the crimes of the Third Reich and Israel's willingness to accept such payments without letting the Germans off the moral hook—to something approaching cordiality. In 1965, Bonn and Tel Aviv established diplomatic relations. In addition to providing Israel with military weapons and technical assistance, Bonn strongly backed Israel in the 1967 Six-Day War. West Germany further elevated its status with the Israeli leadership by rejecting any statute of limitations on "crimes against humanity" and cracking down on neo-Nazi, Holocaust-denying political groups at home. In 1970, Israeli foreign minister Abba Eban paid an official visit to Bonn—a major symbol of reconciliation at the top. But below this level, tensions continued to simmer, at least in Israel. Ordinary Israelis may have been happy enough to buy West German cars and electronic gear—Tel Aviv was full of Volkswagens and Grundig TV sets—but importing German culture was another matter. When the Israel Philharmonic Orchestra announced in 1966 that, due to "a change in attitude on the part of Israel toward the nation that murdered

---

* Curiously enough, it was later revealed by German officials that Moshe Dayan had shown up in Munich in the evening of September 5 to consult on the rescue operation. He had flown in from Tel Aviv and arrived at the Village around 7:30 p.m. But there is no record about what advice he might have given, and his very presence was kept strictly secret.

our people," the orchestra intended to include works by Richard Strauss and Richard Wagner in its repertoire, all hell broke loose. Israel's rightist press (*Hayom*) thundered that performing anything by Strauss or Wagner would amount to an insult to the six million Jews killed in the Holocaust. Obviously in *Hayom*'s view (and in the eyes of the rapidly growing faction of conservative religious Jews), attitudes toward Germany *had not changed*. Lingering hostility to Germany at the popular level also lay behind the dire warnings that some members of the Israeli Olympic team received as they embarked for Munich to participate in the 1972 Games. They dare not go to Germany, the athletes were instructed, for the inveterate Jew-haters over there simply could not be trusted!

In the wake of the carnage at Fürstenfeldbruck, top officials in the Meir government drew their own lessons from what had happened to their nation's delegation at the '72 Games. A group of three experts—Pinchas Kopel, Moshe Kashti, and Avigdor Bartel—was appointed by Golda Meir to investigate the Munich incident in detail. They produced a fifteen-page report that, while highly critical of West German lapses, was almost equally scathing about the performance turned in by Israel's own security agencies. This so-called Kopel Report singled out a number of Israeli security officials "for unbecoming conduct in all matters concerning the security and safety of the Olympic delegation as it was defined before the Munich disaster." On the basis of the Munich episode, the report concluded that the organizational structure in place for Israeli delegations abroad was "not sufficient to address the current situation." Like the German authorities, however, Meir's people were loath to wash their dirty laundry in public. Well after the Games were over, a number of Israeli security officers were quietly dismissed from service. The Kopel Report itself was kept secret—and indeed has not been published in its entirety to this day.

As Israel was trying to come to grips with the horror of what transpired in Munich, the Arab governments faced a delicate challenge of their own: how to keep their distance from the violent act by Black September without seeming to come down too hard on the Palestinians, whose cause was widely popular among Arab populaces across the Middle East. Arab governments also had to worry about being held complicit in the action by Israel, which, the Arab leaders knew, would not hesitate to retaliate against any state it considered co-responsible in this matter.

While the hostage crisis was still unfolding on September 5, Syria's and Lebanon's ambassadors to Bonn hastened to distance their nations from the Black September action; so did the chiefs of the Lebanese, Syrian, and Egyptian Olympic delegations at the Munich Games. The governments of these countries apparently believed that any expression of public sympathy with the fedayeen attack would be taken by Israel and the West as an "admission of political responsibility" for the action. Fearing that their own Olympic delegation might come under attack from angry Germans, Egypt decided to pull out of the Games and bring its team home immediately.

Tellingly, however, the bloody culmination of the hostage drama at Fürstenfeldbruck generated only one public rebuke of the Palestinian killers from an Arab government. Jordan's King Hussein, who of course, had his own bone to pick with Black September, called the killers "morally sick." All the other Arab regimes, far from condemning Black September, or even expressing sorrow over the deaths of the Israeli Olympians, chose to focus their indignation on the West German authorities for failing to resolve the crisis peacefully. Thus, on September 7, Egypt's official governmental spokesman faulted the Germans for "not fulfilling the promises given to Arab commandos [with respect to safe passage out of the country]"—thereby provoking the bloodbath at Fürstenfeldbruck. West Germany, said the Egyptian statement, bore "full responsibility" for the "regrettable" outcome of the crisis. On another occasion, this same spokesman gave vent to a suspicion widely held in the Arab world: the hostages had been killed "by German bullets."

Bonn's ambassador to Egypt hastened to assure his superiors that this harsh criticism of the FRG was mainly for "domestic consumption" and did not reflect the Cairo government's privately held view, but Bonn was nonetheless extremely aggravated by such public rebukes from official Arab sources. Brandt himself chastised the Arab states for not having done more to resolve the crisis, though he stopped short of charging them with complicity in the action, which is what Tel Aviv would have preferred him to do. (We must remember that West Germany was highly dependent on the Arab Middle East for its oil and gas supplies.)

Predictably, media and "man-on-the-street" commentary in the Arab world, mirroring that in Israel, took an even more hostile line toward the Germans than did the official governmental sources. Egypt's *Achbar el Yom* newspaper denounced West Germany as "an American colony that always stands on the side of Israel against the Arabs." A pro-Palestinian newspaper in Beirut proposed that the slaughter at Fürstenfeldbruck derived from a "German-Israeli conspiracy" to discredit the Palestinian cause. Another Jordanian paper, *Annahr*, warned (prophetically) that the Germans' role in the disaster, along with their capture and incarceration of three fedayeen, was likely to invite Black September reprisals against West German targets in the near future.

The PLO, for its part, openly rejoiced in the expressions of Arab rage against West Germany, and in Bonn's wounded response: clearly, Black September had succeeded in driving a wedge between West Germany and the moderate Arab states. But in PLO eyes, this Arab-German rift was just a small part of a much larger strategic victory achieved by the Munich action. Operation Iqrit and Biri'm, declared a PLO spokesman, had been a "100% publicity success," for it had drawn the world's attention to the Palestinian cause in truly spectacular fashion. "Nothing," added the spokesman, "could have shocked the world more—not a bomb in the White House, Mao's death, or an earthquake in Paris." George Habash himself described the Munich operation as "a triumph for Palestine," adding, "Now the war begins in earnest."

It was just such a prospect of a new violent conflict in the Middle East that worried the U.S. government. Washington, albeit not nearly as much as Bonn, was caught in a bind by the Olympic tragedy. On the one hand, America was Israel's strongest ally and possessed an influential Jewish community at home that would, of course, be outraged over the Munich murders. President Richard Nixon, who like Brandt faced a reelection decision in the fall, was worried that the tragedy might turn out to benefit his opponent, Senator George McGovern, in the electoral contest. According to White House correspondent Marvin Kalb, McGovern's call for an immediate U.S. withdrawal from the Games caused Nixon to fret that the senator might be able "to enhance his status with U.S. Jews." (Sure enough, McGovern blamed the Munich attack squarely on Egypt and Lebanon and accused the Nixon administration of basing its Middle East policy not on support for Israel but on "cold war politics.") On the other hand, just as McGovern suggested, the Nixon administration was indeed working to increase its leverage with the moderate Arab states in hopes of combating Soviet influence in the region. Unequivocal support for a tough Israeli retaliation for the Munich attack would only alienate the Arabs and benefit the Soviets.

The conflicting pressures on Washington stemming from the Munich tragedy were evident in a revealing Oval Office conversation between Nixon and his security advisor Henry Kissinger on September 6. (These conversations, of course, were taped, and the transcripts tell us much about how this deeply paranoid president saw the world.) Nixon predictably registered his mindfulness of Jewish pressures at home to make a "big issue" out of the terror attack. "You see [Henry], we've got to show we care on this one because . . . [of] what the Jewish community will do on this. It's going to be the goddamndest thing you've ever saw." Kissinger, for his part, emphasized the dangers of a harsh Israeli response to the killings, especially one that might appear to have Washington's blessing. Citing the worrisome analogy of Austria's military punishment of Serbia following a Bosnian terrorist's assassination of Archduke Franz Ferdinand in 1914, Kissinger expressed concern that the Israelis might also resort to a military strike, thereby precipitating a new Middle East war. "They [the Israelis] are emotional. And this is an enormous provocation. And I don't want them to think they've got you in their hip pocket."

To Kissinger's relief, Nixon agreed. Instead of egging on the Israelis, Washington should, the president thought, encourage Golda Meir to turn the other cheek—call on the International Olympic Committee (IOC) "to go forward with those Games," using as her cover the argument "That's what my boys would have wanted." This response, added Nixon, would make Israel "look good" rather than typically bellicose. "You see, Henry, the trouble with the Jews is that they've always played these things in terms of outrage. You've got the Jewish Defense League raising hell and saying we ought to kill every Arab diplomat. What we have to do here is . . . show an interest. It's my thought that the best thing here is to let [Secretary of State William] Rogers take the lead in the damn thing."

When Kissinger informed the president that Golda Meir wanted the Games to be *cancelled* and that she had asked Washington to recommend this step to the IOC, Nixon sputtered, "They're crazy. They just want to look good, don't they?" (Of course, Nixon was well aware that George McGovern and the hated *New York Times* also favored discontinuing the Games—two more reasons not to support that line.) A cancellation of the Games would indeed be crazy, agreed Kissinger, because this would only play into the hands of the terrorists, making it appear that *they* had stopped the Games. "It's just like these assholes, that tried to stop us running the government," Kissinger added—referring to the March on Washington protest demonstration against the Vietnam War.

Yet while opposing a "provocative" response to the Munich tragedy— say, a cancellation of the Games accompanied by an eye-for-an-eye reprisal from Israel—the Nixon administration was quick to condemn in very sharp terms the Black September attack and to express its sympathy for Israel. (According to Kissinger, Washington's harsh response prompted Egypt to use a "private channel to voice its unhappiness about the tone of our public condemnation of the terrorist attack . . . and to express fear that Israeli retaliation against Lebanon might cause some other countries to invite Soviet military help.") Washington was also not hesitant to push for new steps designed to combat Arab-based terrorism. With respect to U.S.

domestic security, Nixon personally ordered special restrictions on Arabs trying to enter the United States. On the international level, Secretary of State Rogers held consultations with a number of foreign governments "to develop more effective measures to counter terrorism." Although Washington's campaign to work out an effective transnational strategy to counter threats like hostage-taking, kidnapping, bombings of public installations, and (above all) air piracy did not bear much fruit in the first years after the Munich tragedy, they amounted to baby steps in what we now call the "war on international terror."

For Golda Meir's government, the imperative was not to work out long-term international strategies to curtail terror but to act immediately and forcefully to show that Israel would not let Arab terrorist actions like the Munich murders go "unpunished." Unquestionably, the Munich killings played into the hands of Israeli hawks like General Dayan who opposed *any* concessions to the Palestinians and were always happy to find new reasons to crack down on the PLO. On September 8, without consulting Washington, Meir (urged on by Dayan) ordered her air force to launch simultaneous raids on ten PLO targets in Syria and Lebanon. The raids killed over two hundred people, many of them women and children. Commenting on the strikes, Israeli foreign minister Abba Eban said (rather unnecessarily) that the Middle East peace process had been "set back indefinitely" by the Munich murders. The only question now, he added, was how to eliminate the terrorist threat for good.

To this end, Israel followed up on the air strikes with a large-scale ground thrust into southern Lebanon by several armored infantry units. To the shock of the Israeli Defense Force (IDF), the Lebanese army put up fierce resistance, resulting in Israeli casualties and a significant loss of momentum. Although the offensive was extended in time and scope, it ended up bagging only a few "guerillas." In the end then, the operation was something of an embarrassment for the mighty IDF, calling into question its mystique of "infallibility and invincibility."

Israel's attacks on Syria and Lebanon were also a source of frustration for Washington, since they might well turn the Arab states toward the Soviet Union. But the Nixon administration did not feel that it could publicly discipline Israel because that is precisely what the Soviets and Chinese were trying to do. On September 10, the Soviet delegate to the United Nations offered a resolution in the Security Council demanding that Israel end its strikes against Syria and Lebanon. The U.S. delegate, future president George H. W. Bush, vetoed the resolution because it failed to include any reference to the Munich killings. His comments at the UN placed Washington firmly on the side of Israel. There had been "grounds to hope that new opportunities for peace were opening up in the Middle East," he said. "Then came 'Munich'—the senseless act of terrorism there which cast a pall over those hopes. Yet we are now meeting on a complaint [regarding Syria]—a complaint that stands out for its unreality. It makes no reference to the tragic events at Munich. It gives no salve to the wounded conscience of an agonized world."

Predictably, Israel's military retaliation against targets in Lebanon and Syria provoked outrage throughout the Arab world, much to the delight of the PLO. Although the Arab states were not yet in a position to take full-scale military countermeasures against Israel, they began the preparations that would culminate in the so-called Yom Kippur War one year later.

In the meantime, Black September struck again against Israel with a spate of letter bombs dispatched to Israeli diplomats in foreign capitals. One of these bombs killed an agricultural official working in the Israeli embassy in London. West Germany, too, looked like it might be the target of more Arab violence. The nation's intelligence agency warned that Arab terrorists already present in the Federal Republic were apparently planning more attacks on FRG territory, though the specific targets were not known.

The horrific Munich attack, combined with the possibility of more terrorist activity from Arabs down the line, forced Bonn into an increasingly bunker-like posture with respect to the Arab world—within and without. Brandt's government ordered "especially sharp scrutiny" on all Arabs traveling to and even out of the Federal Republic. Henceforth, visitors from all Arab states, regardless of the duration of their stay in the FRG, would be required to have visas. All people of Arab nationality residing illegally in the FRG were to be expelled immediately. Arrest orders went out for dozens of Arabs in West Germany believed to have some connection with Black September. In this connection, over one hundred Arab students in the FRG were rounded up, though only a few were actually deported.

On the popular level, Arabs became targets of open hostility and abuse. In Munich, on the day after the terrorist attack, many locals could be heard cursing "the Arabs" in general and demanding that Gastarbeiter of Arab extraction be fired and deported forthwith. The chief of the criminal division of Munich's police put the matter bluntly: "The Arab—he is simply not to be trusted." But this mentality was hardly restricted to the Olympic atrocity's "ground-zero." Across the Federal Republic, citizens took up the call for a wholesale expulsion of Arab immigrants. "Out with the people from these [Arab] lands!" demanded an angry citizen in a letter to the *Frankfurter Allgemeine Zeitung*. "Get them all out of Germany!" Germans suddenly remembered what it was that they disliked about Arabs and how "inassimilable" they seemed to be—how "unlike us" they were and always would be. This wave of anti-Arab hostility, of course, did not escape the attention of FRG observers in the Arab world. The Beirut paper *L'Orient Le Jour* commented in alarm, "It is not pleasant these days to be an Arab in the Federal Republic. The rampant anti-Semitism, which was supposed to have been stamped out of the German character, has simply shifted from Jews to Arabs."

"Dancing at Dachau"

Following the massacre of the Israeli Olympians at Fürstenfeldbruck, the Munich Games were suspended for another fourteen hours (making the total suspension period twenty-four hours). At the official mourning service for the murdered Israelis, which took place at 10:00 a.m. on September 6, all the participant nations' flags flew at half-mast around the stadium— all, that is, except for those of the Arab nations, which insisted that their flags be flown in the usual fashion. Egypt, of course, was not represented at all, and most athletes from the remaining Arab states chose not to attend the service. (For that matter, some athletes from non-Arab nations also stayed away, reportedly to sleep in, to train, or to play Foosball in the Village recreation center.)

After a solemn performance of the second movement of Beethoven's *Eroica* by the Munich Philharmonic Orchestra, various dignitaries, including FRG president Gustav Heinemann, Munich OC chief Willi Daume, Israeli ambassador Eliashiv Ben-Horin, and Israel's Olympic delegation chief Shmuel Lalkin, addressed the crowd. Heinemann pleased his Israeli colleagues by labeling Black September a "criminal organization" and also chastising "those [Arab] countries that had failed to prevent its actions." By far the most notable speech, however, came from outgoing IOC president Avery Brundage. His comments, a fervent litany of the obsessions and crotchets that had served as his life's credo, deserves extensive quotation here; if nothing else, the tirade showed it was high time for the old man to go:

> Every civilized person recoils in horror at the barbarous criminal intrusion of terrorists into peaceful Olympic precincts. We mourn our Israeli friends[,] victims of this brutal assault. The Olympic flags and the flags of the world fly at half-mast. Sadly, in this imperfect world, the greater and the more important the Olympic Games become, the

more they are open to commercial, political, and now criminal pressure. The Games of the XX Olympiad have been subject to 2 savage attacks. We lost the Rhodesian battle against naked political blackmail. We have only the strength of a great ideal. I am sure that the public will agree that we cannot allow a handful of terrorists to destroy this nucleus of international cooperation and good will we have in the Olympic movement. The Games must go on and we must continue our efforts to keep them clean, pure and honest and try to extend the sportsmanship of the athletic field into other areas.

We declare today a day of mourning and will continue the events one day later than originally scheduled.

Brundage delivered this message with great conviction, hammering on the podium with his fist for emphasis. Some in the crowd gasped in disbelief at his coupling of the Israeli murders with the Rhodesian affair as "attacks" of comparable import for the Olympic movement, though others could be seen nodding in agreement. Brundage's old friend, Liselott Diem, thought this speech was "the greatest moment of his life."

It should be noted that the decision to continue with the Games was certainly not Brundage's alone; it had the unanimous backing of the IOC Executive Committee, which argued that this was the "best way to honor the dead and to show loyalty to the Olympic ideal." Many governments, including those in Bonn and Washington, also took this position. A hastily launched public opinion poll in the FRG registered 78 percent in favor of the continuation decision and only 8 percent against. In the end, though, this decision to go on with the Games turned out to be *extremely* controversial, and it ignited a tortured debate about the place of play in a time of great pain and suffering.

Tellingly, even Willi Daume, perhaps the Munich Games' most ardent booster, was, at least initially, opposed to continuing the festival. In the immediate aftermath of the terror attack, he announced that he would "find it difficult" to recommend to the IOC to go on with the Games. Although, as noted, the Nixon administration strongly favored continuing the Games, some influential figures in Washington (in addition to George McGovern) believed the play should be ceased. Most notably, Senate minority leader Mike Mansfield of Montana argued on the Senate floor that the Games should be cancelled "in memory of the dead." As for the American press, two of the most influential organs, the *New York Times* and the *Los Angeles Times*, editorialized against continuing the festival. The *Times* opined that "it would be a desecration of everything for which the Games supposedly stand to continue the 1972 contests." In response to Brundage's speech, a *Los Angeles Times* commentator wrote, "Incredibly, they're going on with it. It's like having a dance at Dachau."

Brundage received some letters of support for his decision, but (judging from an IOC file on this matter) many more missives in opposition. The letters of protest were often bitter and cutting. "Are eleven Israeli lives so meaningless that the Games must go on as if nothing has happened?" asked one correspondent. Another wrote, "I am completely in disaccord with your thoughts. You are a complete embarrassment to the U.S. In fact, you are a silly old man. This was a very serious episode and you didn't help." A New York woman zeroed in on Brundage's equation of the Israeli deaths with the Rhodesian affair: "It shows a horrifying want of proportion . . . to consider the non-violent tactic of boycott as remotely related to the terrorism of the Black September group." Some of the letter writers also insisted that, if the Games had to go on, the organizers must find ways to honor the slain Israelis. Among the suggestions were to award all the murdered athletes posthumous gold medals; emblazon the Star of David on the Olympic flag; play the Israeli national anthem at every medal ceremony; and, on an uglier note, "Tell the Arabs that for every Jew injured or killed, ten Arabs will be killed or tortured."

The Israeli government, as we noted, was strongly opposed to the Games' continuation, and the decision to go on with the play sparked "stupefaction and incredulity" across the Jewish state. Blazing mad, Golda Meir ordered the rest of the Israeli team to return home immediately. Although Israel's Olympic Committee unanimously accepted this decision, not all were in agreement with it. Delegation chief Shmuel Lalkin, who called the terrorist attack a "barbaric rape of the Olympic spirit," would have preferred to stay on and compete. Race-walker Shaul Ladany tried to talk his colleagues out of leaving. In his view, "abandoning the Olympic arena" was tantamount to handing the Palestinian terrorists "another victory." (Israel, by the way, was not the only non-Arab government to pull its team out of Munich. Ferdinand Marcos ordered the entire Philippine team home in a show of solidarity with the Israelis.)

And what about the athletes whose governments did not act on their behalf—those who faced individually the decision to play or not play in the wake of the horrific events of September 5/6? Willi Daume reported after a brief visit to the Village on the day after the killings that most of the Olympians were in favor of continuing the competitions. They claimed that they wanted to go on not merely for the opportunity to win medals but also in order "to show that understanding among peoples [was] still possible."

No doubt Daume's informal survey was accurate enough. But there were a few athletes who simply found it morally unacceptable to go on competing in light of what had happened. Although he personally had no more games to play in (his team having been eliminated), West German footballer Uli Hoeness argued vehemently that *no one* should continue competing at Munich: "After this terrible tragedy it is an abomination to continue fighting for medals. What sportsman could now take any real pleasure in achieving an athletic victory?" Six members of the Dutch team decided to leave Munich in order to protest, as one of them put it, the "obscene" decision to continue play. Thirteen Norwegian athletes also packed up and left, declaring in a joint statement that they could not continue competing "when eleven of our sports colleagues have been murdered." (Tellingly, however, three of ten boycotting members of the Norwegian handball team returned to play because the International Handball Federation threatened to hold Norway financially responsible for lost gate receipts if Norway had to withdraw from its remaining matches for lack of sufficient players. The three would-be boycotters who rejoined the Norwegian handball team for a match against Japan wore black armbands to show their sympathy for the murdered Israelis.) Not surprisingly, America's Olga Connolly, the feisty political activist who had smuggled peace buttons into the Olympic Village, was appalled by the decision to play on. In the wake of Brundage's announcement she declared, "It seems incredible that after the terrible tragedy of the past few days, in which our brothers, 11 Olympic athletes, were killed, we are kept at the level of playing Ping-Pong." For Connolly, Brundage's "Games Must Go On" dictum was just one more demonstration of the moral and political bankruptcy of the Olympic movement. "Olympic officials speak the words of brotherhood and peace, but this is only political mouthwash," she complained. "When you see it from the inside, you are disgusted to see that the Games, a kind of Circus Maximus, are not conducted for anything else but commercialism, medal counts, and political profit."

Even those athletes who decided to stay on and continue competing were sometimes severely conflicted about their decision. After initially vowing to withdraw from competition, West German middle-distance runner Ellen Tittel decided to run after all, to dedicate her race to the slain Israelis, and to send any medal she might win to Israel. (Alas, she won no medals.) The American runner Steve Prefontaine also declared a preference for leaving Munich when he learned what had happened at Fürstenfeldbruck. "If they loaded us all into a plane right now to take us home, I'd go," the runner reportedly said. But Bill Bowerman and assistant U.S. track coach

Bill Dellinger managed to calm Pre down, and soon he was blowing steam less over the terrorist attack than over the fact that the twenty-four-hour suspension of play would give Lasse Virén another day to recover from the 10,000-meter race before competing (against Pre) in the 5,000-meter event. Albeit devastated by the Munich murders, American marathoners Frank Shorter and Kenny Moore were also relieved that they would get to compete after all. Their zeal to run was not dulled by the ominous news that their British colleagues had received death threats from the Irish Republican Army (IRA), or the knowledge that there was no way that any of the marathoners could be protected from terrorist attacks along the race route. "We have to not let this detract from our performance," said Shorter, "because that's what they [the terrorists] want." In truth, distracting the American marathoners was probably not high on any terrorist's wish list but to think so apparently helped justify the determination to keep focused on competing rather than on the horror that had just engulfed the Games. Moore decided to let that horror serve as a source of strength during the race. As he ran, he would measure his own (paltry) suffering against that which his fellow Olympians from Israel had experienced during their final hours of life. "Every time I would get a stitch in my side, or a cramp running up a hamstring, I would ask myself if this passing ache were comparable to what they felt in that phosphorous conflagration."

On September 7, the remaining members of the Israeli Olympic delegation flew home, along with ten caskets draped in the national colors; David Berger's body was flown back to Cleveland, where his parents still resided. Foreign Minister Walter Scheel saw the Israelis off, shaking the hand of each one and expressing his condolences in the name of the West German government. Representing the Munich OC, ex-mayor Hans-Jochen Vogel accompanied the Israelis to Lod Airport in Tel Aviv, where he participated in a brief mourning ceremony.

Anton Fliegerbauer, the Munich police officer killed at Fürstenfeldbruck, was honored at a large civic funeral on September 8 with Mayor Georg Kronawitter and Bavarian minister-president Alfons Goppel in attendance. Fliegerbauer's death, while lamentable for his family, was actually a godsend for the West German officials and public because it allowed them to claim a shared "victim" status along with the Israelis. Although the precise details of the officer's death remained unclear (was he hit by friendly fire?), at his funeral he was hailed as a hero who had sacrificed his own life in an effort to save the lives of Jews. As if to cement this alleged bond of victimhood, a representative of Golda Meir's government expressed the gratitude of the Israeli people for Fliegerbauer's martyrdom.

Yet, it would probably be safe to say that the Israeli populace as a whole did not see this man's sacrifice, however it had come about, as sufficient cause to let the Germans off the hook for what had happened at Fürsten-feldbruck—much less to consider them joint victims in this tragedy.

Three days after Fliegerbauer's funeral, the bodies of the five Black Septembrists killed at Fürstenfeldbruck were flown to Tripoli, Libya. It had taken considerable time to identify the dead men because the three survivors initially refused to provide any information about their compatriots. West German newspapers published pictures of the men, asking, "Who knows these dead Arabs?" Eventually, the Black September survivors came through with the names, and Bonn, after rejecting a request from Tunisia for the bodies, acceded to a similar offer of burial from Libya, which at that point was already under the dictatorial control of Colonel Muammar Gaddafi. In Tripoli, thousands of mourners clamored to touch the caskets as they were carried through the streets. A group of wealthy Libyans paid for the dead men's relatives to fly to Tripoli so that they could personally honor their "heroic sons" and preside over the erection of a memorial attesting to the nobility of their sacrifice for the Arab cause. Libyan Radio pronounced the five dead Palestinians "martyrs," and the Voice of Palestine broadcast what it claimed was a "last testament" composed by the deceased on the eve of the Munich operation. "We are neither killers nor bandits," said the testament. "We are persecuted people who have no homeland." While skeptical of their chances for success, the fedayeen insisted in their testament that they had been willing "to give up our lives from the very first moment. . . . This time we shall force [the world] to know we are serious." The testament ended with an apology to "the sporting youth of the world" for intruding upon the Munich Games.

> We are asking them to know that there is a people with a twenty-four-year-old case of injustice. It would do no harm to the youth of the world to learn of our plight, if only for a few hours. We are not against any people, but why should our place here [at Munich] be taken by the flag of the occupiers . . . why should the whole world be having fun and entertainment while we suffer with all ears deaf to us?

CHAPTER Seven

The Games Go On

The important thing is not the triumph but the struggle.
—Pierre de Coubertin

Winning isn't the important thing; it's the only thing.
—Vince Lombardi

Immediately after the conclusion of the memorial service for the slain Israeli Olympians, the atmosphere in the stricken host city was tense and gloomy. With backing from Chancellor Willy Brandt, Willi Daume had arranged for the Bundesgrenzschutz to guard the entire Olympic complex day and night, giving the area the look of "an armed camp." Armored cars took up positions at strategic points around the Olympic Village. Because threats were still coming in against Jews, special protections were accorded to officials and physical assets of Jewish cultural and religious institutions in Munich, as well as to the Israeli Olympic attaché, who had stayed behind after the Israeli team returned to Tel Aviv. "Rumors of threats" to the Federal Republic of Germany (FRG) and German Democratic Republic (GDR) Olympic delegations resulted in extra protections for these groups as well. Meanwhile, at Riem Airport all arriving Arabs lacking a permanent residence or relatives in the FRG were immediately turned back.

Much to the frustration of Olympic visitors, the Games' most popular cultural attraction, the Spielstraße, was shut down on grounds that its kind of frivolity was no longer appropriate. The project's artists had not been consulted on this move, and they were up in arms over the Organizing Committee's (OC) decision to shut *them* down while continuing with the athletic competitions. A group of aggrieved Spielstraße artists held a press conference at which they vented their spleen. "Our helplessness vis-à-vis the powers who decide what happens around here is the decisive lesson we're taking away from this entire experience," said one of the artists. Another noted bitterly, "It was clear to us from the outset that the Spielstraße had an alibi function. We were the court jesters, hired on in order to embody the Joyful Games. Now we're no longer wanted."

Not surprisingly, the competitions themselves became caught up in the new mood of extreme tension and wariness. The first post-memorial event, a handball match between Romania and Hungary (two countries with little love for each other), nearly didn't come off because a bomb threat was called in thirty minutes before the scheduled start. The match proceeded only after police cordoned off the venue and thoroughly searched the premises.

A cycling road race on the morning of September 7 added yet another frisson of tension to the proceedings. Seven Irish Republican Army (IRA) activists managed, despite new security protocols, to crash the race. Although three of the interlopers were apprehended at the starting line, another evaded detection and three more jumped into the race during the first lap. One of the intruders caused a massive pileup in an effort to knock an official Irish rider off his bike. The race managed to go on, and no one was seriously injured, but the IRA touted their "peaceful demonstration" as a useful means of reminding the world about British rule in Northern Ireland.

Three days later, on the evening of September 10, it looked as if the Games' worst nightmare might be recurring when someone reported shots being fired near the Moroccan team headquarters in the Olympic Village. Police immediately shut down the complex and launched a search of the area. The putative shooter or shooters were never found, however, and after a few hours the athletes were allowed to move about their beleaguered camp. "We seem to be dealing with a macabre piece of nonsense," said Johnny Klein of this latest alarum in the Village.

At the same time though, strained and wary as the mood in Munich might have been, most of the athletes were fiercely determined to shut out any distracting fears and get back as best they could to the business at hand—the business of competing for Olympic glory. (And it's probably fair to say that most of those athletes *could* take pleasure in winning medals, despite claims by the likes of Uli Hoeness that this would be impossible after the murders of the Israeli Olympians.)

It also needs to be said that the shock over the "Munich Massacre" dissipated rather quickly once the competitions resumed. As Munich's *Süddeutsche Zeitung (SZ)* reported, signs of a "return to normalcy" abounded within a couple days of the killings: not only were crowds once again cheering at the Olympic sites, but also scalpers were back hawking tickets; autograph-seekers were hounding athletes; the Hofbräuhaus was filled to capacity, and the famous City Hall Glockenspiel, after a brief silence, was back charming tourists at the Marienplatz. Citing a line in the *New York Times*, the *SZ* observed that Munich was "in danger of becoming a world-wide symbol of insensitivity."

Back on Track?

Courtesy largely of the Americans, the track and field competition at Munich had frequently been marked by contentiousness and posturing, so perhaps it is not surprising that the Yank team would be the source of another moment of major acrimony once the track events resumed following the terror attack of September 5.

One of the premier running events still to be contested in the final phase of the '72 Games was the men's 400-meter race. Runners from the United States were expected to dominate this event, as they had so often done in the past. Here, the American coaches believed, was a good chance to make up for the series of embarrassments and disappointments that had plagued the U.S. track squad in Munich thus far. As it happened, Americans *did* dominate the race—but managed nonetheless to turn a splendid athletic performance into yet another public relations disaster for Team USA.

Lee Evans, the defending 400-meter Olympic champion from 1968, had failed to qualify for this event in the U.S. trials. Thus, Vince Matthews, the third-place finisher in the trials, joined Californians John Smith and Wayne Collett on a powerful Yank trio entered in the 400 at Munich. Among these three, Smith was considered the strongest contender for a gold medal, followed by Collett and Matthews. The latter, a New York City Neighborhood Youth Corps worker who, due to poverty and lack of connections, had to train by himself at night in a Brooklyn school yard, never felt wanted by the U.S. track establishment. He especially resented rumors that he might be replaced in the 400 by Evans, who had qualified for Munich as a member of the 4 × 400–meter relay team. More broadly, having witnessed the Smith-Carlos "Black Power" demonstration as a member of the U.S. track team in Mexico City, the young New Yorker had come to share his former teammates' belief that racism still ruled American high-level sport and the Olympics. Thus, by his own admission, Matthews carried a major chip on his shoulder into the Munich Games. And yet, as he crouched at the starting line for the 400-meter final, his only concern was to do his best and help his team to a possible sweep; many of his family members, after all, were sitting in the stands.

Shortly after the race began, Smith, running with a slightly injured leg, badly tore a hamstring and tumbled to the track, writhing in pain. So much for an American sweep. After seeing their teammate go down, Collett and Matthews charged into the lead. In the final lap, Matthews pushed ahead of Collett, surprising himself as much as his American rival. Still feeling strong in the last straightaway, Matthews managed to hold off a surging Collett to win by four meters. In third place was Julius Sang, a Kenyan (and the first Black African to medal in the 400).

As soon as they finished the race, Matthews and Collett rushed over to Smith, who was still lying on the track. They helped him up and got him to a medical station. Their elation over their one-two finish was tempered by sympathy for Smith and anger over the medical authorities' failure to come immediately to his aid. Matthews, moreover, was still disgusted by the International Olympic Committee's (IOC) decision to resume the competitions "as if nothing had happened"—that is, to continue unabashed with all the "fanfare of medal presentations, national anthems and flag-raising ceremonies." Why couldn't the athletes "just run their races, pick up their medals in the Village and leave in peace?" he asked.

The two American runners were thus in a somewhat less-than-celebratory mood when, after refusing to dab on some pancake makeup, they were summoned to the awards ceremony. Rather than taking their appointed places on the podium, both men climbed to the top rung reserved for the champion. Collett appeared barefoot and in shorts rather than in the traditional sweat suit; Matthews wore sweats and shoes but left his jacket unzipped. And rather than gaze in solemn reverence at Old Glory and sing along as "The Star-Spangled Banner" was played, they glanced around the stadium, chatting quietly between themselves. As for posture, Matthews kept his hands on his hips when he wasn't stroking his goatee, while Collett fiddled with a pair of old shoes hanging around his neck. Upon stepping off the platform Matthews twirled his gold medal around one of his fingers; Collett briefly raised one fist in what looked like the now-familiar Black Power salute.

In the case of the Smith-Carlos demonstration at Mexico City four years earlier, it had taken the crowd some moments to catch on to what was happening and to show its displeasure. Not so this time. A huge chorus of boos, whistles, and catcalls immediately rained down on the athletes as they left the podium.

Given the massive tragedy that had just befallen these Games, the crowd response to the Matthews-Collett incident seems somewhat over the top. Yet the fans, the vast majority of them Germans, might not have been responding merely to this one incident. Quite possibly, their hyperbolic reaction represented an outburst of pent-up indignation over what they saw as repeated displays of American "arrogance" and petulance in these Games. And on a deeper level, the Munich fans' anger at the American athletes for failing to show proper "Olympic spirit" may also have reflected a submerged sense of shame over their own country's failure to protect the Games from a much more serious defilement.

Whatever the reasons for the crowd's behavior in this instance, it suggested that the Munich organizers' fond hopes that their Games would be free of any Mexico City–style podium antics had been dashed.

But was the Matthews-Collett gesture in Munich '72 really an act of genuine political protest—a reprise, however muted, of the infamous Smith-Carlos demonstration of '68? Or was it more a sign of personal pique? After the fact, the athletes themselves provided contradictory answers to questions regarding their motives. Matthews initially denied that he and Collett were trying to make a "political" statement at all. "We came up [to the podium] with no protest in mind, but the crowd had protest in mind when we left. If people call our talking on the stand a protest, well, some people can watch *Alice in Wonderland* and get pornography out of it." Yet, when pressed, Matthews conceded that his behavior on the stand had "looked cynical," adding that it all "had to do with things that had happened before I got [to Munich]." And two years later, in his memoirs, Matthews portrayed his actions on the podium as a form of political protest after all: "For me, not standing at attention meant that I wasn't going along with a program dictated by Number One: those John Wayne types— my country right or wrong. . . . I just wasn't going along with the program of all those patriotic people, period."

Collett, for his part, initially claimed that his raised-fist gesture was merely a wave to friends in the stands. But a little later, in an interview with Howard Cosell,* he too changed his tune, insisting that his behavior on the podium had political meaning. "I feel that, looking back on it now, my actions on the victory stand probably will mirror the attitude of white America towards blacks—total casual as long as we're not embarrassing them." Defending his failure to show conventional piety during the playing of the national anthem, he added, "I couldn't stand there and sing the words because I don't believe they're true. I wish they were. I think we have the potential to have a beautiful country, but I don't think we do."

Jesse Owens, by contrast, had rarely found occasion to protest racism in the United States, despite having experienced plenty of it himself. In 1968, egged on by Avery Brundage, he had famously chastised Tommie Smith and John Carlos for their Black Power demonstration. Now, in 1972, at the behest of the United States Olympic Committee (USOC), the aging hero of Berlin '36 attempted to coax an apology from Matthews and Collett for their antics on the victory podium. At a meeting with the athletes on the morning following the incident, Owens suggested that a few words of regret from the two runners might possibly "wipe out the stain" of their insulting behavior and avert IOC sanctions against themselves and the U.S. track team. According to Matthews, "Jesse's lecture contained the same twenty-dollar words and phrases that he had tossed around in 1968, about the importance our participation had for the United States and the opportunities that were available to us." Matthews apparently said nothing in response to Owens's oily diplomacy, but an outraged Collett vehemently rejected the elderly star's proposal, along with his offer to "represent" the two athletes before the IOC. Realizing that no apology was in the offing, Owens (again according to Matthews) suggested that the men simply explain to the IOC that they "weren't aware of what [they] were doing." If they would do this, assured Owens, they might not only placate the IOC but also make it possible for him to broker post-Olympics jobs for the two runners with big American corporations anxious to hire famous black athletes. To Matthews, Owens's proposed plea of ignorance was "more of the same old game: we were just a bunch of poor little niggers who had been chewing on loco weed or something and didn't know how to act or talk in

* In a 1976 ABC documentary entitled "Triumph and Tragedy: The Olympic Experience," Cosell linked the earlier Smith-Carlos demonstration in Mexico City with the '72 Black September attack, implying that the one set the stage for the other: "And so the use of the Olympic Games as a forum for protest, which really gained international attention in 1968, grew even further in 1972 and to what some might regard as the *genesis* for the most horrible thing that's ever happened in any Olympiad: the grotesque massacre of eleven Israelis by members of the Black September gang, an offshoot of the Palestinian Liberation Organization."

the white man's world." Matthews reportedly ended the meeting by telling the grand old man of American track where he could stick his groveling "bull shit" and promises of forgiveness and favors from "Whitey."

As it happened, "Whitey"—in the person of Brundage—was anything but in a forgiving mood in the wake of this new (in his words) "disgrace to sport, to the Olympic movement, and to the United States." Without even consulting officials of the USOC on the matter, Brundage convened a session of the IOC Executive Board, which, at his urging, ordered the two Americans to vacate the Olympic Village immediately. Although the athletes were not to be stripped of their medals, they were "banned for life" from all further Olympic competition.

Brundage's anger extended also to USOC president Clifford Buck, who in his view deserved part of the blame for this embarrassment. In a letter to the American official, Brundage fumed over the "disgusting display of your two athletes" during the medal ceremony, noting that this was "the second time the USOC has permitted such occurrences on the athletic field" (the first, of course, being the Smith-Carlos affair). "If such a performance would happen in the future," Brundage warned, "please be advised that the medals will be withheld from the athletes in question."

Stung by Brundage's criticism of the USOC's apparent inability to run a tight Olympic ship, Clifford Buck jumped on Matthews and Collett with some additional punishments of his own. In private letters to the two athletes he wrote,

> After careful consideration, it is the opinion of the USOC officers that because of your demonstrated flagrant disrespect for the flag of your country, and because of the discredit you have brought to our U.S. Olympic team, you are no longer eligible to wear any insignia of the 1972 USA Olympic Team. Accordingly, you will please remove all Olympic patches and insignia from your clothing and competitive apparel.

Buck also issued a press release affirming the USOC's horror over actions like those of Matthews and Collett but insisting at the same time that the committee could not be expected to field a group of athletes *guaranteed* to toe the Olympic line at all times. Noting that "all athletes, regardless of race, color, and economic status" had an "equal opportunity" to compete on American Olympic teams, he concluded, "No method has been devised for a definitive selection process by which we can infallibly detect in advance, and exclude from the team, athletes who will not properly represent their country in their actions." Buck's point, of course, was that if the United States wanted truly integrated and openly selected (not to mention *winning*) Olympic teams, it had better be prepared for a few rough edges.

This was more or less the opinion of Coach Bill Bowerman, too. Although Bowerman thought that Matthews and Collett had "made asses of themselves," he also believed their stunt was "no big deal." And in an interview, he added, "You cannot expect on an Olympic squad of sixty to have everybody act like army privates. They're great athletes. They're great individuals. The fact that some of them did things that the press objected to didn't bother me too much. They're vivid, alive, human animals. They're keenly interested, very competitive, and all different. So why not accept that and enjoy it?"

It wasn't just the German fans, Olympic officials, and much of the U.S. press that displayed a pronounced unwillingness to "accept," much less "enjoy," deviations from accepted pieties on the part of top-level athletes. Many private citizens, the bulk of them Americans, deluged the IOC and USOC with indignant complaints over the antics of Matthews and Collett. Some of these missives were infused with a barely concealed racism. For example, the president of a pipe and foundry company in North Carolina ranted in a letter to Buck about the "two colored ingrates' disgusting performance," claiming it had undone "in two minutes all the goodwill and fine image that our Olympic competitors have built up over the past decades." If the USOC wished continued economic support from the citizenry, this writer added, it had better "make every effort to select a team comprised of patriotic men and women who will compete in the true Olympic sense and not permit selfish and politically motivated individuals such as these two to disgrace our team and our country." An even more outraged correspondent considered the Matthews-Collett incident "the most shameful outrage perpetrated against the American people that I, and probably the whole world, have ever seen." Like his similarly outraged (but perhaps not quite so historically myopic) colleague, this fellow insisted that America must not be so greedy for Olympic medals that it would allow *just anyone* on its teams.

> We demand that the American Olympic Committee hereafter ensures that only those Americans who are willing and able to meet simple standards of courtesy, good manners and respect be allowed to represent this country. Surely those ideals are equivalent requirements for national representation as physical ability; because if *mere brute force* is

the only requirement for such representation, then this country and the whole world are in trouble." (italics in original)

Writing personally to Brundage, another angry American, after thanking the IOC president for banning Matthews and Collett, proposed that Clifford Buck be sent packing, too, on grounds that he "pleaded for the future of people like these athletes," who after all were "not true Americans." Unfortunately, this self-appointed patriot added, "They [the Matthews' and Colletts' of the world] happen to live in our great country but they do not behave as our countrymen."

For the U.S. track and field team, the misery that was Munich continued with the surprising failure of Jim Ryun, America's premier miler, to qualify for the finals in the 1,500-meter race. In a preliminary heat, he got tangled up with another runner and went down hard on the track with about 550 meters to go. He got up and chased the pack, but unlike Lasse Virén in the 10 km event, he was unable to overcome the deficit. American officials immediately demanded a rerun on grounds that Ryun had been tripped, but the IOC, though agreeing that there had been a foul, rejected the American petition.

The U.S. men undoubtedly stood a good chance of finally getting back on track in the 4 × 400–meter relay—the American lineup for this event was considered the strongest in the house—but, as it happened, the American squad didn't get on the track at all. The originally scheduled American lineup for the relay included Matthews and Collett, but their abrupt exclusion from all further Olympic competition obviously meant that they would not be on the starting line. Unavailable, too, was the projected U.S. anchor, John Smith, because of his severe injury. The loss of these three competitors left the United States without enough fast bodies to put on the line for the 4 × 400–meter relay. In Bowerman's view, this U.S. no-show, which he blamed on the ban of Matthews and Collett by the IOC, represented the loss of a sure gold medal for America and yet another case of the Yanks getting "jobbed" by Olympic officials. "Every time we turned around we got jobbed," he complained bitterly.

With the Americans out of the picture in the relay, the race was up for grabs, and it was the powerful Kenyans who grabbed most effectively, with Julius Sang running an astounding 43.5 anchor leg to blow by a West German, a Frenchman, and finally Britain's David Jenkins to bring in the victory.

Arguably the greatest disappointment for the Americans in the final phase of the track and field competition at Munich was not their withdrawal from the 4 × 400 relay, or even the sad fate of Jim Ryun, but the failure of wonder-boy Steve Prefontaine to medal in the 5,000-meter event, a race that he (and his huge following back home) fully expected him to win.

Well before Munich, "Pre" had become a megastar on the American running scene due not only to a string of phenomenal performances in high school and at the University of Oregon but also to his go-for-broke style and aggressive swagger. He insisted on trying to hold the lead from start to finish in every race he ran; any other strategy, such as "drafting" behind a fellow runner to save energy, he considered "cheating." Pre's massive popularity, especially among the ladies, was not hampered by his matinee-idol looks.

At the Olympic trials for the 5,000 in Eugene, Oregon, in July, Pre defied the advice of Coach Bowerman to play it safe and simply qualify for Munich. Once again, he took off like the proverbial mechanical rabbit in a greyhound race and held the lead throughout, setting an American record for the distance. Sounding rather like Mark Spitz before Mexico City, he predicted he'd run ten seconds faster in Munich.

Pre's training runs at the Olympic Stadium in Munich did nothing to dim that confidence. He told reporters that he was doing things on that fast track that even *he* "did not think possible." If everything went according to plan in the final, he said, rivals like Lasse Virén and Kip Keino of Kenya were "going to have to run like hell to beat me. Right now, I feel so good that I don't know how fast I can go and it scares me a little thinking I have that much inside me."

It turned out that what Pre actually had inside him on the eve of the 5,000-meter final was an unusual case of nerves, complicated by a deep sense of sorrow and confusion stemming from the recent mayhem in Munich. He had managed to safely qualify in his heat on September 7, but an observer noted that "the looseness, lift and drive that characterize Prefontaine's style seemed missing."

The 5,000 final on the following day featured an extremely slow pace in the early going, and Pre, very uncharacteristically, chose to stay in the middle of the pack for much of the race. Only in the final mile did he surge into his usual place at the front. Yet this time he could not hold his lead. Lasse Virén and then Mohamed Gammoudi of Tunisia stayed with him for a bit, then vied for the lead themselves in the final lap. Pre tried valiantly to catch the two front-runners, but for once his legs would not obey his brain. Not only did he fail to close the gap, but also he fell completely out of medal contention when Britain's Ian Stewart motored past him in the final few meters. The victor turned out to be Virén, the Finn whom Pre had watched win the 10,000, hoping the man had "shot his wad." Obviously he hadn't: Virén's time of 13.26.04 was a new Olympic record, and with this victory in the 5,000 he became only the fourth man in Olympic history to achieve the middle-distance "double."

For Bill Bowerman, Pre's fourth-place finish in the 5,000 was maddening but not his sole source of frustration. Coach Bill's most famous protégé, it turned out, was wearing Adidas shoes rather than those of Nike, the new company Bowerman had helped found along with a former middle-distance runner and Stanford Business School graduate named Philip Knight. Bowerman's role in the fledgling enterprise was mainly that of designer. Like one of those geeky computer wizards crafting pioneer hardware in a Silicon Valley garage, Bowerman came up with amazing innovations in his home kitchen in Eugene. One of them was a shoe he called "The Vagina" (looking "scary on the outside but feeling wonderful on the inside"); another was the famous "Waffle" sole, made by melting rubber on his wife's waffle-iron. Bowerman had tried repeatedly to get Pre to wear the new waffle Nikes, but the headstrong runner, albeit loyal to his coach, also felt loyal to Adidas, the shoe he had always worn. Moreover, in the months before Munich, he was being just as assiduously courted by an Adidas representative as he was by Bowerman. Caught between these two loyalties, Pre agreed on the eve of the Munich Games to a decision-making contest proposed by the man from Adidas. If Pre could down a glass of wine faster than the Adidas rep, he'd wear Nike; otherwise, it would be Adidas. Naturally, the Bavarian salesman turned out to be the superior drinker, and Pre perforce wore the three-striped German shoes rather than the Nike "Swoosh" in the fateful 5,000. (For the Adidas man, Pre's disappointing finish was no big deal because the three medalists, Virén, Gammoudi, and Stewart, were all wearing his brand. Only later did Nike overtake Adidas in popularity, its aggressive marketing earning it the sobriquet "Swooshtika.")

After the Munich Games, Steve Prefontaine fell into a black hole of depression and even contemplated quitting racing entirely. Within a few months, however, he was out of the bars and back on the track, running being his most effective form of self-medication. He started racing well again and harbored hopes for redemption at the Montreal Olympics in 1976. But Pre never made it to Montreal. On May 30, 1975, he crashed his sports car while driving near his home in Eugene and died almost immediately. Like actor James Dean, whom he resembled in many ways, his untimely death served to feed a posthumous fame. Some thirty years later, two *homage* films were made about this mercurial figure. The better of the two movies, featuring Billy Cruddup as Pre, was appropriately entitled *Without Limits*.

If the American men were having their troubles on the Munich track, their female counterparts were faring even worse. Instead of stacking up their usual respectable pile of gold medals, American women had garnered only a couple of bronzes in the running events after almost all the competitions had been completed. "What's wrong with the American women?" a U.S. coach was asked as the Yank girls moved closer to being shut out of a gold medal in Olympic track and field for the first time ever. "They're doing all their running between 9 and 11 every night in the discotheque at the Olympic Village," the coach replied.

Finally, as the track and field competitions in Munich had almost reached their conclusion, there came some solace for Team USA (if only for the men). Rod Milburn, another of the U.S. squad's large contingent of African Americans, easily won the 110-meter hurdles with a time that equaled the world record. Milburn had almost not made it to Munich at all because in the American trials in Eugene he had hit two hurdles and barely qualified for the team. Milburn, moreover, was one of those American athletes who, like Pre and marathoner Frank Shorter, wondered whether it made sense to continue competing in the aftermath of the horrible slaughter of his fellow Olympians. Telling a reporter for the *New York Times* that the tragedy had "destroyed the whole morale of the U.S. team," he seriously considered going home immediately. Again like his shaken colleagues, however, he ultimately concluded that the best way to "honor" the slain Israelis was not only to stay and compete but also to throw one's all into that competition.

The men's 4 × 100–meter relay, one of the premier track events in the Games, also provided a bit of saving grace for the Americans. Almost always an exciting race to watch, the 100-meter relay in 1972 promised to be especially gripping because the United States and the Soviet Union had both qualified with very strong teams. The U.S. squad was anchored by none other than Eddie Hart, the poor fellow who had missed qualifying for the 100-meter dash final because his coach had given him the wrong starting time for his preliminary heat. To add to the drama, the Soviet team featured as *its* anchor Valery Borzov, the Ukrainian speedster who had recently been crowned, much to Hart's horror, as the "fastest man in the world." Making the race even more meaningful, especially for the home crowd, was the fact that both Germanys had qualified, so this relay would be a German-German duel as well as a USSR/U.S. showdown.

One of the things that make a relay race so exciting to watch is the baton handoff between runners—always a tricky maneuver loaded with potential for humiliating catastrophe. (In the 1936 Berlin Games, one of the runners on the German women's 4 × 100–meter relay team dropped the baton, causing her squad to lose to the Americans. To make matters worse, the unfortunate baton drop occurred right in front of Hitler, who was not amused.) On the occasion of the men's relay in Munich, there were no such snafus, and even the Americans managed not to screw up. In fact, after the first three legs, American runners Larry Black, Robert Taylor, and Gerald Tinker had opened a five-meter lead over the Soviets. In the anchor leg, Hart easily held off Borzov—indeed, increased the margin and ensured thereby a world record total time of 38.19. For Hart, this was certainly a measure of redemption, suggesting as it did that perhaps the "fastest man in the world" was not "a Commie" after all.

As for the fastest German, that man turned out to be Klaus Ehl, anchor of the West German team, which took the bronze medal. Of course, this result proved especially gratifying to the home crowd, which hadn't expected a medal at all.

Even more gratifying, because even less expected, was the victory by the West German women's team in the 4 × 100–meter relay race. The team from the GDR was heavily favored to win this event; the East Germans had set a new European record in their qualifying heat and had as their anchor Renate Stecher, the gold medalist in both the 100- and 200-meter dashes. Stecher's counterpart on the West German team was the redoubtable Heidi Rosendahl, who had already medaled in the long jump and pentathlon, but she was not considered a match for Stecher in a 100-meter race.

And yet, it was Rosenthal who played the key role in West Germany's victory, for in her anchor leg she managed to protect her team's one-meter advantage against a surging Stecher. With this achievement, bespectacled Heidi Rosendahl became, at least in the eyes of the home crowd, the true "Face of the Munich Games."

That face for the Soviets, in track and field at least, undoubtedly was Valery Borzov, but the runner-up for this distinction was certainly Mykola Avilov, winner of the decathlon in '72. Like Borzov's victories in the sprints, Avilov's win in the grueling ten-event decathlon was a novelty, for no Russian had ever placed first. Over the years, Americans had dominated the decathlon, and the United States had a good prospect to do so again at Munich in the person of Jeff Bannister, who had won the U.S. Olympic trials. However, like so many U.S. track and field hopefuls, Bannister had bad luck in Munich. In a high hurdles heat, he hit two of the barriers after being thrown off stride in attempting to evade another competitor who had fallen down in the next lane. Bannister was disqualified and put out of the running for a medal. Yet it cannot be said that Bannister's bad luck was the primary factor in Avilov's good fortune. In second place after the first day of competition, the Russian amazingly posted victories in every one of the events on the concluding day. Overall, he won seven of the ten events and ended up with 8,454 points, a new world record.

The man whose record Avilov had just bested, American Bill Toomey, happened to be in Munich doing commentary for ABC TV. Toomey rushed over to congratulate Avilov—a gesture that, sadly, was hardly characteristic of the American behavior at Munich vis-à-vis their Cold War rivals.

Soviet success in track and field at Munich did not end with the spectacular achievements of Borzov and Avilov. In the men's high jump, another discipline traditionally dominated by the Americans (albeit not in 1960 and 1964), Juri Tarmak edged out East Germany's Stefan Junge and America's Dwight Stones. Victor Saneyev bested an old East German rival, Jörg Drehmel, in the triple jump. Anatoly Bondarchuk set an Olympic record in the hammer throw with a heave of 75.5 meters. On the women's side, Lyudmila Bragina won the 1,500-meter race (the first time that females ran this distance in the Olympics) with a sensational time of 4:01.4, chopping three seconds off the previous world record that she herself had set.

A Run around the Dog

Technically, the marathon is a "track" event, but, of course, like the 50-kilometer race-walk, it could not transpire exclusively or even primarily on the track (that would have been a major bore!), and since its inception as a competitive sport in the late nineteenth century, it had carved out a special niche all its own. In the history of the modern Olympics, the marathon also enjoyed a special place. Traditionally coming on the final day of competition, it became one of the most celebrated and closely watched of all Olympic events. Perhaps this was because it is the most grueling of all footraces. In the vast majority of Olympic running events, the number of competitors who do not finish is minimal, but not so in the marathon. In the 1924 Paris Olympic marathon, twenty-eight of the fifty-eight starters failed to complete the course. Matters improved a bit after that, yet broader statistics still tell a Darwinistic tale: in the twenty-four men's marathons run between 1896 and 1996 (there were no women's Olympic marathons until 1984), only 73.5 percent of the starters managed to finish, and one actually died trying!

Another intriguing aspect of the Olympic marathon, especially in its earlier iterations, involved a proclivity for mismanagement and royal screw-ups. The course for the marathon at the 1900 Paris Games was so labyrinthine and badly marked that two Americans, running in the lead, took some wrong turns and ended up finishing behind a pair of Frenchmen, who, the Americans suspected, might have availed themselves of a shortcut or two. At the St. Louis Games in 1904, the eventual winner, America's Tommie Hicks, was preceded into the stadium by a fellow American named Fred Lorz who had started the race on foot but then switched to a car for nineteen miles before reentering the course on foot shortly before the finish. (Hicks, who had ingested regular doses of strychnine to get him through this ordeal, got his gold medal only after Lorz, an inveterate practical jokester, admitted he had not run the entire race.) In the London Games of 1908, where the now-standard marathon distance of 26.2 miles was first established, an exhausted and disoriented Italian runner who approached the finish in first place was actually *carried* over the line by race officials, who worried that otherwise the tottering fellow might drop dead in front of Queen Alexandra. After much confusion and acrimony, the gold medal was awarded to the second man to cross the line, American John Hayes. Following a string of relatively scandal-free marathons following the London debacle of 1908, Munich '72 would, as we shall see, revive an old pattern.

In the early 1970s, marathon running was just starting its ascendancy to the level of worldwide craze it enjoys today. The fad was coming on especially strong in America, where municipal marathons and running clubs were sprouting up as furiously as the foot-fungus patches in all those newly purchased Nikes. Munich '72, occurring as it did on the cusp of this craze, was expected to profit from all the fuss. The marathon race that year would feature a larger field than ever before and enjoy, for the first time ever, global television coverage. Hoping to maximize its own ratings, ABC Television hired none other than Erich Segal, author of the best-selling *Love Story* tear-jerker and an accomplished amateur runner, to provide color commentary for its coverage of the big race.

An American had not won the Olympic marathon since 1908, but some observers thought that might change in 1972. Team USA had a strong contender in Frank Shorter, an up-and-coming marathoner who had actually been born in Munich (his American father was stationed there in the military following World War II). Shorter came in to Munich with very respectable credentials, having won the marathon in the 1971 Pan American Games and another major marathon in Japan in the same year. The Yale University graduate and University of Florida law student was, as one might expect, a crafty runner, careful not to go out too fast, happy to draft behind other guys until he was ready to move out in front (in short, a sort of anti-Prefontaine). Once Shorter did take the lead, however, he was extremely reluctant to relinquish it, and his exceptionally fluid style helped him avoid cramping up in the late going of a long race. Shorter's friend and teammate Kenny Moore, who had beaten Frank in the Olympic trials, provided the U.S. team with yet another good prospect for a podium finish.

But neither Shorter nor Moore was a clear favorite in Munich—in fact, no one was. The strong and well-balanced field included Ethiopia's Mamo Wolde, who had won in '68 and seemed primed to defend his title. Another gold medal prospect was the Australian Derek Clayton, the world record-holder for the distance. European champion Karel Lismont of Belgium was also in the race; he had never been beaten in a marathon. Finally, Britain's Ron Hall, a professional textile chemist who wore state-of-the-art fishnet singlets and sun-reflecting shorts, was considered capable of winning, especially if the weather was warm and sultry (which in fact it turned out to be).

The course over which some seventy-four runners from thirty-nine countries would toil on that muggy mid-September day in Munich had a whimsical quality about it, in keeping with the overall festival themes of lightness and gaiety. Seen as a whole, the outline of the course resembled the shape of the Games' mascot, Waldi. The "dog's" head faced to the west, while its butt (naturally) pointed east. Runners started and finished with laps around the track in the Olympic Stadium—three at the beginning and one at the end. Along the way, competitors would go by (but probably not notice, much less think about) historically significant sites like Nymphen-burg Palace, where "Mad" King Ludwig II had been born; Brienner Strasse, where the Nazi "Brown House" had recently stood; and Geschwister-Scholl-Platz, named in honor of two University of Munich students who had been executed in 1943 for spreading anti-Nazi propaganda. A sub-stantial part of the course meandered through the leafy Englischer Garten, surely one of the world's most beautiful parks.

For the runners, though, such pleasant and historically rich vistas were not the course's primary attraction: they liked the fact that it was gener-ally flat, abundantly shaded, and distant from any pollution-spewing traf-fic. (For the first time ever, the '72 marathon deployed an electric, rather than gas-powered, pace car to lead the runners.) The only downside of the course for the competitors was the odd fact that it included an uncomfort-able stretch of gravel. Coach Bowerman (of course) complained about this, prompting the German technical staff to ask why *he* should have any say in the layout. To this, Bowerman held up two fingers and replied, "World War One and World War Two."

The race organizers had hoped to see a record time on their fast flat course, and their hopes in this regard might well have been realized had the race not started at 3:00 p.m., the hottest part of an already unseasonably warm and muggy day. With brow-mopping humidity and a temperature in the mid-seventies, the runners naturally stuck to a slow pace in the early going. It was not long, though, before Frank Shorter decided that the pace was simply *too* slow. Having allowed Clayton and Ron Hill to hold the lead in the first phase of the race, he charged to the front of the pack at the 15 km mark, forcing a pickup in the tempo. Comfortable enough with the faster pace, he gradually expanded his lead as the kilometers clicked by, something he was surprised at being able to do so easily. After twenty kilometers, he had increased his lead by some thirty seconds.

Although sweating profusely, Shorter was still running with a very fluid stride, and he compensated for the steady fluid loss by nipping frequently from a plastic bottle marked with the international sign for radiation hazard (a bit of whimsy of his own). Sideline spectators, some of them thrusting paper cups of beer at the passing runners, must have wondered what in hell the front-runner was drinking as he glided by. Shorter's magical pick-me-up turned out to be nothing other than good old Coca Cola, allowed to stand out overnight and go flat so as not to build up gas in the drinker's belly and bowels.

High on Coke and his growing confidence, Shorter pushed his lead at the 40 km mark to about two minutes over his nearest pursuers, now Karel Lismont and Mamo Wolde, who themselves were running about five seconds apart. Barring a severe breakdown, it looked like Shorter had this race in hand, the only question being who would come in second and third.

The tall, gaunt, mustachioed Shorter did not break down—did not even waver or slow his pace as he approached the Olympic Stadium. Upon reaching the tunnel that led into the arena, he must have anticipated the cheers and applause that would undoubtedly greet him—a native son, after all—when he finally burst onto the track for his final lap to the tape.

But what Shorter actually heard as he came out of the tunnel into the glass-roofed arena was a cascade of boos, whistles, and catcalls. What was going on here? Had the Munich fans become so down on Americans that they could not tolerate a victory by *any* of them?

Fortunately, no. Unbeknownst to Shorter, in an eerie echo of 1904, another runner had jumped into the race late and entered the stadium before him. The interloper was a twenty-two-year-old West German student named Norbert Südhaus, who had slipped onto the course undetected about a mile from the stadium. Südhaus had launched this stunt, he explained later, in order to introduce an element of levity into an atmosphere that in his view had become way too somber and down-in-the-dumps. Wearing a tacky homemade bib with the number "72" pinned on it, the stocky young Bavarian certainly did not have the build of a marathon runner, and he looked amazingly fresh and jaunty for a guy who had supposedly just run over forty kilometers. Nonetheless, police and officials lining the final section of the course did not question his legitimacy or try to interfere with him in any way. As for the folks inside the stadium, they initially let out an appreciative roar when Südhaus entered the arena and started around the track. Amazingly, it took race officials a minute or two to realize that the flabby guy in yellow shorts with an unregistered race number was a hoaxer. By the time they made a dash to remove him from the course, Südhaus himself had decided that he had amply made his point, so he simply sprinted through a tunnel on the opposite side of the stadium without ever crossing the finish line. Not at all amused by this piece of conceptual art, the fans in the stands started to boo and hiss, and these were the ugly sounds that greeted poor Shorter as he made his own entry into the stadium. Until the matter was later clarified, he was totally mystified about why he had heard boos upon entering the stadium, only to have those catcalls turn to cheers as he completed his final lap and hit the tape.

Shorter's winning time of 2:12:19.8 set no Olympic (much less world) record, but for him it was a personal best, always a gratifying achievement for a marathoner. Gratifying, too, was the fact that Shorter had convincingly beaten two much more seasoned marathoners, Lismont and Wolde, who finished second and third, respectively. The American was also happy not to have hurt himself, as marathoners often do. (In fact, he claimed not to have overtaxed himself at all, and to have been able to notice some of the attractions on the route, something "I don't usually have time to do.") Finally, Shorter was pleased that two other Americans had finished in the top ten—Kenny Moore in fourth place and Jack Bachelder in ninth. This strong American performance seemed to disprove the recent wisdom that, when it came to long-distance running, the Americans had "lost the use of their legs."

The marathon results notwithstanding, the Americans, men and women, had to be considered the big losers in the track and field competition in Munich. Although Team USA had piled up the largest number of medals (twenty-two), the men had garnered only six gold medals, half their haul of four years earlier in Mexico City and the fewest ever for the American men in a single Summer Olympiad. As for the U.S. women, they ended up being shut out of the gold medal hunt entirely, the first time this had happened since women had entered Olympic track and field competition in 1928. "We were a big bust," conceded U.S. hammer-thrower George Frenn. "We must go to Congress and have the entire U.S. Olympic Committee reconstructed. A thing as important as this to our international prestige must be given more efficient hands and better brains."

Why was the American track performance in Munich so miserable? Was it poor leadership at the top, insufficient funding, team mismanagement, lack of Olympic experience, distractions, morale problems due to the terror attack, getting "jobbed" by officials, or just a string of bad luck? Christopher Brasher, a British Olympian turned sportswriter, thought he had the most convincing answer. The American team, he opined, was "divided against itself just as American society is divided, waging an internal war. I do not think there is any doubt that an unhappy society produces an unhappy team." A sportswriter for the *Los Angeles Times* made a similar point at the conclusion of the track competition: "The separatism that is characterizing our society could be carrying over to the track and field."

No doubt there was something to this analysis. But if social discord and national malaise were really the fundamental cause for this poor performance in track, why hadn't the Americans tanked at Mexico City in 1968, when the social discord at home was even greater? Perhaps the best answer for the "misery of Munich" in track and field for Team USA came from Coach Bowerman himself, who had warned at the start of the Games that Americans were facing stiffer competition than ever before in the classic athletic events and should not be surprised if they suffered setbacks in disciplines they had traditionally dominated.

Cold War on the Hard Court

American basketball coach Hank Iba had issued a similar warning regarding his sport on the eve of the Munich Games, but, as we noted previously, in the early rounds of the '72 tournament Team USA was so dominant that there seemed little cause to worry that the Yanks would not bring home the gold yet again. Or, put in proper imperial terms, America's habit of "lording it over the Olympics like Alexander the Great" was likely to go on unabated.

The U.S. hoopsters continued to cruise as the competition resumed following the terror attack. On September 7, the Americans clobbered Italy

68–38, notching thereby their sixty-third straight Olympic basketball victory. The powerful USSR squad, meanwhile, had major trouble with Cuba in the semi-finals but hung on to eek out a 67–61 win. With equal tournament records of 8-0, the United States and USSR would face each other for the Olympic basketball championship on the morning of September 10, the penultimate day of the Munich Games.

In the early phase of that fateful contest, the U.S. squad played as if the pressure of the moment was getting to them, while the more experienced Soviet team put on a display of brilliant half-court ball perfectly suited to the slow tempo of play. (The Americans might have picked up the pace, but Coach Iba had ordered the normally fast-breaking Yanks to take a more cautious and deliberate approach.) The mastermind behind the Soviet tactic was head coach Vladimir Kondrashkin, a noted tactician famous for his highly disciplined approach to the game. Marching precisely to Kondrashkin's orders, the Soviets established a narrow lead of five points (26–21) at halftime.

For most of the second half, the U.S. men continued to have trouble finding the basket, which allowed the more accurately shooting Soviets to expand their lead to ten points with a little over nine minutes left to play. If this pattern continued, the Yanks would not only lose but also lose by an embarrassingly large margin.

As the final minutes ticked away, however, the Americans finally threw off their jitters and launched a ferocious rally, led by the inspired play of guard Kevin Joyce. With thirty-eight seconds left to play, the Soviet lead had shrunk to one point. Trying to protect that precious margin, the Soviets passed incessantly in the backcourt—and one of those passes, an imprudent cross-court heave by Alexander Belov, ended up in the hands of American guard Doug Collins. Collins immediately drove toward the opposite basket but was taken down by a Soviet pursuer before he could get there. Three seconds remained on the clock at the time of the foul. The American guard had been hit so hard he could barely get off the floor to shoot his allotted two free throws. Despite a dizzy head and the huge pressure, Collins sank both his shots, giving the Americans a 50–49 lead, their first in the entire game. (Collins went on to a successful career in the NBA as player and coach, after which he became a prominent basketball broadcaster.)

Showing a preternatural calmness of their own, the Soviets immediately in-bounded the ball, but after two seconds head referee Renato Righetto, a Brazilian, blew his whistle to stop the play. He had noted a disturbance at the timekeepers' table and wanted an administrative timeout. Soviet coach Kondrashkin, it seems, had called a timeout before Collins went to the free throw line for his first shot. By the rules of Olympic play, a coach desiring a timeout during a free throw situation could choose to take it either before *or after* the first of the two free throw attempts, and Kondrashkin insisted vehemently that he had asked for the latter option. The German game officials, either unaware of this second option or overwhelmed by the excitement of the moment, had assumed that Kondrashkin must have cancelled his request for a timeout when the Soviet players lined up for Collins's second foul shot. The contretemps on the sidelines involved a red-faced Kondrashkin screaming at the timekeeper about his missing timeout. Having sorted matters out with the German officials, referee Righetto now awarded the Soviets their breather. One second remained on the clock.

After the timeout, the Soviets in-bounded the ball once again but were unable to make a play before time ran out. The United States had won, 50–49! The American players rushed off the court, hugging each other and jumping for joy. (An unknown spectator hugging Coach Iba managed to lift his wallet.)

No sooner had the Americans reached the sidelines, however, than they were ordered back on the court by the referee: the game was apparently not over, after all. But this time it was not referee Righetto who made the crucial decision. Prodded by Soviet coaches, R. William Jones, the British secretary-general of the International Amateur Basketball Federation (FIBA), now intervened in the action. Holding three fingers in the air, he insisted that three seconds be put back on the clock because there had been that many seconds remaining in the game when Coach Kondrashkin had originally requested his timeout.

The American players were incredulous. "We couldn't believe that they [the officials] were giving the Russians all these chances," said U.S. forward Mike Bantom. "It was like they were going to let them do it until they got it right."

The Soviets thus got a third chance to "get it right"—and this time they managed to do so. Kondrashkin substituted in Ivan Edeshko, a former handball player, to make the crucial all-or-nothing in-bound toss, basketball's equivalent of football's final-seconds "Hail Mary" pass into the end zone. In what in fact resembled a football maneuver, Edeshko lobbed a full-court pass over the head of American center Tom McMillen in the direction of a sprinting Alexander Belov, who, having elbowed away two American players, caught the ball in his outstretched arms and flicked it deftly into the basket.

With the final score 51–50 in favor of the USSR, it was time for the Soviets to celebrate, and they did so with great abandon. And why not?

They had taken down the mighty Americans in one of the most amazing last-second victories in the history of sport. Their man Belov had gone in a few seconds from being the game's goat to its hero. Who was "Alexander the Great" now?

The USOC immediately appealed the result to FIBA, arguing that "gross irregularities" had occurred at the end of the game, including an "illegal" Soviet timeout and an "arbitrary" addition of three seconds to the clock. Also among the "irregularities" cited by the USOC was the crucial intervention by FIBA chief Jones, who had no right to usurp the game officials' functions during play. (This was true enough, but the imperious Jones ruled FIBA with an iron hand and accepted no limits on his authority.)

A five-person FIBA jury met on Monday, September 11, to consider the American appeal. By a vote of 3–2, the jury rejected the protest. Revealingly, the representatives on the jury from Cuba, Poland, and Hungary voted against the appeal, while delegates from Italy and Puerto Rico voted for it. Like the big game itself, the jury deliberation looked like an extension of the Cold War, with the Soviets winning another battle.

Infuriated by the FIBA verdict, the USOC's Clifford Buck immediately recommended to his Executive Board that the United States suspend indefinitely any further participation in Olympic basketball competition "as a protest against the unconscionable injustice done the USA basketball team in Munich and to preclude the continued recurrence of similar treatment at the hands of the International Amateur Basketball Federation." Aware that such a step might make the United States look like "poor losers," Buck added, "I must say first that we did not lose; and secondly, I do not believe that the American people want their national Olympic Committee to subject our athletes to any more of the gross malfeasance which in my opinion we have experienced at the hands of the FIBA administration."

The USOC Executive Board did not follow through on Buck's intemperate threat, but the American protest did not end with the FIBA appeal and the USOC president's histrionics. At a hasty meeting following their defeat, the American players voted unanimously not to participate in the awards ceremony, where they would have received their silver medals. (Later, they decided that they would *never* accept the medals, and to this day they have not.) Moreover, in January 1973, the USOC lodged an appeal to the IOC to overturn the FIBA verdict of September 11, 1972. This second appeal claimed that the jury ruling "was not based on an objective consideration of all the facts." The appeal was buttressed with affidavits from referee Righetto and the timekeeper stating that they now agreed that there had been "violations of official basketball rules." The IOC, reluctant to tangle with Jones and FIBA, refused to overturn the ruling.

Not surprisingly, it wasn't just American players and officials who were livid over what one U.S. journalist called "The Great Gold Heist" in the Olympic basketball tournament. The American press was filled with irate editorials and letters to the editor about this latest "scandal" in Munich. The IOC was flooded with similar messages. In an Olympic festival where so many of the competitions had been freighted with political meaning, the basketball controversy seemed only to confirm convictions that the entire Olympic system was rigged, rotten, and hopelessly politicized. As one angry American sputtered to the IOC,

> The American public watched in awe as you robbed us of one medal after another in Munich. I am referring, of course, to the cases of Bob Seagren, Rick DeMont, Jim Ryun, numerous boxers and divers, and the U.S. basketball team, all of whose protests and pleas for justice fell upon voluntarily deaf ears. But the latter was the most shocking case of all. I was one of millions of Americans who watched the United States vs. Russia basketball game on television last Saturday evening. We all saw what happened, and therefore you cannot lie to us.
>
> The Munich Games have served to enlighten me. They have demonstrated the fact that you, as an "international" body . . . are merely using the Olympics as a political forum for anti-U.S. sentiment.

Like the American frustrations in track and field, however, the U.S. basketball defeat at the Munich Games should be placed in a broader athletic context. The international competition in basketball *was* getting stronger, and American amateurs could no longer assume unquestioned superiority. As *Tass* writer Yuri Khromov put it, the Soviet victory in Munich "dispelled the myth of American basketball invincibility." America's vulnerability, especially vis-à-vis the USSR and that other East Bloc powerhouse, Yugoslavia, quickly became evident in the major non-Olympic international arena: the quadrennial FIBA World Championships. In 1974, the United States finished third behind Yugoslavia and the USSR; four years later, in 1978, Yugoslavia defeated the USSR for the gold medal and Team USA did not place at all; and in 1982, the Soviets beat the Americans in the championship game.

While over time Americans became more used to seeing their national team challenged, and even vanquished, in international play, in the immediate aftermath of the Munich Games the loss to the Soviets was too bitter a pill to swallow with any grace. In April 1973, the American and Soviet national teams met again, this time on U.S. soil. Billed as "The Revenge Tour," the series was meant by its American sponsors to reassert American superiority and thus expunge the stain of Munich. Throughout the six-game series, both teams played as if these matches were indeed a form of proxy war: the contests were rife with flagrant fouls, bloody noses, black eyes—and, in one case, torn testicles. Each coach accused the other of unsportsmanlike behavior. Team USA did manage to win four of the six games, but there was no sense of distinct superiority: Munich remained unavenged. (At Montreal in 1976, Team USA won the gold medal and the Soviets took the bronze, but the two teams did not meet in the tournament. Arguably, for the Americans, Munich was not really avenged until the "Miracle on the Ice" at Lake Placid in 1980, but that of course involved a different sport.)

"Paki-Bashing"

The epic basketball showdown between the United States and the USSR was hardly the only disputed final at Munich, nor was it even the most violently contested one. This dubious distinction has to go to the championship match in field hockey, which pitted Pakistan, the winner in Mexico City and joint sovereign with India over Olympic hockey since its inception in 1920, against West Germany, a surprise contender. In a bruising and vicious game that has been called "one of the most violent [hockey matches] in history," host West Germany won 1–0 on a penalty shot ten minutes from the concluding whistle. During the match, Pakistan had managed on one occasion to get the ball into their adversary's net, but this "goal" was disallowed by the head referee, an Australian. Over the course of this ugly brawl, one German and two Pakistani players were ejected for egregious fouling. There was literally blood on the turf.

Immediately following the final whistle, Pakistani players and their supporters flew into a violent rage. Believing they had been cheated by biased officiating, the players smashed the goal nets, while Pakistani fans raced onto the field and laid siege to the judges' table, pouring a pitcher of water over the head of René Frank, the Belgian president of the International Hockey Federation (FIH). Team members also physically assaulted a doctor who tried to administer the required post-game drug test. As a final touch, the players tore up their dressing room.

Unlike the American basketballers, the Pakistani hockey players consented to show up for the awards ceremony, but, in an echo of Matthews and Collett, they used this occasion to vent their spleen. Rather than allow their silver medals to be hung decorously around their necks, they grabbed them from the presenter and tossed them contemptuously about in the air. One player even stuck his medal into his shoe, the ultimate insult by a Muslim.

Neither the FIH nor the IOC was amused. Primarily because of their behavior on the podium, the Pakistani players and managers were barred from Olympic competition for life by the IOC; the FIH, for its part, suspended the Pakistani Hockey Federation from all international play for the next four years, which meant exclusion from the next field hockey world championships. The only consolation for Pakistan was the IOC's begrudging decision to allow the players to keep their silver medals.

To the Pakistanis, their treatment in Munich smacked of "Paki-bashing"—the brutal and occasionally lethal pummeling that Pakistani immigrants sometimes received in Britain at the hands of racist thugs. Pakistani newspapers were filled with complaints of host-country favoritism and "neo-colonialism." West German officials were said to have "bought" the referees; the "draconian" IOC and FIH punishments had clearly been imposed "to arrest the dominance in international field hockey by teams from Britain's former colonies." As for FIH president Frank, he was desperately trying, in the words of one Pakistani Olympic official, "to preserve the powers of an imperial dictator in the modern democratic world." According to an angry resident of Karachi, Frank, the IOC, and the West Germans together had "ended the grand symbol of the Olympics" for Pakistan, which, under conditions like those prevailing in Munich, had "no wish to participate further in International Hockey matches."

Of course, not all the finals in the closing days of competition at Munich '72 were as fraught with bitter feelings and political animosities as those on the basketball court and hockey field. The only really nasty thing about the soccer final on September 10 between Hungary and Poland was the weather, which had suddenly turned foul. Torrential rain and near gale-force winds made it difficult for either team to put together effective play combinations. With the wind at their backs throughout the first period, Hungary, which had lost only once in twenty-one Olympic soccer outings going back to 1960, led 1–0 at the interval. But in the second half, with the wind advantage reversed, Poland managed to score two goals and win the game. This was Poland's first gold medal in Olympic football.

The consolation match on the same day between the GDR and USSR to determine the bronze medal winner in soccer turned out to be a ridiculous farce, owing largely to a dumb rule instituted by the Fédération

Internationale de Football Association (FIFA). During the elimination rounds in Olympic soccer there could be no tie games, but at the medal level ties were permitted if the score remained equal following regulation play and two fifteen-minute periods of overtime. In the GDR-USSR match the score was tied 2–2 at the end of regulation play. No doubt aware that they could share the bronze medals with a final tie, the Soviets and East Germans played with exceeding caution during the two overtime periods. The players pushed the ball around in a desultory fashion, keeping their main attention on the clock. The eighty thousand spectators responded at the end of the match with howls of disapproval and for good reason: they had been subjected to a half-hour of utter tedium and had witnessed an insult to the "Olympic spirit" as grievous as anything the Americans had done.

Very different was the stirring match between Japan and the GDR for the gold medal in men's volleyball. Japan had garnered a bronze medal in Tokyo and a silver medal in Mexico City and now hungered for the heavy metal in Munich. The powerful GDR team, having won the International Volleyball Federation championship earlier that year, was considered by some experts to be the stronger of the two clubs. Japan, moreover, had played a three-hour semi-final game the day before and could well be out of steam.

Yet, in the hard-fought final on the night of September 10, Japan ended up prevailing 3–1 after dropping the first set. In the opinion of a West German commentator, the GDR players had simply "lost their nerve" in the face of a relentless Japanese onslaught.

Much to the delight of the three thousand volleyball fans, most of whom stayed in the hall well past midnight to watch the awards ceremony, the Japanese players showed themselves masters of decorum in receiving their gold medals from none other than Avery Brundage, the outgoing IOC president. Although many in the Olympic community were happy enough that the irascible old American was finally stepping down, the volleyball fans, knowing that this was Brundage's last awards ceremony, gave him a standing ovation.

The Virtues of Regimentation?

According to their founder, Pierre de Coubertin, the modern Olympic Games were supposed to be contests between individuals, not nations. But de Coubertin had undercut this ideal by mandating that athletes could compete only as members of organized entities recognized by the IOC, which for all practical purposes meant national teams. Holding to the fiction that the Games were exclusively about individual excellence, the IOC had always discouraged the inclusion of national medal tallies in the official results, but such tallies had nonetheless been part of the modern Olympic story from the beginning. By the time Munich '72 rolled around, the Olympic movement had become well established as a premier measuring rod of national virility and vitality.

When the Munich competitions finally came to an end with the equestrian Grand Prix on September 11, the Soviet Union stood in first place with a total of ninety-nine medals, fifty of them gold (the largest number of golds the USSR ever won). Soviet commentators made much of this magical number fifty, claiming it represented a celebration of the fiftieth anniversary of the Soviet Union, formed in 1922. The Soviets also made a great deal of the fact that they had topped the United States in the Summer Games for the first time since Rome and had done so on the home turf of Washington's most important and loyal continental European ally.

Second-place America finished with ninety-four medals (thirty-three gold). Although the USOC claimed for the record that this showing was "all that reasonably could have been expected," the result was actually a major disappointment for that body—and for the nation as a whole. Many newspapers ran editorials decrying what was generally seen as an inadequate performance in Munich, one that suggested some fundamental deficiencies in the national fiber. (No doubt the disappointment was all the greater because four years earlier, in Mexico City, the United States had beaten the Soviets in the national medal count, 107–91, an achievement that was hailed at the time as a clear reassertion of American supremacy in the athletic cold war.)

Apart from the USSR, the biggest winner in Munich was indubitably the GDR, which, with a population of only eighteen million, came in third with sixty-six medals, twenty of them gold. The GDR leadership was, of course, ecstatic over this result. East German Communist Party (SED) secretary Erich Honecker sent congratulatory telegrams to all the winners and threw an opulent party for "his" Olympians upon their return to East Berlin.

Although the GDR's arch-rival West Germany managed a respectable fourth place, with a total of forty medals (thirteen gold), there was no gainsaying that in the world of high-level sport, *East* Germany was the more powerful Germany. The additional fact that this huge GDR triumph in the German-German athletic wars came on West Germany's own turf served to drive this disparity home all the more painfully.

While the FRG showing vis-à-vis East Germany in Munich could hardly be a source of cheer to the West German athletic establishment,

Olympic officials there struggled mightily to put the matter in the best possible light. When asked if the failure to best the GDR on home ground did not represent "a painful loss of prestige" for the West German sports program, Olympic fund-raising chief Josef Neckermann claimed never to have believed that the FRG's home-field advantage could compensate for the "effective athletic-support methods" that the GDR, as a tightly regulated authoritarian state, could employ. "We lack the potency of a closed society," concluded Neckermann, rather lamely.

The GDR, of course, shared this regimented socio-political system with the other nations in the Soviet-dominated East Bloc, and it is interesting to note that these states, as a whole, also fared well at the Munich Games. In addition to their excellent showings in track and field, Eastern Europeans totally "owned" the weightlifting competition, winning all but one of the nine events in that discipline; they also dominated men's and women's fencing. In the final medal count, Poland, Hungary, and Bulgaria all finished in the top ten; Romania came in thirteenth, Czechoslovakia, eighteenth. If the national medal standings were weighted by population size, these nations would have placed even higher. Observing this reality, one American commentator proposed that the Munich medal standings "might say something about [the virtues of] regimentation."

The Eastern European showings at Munich were especially notable in light of quite lackluster performances on the part of large Western European democracies like Italy, Britain, and France, which finished tenth, twelfth, and seventeenth respectively. If one (again) takes into account population size, these were unimpressive showings indeed.

Among the major Western European democracies, Britain perhaps had the greatest reason to be disappointed with its Munich performance, for it had an illustrious Olympic history and was hoping to burnish this tradition at the 1972 festival. At the time of the Munich Games, Britain had amassed the third-largest number of medals in the history of the modern Olympics and had typically finished among the top five nations in the earlier Olympiads. Starting in the late 1920s, however, Britain had begun to stumble, and its tenth-place finish in the Berlin Games of 1936 had produced much handwringing about "going soft." Yet the problem got worse after World War II. Even in the role of host nation in 1948, Britain could finish only number 12, and it slipped to a lowly eighteenth place in Helsinki in 1952. However, with the achievement of tenth-place finishes in Tokyo and Mexico City, many Britons were beginning to hope that their nation had started to turn things around. Alas, their exceptionally large team of 284 athletes in Munich managed a total of only eighteen medals, of which a mere four were gold (in addition to Mary Peters's win in the pentathlon, the Brits racked up a sailing victory in Kiel and two triumphs in the equestrian competition).

Not surprisingly, this meager medal haul generated a whole new round of handwringing about the inadequacies of Britain's Olympic program and its national sport scene in general. Roger Bannister, who after breaking the four-minute mile in 1954 had gone on to become a respected physician and head of Britain's Sports Council, declared after Munich that, although there had been some "heartening" moments at the '72 Games, "all too many weaknesses had been exposed." Up until 1972, the word "Munich" in Britain had been synonymous mainly with appeasement—Chamberlain's infamous kowtowing to Hitler in 1938. Now, it seemed, "Munich" also meant humiliation of a different sort.

Closing Time

On September 10, 1971, exactly one year before the ceremony to close the Twentieth Summer Games was scheduled to take place, Munich's *Süddeutsche Zeitung* had noted that, despite all the planning and advance work for the '72 Games, many questions remained open. Was enough being done to prepare for the "avalanche of automobiles" expected to clog the city? Would there be adequate lodging for the army of visitors? Would the competition facilities going up on the Oberwiesenfeld prove acceptable to the athletes? And above all, were Olympic and Bavarian officials adequately prepared to handle any "possible emergencies" that might transpire during the Games? The answer to this last question, of course, had become painfully evident one year later—and the ceremony that would bring the ill-starred 1972 Olympic festival to a close somehow had to reflect the sad fate of Munich's would-be "Carefree Games."

Because of the twenty-four-hour interruption following the terror attack on September 5, the closing ceremony took place on Monday, September 11, rather than on the previous day. In the opinion of some of the athletes, this traditional piece of Olympic theater should not have taken place at all. However, Olympic officials rejected calls for dropping the ceremony with the same argument that they had employed for not cancelling the Games altogether: this would have been tantamount to "giving in to terrorism." On the other hand, the closing program could not blithely follow the original script, as if nothing untoward had happened. The organizers thus decided to cut the ceremony almost in half, to about forty-five minutes—and (thankfully) to leave out much of the happy/hokey Bavarian folklore. There was one other important change. The original plan had called for a minute of silence for all Olympic athletes who had been killed in the two world wars of the twentieth century. This idea was changed to include a minute of silence for those killed in the September 5/6 carnage. Tellingly, however, there was no specific reference to murdered "Israelis" or "Jews"—merely to "victims of terror." (The Germans were still hoping not to completely alienate the Arab states.) Avery Brundage also revised his farewell speech to include an oblique reference to the murders. After thanking the Münchners for their generous hospitality, he intoned, "Together we celebrated days of radiant joy and hours of deepest darkness." That was the sum total of acknowledgment with respect to the horrors of September 5/6. Overall, what is remarkable about the closing ceremony is how *little* attention was paid to the greatest tragedy ever to befall an Olympic festival.

Perhaps fittingly, the cold, rainy weather that had blown in at the very end of the competitions stayed around for the closing ceremony. The eighty thousand spectators who filled the stadium were obliged to trade their light summer outfits for the heavier gear of autumn.

Even more fitting, given the festival's vulnerability to gut-wrenching violence, was the fleeting possibility that the closing ceremony itself might be subjected to another, even more heinous, act of terror. Unbeknownst to the thousands of people settling into their seats at the Olympic Stadium that September evening, an anonymous male caller had telephoned the Munich Organizing Committee at 7:00 p.m. with the alarming news that "Arab terrorists" had just stolen his private airplane from its berth at the Malmstein Airfield near Stuttgart. According to the caller, the thieves had loaded a "large bomb" into the plane and were apparently headed with their lethal cargo in the direction of Munich and its Olympic Stadium.

This threat may sound pretty dubious to our jaundiced ears, but to the rattled and nervous Olympic officials it seemed all too credible. A "catastrophe-alarm" procedure instituted in the immediate aftermath of the September 5 incident called for the immediate evacuation of any Olympic venue threatened by attack or sabotage. Willi Daume and Manfred Schreiber now seriously considered applying this emergency procedure to the Olympic Stadium. Before taking this drastic step, however, they consulted with a new member of the Olympic security team, Admiral Armin Zimmermann, general-inspector of the Bundeswehr. Zimmermann advised against the evacuation order, pointing out that it would cause panic and pandemonium in the Olympic complex. He made clear as well that the Bundeswehr was already hot on the case of the missing plane: all radar installations around Munich had been given orders to search for the craft, and two Starfighter combat aircraft based at Neuburg Airbase on the Danube had been put on alert to intercept the plane should it approach the Bavarian capital. Defense Minister Georg Leber himself had taken charge of the operation; he and Zimmermann were determined that, unlike at Fürstenfeldbruck, the federal army, not the Bavarian police, would handle this problem. Although no one commented upon it at the time, this decision was actually a historic moment in the history of the Federal Republic: for the first time since the state's foundation in 1949, the Bundeswehr was being mobilized to meet an *internal* security crisis.

Eighteen minutes after Leber had put the Starfighters on alert, he found probable cause to send them up. Flight controllers near Munich had located an "unidentified craft" approaching local airspace so rapidly that effective interception could be accomplished only by immediate deployment of the jets. At 8:22 p.m., the two Starfighters took off with orders, if necessary, to shoot down the intruding plane.

The jets ended up cruising over Munich for forty-five minutes, looking in vain for the intruder. Although the entire Munich air space had been closed to all incoming planes, a Swiss Air passenger jet managed to land at Riem and a Finnair charter aircraft touched down at Fürstenfeldbruck during the closure period. This Finnair craft had not pre-registered its flight plan, and it was soon established that *this* was the "unidentified" plane heading for Munich noted by the air controllers.

At 9:21 p.m., Secretary Leber broke off the hunt for the mysterious intruder and ordered his jets to return to Neuburg. They had found no purloined aircraft because there had been no theft. In fact, the only private plane to have taken off from Malmstein Airfield during the period in question was a company-owned Cessna that had landed safely at Baden-Baden at 7:24. The company president was sitting at that moment in the Olympic Stadium awaiting the start of the closing ceremony.

The festivities began with the Olympic hymn, followed by the entry of twenty-five Schäffler, members of a historic Munich arts guild who performed every seven years in gratitude for the survival of Munich's population during a medieval plague. Then the (supposed) principal figures in the Games—the athletes—entered the arena. There were far fewer of them now than on opening day, and, per a new "tradition" dating back to Mexico City, they did not march around the track in disciplined team phalanxes but scattered helter-skelter across the infield, where they formed swirling circles and snaking conga lines. Athletes from different countries held hands, embraced, and, in some cases, passionately kissed—a refreshing demonstration of what these Games were supposed to be about (and evidence, no doubt, that the organizers' efforts to prevent "intimate" relations between the athletes had not worked).

There were, of course, no Israelis among the cavorting Olympians on the Munich infield that mid-September evening. The name "Israel" was also missing from the parade of national signs carried into the stadium by dirndl-clad Olympic hostesses. In all the excitement no one seemed to notice that, alone among the banners lining the stadium perimeter, the Israeli flag hung at half-mast. Given the absence of Israeli athletes, none of the revelers in the infield waved the Star of David—though, as if to remedy this deficiency, two members of a film crew shooting the happy scene draped the Israeli flag over their camera stand.

After about ten minutes of directionless activity, the West German national anthem sounded over the loudspeaker system. The official announcer had declared at the beginning of the ceremony that "the Games of the twentieth Olympiad began lightheartedly [but] must end seriously." Now came the serious part, such as it was. The same speaker asked for a moment of silence in honor of "the victims of terror" who had lost their lives during the festival. That old scold, Avery Brundage, now stepped to the microphone to deliver his last hurrah. He concluded,

> I declare the Games of the twentieth Olympiad closed, and, in accordance with tradition, I call upon the youth of all countries to assemble four years from now in Montreal, there to celebrate with us the Games of the twenty-first Olympiad. May they display cheerfulness and concord so that the Olympic torch will be carried on with ever greater eagerness, courage and honor for the good of humanity throughout the ages.

As Brundage walked off the field, his stooped figure was lit by a spotlight and the scoreboard flashed the message "Thank you, Avery Bandage." Was it another wry hoax, or just carelessness, that yielded this misspelling of the departing president's name? In any event, it's probably a good thing that the organizers had decided to discard another farewell gesture to the irascible old man: a request to the audience to stand as one and belt out "For He's a Jolly Good Fellow."

The farewell to Brundage had been fully expected by the spectators, but the organizers still managed to spring one big surprise on the audience at the end of the closing ceremony. In place of the booming martial fireworks displays that traditionally accompany the extinguishing of the

Olympic flame, five long, helium-filled tubes fused together and adorned in the Olympic colors rose up slowly to overarch the entire Olympic complex. The resulting image, of course, was that of a majestic "rainbow"—the symbol of brotherhood, diversity, hope, and, yes, joy.

"The Most Beautiful Olympics Ever Wrecked"

No sooner had the Olympic flame gone out at the stadium than instant assessments of the Munich Games began rolling in. *Sportsworld*, the official journal of the British Olympic Association, pithily declared, "It is an understatement to say that the £300 million spent on Munich '72 did not buy the happiest of Games, embracing, as they did, murder, massacre, dope, disqualification, bad manners, Black Power and, according to the gospel of Avery Brundage, naked political blackmail."

Among the questions raised by these most tragic of Games was whether the Olympic flame, given what had happened on September 5/6 in Munich, should not stay extinguished for good. In a post-Games commentary on Munich, *New York Times* columnist Red Smith put the question this way:

> Now that the gasman cometh, to take the last 10 pfennig out of the meter and turn off the Olympic flame . . . should there be a XXI Olympics? Should Montreal try to do this all over again four years hence? No, unless there is a serious house-cleaning first. The world cannot afford to trust another undertaking of such magnitude to the clutch of atrophied eggheads who made such a botch of this one.

Of course, the Olympic flame did not remain extinguished, but Munich generated a level of soul-searching about safety, modalities of organization, costs, purpose, and the future of the Games that had not been seen in the modern Olympic movement since it was launched in the late nineteenth century.

Looking back on the just-completed Olympic festival, virtually everyone recognized that the terror attack of September 5 had not only redefined this particular Olympiad but also was likely to have a huge impact on all Games in the future. Perhaps, opined one American sportswriter, the problem of terror would now entirely overwhelm the "sanctuary" of Olympism, forcing it ultimately into extinction. "Are athletes [now] to join archdukes and prime ministers as objects of assassination?" he asked. "If so, the Games are doomed, to say nothing of athletics overall."

At the very least, Munich proved that a somewhat casual handling of security matters was no longer acceptable. Montreal had initially planned to copy Munich's "informal" approach to safety. After September 5/6, however, Montreal's planners were determined to make security a central priority. Hoping to undercut calls from some Canadians to abandon the '76 Games entirely, Montreal mayor Jean Drapeau even promised to send in the Canadian army if necessary to keep the Games safe. (On the security front, one of Drapeau's main worries concerned possible attacks by Quebec separatists.) Writing thirty years later about the ongoing threat of terror to the Games, one prominent Olympic official identified this issue as "a consuming challenge that occupies every waking moment—and probably many sleeping moments as well—of the hosts."

The Games of Munich that were supposed to have been "carefree"—but obviously were not—were also meant to have been financially modest—but clearly were not that either. In fact, the Munich Olympics ended up costing DM 1,972 billion ($700 million), roughly three times the outlay for Mexico City. Like the lapses in security, the huge cost of the Munich Games re-raised old questions about financing the Olympics and gave these questions new urgency. Of course, the need for heightened security measures only exacerbated the problem of spiraling expenses. In the case of Montreal, Mayor Drapeau's initial promise of "modest Games" (an echo of Mayor Hans-Jochen Vogel's similar promise for Munich) went by the wayside in part because of a huge outlay for security: the Montreal Games ending up costing nearly $2 billion, leaving the city deeply in the red. Some Olympic critics concluded that escalating costs constituted yet another reason for getting rid of the Games altogether. Wouldn't it be better to have no Games at all than the kind of bloated and extravagant festivals that only the richest cities and nations of the world could afford to host?

Barring this extreme solution, one West German commentator, in drawing up the "lessons of Munich," suggested that in the future the Games should no longer be hosted by single cities but by consortiums of cities and countries working together under the umbrella of the IOC. The funding might come from contributions from every participant nation in the Games, based on national wealth. This would finally make it possible for poorer cities and countries in Africa and South America to host the Games—and might also, perhaps, prevent the Games from being, time after time, spectacles of conspicuous municipal one-upmanship and national prestige.

If the spiraling cost of putting on a modern Olympic festival was said to have reached "crisis" proportions with the bloated Munich Games, biased and incompetent judging had likewise, it was claimed, reached a new nadir in 1972. The conclusion of the '72 festival brought a surge of angry editorials in the world press (or at least the Western world press), as well as a spate of irate letters to the IOC, on the subject of judging. The loudest complaints, not surprisingly, came from the United States, where the "We Wuz Robbed!" syndrome seems to have been omnipresent. In toting up a sarcastic list of "Olympic Awards" for the "Massacre Olympics," *Los Angeles Times* sportswriter Jim Murray gave one of his booby prizes to "the Iron Curtain boxing referees for consistency in performance"—that is, for having consistently awarded winning decisions to fellow countrymen "even if they had to wake them up to do it." In an editorial entitled "Olympic Changes Are Overdue," the same paper fumed,

> The International Olympic Committee makes the rules and calls the shots. If, after the experience of Munich, it does not make reforms to get politics and incompetence out of Olympic judging, it will have to stand blame for transforming the modern Games into what the ancient Games had become before they were finally abolished in the fourth century, a corrupt and meaningless circus.

Typical of the letters to Avery Brundage on this subject was a missive from a Minnesota man who complained that the judging in Munich revealed the Games to be "a springboard for politics" in which biased officiating furthered ideological goals, especially those of the East Bloc nations. The prevalence of corrupt judging in Munich convinced this writer that the Olympics were no longer worthy of interest, let alone financial support. (To letters like this, Brundage invariably provided a stock response: judging at the Olympics, he said, was controlled by the international athletic federations, not the IOC; the athletic federations had made every effort "to select experienced and qualified individuals"; and, considering that there had been 194 contests and several hundred judges at the Munich Games, the number of bad calls was "relatively small." Anyway, concluded Brundage, it was "too much to expect perfection" in this domain.) It is highly doubtful that this response proved satisfactory to the embittered complainers.

Another growing and seemingly intractable problem raised by the Munich Games was the practice of doping. We have seen that the Munich organizers made drug testing a priority for the first time in the modern Games and managed actually to catch some offenders—although the enforcement of the new rules was quite spotty and the punishment inconsistent. All told, one swimmer (the unfortunate Rick DeMont), one basketball player, one judo competitor, three weightlifters, and two cyclists were found guilty of using illegal drugs. Furthermore, fourteen entrants in the modern pentathlon were suspected of having violated a ban on tranquillizers during the competitions, though no action was taken against them. The Russians were rumored to be using a muscle-building drug derived from female placentas, but this rumor remained just that. The most glaring inadequacy in Munich's anti-drug program involved anabolic steroids. The Munich medical commission's inability to test for this substance meant that many "juicers" skated free. Noting this problem, an editorial in the *Times* (London) proposed that the IOC eliminate all those sports in which "systematic" use of steroids was "suspected" but could not yet be detected. Of course, at Munich it was the East Germans who were suspected of having abused steroids most widely. Assessing the strong performance of the bulked-up GDR women in Munich, one British expert cited their "obvious" reliance on anabolic steroids as a "grotesque shadow hanging over the competition" in Munich.

This steroid shadow, and indeed the dark pall cast by a whole host of designer drugs, got even darker after Munich. "Doping" became increasingly rampant in subsequent Olympics in part because the IOC did little to stop it. As Dick Pound, a long-time IOC Executive Board member and anti-doping activist, conceded in 2004, "There was no money available within the IOC [to fight doping] until well into the 1980s under [Juan Antonio] Samaranch, and even then there were other, more demanding priorities. There was no concerted effort to accelerate the fight."

Reflecting in 2006 on a survey about drugs that a small group of Olympians had completed shortly after the '72 Games, in which some of the responders had justified their use of steroids, a strength coach at Michigan State University could comment, "While reading [the '72 survey results], my ears were buzzing with a much too familiar negative ring. If administered today, the survey would probably produce carbon-copy answers or, worse yet, lean even closer to the dark side." The Michigan man concluded that the present "drug epidemic" in Major League Baseball, Olympic track and field, and the Tour de France could be traced back to the deeply inadequate drug testing and enforcement regime launched in Munich in 1972.

For Avery Brundage, who never really understood the problem of drugs, this issue definitely took a back seat to growing commercialism and creeping professionalism among the plethora of evils threatening the "purity" of the modern Olympics. At Munich, Brundage made his last stand against what he saw as excessive merchandizing by corporations as well as violations of the Olympic amateur code by athletes. But his efforts in this domain were ineffective, to put it mildly. The Munich organizers depended heavily on corporate sponsors to fund the Games, and corporate influence on the '72 festival was extensive, if not quite as open and uninhibited as it would later become. If one of the signature moments of the Munich Games was Mark Spitz's unprecedented seventh gold medal in swimming, another was the American athlete's supposedly innocent display of his Adidas shoes to a global TV audience. Following Brundage's departure from the IOC in 1972, future Olympic champions would no longer have to try to hide commercial involvements—indeed, they would flaunt them—and the Games would become true carnivals of commerce, with bevies of multinational companies competing for coin and glory alongside the athletes.

Although pundits groping for the meaning of Munich in its immediate aftermath sometimes shared Brundage's crotchets about commerce and amateurism, most believed that, apart from a new vulnerability to terror, Munich's most troubling legacy was its exacerbation of an old problem—the pervasive incursion of "politics" into all aspects of the Games. The biggest sporting event in the world, it seems, had also become the most attractive stage in the world for the strutting and fretting of all the grievances, animosities, and tensions that ailed poor old planet earth in the waning twentieth century.

At Munich, this "politicization" bugaboo had been most flagrantly evident in the Rhodesian controversy, the various judging scandals, and the nationalistic posturing that infused many of the competitions, especially those with a Cold War edge. Of course, the intense rivalry between the two Germanys had also been a notable feature of Munch '72. In the end, the East Germans, having earlier expressed fears about possibly being maligned and mistreated in "revanchist" Munich, pronounced public satisfaction over their reception in the Bavarian capital. Heinz Schöbel, the GDR's man in the IOC, declared upon the Games' conclusion, "We are impressed and enthusiastic over the appreciative and objective crowds in Munich and Augsburg. For us, the awards ceremonies were especially inspirational, since for the first time in the Summer Olympics we got to see our national flag raised and hear our national anthem played."

Yet despite such encomiums, Munich turned out to be no love-fest between the two Germanys. As we have seen, the East German athletes and Olympic tourists seemed wary and aloof upon arriving in Munich on the eve of the Games. Although they shed some of their stiffness over the course of the festival, they continued for the most part to avoid private contacts with their West German counterparts. The GDR athletes might party with the Russians, New Zealanders, or even the Americans, but there were no "German-German gatherings." As one Bavarian commentator regretfully observed, GDR athletes on their excursions around Munich or into the surrounding countryside were always prevented by their minders from having "any brotherly contacts with the local population."

Given East Berlin's extremely close watch over all GDR visitors to Munich—athletes and spectators alike—it's not surprising that there were no defections from the East German camp. But Munich '72 was by no means free from this particular dimension of Cold War life. Following the Games' conclusion, West German officials quietly revealed that one member of the Romanian men's volleyball team had defected to the West. So, too, had a number of tourists from Poland, Czechoslovakia, and Bulgaria (the exact number was not disclosed). For these individuals, the old ideal of Olympic "sanctuary" clearly took on new meaning.

But what to do about the fact that, as Avery Brundage had complained in his memorial speech on September 6, the "more important" the Olympics became, the more they were subject to political pressures? Barring a displacement of the Games to Mars, and probably not even then, there seemed precious little that could be done about these outside intrusions. If the Black African states had *almost* boycotted Munich, they *did* withdraw from Montreal in '76, this time to protest the inclusion of New Zealand, which maintained rugby ties with South Africa. Whereas Taiwan had shown up for Munich, while the People's Republic of China (PRC) had not, *both* Chinas shunned Montreal because the organizers had naively tried to include teams from each state. The 1980 Moscow Games were boycotted by many Western states (including, most notably, the United States), which generated a tit-for-tat boycott of L.A. '84 by the Soviets and most Eastern European nations. Albania boycotted every Olympiad from 1976 through 1988—an Olympic record (though, in truth, probably not a record that generated much concern, or even notice, by the world community). Of course, the big losers in this boycott mania were the athletes from the stay-at-home countries who were denied the chance to participate in the Games. Perhaps they should have known that the Olympics were not chiefly about *them* in the first place.

With specific reference to the influence of nationalism in the Games, however, some commentators on Munich thought there might be a ray of hope. We have seen that, in advance of the Munich Games, Willi Daume had floated the idea of drastically reducing the presence of national flags and anthems in Olympic ceremony. Daume's gambit had been quickly rejected, but it didn't simply disappear. Following the '72 festival, a *Süd-*

deutsche Zeitung commentator revisited this idea in an essay on the meaning of the Munich Games. Troubled like Daume (and Brundage) by the huge presence of nationalistic "pathos" at Munich, this pundit proposed (once again) eliminating national flag-hoisting and anthem-playing from the awards ceremonies. He claimed that this notion might now have traction because, in the wake of the nationalistic excesses at Munich, some *two-thirds of the IOC membership* favored the proposal.

No doubt this two-thirds figure was somewhat exaggerated, but we do know that many IOC members, including Brundage's successor, Lord Killanin, liked the idea. Asked in one of his first interviews as the new IOC president about how nationalism in the Games might be reduced, Killanin responded, "I am against medal ceremonies with fanfares and the national flags being raised. Most of our members are. The last time we voted on this issue most were in favor of only the Olympic flag being raised, but the proposal didn't get the necessary two-thirds majority. I am sure this [question] will be raised again."

Raised again it was, and more than once, but it never won that two-thirds majority. Too many national Olympic committees had a vested interest in the traditional setup, which offered the prospect of a global stage for their precious national symbols. Moreover, the IOC leadership understood that funding for the Games, whether from individual contributions, corporate sponsorship, or the sale of broadcasting rights, depended largely on keeping *nations*, rather than individuals, at the center of the enterprise. Thus, although Munich '72, with its bitter fights over symbolism between the two Germanys and its proxy wars on turf and court between the Cold War superpowers, had revealed more clearly than ever before the nefarious influence of hyper-nationalism in the Olympic Games, this revelation led nowhere.

In terms of haunting mental pictures of Munich '72, nothing will ever compete with those masked gunmen guarding the Israeli compound in the Olympic Village, or with those burned-out helicopters at Fürstenfeldbruck Airfield, but additional negative imagery (depending on one's point of view) might include Vince Matthews and Wayne Collett posturing on the victory podium; Bob Seagren thrusting his pole at an Olympic official; the GDR and USSR soccer teams playing thirty minutes of meaningless football; Pakistani players and fans running amok after the field hockey final; and FIBA chief Jones holding up three fingers at the (apparent) end of the USA-USSR basketball final.

But of course, there emerged a slew of positive and pleasing images as well from Munich's epochal Olympic festival. One thinks, for example, of the Greek Olympians at the opening day ceremony dancing jauntily into the stadium to the strains of a bouzouki; fans sunbathing on the grassy hillsides of the Oberwiesenfeld, strolling happily through the Spielstraße, and applauding appreciatively in the magnificent Olympic Stadium; Olga Korbut laughing after her amazing performance in gymnastics; Mark Spitz thrusting his arms in the air after his first swimming victory; Ulrike Meyfarth jumping for joy after jumping for gold. Speaking of brilliant athletic performances, Munich saw a record-breaking number of records, Olympic and world. In swimming alone, Munich witnessed twenty-nine Olympic records, twenty of which were also world records. In track and field, eleven world records were set in what one commentator called "the highest standard athletics ever seen in ten days." All this athletic brilliance transpired against the backdrop of the most innovative and spectacular Olympic architecture devised up to that time. Attendance figures for the Munich Games were also impressive. Although the number of foreign visitors was not as high as hoped—for reasons mentioned above—admissions overall totaled an unprecedented 3,307,135 souls, filling almost 90 percent of the available seats. As for the municipality of Munich, it had shown itself, as one American commentator put it, to be "a compassionate city, not the brush-cut, monocle and jackbooted Germany of the Junkers" (of course, in reality, anti-Prussian Munich had never been that, and the "compassion" in question could at times be all too selective).

The citizens of the FRG, despite their anger and despair over what had happened to their "carefree Games," certainly tried to focus on the brighter sides of the Munich '72 experience and to see the Games overall in a positive light. A public opinion poll launched right after the festival ended asked whether the Munich Games, with everything taken into account, should be regarded as "a success" or not. Eighty percent of the respondents answered "yes"; 19 percent, "no." An even higher percentage—86—answered yes to the question "Are you in favor of a continuation of the Olympic Games in the contemporary era?"

Trying to take into account both the inspiring glory and the great tragedy that had been Munich '72, one Bavarian commentator wrote on the day these tumultuous Games ended,

> The Olympic competitive venues set in their fantastic landscape, the athletic achievements, the mood of the international public and the relaxed atmosphere in the Olympic Village—all this had up until September 5 provided the most effective advertising extravaganza possible for the young Federal Republic of Germany and the new Munich. Even

envious spoilsports tended to couch their criticisms of this Olympic festival held under Bavaria's blue heavens in hidden compliments. Thus a foreign journalist commented: "These models of German efficiency somehow managed perfectly to engineer even a quality of spontaneity."

No wonder, then, that those who [in the early going] had complained most loudly about the Games—namely, the radio and TV reporters—were the most saddened, indeed the most offended, by the terror attack of September 5. Thus an ARD reporter could say of these Games on their concluding day: "They were the most beautiful Olympics ever to have been wrecked."

Epilogue

That which we remember is, more often than not, that
which we would like to have been; or that which we hope to be.
Thus our memory and our identity are ever at odds; our
history ever a tall tale told by inattentive idealists.
—Ralph Ellison, *Shadow and Act* (1964)

History, or to be more precise, the history we Germans
have repeatedly mucked up, is a clogged toilet.
We flush and flush, but the shit keeps rising.
—Günter Grass, *Crab Walk* (2002)

Like most modern Olympics, the Munich Summer Olympic festival of 1972 was short (if not sweet)—a mere sixteen days. Unlike virtually all other Olympics, however, Munich '72 has had a very long afterlife. Subsequent episodes of terror and counterterror stemming directly from the Palestinian attack on September 5 served to keep "Munich" before the global mind. So did TV programs, newspaper retrospectives, and major movies. In Germany, memories of the Federal Republic of Germany's (FRG) "darkest day" have been fueled by ongoing recriminations among the officials and politicians who had been responsible for keeping the Munich Games safe. Of course, some people, especially Germans, have made a concerted effort to remember other things—good things—about this crucial episode in postwar German and world history. But the fact is, over the years, Munich '72 has come to resemble nothing so much as a moral/political "Superfund site," slowly leaking its toxins into the atmosphere.

An Endless Cycle of Violence

As of September 7, 1972, the three Palestinian *fedayeen* who had been captured alive at Fürstenfeldbruck—Jamal Al-Gashey, Adnan Al-Gashey, and Mohammed Safady—were undergoing interrogation at three separate Bavarian prisons (Straubing, Landsberg, and Stadelheim). Israel did not request the men's extradition, which indeed Bonn had not expected, given that their crime had occurred on West German soil. Although the prisoners apparently were not physically mistreated, their interrogators pressed them long and hard regarding the organization and leadership of Black September, and their methods of entering West Germany. After visiting the captives, a representative of the Union of Arab Lawyers, based in Cairo, publicly charged that the men were being subjected to "psychological torture" in the form of solitary confinement and sleep deprivation. Arab lawyers from Egypt, Algeria, and Tunisia offered to defend the Palestinians free of charge but were turned down on grounds that only lawyers licensed in the FRG could take the cases.

Meanwhile, authorities in Bonn and Munich worried that the fedayeens' Black September colleagues or other supporters in the Arab world might resort to terror tactics in order to force their release, as indeed had been threatened. Believing that the hijacking of a Lufthansa aircraft was the most likely scenario, the federal Ministry of Interior ordered on September 8 that all employees of Arab nationality working in the West German airline industry be dismissed forthwith.

This seat-of-the-pants security measure was not only ethically and legally dubious—it also proved worthless. In the early morning of October 29, 1972, a Lufthansa Boeing 727 en route from Damascus, Syria, to Frankfurt was hijacked by two Palestinian Black Septembrists just after it left Beirut, one of its stopovers. Sure enough, the motive behind the hijacking was the liberation of the three imprisoned Palestinians. The hijackers, armed with hand grenades and guns, demanded that the aircraft fly directly to Munich. They further ordered the pilot to radio ahead the hijackers' instructions that the three jailed fedayeen be immediately released and transferred to Riem Airport, there to await a rendezvous with their liberators and transport to an (as yet undisclosed) Arab destination. If the German authorities failed to comply with any of their demands, the hijackers threatened to blow up the plane and all its thirteen occupants.

When informed that the plane did not have enough fuel to reach Munich, the hijackers directed it to Cyprus, where it refueled before setting off again for Munich. Upon reaching Munich's airspace at about 11:00 a.m., the hijackers learned that the Bavarians could not have the three fedayeen delivered to Riem for another ninety minutes. The terrorists therefore ordered their pilot to divert to Zagreb, Yugoslavia, demanding now that the prisoners must be transported to Zagreb Airport rather than Riem. The hijackers warned that they would not allow their plane to touch down in Zagreb until they had assurance that their comrades were already at the local airport awaiting pickup.

Despite their fear of just such a scenario, the West German authorities seemed clueless about how to proceed in this newest hostage crisis. They asked Arab diplomats to help mediate a solution, just as they had during the standoff in the Olympic Village. But in this instance, their appeal fell on deaf ears. As a representative of the Arab League in Bonn curtly told the Foreign Office, no accredited Arab diplomat would want to help out given what had recently transpired in Munich. This time, he said, the Germans would be completely on their own.

Left to their own devices, and determined to avoid another bloodbath, the Germans quickly decided that compliance with the terrorists' demands was their best option. On instructions from Chancellor Willy Brandt, the Bavarian authorities immediately released the three captive Palestinians, helicoptered them to Riem Airport, and loaded them on a Lufthansa Condor charter aircraft for a flight to Zagreb. The charter plane, whose passengers included, in addition to the fedayeen, two Bavarian plainclothes policemen and the CEO of Lufthansa Airlines, took off in the direction of Zagreb, but the pilot had orders from Minister of the Interior Hans-Dietrich Genscher not to leave West German airspace until he personally gave the word. Once en route, however, the Lufthansa CEO overruled Genscher and ordered the pilot to fly straight to Zagreb. Meanwhile, the Foreign Office in Bonn alerted its general consul in the Croatian provincial capital to rush to the airport to take charge of the situation from the German end.

By late afternoon, the hijacked 727 was cruising over Zagreb, dangerously low on fuel, awaiting word that the Palestinians were at the airport. Only when that word finally came through, a little before 5:30 p.m., did the hijackers allow their commandeered craft to land. Once the plane had taxied to the terminal, the German consul expected a quick and orderly exchange of the hostages for the Palestinians. He did not know that his superiors had already agreed to allow the hijackers to keep the eleven hostages under their control for a flight to Libya and to release them only upon safely reaching that destination. Brandishing their grenades, the hijackers insisted upon an immediate handover of the three prisoners, fresh tanks of gas, and permission to take off for Tripoli. Unless those demands were met, they would blow up the plane.

With no clear instructions from Bonn about how to proceed under these conditions, the hapless German consul negotiated with the hijackers for two hours before accepting all their conditions. At 7:30 p.m., the Boeing 727, now with three additional passengers on board, took off for Libya.

Several hours later, after the hijacked plane had landed in Tripoli, the German ambassador there was finally able to take charge of the hostages. As for the three Palestinian terrorists, they were not incarcerated in a Libyan prison (as Bonn had naively demanded) but treated as heroes of the Arab people. They spent the next few days telling and retelling the story of how they had found a way for the Palestinian people to participate in the Munich Games.

No sooner had the Palestinian fedayeen settled happily into their new celebrity status in Libya than conspiracy theories regarding their liberation began to swirl around the Middle East (in truth, conspiracy theories are *always* swirling around the Middle East). According to the most popular theory (especially in Israel), the "hijacking" had actually been set up in advance by Bonn and Black September as a "compromise" advantageous to both: Black September would get its comrades back, and Bonn would be free of three troublesome captives whose presence might inspire further acts of terror on German soil.

This theory continues to have wide currency. Journalist Simon Reeve, looking back on the hijacking incident in *One Day in September* (2000), points out that there "are several strange aspects" about the operation that suggest a conspiratorial interpretation, including the facts that the Lufthansa Boeing left Damascus with seven crew members but no passengers and that in Beirut it picked up only thirteen passengers (including the hijackers themselves)—"a surprisingly low figure." Unidentified German officials interviewed by Reeve for his book stated off the record that the incident fit "the pattern of the German government's pragmatic approach to terrorism in the 1970s . . . a time when Germany made secret agreements with Palestinians and other international terrorist groups as a desperate bid to keep them away from German borders." Reeve further asserts that "German, Palestinian, and Israeli sources" provided concrete evidence of a conspiratorial "compromise."

In a more recent treatment of the Olympic terror attack and Israel's "deadly response," *Striking Back* (2005), Israeli author Aaron Klein fully agrees with this interpretation. He adds to it the detail that the liberation operation was carried out by Popular Front for the Liberation of Palestine (PFLP) specialists under the command of Wadi Haddad, a medical doctor who, like his colleague Dr. George Habash, believed in the importance of "spectacular operations [that would] focus the world's attention on the problem of Palestine." Furthermore, Klein accepts as hard fact contemporary speculation among Jewish groups in West Germany that Bonn even *paid* for the job, wiring $5 million to a PFLP account for the simulated "hijacking."

Although this reading of the "strange" hijacking incident may be correct, it is not quite as convincing as it first may seem. The putatively corroborative "sources" mentioned by Reeve and Klein are never cited—and I can find no sign of any "smoking gun" in the German records (which admittedly does not mean that it doesn't exist). Although the hijacking was perhaps convenient for Bonn, its disorderly and improvised character does not suggest a pre-arranged operation. If there was indeed a "pattern" here, that pattern was not just one of chronic appeasement of terrorists but also one of incompetence and mismanagement on the part of the German authorities. (Indeed, given the German record in these matters, one is tempted to conclude that, if the Germans actually had helped to set up this operation, it probably would have gone awry.) Moreover, if there *was* a German conspiracy, the Bavarians don't seem to have been in on it. Although they acquiesced in the handover of the Palestinian prisoners, they were livid about it. In their view, the three fedayeen remained under Bavarian indictment after their transfer to Libya. Munich pressed Bonn for extradition of the men even though Bonn had no extradition treaty with Tripoli. Conceding that the extradition prospects were "doubtful," the Bavarian Ministry of Justice nonetheless maintained that it was necessary to request the fugitives' return to German soil for trial. "We must not write off these terrible acts of murder as long as a judicial reckoning is possible," wrote a representative of the Bavarian Justice Ministry to Bonn.

Taking note of Munich's position, the Foreign Office in Bonn debated the pros and cons of an extradition request. Officials in Bonn agreed that "the faith of German citizens in the rule of law" might be shaken if the West German government did not make every effort to enforce Bavaria's criminal indictment of the fugitive Palestinians. A formal extradition request would furthermore oblige the Libyan government to "declare before the entire world whether it wished to cooperate in the prosecution of a serious crime." On the other hand, not only did Bonn and Tripoli have no extradition treaty, but (as a German legal expert noted), by Libyan law no one could be extradited from its soil for acts that might be deemed "political" in nature. Surely Tripoli would see the Palestinian operation in Munich as a political action. In all likelihood, then, an extradition petition would be fruitless. Instead of demanding extradition, it would be best, concluded the Foreign Office in Bonn, to allow the Libyans to take over the prosecution of the fedayeen themselves.

Of course, as the Foreign Office well knew, there was little chance that the Libyan authorities would undertake any prosecution of men who were being hailed as heroes across the Arab world. For all practical purposes, the Munich murderers had escaped justice.

It was just this sorry reality that outraged the Israelis. Prime Minister Golda Meir wrote in her memoirs that she felt "literally physically sickened when the Arabs who had murdered the eleven Israeli athletes at the Olympic Games in 1972 were set free in a blaze of publicity and flown to Libya." Whereas Meir's government (or most of it, anyway) had resisted openly criticizing West Germany for its handling of the hostage crisis in Munich, Tel Aviv now publicly denounced Bonn for releasing the three terrorists. Ambassador Eliashiv Ben-Horin, who was immediately recalled "for consultations" by Meir, declared upon leaving, "The release of the three terrorists is unbelievable. It is not just a question of capitulation to Arab threats. Three murderers . . . are now free . . . to murder more Israelis. . . . One should not be surprised by the shock and disappointment evoked in Israel by the German decision."

The Germans, however, were in fact quite shocked by the severity of the Israeli response. Noting that the release of the terrorists had produced "a serious crisis in German-Israeli relations," a West German Foreign Office memo complained of "an unprecedentedly hostile campaign in the Israeli media against the federal government," replete with "personal attacks against the chancellor and comparisons with the Nazi era." The Foreign Office report also made note of anti-German demonstrations at the West German embassy in Tel Aviv and a last-minute cancellation of a trip to Israel by a West Berlin choir group. Although a personal letter from Brandt to Meir in late November had "helped ease tensions at the official level," relations between the two countries remained strained. Golda Meir herself indicated as much when, in a statement on December 12, 1972, she questioned "whether there would ever be a generation that might experience normal relations between the Germans and the Jewish people."

The Meir government's rage over West Germany's freeing of the "murderers of Munich," along with its corollary conviction that the surviving perpetrators of this crime would never be called to account unless Israel acted on its own, prompted the prime minister's fateful decision in November 1972 to authorize the tracking down and assassination of any and all Black September terrorists involved in the Munich killings. In addition to eliminating those responsible for Munich, Israel hoped with this operation to throw terror into the ranks of the Palestine Liberation Organization (PLO) and significantly degrade its capacity to strike at Israel. In fact, it was this latter goal that was the more important motive for the operation.

The "Wrath of God" and "Spring of Youth" campaigns carried out over the next twenty years by various Mossad hit squads have been extensively chronicled in memoirs, monographs, and films, so there is no need to rehash the details here. It *is* necessary, however, to make several general points about the operation.

First, although Mossad killed many of the figures connected (or allegedly connected) to the Munich murders, it by no means got them all. In fact, Mossad seems to have failed to get *any* of the three surviving members of the Black September commando unit that had attacked the Munich Games—nor did Mossad manage to track down the key figures in the organization and planning of the terror attack; most importantly, Abu Daoud, Abu Iyad, and Fuad al-Shamali eluded the hunters.*

Second, just as in Israel's retribution raids against targets in Lebanon and Syria immediately after the Munich attack, the protracted assassination campaign exacted considerable "collateral damage." Mossad's initial effort to kill Ali Hassan Salameh, a Daoud assistant whom Israel called the "mastermind" of the Munich attack (a charge denied by Black September), resulted in the murder in Norway of a Moroccan waiter whose only crime was to *look like* Salameh. Some six years later, Mossad agents did manage to kill Salameh in Beirut with a massive car bomb but in the process also killed four innocent bystanders and injured eighteen others. At the beginning of its campaign, Mossad had vowed not to act "with the same disregard for innocent lives displayed by the men [they were] hunting," but in the heat of the hunt that vow seems to have fallen by the wayside.

Third, and most important, Meir's larger strategic goal of making Israel safer by eliminating the Munich killers ended up having the opposite effect. By further enraging the Arab world, the state-sponsored assassina-

---

* Fuad al-Shamali died in August 1972 from cancer. Mohammed Oudeh (Abu Daoud) survived a Mossad assassination attempt in 1981 in Warsaw; he lived mainly in Damascus until his death on July 3, 2010, from kidney failure at age 73. He never expressed remorse for his role in the Munich attack, stating in an interview in 2008 that he would "do it all over again," if he had the chance. In his view, "Munich" put the Palestinian cause on the map.

tion campaign added yet more fuel to the fires of hatred in the Middle East, helping to perpetuate a seemingly endless cycle of attack and retribution.

The cycle of violence took another, very ugly, turn in October 1973 with the so-called Yom Kippur War. Egyptian president Anwar Sadat, embittered over Israeli's retaliation against Arabs in the wake of Munich, and anxious to regain the Sinai region occupied by Israel since the 1967 war, sent eighty thousand Egyptian troops across the Suez Canal on October 6, 1973. Caught off guard, the Israeli army fell back into the Sinai, a retreat that stunned the world. However, aided by an emergency airlift of arms from the United States, the Israeli Defense Force (IDF) managed to repulse the Egyptians after two weeks' hard fighting. The war came to an end on October 26 with a peace settlement brokered by Washington.

But another kind of war was just beginning. Deeply angered by Washington's support of Israel, Saudi Arabia (which had bankrolled Sadat's attack), along with nine other Arab members of the recently formed OPEC oil cartel, clamped an embargo on oil shipments to American ports. The embargo created an artificial oil shortfall around the globe resulting in the quadrupling of world oil prices, from $3 a barrel to $12. In the United States, customers were soon spending three times as much for gasoline as they had before the war.

One of the unforeseen consequences of this "oil crisis" was a sudden demand for smaller, more fuel-efficient cars, even in profligate America. As we know, Japanese and European car makers were in a much better position to thrive in this new atmosphere than was Detroit, which continued to resist making the necessary adaptations to the changed environment for years. Thus, in a way, what happened in Munich in 1972 constituted an important link in the chain of events that helped to dramatically weaken the American auto industry. It turns out that Detroit's loss to Munich in the competition to hold the '72 Summer Olympics presaged a much more critical setback for Motown in the race to stay afloat in the new world of high-priced oil.

In the FRG, the pressing issue in the wake of the Munich Games was dealing with all the recriminations and criticism stemming from Germany's handling of the hostage crisis. Although the West German government continued to claim for the record that Bavarian security officials had acted responsibly throughout the ordeal, Bonn knew that, among other inadequacies, the FRG's lack of a trained counterterrorism unit had critically hampered the response in Munich. As early as September 10, 1972, Interior Minister Genscher disclosed that he had instructed Bonn's Federal Criminal Office to prepare for the creation of a special antiterror unit that would be at the disposal of West Germany's individual states. A little later, Genscher tasked Colonel Ulrich Wegener, a trusted aide who had served as his liaison to the Bundesgrenzschutz during the Olympics, with the job of building up this agency. In the face of ongoing objections from some politicians that a federal antiterrorist unit would inevitably rekindle memories of the Nazi SS or Gestapo, Wegener pressed on with the project. To deter domestic critics of the idea, he drew personnel for the new unit from the various state police forces rather than from the federal army, as was the model in most Special Forces around the world. On April 17, 1973, this new force, christened Bundesgrenzschutzgruppe 9 (GSG-9), was formally added to the existing eight Bundesgrenzschutz units and stationed at Saint Augustine-Hangelar, near Bonn.

Some four years after its creation, GSG-9 achieved great distinction when, on the airport tarmac at Mogadishu, Somalia, it stormed a Lufthansa passenger plane that had been hijacked by four Palestinian terrorists, who were threatening to blow up the plane, along with its passengers and crew, unless Bonn freed several imprisoned members of the Rote Armee Fraktion (RAF) terrorist group. The antiterrorist commandos managed to rescue all the hostages and kill three of the hijackers, while suffering only one injury themselves and causing one minor injury to a flight attendant. Comparing this result with what happened at Fürstenfeldbruck in September 1972, one can only conclude that it's extremely unfortunate that GSG-9 had not been created a few years earlier.

Accountability, Compensation, and Commemoration

Meanwhile, worldwide criticism of the German authorities' handling of the Olympic hostage crisis was so intense that the Federal Ministry of Justice in Bonn privately considered the possibility of lodging formal charges of gross negligence against the Bavarian authorities who led the police operation. In the end, such charges did not come to pass, leaving it to Bavaria (specifically, the state Interior Ministry) to conduct its own investigation into security planning and police practices in connection with the Munich Games. While the investigation was still proceeding, a chemical expert employed by the Federal Criminal Office made headlines by asserting that the hostages might have been saved had the Bavarian authorities authorized the use of poison gas against the terrorists, as he had allegedly suggested. Manfred Schreiber dismissed this proposition as absurd. As for Bavaria's official investigation into the tragedy, it eventually produced a compendious and very detailed document that (not surprisingly) absolved the authorities of any significant failings in the hostage crisis.

Well before this report was completed, Bonn and the Munich Organizing Committee (OC), perhaps in hopes of fending off financial claims against them by relatives of the victims of the Olympic tragedy, dispatched compensation payments in the direction of Israel. Willi Daume turned over insurance monies received by the OC (for damages to Olympic structures to the Israeli Olympic Committee) for the construction of a sports center in honor of the eleven slain Israeli Olympians. A Soforthilfe (Emergency Relief) fund established by the federal government in Bonn sent some DM 3.2 million to the Israeli Red Cross for distribution among the thirteen parents, seven widows, and fourteen children of the slain Israeli Olympians. Upon receiving her payoff of DM 400,000 from the Germans, Shoshona Shapira, widow of the murdered athletic trainer Amitzur Shapira, made it clear that the Israeli families were not going to be bought off so easily: "In light of the six million murdered Jews [in the Third Reich], the Germans should have been more diligent [in protecting Israelis during the Games]," she declared. Some of the relatives also faulted their own government for not being more critical of the Germans' handling of the hostage crisis and for not pursuing more aggressively the "truth" behind the killings. They suspected that a "deal" had been struck between Bonn and Tel Aviv whereby the Germans would be let off the hook in the Munich catastrophe in exchange for some kind of "reward" to Israel.

In fact, what the victims' relatives wanted from the Germans was not just substantial financial compensation (though they certainly did want that) but also an honest and detailed accounting of the events that led to the deaths of their loved ones on September 5/6, 1972. One question that certainly begged for clarification concerned the death of David Berger, who, as we recall, was among the hostages found dead in one of the burned helicopters following the firefight. A lawyer retained by the relatives claimed to have been told by unnamed German pathologists that Berger had still been alive an hour after the fighting at Fürstenfeldbruck—and had died of smoke inhalation rather than gunshot wounds. This suggested that he might have been saved had the Germans rushed the helicopters as soon as the shooting ended.

With specific regard to material compensation, in 1973 an Israeli lawyer sought DM 1 million in compensation from German sources for each of the eleven families. The compensation demand was later increased to a total of about DM 40 million. After their initial payouts, however, the

Germans proved reluctant to sweeten the pot, arguing that there were no legal grounds for compensation in any amount.

Bonn and Munich also stonewalled when it came to providing the detailed files demanded by Ankie Spitzer (wife of Andrei) and other victims' relatives. The relatives pushed hard for the files following a report in the Israeli newspaper *Yedioth Ahronoth* that survivors among the Israeli Olympic team had received classified reports from the Bavarian Prosecutor's Office saying that at least eight of the hostages had been killed by police bullets. But the Bavarian Justice Ministry claimed for years that there *were no* files on the case and then, in the early 1980s, switched to the position that files had once existed but were destroyed in 1978 when the routine period for holding such materials had run out. The ministry asserted, however, that the original ballistics report had shown that the bullets fired into the helicopters had all come from AK 47s, weapons used exclusively by the terrorists.

In September 1992, the story took a new twist when the Bavarian Justice Ministry announced that the ballistics record previously reported as destroyed had resurfaced and—as the ministry had earlier asserted—indeed proved that all the Israeli hostages had been killed by the Palestinian terrorists. The ministry dismissed charges of police involvement in the hostages' death as "a disinformation campaign" waged by the relatives in order to win damages amounting to some DM 40 million ($29 million). Finally, the Bavarian officials also asserted that relatives of the slain Olympians had not approached the Prosecutor's Office for the relevant documents until August 20, 1992, so there could be "no question of information being denied for twenty years and the 'truth' being hushed up."

Yet the German wall of silence was beginning to show signs of cracks. An anonymous whistleblower inside one of the Bavarian ministries secretly sent Ankie Spitzer a parcel of eighty pages of documents from ballistics and pathology reports on the Fürstenfeldbruck disaster. The parcel also contained an annex listing hundreds of other documents. Using this incriminating material as a lever, a lawyer for the relatives managed to gain brief access to voluminous files in the Bavarian archives relating to the Fürstenfeldbruck operation. According to the lawyer, Pinchas Zeltzer, the files provided graphic proof of blunder after blunder on the part of the Bavarian authorities. Zeltzer also insisted that a pathology report showed that David Berger had died of smoke inhalation rather than terrorists' bullets. Moreover, on the basis of newly available ballistics evidence, Zeltzer and Spitzer came away convinced that "one or possibly two" of the Israeli hostages had been killed by German sniper fire, not by terrorists' grenades or bullets.

Although this last assumption lacked conclusive proof—the evidence in the Bavarian archives was and remains extremely ambiguous and confusing—the revelations contained in the files were so damaging to the German side that the relatives decided to take legal action against the federal government, the state of Bavaria, and the Munich municipality. To this end, they hired a Munich law firm, which pursued the case in the Bavarian court system, starting at the bottom. Very quickly, a lower court threw the case out on grounds that a three-year statute of limitations had elapsed. The relatives appealed this decision, arguing that the statute of limitations should not have begun until *after* the relevant documentation had been made available to them. A higher court rejected this appeal.

Undeterred, in early 2000 the relatives appealed their case to the highest Bavarian court. While the matter was still pending, Bavarian prime minister Edmund Stoiber proposed an out-of-court settlement that had originally been advanced by Chancellor Gerhard Schröder in Berlin. On April 31, 2001, Stoiber announced that Berlin, Bavaria, and Munich together were offering to pay a total of DM 6 million in compensation to the families. This offer included an additional DM 1.2 million for the families' legal fees incurred over the past twenty-eight years of seeking compensation.

Stoiber's offer occasioned nothing but contempt from the families. "The connotation of 6 million is horrible and I'm furious," said Ilana Romano, widow of wrestler Yossef Romano. However, not long after Stoiber's awkward attempt at an out-of-court settlement, Bavaria's highest court also rejected the relatives' suit. They had now reached the legal end of the line.

About one year later, on the occasion of the thirtieth anniversary of the Munich Games, the Germans were still holding firm to their position that they bore no legal or financial responsibility for the deaths of the eleven Israeli Olympians at the Munich Games. During a ceremony at Fürstenfeldbruck, federal interior minister Otto Schily noted that the German government had already paid some $3 million in compensation to the families of the victims. But he added that such payments were not "an admission of guilt; [they were] a humanitarian gesture."

In addition to financial compensation and an official acknowledgment from the German authorities that they had inadequately protected the Israeli Olympians and badly mishandled the attempt to rescue them, the families pushed for a worthy memorialization of their slain loved ones at the Olympic site. Here, too, they ran into resistance, albeit not as obdurate.

Exactly one year after the terror attack, representatives from the Munich OC, the Bavarian government, and the Israeli Cultural Office of Bavaria gathered at Connollystrasse 31 to reflect on the tragedy of September 5/6, 1972—a horror that Schreiber, Daume, and Bruno Merk continued to allude to in delicate circumlocutions such as "the events of that time," or "those unfortunate occurrences." Schreiber, tone deaf as ever, took advantage of this occasion to repeat his mantra that "decisions of the Israeli government" had from the outset doomed all German efforts to free the hostages.

In the run-up to this first anniversary commemoration, Bavarian authorities had been tossing around various plans to build a physical memorial to the Israeli Olympians either on the Olympic grounds or perhaps on the site of a former synagogue destroyed during the 1938 "Night of the Crystals" pogrom. Immediately after the Games, the OC (in the person of Hans-Jochen Vogel) had rejected a proposal from some contrite West Germans to rename the Olympic Stadium in honor of Moshe Weinberg. Such a move, said Vogel, would serve only to perpetuate painful memories of the tragedy at the Olympic site. As for a physical monument, it quickly became evident that no West German agency, public or private, wished to pony up the funds necessary for a major memorial.

At this point, the former Israeli team lodgings, like all the other structures in the men's Village, legally belonged to the Bayerische Hausbau, a semi-public agency whose job was to sell off all the units to private buyers on the open market. Yet, it was understood from the outset that Connollystrasse 31 was a special case—it should not be sold off in this way. Instead, it should somehow serve the needs of historical commemoration and education. But how, precisely, should this noble goal be actualized? Early on, the Hausbau had rejected a number of proposals from private bidders whose sole intent seemed to be "to make money out of tragic history." In subsequent months, the agency considered and rejected plans to convert #31 into an international youth library or hostel. Hanns Lamm, president of the Jewish Cultural Community of Bavaria, proposed that the complex be taken over as a guest house by the Institut für Zeitgeschichte, a prestigious Munich-based research institution focusing on the Nazi and postwar eras. But the Institut said it didn't need a guest house, and in any event, there wasn't sufficient funding. Deeply frustrated, Lamm complained, "I can't even knock on a door without getting it slammed in my face." Thus, at the time of the first anniversary of the "Munich Massacre," the only changes to have occurred at Connollystrasse 31 involved the installation of a small plaque listing the names of the eleven Israeli victims, along with a plastering over of the bullet holes and a fresh coat of paint. (That first plaque, we should add, contained errors in the list of victims and featured a cross rather than a Star of David; following understandable objections from Israel and the local Jewish community, this plaque gave way to a new one commissioned by the Central Council of Jews in Germany.)* In the view of the Foreign Office, the Connollystrasse plaque was all that was needed by way of a memorial for the slain Israeli Olympians; it saw "no need for further German initiatives" in this area.

The physical aspect of Connollystrasse 31 has remained unchanged through the decades. However, by the time the second anniversary of the murders rolled around, the infamous apartment had a new tenant. The Munich OC bought the apartment for DM 500,000 from the Hausbau and presented it free of charge to the Max Plank Institute, with the provision that it be used "in the spirit of international understanding." The institute accordingly turned it into a guest house for visiting foreign scientists. Alas, the first occupants found their lodgings less than ideal. They were constantly bothered by nosy sightseers peering in their windows or demanding to be allowed inside to inspect the murder scene at close quarters.

The families of the murder victims, meanwhile, pressed for memorialization of their loved ones not only from the Germans but also from the International Olympic Committee (IOC). More specifically, they wanted a minute of silence for the Israeli Olympians to be observed during the opening ceremonies at future Olympic festivals, summer and winter. The IOC repeatedly rejected the families' petitions, citing their well-worn—and typically hypocritical—argument that "politics" must not be allowed to intrude upon the Games. (This concern did not prevent the committee from allowing a tattered flag from New York's World Trade Center to be carried in the opening ceremony at the 2002 Salt Lake City Winter Games: presumably the terror attacks on September 11, 2001, had nothing to do with "politics.") Finally, after twenty-four years of stonewalling, the IOC agreed to a rather low-key acknowledgment of the Munich murders by inviting children of the slain Israeli Olympians to attend the 1996 Atlanta Summer Games. Moreover, independent of the IOC, a commemorative service for the eleven Israelis took place during the '96 Games at the Martin Luther King Memorial in downtown Atlanta.

---

* It was not until 1995 that a more ambitious memorial finally materialized on the Olympic grounds. A balance-beam-like rectangular sculpture by the German artist Fritz König entitled "Klagebalken" (Wailing Beam) went up at the entrance to the main Olympic concourse. The DM 500,000 price tag was covered by the city of Munich. Four years later, a smaller memorial was unveiled at Fürstenfeldbruck.

Ironically, participants at this event at the King Memorial were obliged to mark a second, and much more recent, Olympic tragedy: the bombing two days earlier at Atlanta's Centennial Olympic Park that killed 2 people and injured 111. "It is being said that Saturday morning's act of violence and terror has destroyed the innocence of the Atlanta Games," said Stephen Selig, president of the Atlanta Jewish Federation. "But the fourteen children of the Munich eleven are here tonight to tell us that the innocence was lost long ago." If, in the view of many observers, the Atlanta bombing was "Munich all over again," added Rabbi Arnold Goodman, there was a sobering and vital difference. In Munich, "the Israelis were the target victims as Palestinians brought their political feud into the Olympic Village. They were not chosen at random. The victims in Centennial Park happened to be at the wrong place when the bomb went off."

In September 2000, Matan Vilnai, Israel's minister of sport, appealed to the IOC yet again to honor the Munich Olympians with a minute of silence at the upcoming Sydney Games. Speculation in the press that this time the appeal would be granted prompted Yasser Arafat's Palestinian Authority to call upon Arab states to boycott the Sydney Games. But in fact, the IOC turned down Vilnai's petition, as it had all others before it, leaving any memorialization of the Munich tragedy up to Sydney's Jewish community. During the 2000 Games, officials of a local Jewish college unveiled a memorial to the victims of the '72 terror attack. As the veil came off the memorial, Vilnai declared, echoing his people's stance on the Holocaust, "We will never forget these cold-blooded murders, nor forgive them."

Munich '72 and the "Arc of Terror"

Although the international Olympic movement over the years seemed intent upon forgetting or ignoring what had happened at the Munich Games on September 5/6, 1972, that experience in fact exerted a huge influence on every subsequent Olympic festival. The IOC and future host cities "remembered" Munich by doing everything in their power to ensure that "another Munich" would not occur. After '72, security became *the* obsession at the Games, even at the risk of turning these self-proclaimed celebrations of peaceful play and international conviviality into something approaching inmate competitions in a prison yard.

As we noted above, the organizers of Montreal's Games in 1976 decided in the wake of the Munich horror to make security their number 1 priority. They did just that by deploying some sixteen thousand military troops and police to patrol the Olympic grounds around the clock. The perimeter around Montreal's Olympic Village featured a high, barbwire-topped fence guarded by machinegun-toting soldiers stationed every fifty yards. The bill for security at Montreal came to $100 million, fifty times the outlay for Munich.

And that was just the beginning. Whereas earlier Olympic host cities had tried to outdo their predecessors in terms of architecture, now they seemed intent upon spending record amounts on security. At the 1992 Barcelona Games, the host city deployed a massive security force bolstered by fifty thousand specially trained experts. Barcelona's Olympic Village bristled with high-tech electronic surveillance gear along with armed patrols. The cost for all this was approximately $300 million.

For the Atlanta Games four years later, the organizers actually spent more on security than on any other budget item—an Olympics first. Alas, those safety precautions focused almost exclusively on the Olympic competition venues, not on the downtown Centennial Park, which (shades of Munich) was kept relatively free of obtrusive security measures so as not to spoil "the party atmosphere" in the city. The way was thus clear for Eric Rudolph, a fundamentalist Christian zealot who was determined to strike out against the "holocaust" of abortion by bombing a park full of people, to wreck—or at least cast an ugly pall over—the Modern Olympics' one hundredth anniversary party in Atlanta.

On the eve of the 2004 Athens Games, a former U.S. State Department security expert who had compiled a data base on terrorism pointed out that there had been "more than 170 terrorist events involving athletes or athletic events since the 1972 Munich Olympics." And he added, "To protect an event the size of the Olympics, you have to know what the bad guys know about what has worked in the past." Hoping to allay widespread foreign fears that "bad guys" of one stripe or another might successfully crash their Olympic party, the Athens organizers preemptively incarcerated local leftist radicals and stepped up police surveillance of the city's Muslim areas. During the Games, some seven thousand heavily armed soldiers patrolled the streets. Yet these draconian measures were not enough for the Israelis, who brought their own security team to Athens, as indeed they had done at every Olympic festival since 1972. "Since Munich we are always taking extra [security] measures," said Ephraim Zinger, director general of the Israeli Olympic Committee.

No one knows how much the Chinese spent to protect the 2008 Beijing Games, but like everything else about that festival the security expenditure was undoubtedly outsized. The safety budget would have had to have been huge, for some one hundred thousand soldiers augmented

Beijing's regular police force to guard the Games. Surface-to-air missiles were stationed around prominent Olympic sites like the "Bird's Nest" Stadium and the "Water Cube" Aquatics Center. Police accompanied by bomb-sniffing dogs patrolled every railway and subway station in the city. The security checks at Beijing's Olympic venues were even stricter than those imposed at Tel Aviv's Ben-Gurion Airport, noted an Israeli journalist, obviously much impressed.

While enhanced security measures at all the post-1972 Olympics may have helped to prevent another terrorist attack on the scale of the Munich Massacre, the decades since then have of course been rife with all sorts of terrorist activity aimed at targets unconnected to the Olympics or other high-profile sporting events. Many of those episodes have, in the manner of the Atlanta bombing, evoked memories of and analogies to the Munich tragedy. And rather like that other infamous Munich episode—the 1938 conference in which Neville Chamberlain and Édouard Daladier fatefully appeased Hitler—much of this fevered analogizing was not rendered more accurate by its sincerity.

Such was certainly the case with the reaction to a vicious bombing of Munich's annual Oktoberfest on September 26, 1980. The pipe-bomb explosion, which killed thirteen people and injured over two hundred, was the deadliest terror episode in postwar German history after the Munich Massacre. This time, though, the alleged perpetrator, a right-wing extremist named Gondolf Köhler, was a home-grown terrorist, and his victims were not preselected members of a particular group but any and all Oktoberfest revelers who had the bad luck to be in the proximity of the dustbin in which the killer (who himself was blown to bits in the blast) had deposited his lethal mixture of TNT and mortar shells. The differences between the Oktoberfest mayhem and the Olympic tragedy did not prevent commentators from drawing analogies between the two events. Yet, however dubious the parallels were, shell-shocked Münchners might be forgiven for wondering if their beautiful city was not cursed: first, their joyful Olympic Games had been plunged into sorrow, and now, eight years later, their annual celebration of beer and good cheer had been turned into a bloodbath.

The upsurge of right-wing anti-immigrant violence following Germany's reunification in 1990 likewise evoked memories of Munich. During a ceremony at Connollystrasse 31 marking the twentieth anniversary of the Olympic massacre, Munich deputy mayor Christian Ude declaimed that recent firebomb attacks on refuge shelters in eastern Germany showed that the "lessons of Munich"—namely, the evils of xenophobic hatred and a corollary need for cross-cultural tolerance—were as pertinent as ever. Yet, of course, such "lessons" were bound to be lost on all those racist and religious fanatics who believed that *not* killing for their cause was the "true" evil.

For those who had experienced the Munich hostage drama firsthand, the horrific terror attacks in the United States on September 11, 2001—though very different from Munich in scope, motivation, and mode of operation—brought back painful memories, along with fresh reflections on the place of the Munich Olympic tragedy on the continuum of modern terrorism. "It [the destruction of New York City's World Trade Center] is bringing back a whole lot of awful memories," said Willye White, a member of the U.S. Olympic team at Munich. "Those people in the air, it was like equating their lives with the Israeli athletes and the feeling that they were going to die. It's all very painful."

Although terrorism related to the Middle East conflict had obviously been around long before Munich, for veterans of the Olympic tragedy like White, the '72 episode seemed to be the true beginning of an "arc of terror" that had reached a new level of horror on September 11, 2001. "This is where we were introduced to terrorism," said White. "[Munich generated] memories that you never shake." Upon watching the 9/11 horror unfold on his TV set, Jim McKay, the anchor of ABC's coverage of the Munich disaster twenty-nine years earlier, experienced exactly the same sensation. "My instant thought was of Munich," McKay said. And he added, more than a little hyperbolically and confusedly, Munich was "the fuse that ignited Arab terrorism."

In the immediate aftermath of 9/11, Arthur Cohn, producer of the Oscar-winning documentary *One Day in September* (2000), noted that his film was being rerun in France and Germany, adding that the movie should also be "required viewing as a teaching tool" in the United States. "Nothing was learned from Munich," he stated. "Hopefully, people will learn that terror at their doorstep with suicide bombers who are without dignity and without any respect for human life is a wake-up call. If we don't learn from it now, we will be forever cursed."

As if to take up Cohn's challenge, ABC produced a new hour-long documentary on the Munich Massacre and aired it on September 1, 2002, just in time for the thirtieth anniversary of the Munich Games. Commenting on the upcoming TV docudrama, a journalist for *USA Today* suggested that "if you and your kids or anyone you know has doubts about how some 3,000 people came to die on September 11 [2001]," this film was "something to consider." (To consider, yes, but hopefully with a more critical eye for the differences between the two terror attacks and the putative causal relationship between them.)

The "arc of terror" reaching from Munich to 9/11 was also much on the mind of Steven Spielberg when he set out to make his own film, *Munich* (2005), which, despite the title, focuses more on the Israeli reprisal campaign than on the '72 Games. Spielberg's motivation in making the film seems to have been as muddled as the film itself turned out to be. The director told an interviewer that he saw his movie as "a prayer for peace" in the Middle East, his own small effort to promote understanding and reconciliation between two peoples, Jews and Palestinians, who both had suffered persecution. While not harboring illusions that his film could "solve the stalemate in the Middle East," he hoped to portray the contenders on both sides not as "demons" but as beleaguered "individuals with families," thereby breaking down mutually inflammatory stereotypes. But Spielberg's second motivation—to "pay tribute" to eleven Israeli Olympians who had been "largely forgotten" outside their homeland and shrouded in deliberate and "ever louder silence" by the IOC—was, while worthy enough, a little too one-sided to effectively serve his first goal of promoting mutual understanding. Moreover, Spielberg's film does little to help the viewer understand why the Palestinians seized the Israeli Olympians in the first place, or how the day-long hostage drama ended up in such a bloody mess. As for Israel's campaign to exterminate the Black September terrorists, *Munich* deals with the complicated moral questions raised by this project by endowing the macho Mossad hunters with guilt complexes they probably did not have, while simultaneously ignoring the fact that the campaign's purpose was as much to weaken the PLO's operational capacity as to settle old scores.

Cost-Benefit Analyses: A "Convenient Fable"?

While most of the rumination on the Munich Olympics in subsequent decades has understandably focused on the terror attack and its legacy, the German officials responsible for putting on the festival threw themselves over the years into an activity that they hoped might eventually mitigate all those lingering bad memories of their ill-starred Games. They conducted periodic cost-benefit analyses of the entire '72 enterprise in the apparent belief that these would prove the Games to have been an enormous boon to West Germany and Munich, and therefore "worth" all the organizational effort, financial expenditure, and even those lamentable "dark" moments.

At the same time, the city of Munich sponsored anniversary celebrations of the Games that called attention to stellar athletic achievement, innovative architecture, and cultural creativity. Commenting on this process in 1973, *Der Spiegel* wondered whether, over the generations, strategic memory repression and skillful reworking of the past might ultimately do for the Munich Games what these forces had sometimes done for other bits of problematical history—create a "convenient fable."

One year after the Games had concluded, the prospects for achieving such an outcome did not look good. The Munich OC, which remained in existence until 1977, found itself faced with dozens of lawsuits from malcontented former Olympic employees and even from its own advertising chief, who charged that the committee had sold off his copyrighted Glückspirale (lottery) concept to the Bundesliga without his permission. Moreover, the Bundesrechnungshof (Federal Accounting Court) had discovered numerous irregularities in the OC's books. To make matters worse, the OC was still sitting on all kinds of Olympics-related paraphernalia that it had been unable to unload on an unsuspecting public: seven hundred thousand clothes hangers, one thousand rolls of toilet paper, two million cleaning rags, a whole warehouse of souvenirs, and an entire television studio. Above all, the OC's plan to sell off some 2,621 apartments in the men's Olympic Village was not going well. The units, still undergoing renovation, were generally perceived by would-be buyers as too costly for their small size and minimal accoutrements. As for the rest of the Olympic physical plant, parts of it, such as the Equestrian Center and rowing complex, were already looking long in the tooth.

And, of course, all the Olympic buildings had to be maintained and kept operational in the hope that they could find regular users and eventually become self-sustaining. The OC fought in the courts with the city of Munich and the Bavarian government over who should pay the upkeep costs. Maintenance and utility expenses for the Olympic buildings were especially high because of their technological complexity. The biggest offender here, not surprisingly, was the high-tech glass roof covering part of the Olympic Stadium and the adjoining Schwimmhalle and Sporthalle. The roofing over the latter two buildings was actually double-layered, and it was discovered about a year after the Games that the inner layer of Plexiglas was turning brown, shrinking, and falling apart. Experts blamed this alarming development on a buildup of temperatures between the two layers. They cautioned that if remedial measures were not taken soon, the inner panes might come loose and drop into the buildings.

One might have thought that the builders could have foreseen this problem—and sure enough, a parliamentary investigation committee came to the conclusion that the builders *had known in advance* that their design was flawed but had stuck to it in order to stay on their construction schedule. Chief architect Günter Behnisch was called in to testify on the matter; he stoutly denied any wrongdoing, as did the roof designer, Frei Otto.

When it came to possible remedial action, Behnisch opposed the measure that most experts favored—a further darkening of the roof's outer panels, so as to reduce temperatures between the layers. Behnisch cautioned that this measure would diminish the roof's transparency, which was its best quality. In the end, though, this was the remedy the Olympic Bau-Gesellschaft chose. In 1974, the outer panes were darkened and covered with a thin layer of steel wool. The DM 2.1 million repair cost for this was jointly born by the Bau-Gesellschaft and the builders. Lamentably, the operation indeed brought a significant reduction in the roof's translucence and thus a rather gloomy atmosphere inside the buildings.

Once repaired, though, Munich's iconic roof complex managed to withstand the tests of time and weather much better than most experts had expected. An evaluation of the structure undertaken some ten years after the Games found the fabulous *Dach* to be in such good shape that it might last until the year 2050!

But if the Olympic roof was apparently not going to fall in any time soon, the question remained whether the spaces under it, along with the other Olympic venues, would get enough use to make them self-sustaining. The OC was determined that Munich's Olympic facilities must not become deserted "ruins," as was the case with the Olympic structures in many other host cities. The Olympics' gift to Munich must be a gift that kept on giving. But achieving this ideal was very difficult, especially in the early going. The Equestrian Center and rowing facility found few users in the first years after the Games. The Sporthalle witnessed a number of attractions, including dog shows, a six-day bicycle race, an exhibition of rare coins, a Mormon convention, and a Rolling Stones concert. However, with the exception of the Stones concert, these events did not bring in much income. Moreover, the utilities costs for these affairs prompted the Olympic grounds' new concessionaire, Olympiapark Gmbh (OPG), to cut back on the number of events it would sponsor. The OPG chief admitted that, without subsidies from the city, he could put on "no events at all." Thus, by the end of 1973, despite 2.1 million paying visits to the Olympic Park as a whole and many soccer matches in the Olympic Stadium (which became home to the Bayern-München Football Club and was also scheduled to host some of the 1974 World Cup games, including the final),* the outlook for a self-sustaining post-Games Olympic enterprise seemed doubtful.

On the other hand, after two more years of post-Olympic bean-counting, ongoing assessments of the financial liabilities left over from the '72 Games were looking better than they had when the festival ended. A final accounting in February 1976 by a Bundestag financial committee showed that total costs for the Munich Olympics had come to DM 1.93 billion, slightly less than the DM 2 billion estimated in late 1972. Since income from all sources directly related to the Games had amounted to DM 1.324 billion (roughly two-thirds of the total price tag), West German tax payers were in hock only about DM 592 million. Given the huge scope of the Olympic enterprise, this was a good outcome, concluded the Bundestag committee.

The Munich OC came to the same happy conclusion in its own cost-benefit analyses. Following its final meeting in June 1977, the committee proclaimed that the Games had been "brilliantly organized" and had constituted "a sensible investment" for the city, state, and nation. Unlike the recently completed '76 Games in Montreal, Munich's festival had not been "a financial fiasco." The OC's own budget deficit was only DM 61 million, instead of the DM 91 million originally forecast.

Of the OC's DM 61 million debt, the city of Munich was liable for a mere DM 14.8 million, a drop in the municipal bucket. Thus, it was Willi Daume's modest conclusion that Munich was "the big winner" coming out of the '72 Games. For an investment of roughly DM 150 million, he noted, the city had gotten "the most beautiful sport-park in the world," along with "6000 new residences, 1,800 student apartments, three schools, 4.2 kilometers of additional U-Bahn track, and lots of new surface roads." Although many of the residences in the former men's Village remained to be sold, Daume insisted that the area was starting to show signs of "urban life." The athletic facilities, too, he said, were coming in for more and more use—for competitions, university events, and training academies. Above all,

---

* Although initially pleased with its new home, Bayern-München eventually found the Olympic Stadium inadequate for its needs. In 2000, Bayern-München's Franz Beckenbauer demanded that the stadium be fully remodeled or even replaced by a new one. When that didn't happen—the complex stood under a historical protection law—Bayern-München decamped in 2005 for the swankier and fully up-to-date Allianz Stadium north of Munich, named for a giant insurance company that had played a major financial role in the Third Reich. Since Bayern's move, the Olympic Stadium has become something of a white elephant.

the people of Munich were coming to realize what a recreational treasure trove they had in their own backyard.

Daume, for all his hyperbole, was telling the truth about a gradual turn-around in the fortunes of Munich's post-Olympic inheritance (at least its physical legacy). A comprehensive report on the Olympic Park published in summer 1977 showed that over twenty-one million paying customers had attended some five hundred events at the park in the five years since the conclusion of the '72 Games. Over 9.4 million patrons had watched events in the Olympic Stadium. Moreover, the 800,000-square-meter facility, now Europe's largest "recreation and sports-center," had attracted millions more visitors who, without having to pay, had simply come to walk around the beautiful grounds, admire the spectacular architecture, and sprawl on the grassy hillsides in the sun. On the basis of this report, the OC proudly concluded that, while Rome, Tokyo, Mexico City, and now Montreal had suffered "negative experiences" in terms of their post-Olympic physical and financial aftermaths, Munich had not.

By the end of the decade, moreover, even that problem child in the Olympic inventory, the men's Village, had ceased to be a source of worry. As of late 1979, virtually all the remaining apartments had been unloaded: the Village had stopped being a "stone desert" and really *was* pulsing with "urban life." Why the turn-around? No doubt Munich's ever more chronic housing shortage had something to do with it, but the main reason was that young families were discovering that the Village was a perfect place to raise kids. It was convenient, safe, and cozy. Not only could the *Kinder* play unsupervised in the tranquil Village lanes, but they could also swim in the artificial "Olympic Lake" and go skiing in wintertime on the rubble-filled "Olympic Mountain." (Life was admittedly rather less copasetic in the part of the Village that became student housing. In August 2007, a student party segued into a small riot during which many of the apartments were severely vandalized.)

The process of drawing up meticulous cost-benefit analyses of Munich's Olympic legacy continued apace down through the years—the conclusions getting ever rosier. On the occasion of the tenth anniversary of the Games, Munich mayor Erich Kiesl could confirm, unambiguously, that the city's investment in the enterprise had been well worthwhile, because the Olympic facilities—"now a centerpiece in the athletic and recreational agendas of all Münchner"—had continued to grow in popularity and financial productivity. In the last ten years, "around 43 million paying customers had attended athletic, cultural, and commercial events at the Olympic Park," Kiesl noted. He was proud to say that the Olympic facilities had also helped Munich burnish its status as an international tourist destination and convention center. Concluding his remarks, the mayor could not resist pointing out that, without the Olympics, Munich would not have gotten its splendid new stadium and, without that stadium, it would not have been able to host several of the 1974 Fédération Internationale de Football Association (FIFA) World Cup matches, including the final, which West Germany (led by Bayern-München's own Franz Beckenbauer) gloriously won. The implication was obvious: no Olympics, no World Cup championship!

Ten years down the line, the '72 Games cast such a rosy glow, at least in the eyes Munich's municipal leadership, that the Kiesl administration decided to lay on a tenth anniversary celebration—a birthday fête for Munich's one and only Olympic party. Guests at the sold out Olympiahalle applauded West Germany's medal winners from '72 as they paraded across the stage to the stirring strains of the Olympic fanfare. A troupe of children dressed in outfits symbolizing the five continents represented in the Olympics danced and sang. Film clips from the athletic competitions—mostly, of course, West German victories, which made for a shorter film—played across a huge screen at the back of the stage. Master of Ceremonies Dieter Kürten, a popular TV sports commentator, chatted with the gold medal winners, who agreed that, for them, "Olympia" had been the "highest moment" in their lives. During the final hour, Julia Migenes, West Germany's premier pop diva, belted out show tunes "from the dramatic to the farcical." When it was all over, at a command from Kürten, audience members flicked on disposable cigarette lighters and held them aloft, "like 8000 glow-worms." Throughout it all, there was nary a mention of eleven dead Israeli Olympians.

The city sponsored a second Olympic birthday party at year 20, though this one was not as glitzy as number 10. During a gathering at the Olympic Park, Mayor Georg Kronawitter (who had returned to office in 1984) declared, "The Olympic Festival of 1972 constituted the standout event of the postwar era [for Munich]; it was coupled with an unbelievable building boom and the explosion-like development of our city." Moreover, by virtue of its sprawling Olympic complex, Munich had become, in one fell swoop, "West Germany's sports capital."

The two chief officials responsible for bringing the '72 Games to Munich and organizing them were absent from the first and tenth anniversary celebrations, but Daume was present for number 20, where he was fêted along with the athletes. Although over the years he and Vogel had not said much about the tragedy that so clouded the Games' memory, they did speak up frequently regarding the sunnier side of the Olympic legacy. Daume, who died in 1996 at age 82, went to his grave insisting that the tragedy of September 5/6 should not be allowed to obscure the greatness and gloriousness of the Munich Games. (In 1997, Munich honored Daume with a square named after him in the Olympic Park.) As for Vogel, he produced a second set of memoirs in 1996 in which he reiterated his belief that none of the principal German actors in the hostage crisis "had reason to level criticism against themselves or any other relevant officials." Anyway, he agreed with his colleagues that the Olympic enterprise had been a great success overall and "well worth" all the effort it had required. His fellow Münchners, he added, felt much the same way. "Twenty-eight years after [the Games], and now in my retirement, I still hear [praise for the Games] in encounters in the U-Bahn or at events at the Oberwiesenfeld."

Vogel was hardly the only West German politician to give a hearty thumbs-up to Munich '72. The redoubtable Franz Josef Strauß, no friend of the mayor's, did the same. As early as 1973, Strauß opined on a TV show that the affair had been so wondrous and impressive that Munich should *apply again* to host the Games in the near future.* But next time, he added, the security procedures would have to be "significantly sharpened."

Clearly, had it been up to Messieurs Strauß, Daume, Vogel, Schreiber, and colleagues, our sense of the Munich Olympics might indeed have amounted to something like a "convenient fable." But in the end, the view of Munich '72 as an essentially positive and valuable experience, a legacy of which the German people could be unambiguously proud, hardly became the "dominant narrative" on this episode. The world outside Munich and the FRG was clearly not prepared to endorse such an interpretation—and, ex-Mayor Vogel's encounters on the Munich U-Bahn notwithstanding, this largely favorable perspective on the Games did not end up as the prevailing narrative among influential elements of the West German media either.

As for rival East Germany, its state-run media, of course, had their own take on Munich '72. Although dramatically different from the positive cost-benefit analyses proposed by the likes of Daume and Vogel, the Eastern line was, in its way, as tendentious and blinkered as anything generated

---

* This idea was not quite as weird as it may seem. After all, Berlin, which carried much heavier historical baggage than Munich, applied in 1993 to host the Games a second time (in 2000). Berlin's bid failed not so much because of the city's problematical past but because its application campaign was badly run. Its first boss was caught with his hands in the till, while his successor was discovered to be compiling a secret file on the drinking habits and sexual preferences of IOC members.

by the self-justifying men of Munich. Apart from mass media outlets, East Berlin's dogma on Munich found expression in a volume of commentaries and recollections compiled by the "Society for the Promotion of the Olympic Ideal in the GDR." Entitled *Spiele der XX. Olympiade München 1972*, the book appeared in 1973—the very same year in which the West German Olympic Society put out an equivalent volume with exactly the same title. (Here, then, was another example of the "memory duels" between the two Germanys during the Cold War.) Unlike the West German volume, which offered no single perspective on the Games, including on the terror episode, the Eastern retrospective advanced just one take-home message: the Munich Games, while a supreme demonstration of socialist-world athletic supremacy, had also amounted to a revealing display of "imperialistic machinations" on the part of the FRG and its Western allies. But above all, these Games had to be remembered for the horror that had unfolded in the Olympic Village and Fürstenfeldbruck, and the chief parties responsible for this horror were Israel itself and the West German hosts, who had "willfully allowed" the catastrophe to happen.

Although this "blame the victim" line regarding Israel hardly became the dominant approach to the Olympic tragedy in the FRG, West German media critics did not need any prompting from the East to recall—and even to dwell upon—the horror at the center of the '72 experience and the role of their own government in compounding that horror. Memories of the debacles in the Village and at Fürstenfeldbruck were kept alive also by sectarian strife among some of the principal German actors. The party infighting that broke out in the immediate aftermath of the Olympic embarrassment continued apace, periodically tearing the scab off this never-quite-healed wound. In 1980, eight years down the road, Franz Josef Strauß, who for years had said little about the terror episode (perhaps not wishing to call attention to his own less-than-heroic role in this affair) suddenly, and quite venomously, attacked the Social Democratic Party (SPD)–controlled Munich Police and its vice president, Georg Wolf. Labeling Wolf "the Failure of Fürstenfeldbruck," Strauß now claimed that Wolf had ordered armored cars to *Riem Airport* rather than to Fürstenfeldbruck. He went on to assert, in his colorful manner, that the officials in charge of the rescue operation—including Schreiber and Genscher—were capable of nothing more than "sharpening pencils and stacking toilet rolls." SPD and Free Democratic Party (FDP) spokesmen immediately fired back, suggesting that Strauß's "shabby" comments derived from a need to deflect attention from his own behavior. In the Bavarian Landtag, an FDP delegate recalled a report from the field that had Strauss cowering in a corner (when not demanding beer) amidst the firefight at Fürstenfeldbruck. Another FDP delegate pointedly asked, "Does Strauß have all his cups in his cupboard?"

In the same year that Strauß rounded on his political enemies and the Munich Police, a judicial ruling in a Munich court relating to the bloody rioting around the Karlstor at the beginning of the '72 Games provided a reminder that the Palestinian attack was not the only assault against Munich's hopes for a joyous and peaceful Olympiad. More specifically, Bavaria's highest court upheld two lower court rulings that one Dieter Vogelmann, a former physics student indicted five years earlier for having participated in the '72 riot, must serve a year in prison for "breach of the peace." Normally, West German courts granted probation in cases involving one year or less of jail time, but the Bavarian High Court justified the unusually harsh punishment for Vogelmann with the odd argument that actions that "might discredit the concept of the Olympic peace must not be allowed to gain public acceptance." Leniency in this case, said the court, "could lead to misunderstandings in the general populace." (Who knew? Maybe someday Munich might indeed apply to host another Olympic festival.)

Of course, it was not latter-day reports on the Karlstor rioting, intriguing as these might have been, that were the major factor in lodging those less-than-happy recollections of Munich '72 in the national memory bank. It was the "Munich Massacre" that most Germans could not forget, though many may have wished fervently to do so. The horror images stayed in people's minds in part because the experiences that had immediately preceded them were often exceedingly happy. This was particularly true for people who had been part of the show. Interviewed ten years after the event, a West German female gymnast recalled "an indescribable glimmer in the air, which then was snuffed out like a candle."

But the main reason that the "shadow over Munich" remained intact (and as crepuscular as ever), is that West Germany's mainstream media dutifully revisited this doleful episode every few years, almost sadomasochistically rehashing the sorry story in all its agonizing detail—and, in addition, often engaging in some not-very-helpful Monday-morning quarterbacking.

For example, a full-page "what we know now" account of the hostage crisis that appeared in the *Süddeutsche Zeitung* on the tenth anniversary of the terror attack pointed out that there had been *twenty-one well-trained sharpshooters* on hand at the Fürstenfeldbruck Military School, experts who could have been deployed to the nearby airfield to deal with the terrorists if the officials in charge of the operation had only given the order. Earlier, at the Olympic Village, a second assault on the Israeli compound, this one much better prepared and organized than the hapless "Operation Sunshine," had been "all set to go" when Interior Minister Genscher suddenly scuttled it by insisting upon yet another futile round of negotiations.

Even three decades down the road, well after the FRG had swallowed the defunct and discredited German Democratic Republic (GDR), the thirtieth anniversary of the '72 Olympic tragedy brought forth extensive commentary on what was still being called "the darkest day in the history of the Federal Republic." On September 5, 2002, the *Süddeutsche Zeitung* profiled a Dutch middle-distance runner, Jos Hermans, who had elected not to compete in his event when he learned that an Israeli Olympian, Moshe Weinberg, had been murdered in the Village. "How many corpses do you have to have before you say [regarding the continuation of the competitions] 'No, not with me!'" By way of contrast, the paper also looked back at the behavior of former Village "mayor" Walther Tröger, who, the article pointed out, had not bothered to attend the memorial service for the murdered Israelis, preferring instead to watch the spectacle on TV. "I think my friends in Israel found this ceremony dignified and appropriate," Tröger told his interviewer.

However Tröger's Israeli "friends" might have assessed the memorial ceremony back in September 1972, the German reporter thirty years later thought Tröger's comment sounded "like the formulation of a politician"—more precisely, like one of the over-optimistic and self-serving blandishments typically served up by former chancellor Helmut Kohl.

As the West German chancellor who presided over German reunification in 1990, Helmut Kohl had famously promised that unification with the more prosperous West would quickly produce "blooming landscapes" in the former East German states. As we know, the Eastern landscape did *not* bloom, or at least not for a long while. The organizers of the Munich Olympic Games had also promised something like a great bloom—a summer of love—and the promised love and good cheer were undoubtedly there for a brief moment. And yet, of course, sorrow and tragedy remain the dominant motifs when it comes to Munich's Games. This epochal moment in the history of Germany and the world in the modern era is highly unlikely *ever* to become a convenient fable.

Notes

Abbreviations Used in Notes

AA	Auswärtiges Amt
ABC	Avery Brundage Collection
BAB	Bundesarchiv Berlin
BAK	Bundesarchiv Koblenz
BayHstaA	Bayerisches Hauptstaatsarchiv, München
BGS	Bundesgrenzschutz
BLVS	Bayerisches Landesamt für Verfassungsschutz
BMI	Bundesministerium des Innern
BPA	Bundespresseamt
BSMI	Bayerisches Staatsministerium des Innern
BSMJ	Bayerisches Staatsministerium der Justiz
DDR	Deutsche Demokratische Republik
dpa	Deutsche Presse-Agentur
DSHA	Deutsche Sporthochschule Archiv, Köln
FAZ	*Frankfurter Allgemeine Zeitung*
IfZG	Institut für Zeitgeschichte, München
IOCA	International Olympic Committee Archive, Lausanne
JO	Jeux Olympiques
MInn	Ministerium des Innern
MM	*Münchner Merkur*
NA	National Archives, College Park, Maryland
ND	*Neues Deutschland*
NOK	Nationales Olympisches Komitte
NYT	*New York Times*
OC	Munich Olympic Organizing Committee

PAAA   Politisches Archiv im Auswärtigen Amt
SAM   Stadtarchiv München
sid   sportinformationdienst
STAM   Staatsarchiv München
SZ   *Süddeutsche Zeitung*
UIA   University of Illinois Archive

Introduction

1   "laid back" and "charming": John Skow, "The Games of Munich," *Playboy*, April
     1973, 143–47.
2   "Nazi Games" had helped advertise and promote the Third Reich.: On the 1936
     Games, see David Clay Large, *Nazi Games: The German Olympics of 1936* (New York,
     2007); Richard D. Mandell, *The Nazi Olympics* (New York, 1971; Urbana, 1987);
     Duff Hart-Davis, *Hitler's Games: The 1936 Olympics* (London, 1986); Arnd Krüger,
     Die Olympische Spiele 1936 und die Weltmeinung (Berlin, 1972); and Guy Walters,
     Berlin Games (London, 2007).
2   a byword for appeasement ever after).: On Nazi Munich, see David Clay Large,
     Where Ghosts Walked: Munich's Road to the Third Reich (New York, 1997), 231–346.
2   "Cheerful Games"): Organizing Committee for the XX. Olympiad Munich 1972,
     Die Spiele: The Official Report, 3 vols. (Munich, 1972), 1:28; Arnd Krüger, "Berlins
     Schatten über München," *Leistungsport* 4 (1972): 252–53.
3   "Olympic ideal to German soil.": P. Collier, "Late Night Show from Munich: A
     Review," *Ramparts*, November 1972, 50.
3   "azure skies of Bavaria.": Organizing Committee, *Die Spiele*, 1:32.
3   "Nothing happens at night,": "Ich werde heute noch für Palästina sterben," *Der
     Spiegel* 38 (1972): 27. See also Alexander Wolff, "When the Terror Began," *Sports
     Illustrated*, August 26, 2002, 61.
4   "need not fear comparisons.": BPA release, August 29, 1972, quoted in Noel Cary,
     "Murder and Memory at the Munich Olympics," unpublished conference paper,
     2001.
5   "world's trust" was "not undeserved.": William Shirer, "From Jesse Owens to the
     Summer of '72," *Saturday Review*, March 25, 1972, 40.
7   tranquility of the Munich Games.: "Die Entwicklung aussenpolitischer Stör-
     felder auf die Olympischen Spiele, Zwischenbericht Juni 1970–Juni 1971," MInn
     88598, BayHstaA. On Black Nationalism among GIs in West Germany in this
     period, see Maria Höhn and Martin Klimke, *A Breath of Freedom: The Civil Rights
     Struggle, African American GIs, and Germany* (New York, 2010), 107–22.
8   to the back burner.: See, for example, Wolff, "When the Terror Began."
8   "terror" and "terrorist.": Mohammed Oudeh (a.k.a. Abu Daoud), one of the plan-
     ners of the Munich attack, always insisted that the action was a legitimate mili-
     tary operation rather than a terrorist act. See Dina Kraft, "Mohammed Oudeh,
     Who Planned '72 Munich Attack, Is Dead at 73," *NYT*, July 3, 2010.

9   act in a particular way.: For a good discussion of varying definitions of terrorism, see Anthony J. Marsella, "Reflections on International Terrorism: Issues, Concepts, Directions," in *Understanding Terrorism: Psychological Roots, Consequences, and Interventions*, ed. Fathali M. Moghaddam and Anthony Marsella, 11–48 (Washington, D.C., 2004).

9   not an act of terror.: On the King David Hotel bombing, see, above all, Thurston Clarke, *By Blood and Fire* (New York, 1981); for Netanyahu's justification of the action, see "King David Hotel Bombing," last modified June 6, 2011, http://wikipedia.org/.

10   German political and cultural issues at stake.: A case in point is the recent study by Kay Schiller and Christopher Young, *The 1972 Munich Olympics and the Making of Modern Germany* (Berkeley, 2010).

10   at the Mexico City Games of 1968.: On race and the Mexico City Games, see Richard Hoffer, *Something in the Air: American Passion and Defiance in the 1968 Mexico City Olympics* (New York, 2009).

11   not to this book.: The best encyclopedic source on the athletic events at Munich (and on all the other summer Olympiads) remains David Wallechinsky, *The Complete Book of the Summer Olympics: Athens 2004 Edition* (Wilmington, Del., 2004). See also Organizing Committee, *Die Spiele*; Volker Kluge, *Olympische Sommerspiele. Die Chronik III. Mexiko-Stadt 1968–Los Angeles 1984* (Berlin, 2000), 208–435. For narrative accounts of some of the athletic events at the Munich Games, see Christopher Brasher, *Munich 1972* (London, 1972); and Richard D. Mandell's diary of his visit to the '72 Games, *The Olympics of 1972: A Munich Diary* (Chapel Hill, N.C., 1991).

13   "cheese and eat it.": Simon quoted in Allen Guttmann, *The Olympics: A History of the Modern Games*, 2nd ed. (Urbana, 2002), 142.

13   "than a few years.": Brundage quoted in Michael Payne, *Olympic Turnaround: How the Olympic Games Stepped Back from the Brink of Extinction to Become the World's Best Known Brand* (Westport, Conn., 2006), 5–6.

13   "writing the Olympic obituary,": Payne, *Olympic Turnaround*, 6; see also Jeré Longman, "Juan Antonio Samaranch, Who Transformed the Olympics, Dies at 89," *NYT*, April 21, 2010. Samaranch's marketing director, Michael Payne, was responsible for negotiating the multi-million-dollar TV deals that, for better or worse, "saved" the modern Olympic movement. For details, see his memoir, *Olympic Turnaround*.

Chapter 1: The Decision for Munich

15   "*Habemus Papam.*": "OB Vogel: Wie er die Spiele nach München brachte," *Abendzeitung*, August 8/9, 1992; D. Mülders, "Warum München?" unpublished manuscript, 1.1 Bewerbung, DSHA.

16   would go to Sapporo, Japan.: Hans-Jochen Vogel, *Die Amtskette: Meine 12 Münchner Jahre. Ein Erlebnisbericht* (Munich, 1972), 106–7; "Die Olympischen Spiele 1972 in München," *FAZ*, April 27, 1966.

17   German Olympic agency recognized by the IOC.: On the status of the two Germanys in the international sporting world and their struggle for athletic preeminence, see, inter alia, Martin H. Geyer, "On the Road to German 'Postnationalism'? Athletic Competition between the Two German States in the Era of Konrad Adenauer," *German Politics and Society* 25, no. 2 (Summer 2007): 143–48; Tobias Blasius, *Olympische Bewegung: Kalter Krieg und Deutschlandpolitik 1949–1972* (Frankfurt am Main, Germany, 2001); G. A. Carr, "The Involvement of Politics in the Sporting Relationships of East and West Germany, 1945-1962," *Journal of Sport History* 7, no. 1 (Spring 1980): 40–46; Uta Andrea Balbier, "'A Game, a Competition, an Instrument?': High Performance, Cultural Diplomacy and German Sport from 1950 to 1972," *International Journal of the History of Sport* 26, no. 4 (March 2009): 539–55; Ulrich Pabst, *Sport: Medium der Politik?* (Berlin/Munich, 1980); Horst Geyer, *Olympische Spiele 1896–1996: Ein deutsches Politikum* (Münster, Germany, 1996); and Schiller and Young, *The 1972 Munich Olympics*, 157–86.

17   "politics" into the Olympic movement.: Geyer, *Olympische Spiele 1896–1996*, 97–98.

18   "warfare without weapons.": On the modern Olympics as an arena of nationalism and political conflict, see, inter alia, Guttmann, *The Olympics*; John Lucas, *The Modern Olympic Games* (Cranbury, N.J., 1980); Richard Espy, *The Politics of the Olympic Games* (Berkeley, 1979); Christopher R. Hill, *Olympic Politics* (Manchester, UK, 1992); Peter J. Graham and Horst Ueberhorst, eds., *The Modern Olympics* (West Point, N.Y., 1976); Andreas Höfer, *Der Olympische Friede: Anspruch und Wirklichkeit einer Idee* (Sankt Augustin, Germany, 1994); and John MacAloon, *This Great Symbol: Pierre de Coubertin and the Origins of the Modern Olympic Games* (Chicago, 1981).

18   elected to boycott that festival.: Guttmann, *The Olympics*, 151.

18   "failed to master.": Quoted in Blasius, *Olympische Bewegung*, 159.

18   "my baby.": Brundage's reference to the unified German team as his "baby" was noted, with scorn, by GDR sports officials. See Besuch in Lausanne, March 24, 1965, DY30/IVA2/18, BAB. On Brundage's infatuation with the unified team, see Allen Guttmann, *The Games Must Go On: Avery Brundage and the Olympic Movement* (New York, 1984), 155. Brundage's correspondence also reveals dogged support for the unified German Olympic team experiment.

19   "Let us plough . . . as never before"): Martin H. Geyer, "Der Kampf um nationale Repräsentation: Deutsch-deutsche Sportbeziehungen und die 'Hallstein-Doktrin,'" *Vierteljahrshefte für Zeitgeschichte* 44 (1996): 69–70; see also Gunter Holzweißig, *Diplomatie im Trainingsanzug: Sport als politisches Instrument der DDR in der innerdeutschen und internationalen Beziehungen* (Munich/Vienna, 1981), 35–36.

21   trademark "pig's head.": Quoted in Geyer, "Der Kampf," 152.

21   "beneath the dignity . . . [the five-ringed flag],": Quoted in Geyer, "Der Kampf," 71; see also Holzweißig, *Diplomatie*, 36.

22   "on the territory of the Soviet Occupation Zone": Carr, "The Involvement of Politics," 47–48.

23   "life for the workers.": Geyer, *Olympische Spiele 1896–1996*, 93.

23   "name of our Republic.": Quoted in Blasius, *Olympische Bewegung*, 151.

24   national youth-development initiative.: Erich Honecker, *Aus meinem Leben* (Berlin, 1980), 222; Geyer, "Der Kampf," 64.

24   nurseries of athletic talent.: The German College of Physical Culture and Sport greatly impressed West German sports officials when they visited it in 1953. See Dr. Werner Kürbs, "Bericht über meinen Besuch der deutschen Hochschule für Körperkultur," December 10, 1953, B10/1758, BAK.

24   "All Germans at a common table.": Carr, "The Involvement of Politics," 41.

24   West Germany deployed "professionals": Honecker, *Aus meinem Leben*, 223–24; Geyer, "Der Kampf," 58.

25   "golden girl": "Ingrid Kraemers perfekter Triumpf," August 28, 1960, *ND*.

25   more so as time went on.: On problems within the unified German team, see Andreas Höfer, "Querelle d'allemand: Die gesamtdeutschen Olympiamannschaften, 1956–1964," in *Deutschland in der Olympischen Bewegung: Eine Zwischenbilanz*, ed. Manfred Lämmer, 209–59 (Frankfurt am Main, Germany, 1999).

25   "along well with each other.": Quoted in David Maraniss, *Rome 1960: The Olympics That Changed the World* (New York, 2008), 156.

26   another Brundage baby.: In a meeting on August 10, 1965, with the GDR's Heinz Schöbel, Brundage expressed enthusiasm for the idea that a Berlin-Berlin Olympiad could give East Germany a chance to tear down its Wall without losing face. See Ewald Bericht, August 12, 1965, DY30/IVA2/18/3, BAB.

26   bring the Olympics to Munich.: In 1963, Willi Daume proposed that, if the Berlin Wall were still standing in 1968, a Berlin-Berlin Olympic festival would render that barrier "absurd." See Daume to Höcherl, January 23, 1963, Abt. 4/Nr. 1599, PAAA.

26   industrial city of Dortmund.: On Daume's early life and career as a sports functionary in the young Federal Republic, see Jan C. Rode, *Willi Daume und die Entwicklung des Sports in der Bundesrepublik Deutschland zwischen 1945 und 1970* (Göttingen, Germany, 2010).

27   "and great loyalty.": Quoted in Rode, *Willi Daume*, 38.

27   desperately wanted to avoid.: Rode, *Willi Daume*, 39–40.

28   fining him DM 1000.: Rode, *Willi Daume*, 45.

28   "rejected Nazism in his heart.": Quoted in Rode, *Willi Daume*, 46.

28   "young and charming wife.": Quoted in Arnd Krüger, "Deutschland und die Olympische Bewegung (1945–1980)," in *Geschichte der Leibesübungen*, ed. Horst Ueberhorst (Bonn, 1982), Band 3/2, 1982, note 113, 1080. Actually, Ritter von Halt need not have introduced Daume to Brundage, for the two men had known each other since the 1936 Berlin Olympics. For a biography of von Halt, see Peter Heimerzheim, *Karl Ritter von Halt: Leben zwischen Sport und Politik* (Sankt Augustin, Germany, 1999).

29   "an excellent idea.": Daume to Höcherl, January 23, 1963, Abt. 4/Nr. 1599, PAAA.

29   that other Berlin across the Wall.: Blasius, *Olympische Bewegung*, 292.

30   "deceptive charade.": "Bericht über die Reise der NOK-Delegation nach Lausanne in der Zeit," 4–8 Juni 1963, DY/30/IVA2/18, BAB.

30   but as "Ostdeutschland.": Blasius, *Olympische Bewegung*, 260–63.

31   "[to participate] in Olympic Games.": Daume speech at an assembly of the West German National Olympic Committee, December 18, 1965, in Protokoll, File 1/1, NOK-Archiv, Frankfurt.

31   "became great nonetheless.": "O'zapft is," *Der Spiegel* 39 (1964): 42.

31   "best-dressed girls in Germany.": "Munich: Olympic City Where Pleasure Has Become a Way of Life," *Times*, June 6, 1972.

31   less than three months away.: Vogel, *Die Amtskette*, 95–100.

32   "host the Olympic Games.": Vogel, *Die Amtskette*, 95.

32   "do something for the West Germans.": Vogel, *Die Amtskette*, 95.

32   "serious contenders."; "almost insurmountable.": Vogel, *Die Amtskette*, 96–97.

33   even be an issue by 1972.: Vogel, *Die Amtskette*, 98.

34   "had never existed at all.": Quoted in Nina Krieg, "'Die Weltstadt mit Herz': Ein Überblick 1957 bis 1990," in *Geschichte der Stadt München*, ed. Richard Bauer (Munich, 1992), 419.

34   from Bonn was forthcoming.: "Olympia in München kostet zuviel Geld," *Handelsblatt*, December 6, 1965.

34   hosting an Olympic festival.: Strauß declared in a speech on March 16, 1966, that the Games would provide opportunities for thousands of Olympic guests—Russians, Chinese, Americans, Africans—to "learn the truth about the new Germany." See "Information über die Bewerbung der Stadt München für die Sommerspiele 1972," DR150/132, BAK.

34   were virtually zero.: Blasius, *Olympische Bewegung*, 295–97.

35   crucial meeting with Erhard's government.: On this meeting in Bonn, see Vogel, *Die Amtskette*, 99; see also Protokoll (Althammer), November 29, 1965, B106/30598, BAK.

35   "horn of distress.": Vogel, *Die Amtskette*, 99.

36   "despite its budgetary situation.": "Tun sie Alles für Olympia in München," sid, November 30, 1965, B106/3060, BAK.

36   including those from the GDR.: Von Hovra to Vogel, December 8, 1965, B106/36167, BAK; Vogel to Zanch (IOC), March 25, 1966, B106/36167, BAK.

36   "only German city that is Olympia-worthy.": "Nur Berlin Olympia-reif," sid, November 29, 1965, B106/30601, BAK.

36   "beyond its financial resources.": "Auch Hannover überrascht," sid, November 29, 1965, B106/30601, BAK.

37   "going to need it!": "Man muss München nur Glück wünchen," sid, November 30, 1965, B106/30601, BAK.

37   for both athletes and spectators?: Vogel stressed the virtues of a downsized Olympic festival in a press conference on December 17, 1965. See sid, December 18, 1965, B106/30601, BAK.

37   "sensible modesty": Vogel, *Die Amtskette*, 109–10.

38   "unity of sport and art,": "Kurzfassung der Bewerbung der Landeshauptstadt München um die Austragung der Olympischen Spiele 1972," Stk. 14–30, BayHstaA.

40   "a kind of German paradise?": "Kurzfassung der Bewerbung." See also "Olympische Bewerbung mit einem Dichterwort," sid, December 18, 1965, B106/30601, BAK.

40   *very heart* of the old German evil?: Vogel, *Die Amtskette*, 100. See also "Was sagt die Welt zur Wahl Münchens? Das Ja zur Olympia-Stadt 1972 überwiegt," *MM*, April 28, 1966.

41 speak of "national prestige,": "Die Olympische Vorentscheidung ist gefallen," *SZ*, December 21, 1965.

41 "champions of forgetting.": "Das Streiflicht," *SZ*, April 27, 1966.

41 on financial grounds.: "Wien zieht Olympia-Bewerbung endgültig zurück," *Die Welt*, December 22, 1965.

41 construction of new housing.: "Keine Bewerbung aus Moskau!" sid, November 30, 1965, B106/30601, BAK.

41 "sovereign rights in Moscow.": "Deutscher Turn- und Sportbund," March 19, 1966, DR/150/132, BAK.

41 "greatest automobile city in the world": "Fingerhaken um die Olympia-Stadt," *Die Zeit*, April 22, 1966. For an assessment by Munich boosters of their Olympic chances, see "Betrachtung der Chancen für München," March 11, 1966, B145/6947, BAK.

42 "than we can chew.": Franz Gleissner et al. to Vogel, March 24, 1966, Stk. 14030, BayHstaA.

42 "the factors involved.": Vogel to Gleissner, March 25, 1966, Stk. 14030, BayHstaA.

43 "criminal political agenda.": "Deutscher Turn- und Sportbund, Information über die Bewerbung der Stadt München für die Olympische Sommerspiele 1972," March 16, 1966, DR/150/132, BAB.

43 "selection of Munich.": "Deutscher Turn- und Sportbund, Information."

43 "German organizational talent": Sylvio de Magalhaes Padilha to Vogel, February 6, 1966, Olympiade 1972/562, SAM. Quoted in Schiller and Young, *The 1972 Munich Olympics*, 61.

44 anticommunist activity and agitation.: "Deutscher Turn- und Sportbund, Argumentation zur Bewerbung der Stadt München für die Olympischen Sommerspiele 1972," March 16, 1966, DR510/132, BAB.

44 center of subversion.): Ian Johnson, *A Mosque in Munich, Nazis, the CIA, and the Rise of the Muslim Brotherhood in the West* (Boston, 2010), 37.

44 "against the Socialist lands.": "Deutscher Turn- und Sportbund, Argumentation."

45 "new scandals.": "Deutscher Turn- und Sportbund, Argumentation."

45 Andrianov eventually came around.: "Der süßsaure Apfel, in den München biß," *Die Welt*, April 28, 1966. See also "Am Tiber floß das Bier aus Bayern," *Die Welt*, April 28, 1966.

46 "your valuable advice.": Vogel to Brundage, December 20, 1965, ABC, Box 182, UIA.

46 than the former chancellor.: Vogel, *Die Amtskette*, 102.

47 Montreal and Detroit.: Vogel, *Die Amtskette*, 104.

47 as all other Olympic participants.: The Brundage letter is discussed in Vogel's letter to Erhard, April 20, 1966, B106/3617, BAK.

48 with Bonn's apparent accommodation.: Vogel, *Die Amtskette*, 103.

48 "proprietor at Oktoberfest.": Vogel, *Die Amtskette*, 104.

48 "mentality of the IOC.": Vogel, *Die Amtskette*, 106.

48 per day per competitor.: Address of the Lord Mayor, Dr. Hans-Jochen Vogel, to the International Olympic Committee in Rome on April 26, 1966, Stk. 1430, BayHstaA.

Chapter 2: "We Just Slid Into It"

51   "would be sensible.": "Ein Konstrukteur über Münchens olympischer Architektur," *SZ*, January 26, 1968.

52   "We just slid into it,": "Wir sind da so hineingeschlittert," *Der Spiegel* 31 (1972): 28.

52   a bit "Olympian" himself.: Vogel, *Die Amtskette*, 108.

52   "started to tick.": Vogel, *Die Amtskette*. See also "München: Olympiastadt 1972, Organisationskomitee für die Spiele der XX. Olympiade München," April 17, 1968, Stk. 1430, BayHstaA.

52   "between East and West.": Daume interview, April 29, 1966, sid, B106/30601, BAK.

53   "symbol for the entire business?": "Der süßsaure Apfel, in den München biß," *Die Welt*, April 28, 1966.

53   "can come in.": "Auch Nachts tickt es hinter den Vorhängen," *SZ*, May 3, 1966.

53   according to Nazi principles.: On von Mengden, see Hajo Bernett, *Guido von Mengden. 'Generalstabschef des deutschen Sports'* (Berlin, 1967).

54   Munich's organizational team.: "Bundesfinanzminister übernimmt Vorsitz," sid, August 3, 1967, B106/30601, BAK.

54   disciplines in Olympic play.: Vogel, *Die Amtskette*, 127.

54   proved to be extremely expensive.: "Wir sind da so hineingeschlittert"; see also "In München wird die Perfektion erwartet," *FAZ*, October 11, 1968.

55   on the prospective host city.: Vogel, *Die Amtskette*, 128.

55   "Auschwitz any longer.": Quoted in Geert Mak, *In Europe: Travels through the Twentieth Century* (New York, 2008), 649.

56   "small-mindedness."): Daume interview, November 29, 1966, sid, B106/30601, BAK.

56   in its own right?: Vogel, *Die Amtskette*, 123.

57   Otl Aicher: On Aicher, see Mandell, *The Olympics of 1972*, 154–56; Markus Rathgeb, *Otl Aicher* (London, 2006); "Das heitere Schau-Bild der Olympischen Spiele," *MM*, May 21, 1967; and Schiller and Young, *The 1972 Munich Olympics*, 95–104. For a sampling of Aicher's own theoretical writing, see Aicher, "Olympia und Kunst," in *Auf der Suche nach der Olympischen Idee: Facetten der Forschung von Athen bis Atlanta*, ed. Norbert Müller and Manfred Messing, 16–22 (Kassel, Germany, 1996).

57   "politics with color,": "Wir sind da so hineingeschlittert," 32.

58   *she* be doing?: Skow, "The Games of Munich," 145.

58   "design in the world.": Quoted in Mandell, *The Olympics of 1972*, 156.

59   too much time at a desk.): "Hurra für Kokoschka," *Die Zeit*, March 28, 1969.

59   vertigo-inducing Olympic emblem.: "Münchner Olympia-Grafiker fühlen sich dupiert," *Die Welt*, February 25, 1970.

59   "no new territory in the graphic arts,": "8000-Mark Mißverständniß," *Die Zeit*, April 17, 1970. See also "Olympia an allen Strassenecken," *MM*, April 10, 1970; and "Werbung mit 190,000 Zeltdächern," *SZ*, April 10, 1970.

59   "just plain stupidity."): "Sonderprogram für prominente ausländische Gäste anläßlich der Olympiade München 1972," Stk. 14032, BayHstaA.

60 "official mascot": On the history of Olympic mascots, see Tara Magdalinski, "Cute, Loveable Characters: The Place and Significance of Mascots in the Olympic Movement," *Olympika* 8 (2004): 75–92.

60 "to the general public.": Maps of World, "Olympic Mascots," accessed September 1, 2011, http://www.mapsofworld.com/olympic-trivia/olympic-mascot.html.

60 "joy of the Olympic festival.": Maps of World, "Olympic Mascots."

60 "new Germany" had to offer.: "Ein olympisches Fest der Künste plant München für das Jahr 1972," *SZ*, May 3, 1966. For a rather jaundiced British take on Munich's cultural plans, see the British Council, "Olympic Games 1972," June 10, 1968, Correspondence 1968–1972, IOCA.

60 had promised to do.: "Großes Fest," *Der Spiegel* 33 (1970): 116–17.

60 into full reality.: "Auf den Dackel gekommen," *Die Zeit*, September 3, 1971.

61 part of the art.: On the Spielstraße, see "Mimen balgen sich zu Beethoven," *SZ*, August 29, 1972; "Großes Fest"; "Eine Theaterstraße für Olympia 1972," *Welt am Sonntag*, May 8, 1969.

61 a measure of sobriety.: Vogel, *Die Amtskette*, 110.

61 They rejected it.: "Auf den Dackel gekommen."

62 Mothers of Invention.: Schiller and Young, *The 1972 Munich Olympics*, 152.

63 "mockery of the Olympic Spirit.": Deutsches Kulturwerk to Lübke, October 26, 1967, B122/5236, BAK.

63 "dangerous to youth.": Zimmer to Lübke, October 12, 1967, B122/5236, BAK.

63 "for the Olympic Games.": Döring to Zimmer, October 12, 1967, B122/5236, BAK.

63 program of offerings.: "Für Schwimmer ein sonniges Motiv," *Der Spiegel* 36 (1971): 116.

64 "dribble art").: "Für Schwimmer ein sonniges Motiv."

64 "saddle put in too,": Quoted in Janie Hampton, *The Austerity Olympics: When the Games Came to London in 1948* (London, 2008), 76.

65 was hopelessly unrealistic.: Vogel, *Die Amtskette*, 118.

65 tune of DM 288 million.: Vogel, *Die Amtskette*, 115. On the Glückspirale, see also Organizing Committee, *Die Spiele*, 1:66.

65 beating out NBC.: Westerhof to Brundage, February 4, 1969, ABC, Box 185, UIA.

65 earn from advertisers.: "Die Olympische Spiele als Verkaufsobjekt. Der Handel mit den Fernsehenrechten," *SZ*, September 24, 1969.

65 "healthy profit left over.": Roone Arledge, *Roone: A Memoir* (New York, 2003), 122–23.

66 official Olympic emblem.: For promises to avoid excessive commercialization, see Westerhof to OC, January 9, 1969, JO Eté 1972, Cojo Comité, 1966–1969, IOCA.

66 for this privilege.: "The Race for Olympic Gold," *Business Week*, September 11, 1971, 20.

66 Aktion Sparschwein: "Handfeste Ziele," *Der Spiegel* 24 (1969): 140.

66 on those products.: "Protokoll der 14. Sitzung des Presseausschusses am 26.8.71," *Förderverein*, SAM.

66 "to solicit alcoholic beverages.": Siegfried Heinrich to George Ballantine and Son, Ltd., June 16, 1972, *Förderverein*, SAM.

67   bottle of Coke.: On Coca-Cola at the Berlin Games, see Large, *Nazi Games*, 185–86.

67   "relevant experience" in previous Games.: "Keine Pause mehr bei Coca-Cola," *Sportkontakt*, November 2, 1970, *Förderverein*, SAM.

68   "try it themselves.": "The Race for Olympic Gold," 20.

68   Olympic motor pool.: Schiller and Young, *The 1972 Munich Olympics*, 30.

68   German sporting goods manufacturer Adidas.: For a good study of Adidas and Puma, see Barbara Smit, *Sneaker Wars: The Enemy Brothers Who Founded Adidas and Puma and the Family Feud That Forever Changed the Business of Sport* (New York, 2008).

68–69   "walking Litfaß pillars [billboards]": "Daume wollte neuen Skandal vermeiden," *Abendzeitung 8-Uhr-Blatt*, June 23, 1972.

69   "sporting goods industry.": "Daume wollte neuen Skandal vermeiden."

69   "financing of the Games.": "Medaillensegen schon vor den Spielen," *SZ*, November 6, 1969.

69   "unsuitable" to carry the Olympic logo.: "The Race for Olympic Gold."

70   going entirely to the OC: On the coins, see Vogel, *Die Amtskette*, 129–30; see also "Olympische Zehnmarkstücke," *MM*, January 11, 1968.

70   honor at the Olympic complex.: Vogel, *Die Amtskette*, 129.

71   not to nations.: "Minutes of the Meeting of the Executive Board," February 21–23, 1970, IOCA.

71   unsure about their interest.: For the poll data, see Hartmut Becker, "Die Einstellung der Bevölkerung der Bundesrepublik zu den Olympischen Spielen in München," *Die Leibeserziehung* 21, no. 8 (August 1972): 283–84.

71   "World Mountain"; "World Rabbit Farm": "Olympiahasen als Goldesel," *SZ*, February 17/18, 1968.

74   no time to think small.: Vogel, *Die Amtskette*, 119.

74   statement of the century.: "Ein Wettbewerb für die Olympia-Sportanlagen," *SZ*, December 5, 1966.

75   "atmosphere of the Reichssportfeld,": Erdmann Kimmig, "Mü-Olympiade und Wettbewerb," *Der Baumeister*, February 1988, 104.

75   a "conceptual fantasy.": Vogel, *Die Amtskette*, 120.

76   "totally inappropriate.": Vogel, *Die Amtskette*, 121–23.

76   "purpose and content.": Behnisch & Partner, "Anlagen und Bauten für die Spiele der XX. Olympiade München 1972," Behnisch & Partner, Freie Architekten BDA, Munich, 1976, 1. See also the Behnisch interview in Heinrich Klotz, *Architektur in der Bundesrepublik. Gespräche mit Günter Behnisch, Wolfgang Döring, Helmut Hentrich, Hans Kammerer, Frei Otto, Oswald Ungers* (Frankfurt am Main, Germany, 1977).

77   "of the host country.": "Report on Foundation-Stone Laying Ceremony," July 22, 1969, JO Eté 1972, Cojo-Comité d'Organisation 1966–1969, IOCA.

77   guests from Eastern Europe.: "Olympia-Grundstein verschwunden," *MM*, October 20, 1969.

78   "carry out your plans.": Brundage to Vogel, February 3, 1969, JO Eté 1972, Cojo-Comité d'Organisation 1966–1969, IOCA. During his stay in Munich, Brundage was honored at a reception hosted by Mayor Vogel, who called the American "a

Münchner with special status." See "IOC-Präsident Brundage in München," *SZ*, January 28, 1969.

78   "the general public.": Klotz, *Architektur in der Bundesrepublik*, 219–20.

79   huge cost overruns at the Oberwiesenfeld.: See, for example, "Neue Olympia-Rechnung für 1972," *SZ*, October 16/17, 1971.

79   "incompetent experts from the city,": Vogel, *Die Amtskette*, 127.

80   staggeringly high.: "Die wollen Franz Josef, die haben ihn," *Der Spiegel* 46 (1972): 34–43; "Bavarian Gamesmanship over Olympic Village," *Guardian*, December 7, 1972.

80   a few kilometers north of Munich.: "Construction for the Games of the XXth Olympiad in Munich," IOC Correspondence, 1970–1972, IOCA.

80   asking price "astronomically.": Vogel, *Die Amtskette*, 125.

81   "Holy Trinity East-West.": "Väterchen kann ruhig schlafen," *Der Spiegel* 16 (1969): 10.

81   "into this conception.": "Väterchen kann ruhig schlafen." On Father Tim, see also "Der schlaue Donkosak als Mönch," *FAZ*, July 18, 1968.

81   "sleep in peace,": "Väterchen kann ruhig schlafen."

82   "and motor traffic"; "massage cabins.": "Construction for the Games."

82   "giant war game,": Vincent Matthews, *My Race Be Won* (New York, 1974), 292.

83   "aggressiveness of the women!": "Fun and Games at the Olympics," *Sunday Daily Telegraph*, March 2, 1971.

83   "villages to the death.": "To Segregate or Not to Segregate the Sexes," *Sun* (Sydney), March 15, 1971.

84   "to Munich in 1972.": "Plans for the Organization of the Press Services at the 1972 Olympic Games in Munich," JO Eté 1972, Cojo Comité d'Organisation, 1966–1969, IOCA.

84   "members of the press.": "Plans for the Organization of the Press Services."

84   "20 feet from the bar.": Skow, "The Games of Munich," 145.

85   "prostitute-free zone,": "Kampf dem Koller," *Der Spiegel* 33 (1972): 93.

85   TV sets around the globe.: On the importance of TV to the Olympic movement, see Stephen R. Wenn, "Growing Pains: The Olympic Movement and Television," *Olympika* 4 (1995): 1–22.

85   "110 radio systems.": "Plans for the Organization of the Press Services."

85   broadcasting facilities for 1972.: "Knall, Schuß, bums, raus, weg," *Der Spiegel* 36 (1972): 24–27.

85   "color curtain": "Europe 'Color Barrier' Is Lifted for the Olympics," *Chicago Tribune*, July 23, 1972.

86   "tough luck for him!": "Dabeisein heißt: Alles oder Nichts," *Der Spiegel* 36 (1972): 28.

86   "rolling toward Munich.": "Teure Spiele verstimmen Bonn," *Die Zeit*, April 16, 1971.

86   "park-like setting": For progress reports on the Olympic construction, see "Spaziergang durch die Olympische Landschaft," *SZ*, April 22, 1969; "Construction Report on the XXth Games, 1970," IOC Correspondence 1970–1972, IOCA; and "Olympics by the Lake," *Guardian*, April 1, 1971.

87   "off to the world!" "Brandt Vorsitzender des Olympia-Beirats, Melding von 24.3.70," DY30/IVA2/18, BAB.
87   "native-only" employment policy.: "Olympics by the Lake."
87   Munich's reconstruction in the decades after World War II.: On the postwar reconstruction of Munich, see, inter alia, Jeffry M. Diefendorf, *In the Wake of War: The Reconstruction of German Cities after World War II* (New York, 1993); Gavriel D. Rosenfeld, *Munich and Memory: Architecture, Monuments, and the Legacy of the Third Reich* (Berkeley, Calif., 2000); Nina Krieg, "'Solang der Alte Peter . . .': Die vermeintliche Wiedergeburt Alt Münchens nach 1945," in Bauer, *Geschichte der Stadt München*, 394–412; and Large, *Where Ghosts Walked*, 348–61.
88   the early postwar period.: Diefendorf, *In the Wake of War*, 91.
89   citing a lack of funds.: Rosenfeld, *Munich and Memory*, 126.
89   function in the Third Reich.: "Ratloß vor dem steinernen Größenwahn," *SZ*, May 2, 1994; see also "Kein Rauch ohne Feuer, kein Gedenken ohne Reue," *SZ*, November 9, 1995.
90   "Munich Is Munich Again.": Krieg, "'Solang der Alte Peter,'" 411.
90   municipal coat of arms.: Rosenfeld, *Munich and Memory*, 157.
90   "catastrophic" dystopia.): Brian Ladd, *Autophobia: Love and Hate in the Automotive Age* (Chicago, 2008), 89–90.
90   before the opening of the Games.: On plans for the Olympic subway line and its early construction, see "Sie müssen vor dem Startschuß am Ziel sein," *SZ*, August 30, 1969; on funding for Olympic public transit, see "Plus de 2 milliards de francs pour des transports en commune," *La Tribune de Genève*, June 28, 1971.
91   Fußgängerzone (pedestrian mall) in the inner city.: "Sie müssen vor dem Startschuß am Ziel sein."
92   "representative" look: "Sie müssen vor dem Startschuß am Ziel sein."
92   its "prettiest" face.: "Stadt will Rathaus-Balkon für eine Million renovieren," *MM*, August 20, 1970.
92   "[had] grown prohibitive.": "Munich: Olympic City Where Pleasure Has Become a Way of Life," *Times*, June 30, 1971.
92   "their" Munich would still exist.: "München: Weltstadt mit zerissenem Herzen," *Die Welt*, September 16, 1969.

Chapter 3: On the Eve of the Games

94   only on themselves.: Albert Hourani, *A History of the Arab Peoples* (Cambridge, Mass., 1991), 411–15; Avi Shlaim, *Israel and Palestine* (London, 2009), 256, 308; David K. Shipler, *Arab and Jew: Wounded Spirits in a Promised Land* (New York, 2002), passim.
94   Munich's joyous festival.: "Jetzt können die Chinesen kommen," *Tageszeitung* (Munich), October 25, 1972; "Entsendet Peking 1972 Olympiakämpfer nach München?" *Stimmen aus aller Welt*, May 7, 1972, Stk. 14032, BayHstaA.
94   "the Taiwan problem,": Daume to Brundage, November 30, 1966, ABC, Box 54, UIA; Brundage to Daume, October 27, 1971, ABC, Box 183, UIA; "Keine Peking-Ente für München," *Die Zeit*, August 13, 1971.

94 Ostpolitik: There is an enormous literature on Brandt's Ostpolitik. See, inter alia, Brandt's memoir, *People and Places: The Years 1960–1973* (Boston, 1976), 165–97; Manfred Görtermacher, *Geschichte der Bundesrepublik Deutschland. Von der Gründung bis zur Gegenwart* (Munich, 1999), 523–63; Peter Meersburger, *Willy Brandt, 1913–1992. Visionär und Realist* (Stuttgart, Germany, 2002), 486–656; Gregor Schöllgen, *Geschichte der Weltpolitik von Hitler bis Gorbatschow 1941–1991* (Munich, 1996), 245–92; and Mary Sarotte, *Dealing with the Devil: East Germany, Détente and Ostpolitik, 1969–1973* (Chapel Hill, N.C., 2001).

95 "giant inflatable cock" tour.): Keith Richards, *Life* (New York, 2010), 12.

95 Shah of Iran.: Vogel, *Die Amtskette*, 179–91; Manfred Schreiber, "Das Jahr 1968 in München," in *1968. 30 Jahre danach*, ed. Venenz Schubert, 35–41 (St. Ottilien, Germany, 1999).

95 out into the night.: Schreiber, "Das Jahr 1968."

96 on the host city.: "Mexiko als Maßstab für München," *SZ*, October 23, 1968.

96 "Games of fascist Germany.": "Ostberliner Kampagne," 1968 B106/3619, BAK. See also "Minen gegen München," *Rheinischer Merkur*, November 15, 1968. For a virulent Czech attack against Munich and the prospect of an Olympiad there, see *Narodni Vibory*, February 24, 1971, which condemned the Bavarian city as a center of "revanchist" gatherings, "fascistic" tendencies, and "criminal organizations." The paper is quoted in BPA, Echo Olympia '72, May 7, 1971, Stk. 14032, BayHstaA.

96 "Games of 1936 offered.": "Ist 2 mal 36 vielleicht '72?" *ND*, December 12, 1968. The *ND* position was parroted by the Communist Party of Switzerland, whose house organ, *Vorwärts*, warned that the Munich Games would be politically "misused" to a degree that "put even the Nazi Olympics of 1936 in the shadow." See "Wieder Nazi Olympiade?" *Vorwärts*, June 3, 1971.

97 still up in the air.: On the squabbles between the two Germanys over Olympic representation, see Christopher Young, "Munich 1972: Re-presenting the Nation," in *National Identity and Global Sports: Culture, Politics, and Spectacle in the Olympics and the Football World Cup*, ed. Alan Tomlinson and Christopher Young, 117–31 (Albany, 2006).

97 "breach of public order": "Keine Gefahr für Spiele in München," *Die Welt*, October 15, 1968.

97 "lose all credibility.": "Olympische Spiele in München: Flagge, Hymne und Emblem der 'DDR,'" B1/391, PAAA.

97 "everything possible": "Olympische Spiele in München." See also the Foreign Office memos, "Kabinettsitzung vom 23.10.68: Beschluß des IOC betreffend das NOK der DDR," B1/391, PAAA; and "Auswirkungen des IOC-Beschlußes von Mexiko auf die Deutschlandpolitik," December 9, 1968, B1/391, PAAA. "Kontakte mit Brundage," September 11, 1968, B2/195, PAAA.

98 "peoples of the world.": "Keine Gefahr für Spiele in München."

98 "nefarious political purposes.": "Olympia mit Hammer und Zirkel?" *Die Welt*, October 15, 1968.

98 unity of all peoples.: "1972 ohne Flaggen und Hymnen," *Düsseldorfer Nachrichten*, January 29, 1969.

99   sign off on it.: "1972 ohne Flaggen und Hymnen."

99   "ritual since 1896.": Ulbricht quoted in "Ostberliner Kampagne gegen die Olympischen Sommerspiele 1972 in München," November 13, 1968, B106/36119, BAK.

99   also cry foul.: "Ostberliner Propaganda gegen die Olympischen Spiele," March 6, 1969, B106/36119, BAK.

99   "by [Moscow's] oppression.": "Feldzug gegen Hammer und Zirkel?" *Die Zeit*, June 20, 1969.

99   internationalist homogeneity.: "Feldzug gegen Hammer und Zirkel?"

100   ideological, or racial principles.: "Beschlußentwurf zu den Olympischen Spielen 1972 in München," DY30/IVA2/18, BAB; "Rede des Delegationsleiters einer Beratung auf die Ebene von Stellvertreter der Außenministern der Staaten des Warschauer Vertrages," undated, DY30/IVA2/18, BAB; *Sowjetski Sport*, April 8, 1971, DY30/IVA2/18, BAB.

100   "propaganda stations" in Munich.: "Revanchismus statt olympischer Idee," *ND*, August 11, 1969.

100   "has ever sent abroad.": "Olympic Boycott?" *Sunday Times*, February 28, 1971.

101   of the world together.: Brundage to Radio Liberty Committee, April 20, 1971, ABC, Box 183, UIA.

101   "activities of Radio Liberty.": Sargent to Brundage, May 7, 1971, ABC, Box 183, UIA.

101   "in the Olympic spirit.": Clay to Brundage, April 29, 1971, ABC, Box 183, UIA.

101   "[would] be appreciated.": Brundage to Clay, May 1, 1971, ABC, Box 183, UIA.

102   "revanchists of the worst sort.": "Ist 2 mal 36 vielleicht '72?" *ND*, December 9, 1968.

102   "peace and [international] friendship.": "Erklärung des Olympischen Komitees der UdSSR," DR150/696, BAB.

102   Bonn and the host city.: "Konzeption für den Besuch einer offiziellen Delegation des NOK der DDR beim Organisationskomitee der XX. Olympischen Sommerspiele in München (vom 26. bis 28. April 1971)," DR150/696, BAB; "Bericht über die Reise der Sportfreunde Moke und Mainschack zum Organisationskomitee der Spiele der XX. Olympiade in München in der Zeit vom 14.4–17.4.71," DR510/700, BAB.

102   *Deutsches Mosaik*: Deutsche Olympische Gesellschaft, ed., *Deutsches Mosaik: Ein Lesebuch für Zeitgenossen* (Hannover, Germany, 1971).

103   whitewashed or ignored.: "Konzeption für den Besuch." For Polish criticism of the "Olympic Reader," see Przeglad Sportowy, April 3, 1971, quoted in BPA, "Olympisches Echo '72," May 7, 1971, Stk. 14032, BayHstaA.

103   "misuse of the Olympic Games.": "Konzeption für den Besuch."

103   "play it often enough!": Quoted in "Politik unters Zeltdach," *Der Spiegel* 35 (1972): 38.

103   "political schooling."): BMI to President of OC, November 2, 1969, B106/36169, BAK.

104   on behalf of the Munich OC.: "Grundsatzerklärung gegenüber dem IOC," undated, B106/3617, BAK.

104   "and worthily represented.": "Olympiatips aus Ostberlin," *Der Spiegel* 48 (1971): 161.

104   presence felt in Munich.: "Gefahr für die Olympiade," *Christ und Welt*, April 2, 1971.

104   closer together economically.: "Wie Westländer," *Der Spiegel* 29 (1972): 31.

105   "Russia's position" on the Munich Games.: "Wir sind da so hineingeschlittert," 30.

105   "self-image as a great sports nation.": "Weiche Welle," *Der Spiegel* 10 (1971): 138.

105   Warsaw to sign the treaty.: Brandt, *People and Places*, 398–401.

105   part of the Germans.: Terence Prittie, *Willy Brandt: Portrait of a Statesman* (New York, 1974), 254–55.

106   "betraying Germany to Moscow!": Prittie, *Willy Brandt*, 268.

107   vis-à-vis the East.: A GDR assessment of Brandt's regime argued that, although it was less "impertinent" than previous Bonn governments, it had not given up the old FRG goal of undermining the GDR. See "Sportpolitische Argumentation für die weitere Vorbereitung unserer Olympiakader auf die Olympische Spiele 1972 in Sapporo und München," DY30/IVA2/8, BAB.

107   "political-ideological situation": "Einige politisch-ideologische Aspekte von den Olympischen Sommerspielen 1972 in München," undated, DR150/696, BAB.

108   "both sides of the Fatherland."): Daume radio interview, *Deutschland-Echo*, February 12, 1971, DY30/IVA2/18, BAB.

108   "friends with the Germans.": "Pressemitteilung des Organisationskomitees," December 10, 1971, B145/8061, BAK.

109   "important human interaction.": Daume radio interview, File 1.1 Bewerbung, DSHA.

109   requisite invitations.: Daume radio interview, File 1.1 Bewerbung, DSHA.

110   in advance of the Games.: AA to General Secretary of Deutsche Sportbund, August 19, 1970, B145/8601, BAK.

110   "Sport in Africa.": AA to General Secretary of Deutsche Sportbund, November 17, 1970, B145/8601, BAK.

110   Yanks must go to Berlin.: Max Schmeling, *An Autobiography* (Chicago, 1978), 110.

111   docked in New York Harbor.: Schiller and Young, *The 1972 Munich Olympics*, 71.

111   freshly tapped Weißbier.: Klein letter (no salutation), September 13, 1971, B145/8061, BAK.

112   "states with differing political outlooks.": Merk to President of Bavarian Landtag, August 16, 1971, MInn 88598, BayHstaA.

113   "Federal Government as well.": "Ergebnisniederschrift über die Sitzung am 10.2.71 in München," February 23, 1971, B106/78702, BAK.

113   blueprint for the "Olys.": "Konzeption für den Ordnungsdienst," December 1970, B106/88817, BAK.

114   in the English language.: On recruitment goals, see OC to BMI, August 26, 1970, B106/88817, BAK.

115   threshold might be.: "Abordnung der Polizeikräften des Bundes (BGS) und der Länder zur Verstärkung der bayerischen Polizei anläßlich der XX. Olympischen Spiele 1972 in München, 5.2.71," B106/88817, BAK.

115 "Foreign Political Danger Zones in Regard to the Olympic Games,": "Die Ent-wicklung außenpolitischer Störfelder auf die Olympischen Spiele, Zwischenbericht, Juni 1970–Juni 1971," MInn 88598, BayHstaA.

117 from one danger zone to another.: "Die Entwicklung außenpolitischer Störfelder auf die Olympischen Spiele, Zwischenbericht, Juni–Dezember 1971," MInn 88598, BayHstaA.

119 no sign of going away soon.: Avery Brundage also held the view that the Taiwan issue made Beijing's participation in the Olympic movement very doubtful for the foreseeable future. See Brundage to Daume, October 27, 1971, ABC, Box 183, UIA.

120 Turkish terrorists to assist them.: "Information," BLVS, April 1, 1972–June 30, 1972, MInn 88598, BayHstaA.

120 would they surrender alive.: Manfred Schreiber, "Konzeption für den Ordnungs-dienst," June 12, 1970, B185/3230, BAK; see also "Ich werde heute noch für Palästina sterben," 23.

120 to put on?: See Wolff, "When the Terror Began," 61.

121 home-grown leftist terror).: "Ergebnisprotokoll über die Besprechung am 3.11.70 im MInn wegen der politischen Agitation der DDR im Zusammenhang mit den Olympischen Spielen in München," B106/78702, BAK.

121 "party during the Games.": "Information," BLVS, April 1, 1972–June 30, 1972, MInn 88598, BayHstaA. For perceived German Communist groups' threats to the security of the Games, see also "Durchgeführte und geplante Aktionen an-läßlich der Olympischen Spielen in München," B106/85169, BAK.

121 Rote Armee Fraktion (RAF): The best study on the RAF remains Stefan Aust's *Der Baader-Meinhof Komplex* (Munich, 1989).

121 Criminal Investigations Agency in Munich.: See Aust, *Der Baader-Meinhof Komplex*, 233.

121 "had just begun.": "Information," BLVS, April 1, 1972–June 30, 1972, MInn 88598, BayHstaA.

122 DM 30 million.: "Drohbrief, Baader-Meinhof Bande," July 30, 1972, B106/78702, BAK.

122 invasion of Cambodia.: Vogel, *Die Amtskette*, 191.

122 President Richard Nixon himself.: "Stuttgart Staatsministerium," August 9, 1972, B106/78702, BAK.

122 "criminal aggression.": "Informationsaustausch, Sicherheitslage," August 25, 1972, B106/78702, BAK.

122 National Vietnam Committee,: "Demonstration anläßlich der Eröffnung der Olympischen Spiele," August 23, 1972, B106/78702, BAK.

122 going on in the Olympic Stadium.: "Hippie-Treffen," undated, B106/78702, BAK.

122 "long-distance spitting.": "Goldmedaille für Weitspucken," *Düsseldorfer Nachrichten*, January 26, 1971; "Sie warden uns lynchen," *Die Zeit*, March 1, 1970.

123 "fiasco,": Vogel, *Die Amtskette*, 194–95.

123 "Day of German Unity" rally: "Information," BLVS, April 1, 1972–June 1, 1972, MInn 88598, BayHstaA.

123   "Congress of Nationalist European Youth,": Demokratische Aktion, "Neo-faschisten wollen Olympische Spiele stören," January 4, 1972, B106/78702, BAK.

123   "Soviet delegation" to the Olympics.: "Lagebericht," August 28, 1972, B106/78702, BAK.

123   "Rhodesia not play.": "Anonyme Bombendrohung gegen das Olympische Dorf," August 22, 1972, B106/78702, BAK.

123   "a day of war": "Lagebericht: Innere Sicherheit," August 25, 1972, B106/85169, BAK.

123   "packed Olympic Stadium.": "Lagebericht," August 23, 1972, B106/85169, BAK.

124   "completely exterminated.": "Nichtdurchführung der Olympischen Spiele in München," undated, B106/78702, BAK.

124   "400 will be criminals,": "Banden terrorisieren die Olympia-Stadt," *Kölner Stadt Anzeiger*, June 26, 1971.

124   bigger game to come.: "Vorolympische Glanzleistungen der Taschendiebe," August 21, 1972, B106/78702, BAK.

124   carelessness of Olympic guests.: "Hochkonjunktur für Autoknacken," August 21, 1972, B106/78702, BAK.

125   down well in Egypt.): "Aegyptische Beschwerungen gegen unberechtichte Verünglimpfung Aegypten am Rand der Olympischen Spiele," undated, B36/525, PAAA.

125   "offenses during the Games.": "Hochkonjunktur für Autoknacken."

125   "Games in 1936.": "Das Sicherheitskonzept für die Olympischen Spiele," Staatsanwaltschaft 37430, STAM.

125   near the Bavarian capital.: "Vorbereitungen im Zuständigkeitsbereich der Strafverfolgunsbehörde," January 20, 1972, Staatsanwaltschaft 33350, STAM.

125   command of the Bavarian authorities.: "Sprechzettel für die Innenministerkonferenz," January 29, 1971, B106/88817, BAK.

126   "domestic and foreign, during the Games.": "Sicherheitsmaßnahmen im Zusammenhang mit den Olympischen Spielen," July 17, 1972, B106/7802, BAK.

126   "right-wing radical": "U.S.-Staatsangehöriger Gregg Kennet," July 17, 1972, B106/7802, BAK.

126   speeches augmented by loudspeakers.: "Vorbeugende Maßnahmen eines ungestörten Verlaufs der Olympischen Spiele," BSMI, June 26, 1972, MInn 88612/1, BayHstaA.

126   any special precautions for Israel's delegation.: "Das Sicherheitskonzept für die Olympischen Spiele."

127   would "proceed normally.": "Polizeiverbände aus aller Bundesländer in München," August 23, 1972, B106/78702, BAK.

127   bountiful good cheer.: "Die Rhodesier in München," *Die Zeit*, January 28, 1972. For a study of Rhodesian participation in the Olympics, see Andrew Novak, "Rhodesia's 'Rebel and Racist' Olympic Team: Olympic Glory, National Legitimacy and the Clash of Politics and Sport," *International Journal for the History of Sport* 23, no. 8 (December 2006): 1369–88.

127   "situation is resolved,": "Schamrot warden," *Der Spiegel* 36 (1972): 22; see also "Rhodesian zu Olympischen Spielen nach München eingeladen," BPA, Echo

Olympia, March 29, 1971, Stk. 14032, BayHstaA; and "Rhodesia Approved by Africans, Says Germany," *Daily Telegraph*, April 3, 1971.

127   from those regimes.: "Brundage droht afrikanischen Staaten mit Ausschluß von den Olympischen Spielen," *SZ*, August 17, 1972.

127   racist regime of Ian Smith.: AA, "Teilnahme Rhodesians an den Olympischen Spielen," July 24, 1972, B1/391, PAAA; see also "Sieg, Sieg," *Der Spiegel* 36 (1972): 40–44.

127   "solidarity" with the Black African states.: "Fall Rhodesien," MM, July 23, 1972.

128   come to Munich for the Games.: "Schamrot warden."

128   "conduct of the Olympic Games.": AA, "Abteilung D IV, Gespräch mit Präsident Daume über die Teilnahme Rhodesiens an den Olympischen Spielen," June 29, 1972, B1/391, PAAA.

128   "would not alter the illegal status": "Aide-Memoire, Rhodesia and the Olympic Games," July 13, 1972, B1/391, PAAA.

128   African friends to participate in the Games.: Brandt to Brundage, August 18, 1972, ABC, Box 182, UIA.

128   plenary session on August 22.: For the minutes of these meetings, see "Minutes of the Meeting of the Executive Board," August 21–22, 1972, IOCA.

128   "some South American teams.": "Minutes," August 22, 1972, IOCA.

129   decided to exclude Rhodesia.: "Rhodesia Expelled from Munich Games by Narrow Vote," *Times*, August 23, 1972.

129   "to the pipes of politics,": FAZ quoted in "Ein Geschenk der Deutschen an sich selbst," *Der Spiegel* 35 (1972): 28.

129   "blow out the Olympic Torch,": "Olympic Disgrace," *Los Angeles Herald Examiner*, August 24, 1972.

129   "differently than Caucasians.": A. Keksis to IOC, August 28, 1972, JO Eté, Cojo Comité d'Organisation, Correspondence 1972–1977, IOCA.

129   "before the 1976 Olympiad.": Davis to IOC, September 22, 1972, JO Eté, Cojo Comité d'Organisation, Correspondence 1972–1977, IOCA.

129   "met every requirement?": Larkin to IOC, August 22, 1972, JO Eté, Cojo Comité d'Organisation, Correspondence 1972–1977, IOCA.

129   "as I am.": Berkhout to Brundage, ABC, Box 182, UIA.

130   expelled from the IOC.: "IOC Will Examine Motives behind Rhodesia Issue," *Times*, August 26, 1972.

130   "a few black athletes representing the U.S.": USOC, "Exclusion of Rhodesia from the 1972 Olympic Games," ABC, Box 183, UIA.

130   "pack up and leave,": Matthews, *My Race Be Won*, 312.

130   1968 Mexico City Olympics.: Tex Maule, "Switcheroo from Yes to Nyet," *Sports Illustrated*, April 29, 1968, 28–29.

130   "political demonstrations": "Many U.S. Athletes Have Some Surprises in Store for the Olympics," *Wall Street Journal*, May 15, 1972.

131   "what not to do,": "Many U.S. Athletes."

131   "way of life against another,": "Many U.S. Athletes."

131   "misleading facades.": "Many U.S. Athletes." See also "Jack Scott, a Prominent Critic of Sports Excesses, Dies at 57," *NYT*, February 3, 2000.

131   Munich after all.: "Mr. Nixon on Olympus," *Newsweek*, June 26, 1972.

132   "pertinent to their needs.": "Many U.S. Athletes."

132   one in ten proved faulty.: "Verlauf des Fackellaufs," File 3.2. Fackellauf, DSHA; see also Schiller and Young, *The 1972 Munich Olympics*, 75.

132   promote Ostpolitik on the Olympic level.: AA, "Gespräch des Bundesministers mit . . . Daume," January 25, 1971, B/391, PAAA.

132   African nations to be included on the route.: "Niederschrift über die 2. Sitzung des Ausschußes für die Olympische Fackellauf am 15.6.70," B106/30673, BAK.

133   leave Berlin off the route for '72.: "Niederschrift über die 2 sitzung."

133   "hold the door open": "Daume: Wir wollten die Türe öffnen," *MM*, January 19, 1971.

133   "intervention by Moscow": "Staatsanwaltschaft bei dem Landgericht München, Olympische Spiele in München," January 20, 1972, Staatsanwaltschaft 33350, STAM.

133   central to his Olympic diplomacy.: Daume to Schöbel, October 27, 1967, DR 510/703, BAB; "Olympisches Feuer durch die DDR nach München?" *MM*, March 4, 1970; "Willi Daumes Wunsch: Olympische Fackellauf 1972 durch die DDR," sid, June 28, 1970, File 3.2 Fackellauf, DSHA.

134   thought permissible or desirable.: Ewald to Hellman, November 17, 1969, DR 510/703, BAB; "Olympics Worry East Germans," *Chicago Daily News*, July 7, 1971.

134   passport stolen in Romania.: "Verlauf des Fackellaufs"; "Olympic Flame starts its journey," *Times*, July 29, 1972.

134   three days ahead of schedule.: "Prank Fails to Deter Torch's Arrival," *NYT*, August 26, 1972.

134   all over Germany in 1936.: "Olympischer Tag in Athen," sid, July 30, 1972, File 3.2 Fackellauf, DSHA.

135   "international indifference,": Kozlovieski quoted in "IOC will examine motives," *Times*, August 26, 1972.

135   "it's already there.": "Olympic Overture: Flags and Flak," *Sports Illustrated*, September 18, 1972, 19.

135   private makeup ceremony.: Shaul P. Ladany, *King of the Road* (Jerusalem, 2008), 293–94.

135   "slide comfortably along.": "Olympic Overture."

136   "for after-duty hours,": Matthews, *My Race Be Won*, 322.

136   "no barbed wire.": Kenny Moore, *Bowerman and the Men of Oregon* (Eugene, Oreg., 2006), 284.

136   "harlots, and newspapermen,"; "strong umbrage": Moore, *Bowerman and the Men of Oregon*, 285.

136   *seventy-five-mile radius* of Munich.: "Olympic Travel Scheme Robbery," *Guardian*, May 5, 1971; "1972 Olympic Games: Tickets, Lodgings Americans' Problem," *NYT*, May 21, 1971; "Yankee Stay Home!" *Sports Illustrated*, May 31, 1971, 36.

137   "to attend the Games."): Brundage to Daume, June 28, 1971, ABC, Box 183, UIA.

137   "buy blind.": "Munich Eases Squeeze on Games Dates," *Daily Telegraph*, January 19, 1971; "Olympic Organizers Bow to Protests," *Times*, January 19, 1971.

137   high-profile West Germans.: "Das Olympische Bett-Rennen," *SZ*, January 21, 1970; "Vorolympischer Kampf um Olympische Betten," *MM*, July 4/5, 1970.

137   livelihoods of local innkeepers.): "USA-Hotelkonzerne schon im Vormarsch," *ND*, December 8, 1968.

137   "in a phone-booth,": "1972 Olympic Games," *NYT*, May 21, 1971.

137   "nearly 4.5 million tickets.": "Too Few Tickets," *Guardian*, December 30, 1970.

137   only forty-five thousand actual seats.: "Yankee Stay Home!" See also complaints about tickets from the American Automobile Association in a letter to Brundage, May 21, 1971, ABC, Box 183, UIA.

138   their own party.: "Beim Bau die ersten Rekorde. Bayern bangen um 'ihre' Karten," *Frankfurter Neue Presse*, August 25, 1970.

138   "making their marks.": "Yankee Stay Home!"

138   "clip-joint owners.": "Lid's On in Munich for Olympic Visitors," *Chicago Sunday Times*, July 23, 1972.

138   "jail during the Games,": "Lid's On in Munich."

138   "Games they deserved.": "Ein Geschenk der Deutschen an sich selbst."

Chapter 4: Let the Games Begin

141   "an augury of happiness?": Mandell, *The Olympics of 1972*, 46.

142   "with a light hand.": "Gestaltung des Olympischen Zeremoniells," B106/30673, BAK; see also "Die geplante Eröffnungs- und Schlußfeier der Olympischen Spiele 1972 in München," File 3.3 Eröffungsfeier–Schlußfeier, DSHA.

142   Rhodesia's exclusion from the Games.: Although Zeffirelli "despised" the Rhodesian government and sympathized with Black Africa's cause, he declared, "I consider it unacceptable that the Olympic Games have become a platform for political protests." See "IOC Will Examine Motives behind Rhodesian Issue," *Times*, August 26, 1972.

142   parameters for Olympic opening ceremonies.: Berlioux to Daume, June 25, 1971, IOC Correspondence 1970–1972, IOCA.

143   opening ceremonies over the years.: On the '72 opening ceremony, see Organizing Committee, *Die Spiele*, 1:77–87; and Mandell, *The Olympics of 1972*, 40–58. For an analysis of the Munich opening ceremony within the context of German political culture, see Uta Andrea Balbier, "'Die Welt das moderne Deutschland vorstellen': Die Eröffnungsfeier der Spiele der XX. Olympiade in München 1972," in *Auswärtige Repräsentationen. Deutsche Kulturdiplomatie nach 1945*, ed. Johannes Paulmann, 105–19 (Cologne, Germany, 2005).

143   "not to embarrass anybody.": "Sing cucu nu," *Der Spiegel* 35 (1972): 46; on Edelhagen, see "Erhabenster Tag," *Der Spiegel* 37 (1972): 44.

144   "proof of our indestructibility.": Ladany, *King of the Road*, 288.

144   "cheering the Jewish athletes.": ABC Television Documentary, *Our Greatest Hopes, Our Worst Fears: The Tragedy of the Munich Games* (2002).

145   "path of peace.": "Olga Connolly's Story: A Dream about Peace," *NYT*, August 27, 1972.

145 "demonstratively warm" greeting.: "Athleten marschieren in lockerem Tritt," *SZ*, August 28, 1972. See also "XX. Sommerspiele feierlich eröffnet," *ND*, August 28, 1972.

145 other socialist nations.: "Athleten marschieren."

146 one thousand Olympic visitors.: "Unvermindert starke Polemik in der DDR," BPA, Echo Olympia '72, Stk. 6523, BayHstaA; "Olympics Worry East Germans," *Chicago Daily News*, July 7, 1971.

146 any other family member.: "'Des ist, wia wenn's d'Mauer dabeihätten,'" *Der Spiegel* 37 (1972): 26–27.

146 "own Olympic athletes.": "'Des ist, wia wenn's d'Mauer dabeihätten,'" 27.

146 "Wall along with them.": "'Des ist, wia wenn's d'Mauer dabeihätten,'" 27.

147 "behave over here.": "'Des ist, wia wenn's d'Mauer dabeihätten,'" 27.

147 "imposed on them,": "'Des ist, wia wenn's d'Mauer dabeihätten,'" 27. On GDR athletes and fans at Munich, see also ". . . daß dies ja auch Deutsche sind," *Süd- westpresse*, September 1, 1972; and "Genossen bringen Stallwärme ins Dorf," *SZ*, September 1, 1972.

147 Jaunty pop songs.: "Sing cucu nu."

148 "the Berlin Olympics of 1936."): Danish paper cited in dpa Überseedienst, July 7, 1972, B106/1824, BAK; see also Geyer, "On the Road," 255.

148 "also *our* victories.": "Ihre Siege auch unsere Siege?" *Die Zeit*, March 24, 1972.

149 a huge Olympic flag.: Organizing Committee, *Die Spiele*, 1:77–80; see also Patrick Danne, "Die Mannschaft der Bundesrepublik Deutschland bei den Sommerspielen der XX. Olympiade in München 1972," *Diplomarbeit*, Deutsche Sporthochschule Köln (2001): 34–37.

150 "true spirit of Olympic sportsmanship": Organizing Committee, *Die Spiele*, 1:77.

150 "next Olympiad returns.": Organizing Committee, *Die Spiele*, 1:77.

150 "was out of place.": Arthur Daley, "With Matchless Pageantry," *NYT*, August 27, 1972.

151 synonymous with appeasement.: Red Smith, "Flame Glows amid Pageantry," *NYT*, August 27, 1972.

151 "youth of the world.": "Athleten marschieren."

151 "application in 1965.": Quoted in Schiller and Young, *The 1972 Munich Olympics*, 123.

151 "our city has ever experienced,": Quoted in Deutsche Olympische Gesellschaft, ed., *Die Spiele der XX. Olympiade München und Kiel und die XI. Olympische Winterspiele in Sapporo 1972* (Freiburg, Germany, 1972), 14.

151 many people cried.]: Quoted in Deutsche Olympische Gesellschaft, *Die Spiele der XX. Olympiade*.

151 cover the '72 Olympics.: "Leni Riefenstahl Returns to the Olympics," *NYT*, August 24, 1972.

152 withdraw the offer.: Leni Riefenstahl, *A Memoir* (New York, 1992), 579–80.

152 "in 1936 in Berlin.": "Athleten marschieren."

152 "a modern industrial nation.": "Athleten marschieren."

152 "Piss off to the GDR!": "Athleten marschieren." On the demonstration, see also "Rote Fähnchen im Olympischen Flaggenwald," *SZ*, September 1, 1972.

153   to attend the Games.: "Athleten marschieren." On foreign dignitaries to be received by Brandt, see "Zusammentreffen des Bundeskanzlers mit ausländischen Staats- und Regierungschefs," June 30, 1972, B145/8062, BAK.

153   "Munich gleamed,": Thomas Mann, "Gladius Dei," in *Die Erzählungen. Werke. Taschenbuchausgabe in zwölf Bänden* (Frankfurt am Main, Germany, 1967), 1:149.

154   "Get fit, screw more often!": "Trimm Dich," *Der Spiegel* 37 (1972): 49–50.

154   "the erotic world class.": "Trimm Dich," 50.

154   medals were handed out.: "To Münchners, Foreigners Are an Olympic Nuisance," *NYT*, August 24, 1972.

154   "I bite Prussians.": Horace Sutton, "Munich: Joie de Vivre with an Umlaut," *Sports Illustrated*, March 25, 1972, 49.

154   "our King Ludwig.": Sutton, "Munich."

155   "Why can't *you*?": "To Münchners, Foreigners Are an Olympic Nuisance."

155   "had no right hand.": Quoted in Wallechinsky, *The Complete Book*, 559.

155   in the third round.: "Basketball, Boxing and Soccer Help Open Competition in Olympics Today," *NYT*, August 27, 1972.

156   "and on your chin.": "Stevenson the Big Hit," *Sportsworld*, August 27–September 10, 1972, 42.

156   "they could give me.": "Basketball, Boxing and Soccer Help Open Competition."

156   was seriously overmatched.: "Inkognito k.o.," *Der Spiegel* 37 (1972): 36.

156   color their verdicts.: "Schande, Schande, Schande," *Time*, September 11, 1972, 66.

157   "that job in Boston,": Red Smith, "Biggest Steal since the Brink's Job," *NYT*, August 30, 1972. An irate American wrote Brundage that the Jones decision "made a mockery of the boxing competition at the Olympics." Klein to Brundage, ABC, Box 182, UIA. According to the *New York Times*, Jones received scores of phone calls, telegrams, and condolence letters following his loss to Tregubov. "Sympathy for Reggie," *NYT*, August 30, 1972.

157   an African judge.: "Inkognito k.o.," 36.

157   "stayed there twitching": Mandell, *The Olympics of 1972*, 102.

157   West German boxing champions.: "Inkognito k.o.," 37.

158   "must live in the Village.": Quoted in "Low Blows from Munich," *Time*, June 26, 1972.

158   "But for the grace of God,": Red Smith, "Olympic Chiefs Should Set Youth Example," *NYT*, June 25, 1972.

158   "represent his country.": Aspin to Brundage, July 14, 1972, ABC, Box 182, UIA.

158   "of change and progress.": Lieber to Brundage, June 23, 1972, ABC, Box 182, UIA.

158   "at the Olympic Village.": "Low Blows," 62.

159   "in the Cincinnati area.": Schevre to Brundage, June 28, 1972, ABC, Box 182, UIA.

159   "alongside convicted felons?": Pettigrew to Brundage, August 4, 1972, ABC, Box 182, UIA.

159   "with adolescent pox": Mandell, *The Olympics of 1972*, 85.

159   in the wrestling competition.: "Schande, Schande, Schande," 67. See also "Referee Dismissed in Dispute over Taylor's Loss," *NYT*, August 28, 1972.

160   to bring home the gold.: David Zang, "An Oregon Hippie in Uncle Sam's Court: A Vietnam Era Fable," *Proceedings of the North American Society for Sport History* (1998): 62–70.

161   ended in a scoreless tie.: "An Olympic First," *NYT*, August 28, 1972.

162   West Germany's Olympia-Sporthilfe.: "Auf Ehrenwort," *Der Spiegel* 33 (1972): 92–94.

162   "played as if they were.": "Versöhnlicher Abschied der deutschen Elf," *SZ*, September 10, 1972.

163   black boycott of the Mexico City Olympics).: See Damion Thomas, "Let the Games Begin: Sport, U.S. Race Relations and Cold War Politics," *International Journal of the History of Sport* 24, no. 2 (February 2007): 151–71, 166. See also Hoffer, *Something in the Air*, 61.

164   "going to happen that way.": "U.S. Five Risking 36-Year Streak," *NYT*, August 27, 1972.

165   opening day ceremony.: Lawrence Terry, interview with author, April 2010.

165   twice-daily training sessions.: "U.S. Eight Gains Silver Medal behind New Zealand in Rowing," *NYT*, September 3, 1972.

165   "dream kitchen.": "U.S. Eight Gains Silver Medal." Altogether, the Kiwis raised £21,000 in order to participate in the Munich Games. See "Kiwis' magnificent eight," *Sportsworld*, August 27–September 10, 1972, 63.

167   "more than I could take in.": Wallechinsky, *The Complete Book*, 847.

167   mishap or other.: Olga Korbut, *My Story* (London, 1992), 64–65.

167   never her specialty.: Korbut, *My Story*, 68–70; "Petite Russian Is Big Winner in Gymnastics," *NYT*, September 1, 1972.

168   "lasted several years.": "Olga: I Was a Sex Slave," *Scottish Daily Record and Sunday Mail*, May 25, 1999.

168   "probable is it?": Arthur Daley, "An Excellent Mark in Swimming," *NYT*, August 24, 1972.

169   "winning is.": "Spitz über Alles in Deutschland," *Time*, September 11, 1972, 65. See also the authorized biography of Spitz by Richard Foster, *Mark Spitz: The Extraordinary Life of an Olympic Champion* (Santa Monica, Calif., 2008).

169   "God likes a winner.": "Big Splash at Munich," *NYT*, August 29, 1972.

170   "Now he's a man.": "An Excellent Mark."

170   "one of my aunts.": "Spitz über Alles."

171   "believe this place?": "Mark Spitz and the Qwest for Gold," *Sports Illustrated*, September 4, 1972, 21.

171   not be Munich's fault.: "An Excellent Mark."

171   "Better die than lose,": "Der Einzelgänger," *Der Spiegel* 37 (1972): 38.

171   "a lead-vest on.": "Der Einzelgänger."

171   be immediately disqualified.: "Report from the Eligibility Commission, IOC Executive Committee Minutes," September 1, 1972, IOCA.

172   "have their medals back.'": Foster, *Mark Spitz*, 179.

172   "settle the matter.": Smit, *Sneaker Wars*, 104.

172   "public outcry": "Report from the Eligibility Commission."

172   "Superman of Swimming.": "Verliert Olympia-Star Spitz seine drei Goldmedaillen?" *Abendzeitung* (Munich), August 31, 1972.

173   "limits of life's possibilities.": Mandell, *The Olympics of 1972*, 81.

173   "I'll be a failure.": "Spitz's Score: 6 Finals, 6 Gold Medals, 6 Records," *NYT*, September 4, 1972.

174   earn more premiums.: "Sport Wunderkind," *Time*, June 5, 1972, 95.

174   "gained their respect,": Quoted in George Plimpton, *George Plimpton on Sports* (Guilford, Conn., 2003), 260.

174   "a one-woman Olympic team.": Quoted in Dennis Phillips, "Australian Women at the Olympics: Achievement and Alienation," *Sporting Traditions* 6, no. 2 (May 1990), 195–96.

175   "greatest success story."): Phillips, "Australian Women at the Olympics," 182.

175   Australian Tourist Board!): "Swimming," *Sportsworld*, August 27–September 10, 1972, 71.

175   "tough to beat now.": Neil Amdurs, "Spitz Leads U.S. to World Marks; Miss King Gets Diving Medal at Olympics: U.S. Swimmers Crack Two World Records," *NYT*, August 29, 1972.

175   "is not Gould.": Quoted in Wallechinsky, *The Complete Book*, 127.

176   "do another good one.": "Shane Gould Wins Third Gold Medal," *NYT*, September 2, 1972.

176   "When you're 23, you quit."): Plimpton, *George Plimpton on Sports*, 260.

177   after his race.: "Medication Rule Trips U.S. Youth," *NYT*, September 5, 1972.

177   in the matter at all.: Medical Commission of the IOC, *Doping* (Munich, 1972), 30–31.

177   overdose of powerful amphetamines.: Thomas M. Hunt, "Sports, Drugs, and the Cold War: The Conundrum of Olympic Doping Policy, 1970–1979," *Olympika* 16 (2007): 19.

178   (too much booze).: Hoffer, *Something in the Air*, 238.

178   "and following the Olympic Games.": Quoted in Hunt, "Sports, Drugs," 20.

178   "if we can avoid it.": Hunt, "Sports, Drugs," 20–21.

178   "his steroids or mine.": Hunt, "Sports, Drugs," 22.

179   them brief suspensions.: "West Germans in Drug Taking Tangle," *Times*, June 16, 1961.

179   "are virtually impossible.": Quoted in Hunt, "Sports, Drugs," 23.

179   to the IOC Medical Commission.: "DeMont's Case Is Latest Controversy Involving American Games Officials," *NYT*, September 5, 1972; Hunt, "Sports, Drugs," 24.

180   "consistent in its work.": "Report from the Medical Commission," September 6, 1972, Minutes of the Executive Board, IOCA.

180   "cease using Marax.": DeMont to de Merode, September 4, 1972, ABC, Box 185, UIA.

180   "severely reprimanded.": Brundage to Buck, September 4, 1972, ABC, Box 185, UIA.

181   "someone else's neglect,": Press release, September 10, 1972, ABC, Box 185, UIA.

181   "image of manipulation.": "Olympia-Skandal im Modernen Fünfkampf," sid, October 9, 1972, DSHA; see also "Report from the Medical Commission."

181   called Oral-Turinabol.: John Hoberman, *Mortal Engines: The Science of Performance and the Dehumanization of Sport* (New York, 1992), 217.

181 severe depression, and other afflictions.: The head of the East German sports program from the sixties into the eighties, Manfred Ewald, pioneered the system whereby top athletes were given highly dangerous performance-enhancing drugs. In July 2000, Ewald and Dr. Manfred Hoepner, the GDR's chief sports doctor, were convicted of being accessories to "intentional bodily harm of athletes, including minors." Both men received probation. Ewald died two years later. See "East Germany's Doping Chief, Manfred Ewald, Is Dead at 76," *NYT*, October 23, 2002.

182 connection with the Munich Olympics.: Steven Ungerleider, *Faust's Gold: Inside the East German Doping Machine* (New York, 2001), 46–47.

182 powerful Siemens computers.: "The Push-Button Games," *Sportsworld*, August 1972, 46. See also "Starting Blocks that Stop the Cheats," *Daily Mail*, October 1, 1971.

182 worth the huge expense.: "1972 Olympics: Athletes vs. Architecture?" *Chicago Tribune*, August 29, 1972; "Big Talk at Munich Is the Cost of Big Roof," *NYT*, September 3, 1972.

182 previously sovereign Soviets.: "Sportswunderland," *Time*, June 5, 1972, 95.

183 Championships in Helsinki.: "America's Lag in Pre-Olympic Effort Charts," *Chicago Tribune*, August 29, 1971.

183 "no question about it.": "U.S. Trackmen in Trouble for Olympics in Munich," *Los Angeles Times*, February 14, 1972.

183 "going to do.": "Bowerman Fires Salvos All Around the Games," *NYT*, August 30, 1972.

183 "anything *they* want.": "Bowerman Fires Salvos."

183 "to talk about it.": "2 U.S. Sprinters Shut Out in Mix-up," *NYT*, September 1, 1972; "Saved by a Very Fast Wottle," *Sports Illustrated*, September 5, 1972, 72.

184 "go on being?": "Spitz über Alles," 64.

184 "an American tragedy,": Arledge, *Roone*, 124.

184 "typical USOC copout,": Matthews, *My Race Be Won*, 238–39.

184 "time to warm up.": "2 U.S. Sprinters Shut Out."

184 "of any in Munich.": "Germans Protest the Behavior of 'Arrogant' Americans," *NYT*, September 2, 1972.

185 even going full throttle.: "Borzov Gives the Soviet Union Its First Olympic Sprint Crown," *NYT*, September 2, 1972.

185 car or aircraft designers.: Quoted in Wallechinsky, *The Complete Book*, 207.

185 "are making progress,": "Borzov Gives the Soviet Union."

185 "well preserved cadaver.": Red Smith, "The Fastest Human Is a Commie," *NYT*, September 2, 1972.

185 "double on them.": Matthews, *My Race Be Won*, 331–32.

186 the 800 in Olympic history.: "Arzhanov Gets 2nd Place; American Swimmers Win," *NYT*, September 3, 1972; "Saved by a Very Fast Wottle," 21.

186 until his event was over.: "Sex at the Olympics: A Great Debate," *NYT*, September 3, 1972; "Olympic Notes," *Track and Field News*, December 8, 1972, 6.

188 "I had six weeks.": "Seagren Defeated," *NYT*, September 3, 1972.

188 previous two years.: Wallechinsky, *The Complete Book*, 435.

188   "muscle-bound deformity": "Das Selbstbildnis wurde zerschossen," *SZ*, September 12, 1972. On Rosendahl, see also Horst Bienek, "Die Brille," in Deutsche Olympische Gesellschaft, *Die Spiele der XX. Olympiade München und Kiel*, 70; and Gerd Osenberg, *Heidi Rosendahl: Springer + Sprinter* (Munich, 1973).

189   the standing world record.: "Sensation Nummer 1: Ulrike Meyfarth," sid, September 11, 1972.

189   perfected by the Americans.): "The Push-Button Games," 47.

190   football field in distance.: "Virén, a Finn, Gets Up from Knockdown to Win 10,000-Meter Run Title and Set World Record," *NYT*, September 4, 1972; see also Moore, *Bowerman*, 287.

190   "shot his wad.": Moore, *Bowerman*, 287.

190   "our socialist way of life."): "Vorlage an das Sekretariat des ZK," December 12, 1970, DY 30/IVA2/8, BAB.

190   frolicsome new Munich.: "Sport und Hohn mit schönen Hexen," *Der Spiegel* 37 (1972): 137.

190   "Kultur-Olympiade.": "Finale in den Spielstätten der Musen," *SZ*, September 11, 1972.

191   "German Excavation at Olympia.": "Finale in den Spielstätten."

192   "happy" indeed.: Ursula von Kardorff, "Tips, wie mann Olympia genießt," *Abendzeitung* (Munich), August 31, 1972.

Chapter 5: Invasion of the Sanctuary

193   "for something like this.": Hans-Jochen Vogel, "Wir wurden auf so etwas in keiner Weise vorbereitet," *Das Parlament* 15 (2005): 6.

193   "Olympics of Terror.": McKay quoted in Aaron J. Klein, *Striking Back: The 1972 Munich Olympics Massacre and Israel's Deadly Response* (New York, 2005), 48.

194   "Streets free to the Communists!": "Kommunisten stürmen Karlstor," *SZ*, September 3, 1972.

194   was not known.: "Information des BLVS" (July 1, 1972–September 30, 1972), MInn 88598, BayHstaA.

195   of course, hyper-sensitive.: "Horror and Death at the Olympics," *Time*, September 18, 1972, 22.

195   "to get into the Village,": "BPA/Nachrichtenzentrale," September 4, 1972, B106/85168, BAK.

195   deploy any fakery.: Mandell, *The Olympics of 1972*, 33–34.

195   must be working undercover.: Quoted in Klein, *Striking Back*, 27.

196   "Nothing happens at night,": "Ich werde heute noch für Palästina sterben," *Der Spiegel* 38 (1972): 27.

196   refugee camps in Lebanon.: On Black September's operational planning for the Munich attack, see Abu Daoud, *Palestine: de Jérusalem à Munich* (Paris, 1999), passim; Klein, *Striking Back*, 35–49; and Simon Reeve, *One Day in September* (New York, 2000), 20–47. Also useful are the interrogation records of the three surviving Palestinian guerillas: "Vernehmungen in Stadelheim (September 14, 1972) und Kaisheim (September 20, 1972)," B141/30899 and B141/37488, BAK.

197   organization calling itself Black September.: There is now a substantial litera-
ture on Black September. See, inter alia, Christopher Dobson, *Black September: Its Short, Violent History* (New York, 1974); J. K. Cooley, *"Green March, Black September": The Story of the Palestinian Arabs* (London, 1973), passim; Benny Morris, *Righteous Victims: A Story of the Zionist-Arab Conflict 1881–1999* (New York, 1999), 379–86; Kai Bird, *Crossing Mandelbaum Gate: Coming of Age between Arabs and Israelis, 1956–1978* (New York, 2010), 243–47; and "Black September's Ruthless Few," *Time*, September 18, 1972, 33.

198   "for lunch instead.": Quoted in Reeve, *One Day*, 20–21.

198   quietly left for Damascus.): Bird, *Crossing Mandelbaum Gate*, 281.

198   bête-noir of the Palestinian Arabs.: Morris, *Righteous Victims*, 379.

199   machinery for Israel.: "Schwarzer September am Rhein und Ruhr," *Der Spiegel* 38 (1972): 24.

199   in specialized operations.: Reeve, *One Day*, 37.

200   missions of World War II.): On the Lod Airport massacre, see Reeve, *One Day*, 37–38; Morris, *Righteous Victims*, 380; Bird, *Crossing Mandelbaum Gate*, 281; and Mark Schreiber, *Shocking Crimes of Postwar Japan* (New York, 1996), 215–17.

200   "didn't deserve to exist.": Quoted in Reeve, *One Day*, 39.

200   "They did not exist.": Quoted in Bird, *Crossing Mandelbaum Gate*, 258–59.

201   sunny afternoon in Rome.: Reeve, *One Day*, 39.

201   "moral legitimacy": On the complicated relationship between Bonn and Tel Aviv, see Lily Gardner Feldman, *The Special Relationship between West Germany and Israel* (Boston, 1984); see also "40 Jahre diplomatische Beziehungen zu Israel," *Das Parlament* (April 2005): 5–8.

201   on the side of the PLO.: "München: Ein Sieg der Partisanen im Nahost?" *Der Spiegel* 39 (1972): 101.

202   about a half-hour later.: For my account of the Village takeover, I have drawn on the interrogation records of the Palestinian survivors in B141/37488 and 30899, BAK; see also a report by the Bavarian Interior Ministry dated September 7, 1972, in B36/501, PAAA; and testimony gathered in a legal inquiry into the actions of Munich police officials Manfred Schreiber and Georg Wolf, "Sachverhaltsrekonstruktion des Staatsanwaltschaft München I zur Begründung des Ermittlungsverfahren gegen Schreiber und Wolf, Verfügung vom 5.2.73," B106/146541, BAK. Valuable also is "Die Olympische Tragödie (Das Attentat). Die Chronik vom Olympischen Dorf nach Fürstenfeldbruck," *Die Spiele der XX. Olympiade München*, accessed August 2, 2011, http://www.olympia72.de/attentat2.html. Reeve, *One Day*, and Klein, *Striking Back*, are especially useful for the Israeli side of things, as is the memoir by Ladany, *King of the Road*. For interpretations and self-justifications by the German players, I've relied on BSMI, ed., "Erfahrungsbericht über die Vorbereitung und Durchführung des Einsatzes der Polizei anläßlich der Spiele der XX. Olympiade München und Augsburg 1972," Pol/462, STAM; Hans-Dietrich Genscher, *Erinnerungen* (Berlin, 1995); "Pressekonferenz Polizeipräsident Manfred Schreiber am 5.9.72," accessed May 10, 2009, http://www.olympia72.de/; "Interview Willi Daume am 11.9.72," accessed May 10, 2009, http://www.olympia72.de/; "Pressekonferenz der politisch

Verantwortlichen (Merk, Vogel, Schreiber) am 6.9.72 um 2:30 Uhr," *Die Spiele der XX. Olympiade München*, accessed August 2, 2011, http://www.olympia72.de/pressekonferenz.html; and Matthias Dahlke, *Der Anschlag auf Olympia '72* (Munich, 2006). Sebastian Denkhardt, Uli Weidenbach, and Manfred Oldenburg's *Der Olympia-Mord. München '72–die wahre Geschichte* (TV Documentary, Germany, 2006), provides a good visual chronicle of the events in the Olympic Village and in Fürstenfeldbruck.

202   took no action.: "Die Olympische Tragödie (Das Attentat)," 2.

203   gathering point for hostages.): One of the Palestinian commando survivors later asserted that Issa had at first mistakenly taken his men to a section of the Connollystrasse complex that housed only athletes from Hong Kong, but this would seem odd given Issa's foreknowledge of the facility's layout. See "Vernehmungsprotokoll Badran [Adnan Al-Gashey] vom 19.9.72," B141/37488, BAK.

205   another terrorist shot him dead.: According to the testimony of one of the survivors, it was "Tony" who murdered Romano. See "Vernehmungsprotokoll Badran."

205   "does change things,": Moore, *Bowerman*, 290. Curiously, Ladany's own memoir, *King of the Road*, does not mention his encounter with Bowerman.

206   "You've got it!": Moore, *Bowerman*, 290.

206   "violation of security."; "in trouble.": Moore, *Bowerman*, 290, 292.

206   "again in danger.": Genscher made these comments in an interview in the late 1990s for the film *One Day in September*, directed by Kevin MacDonald and produced by three-time Oscar winner Arthur Cohn.

206   line with Golda Meir.: Genscher, *Erinnerungen*, 150.

207   "absolute blackout": BPA, München, September 5, 1972, B106/85168, BAK.

207   "going on in Munich,": BPA, München, September 5, 1972, B106/85168, BAK.

208   "being held responsible.": "Die Olympische Tragödie (Das Attentat)," 3; see also "Ich werde heute noch für Palästina sterben," 27.

208   feared would be the case.: Genscher, *Erinnerungen*, 150–52.

209   "soliciting his advice.": Genscher, *Erinnerungen*, 151.

209   "our delegation hostage.": Klein, *Striking Back*, 47.

210   "hostages will die.": Reeve, *One Day*, 15.

210   "not about money.": "Pressekonferenz Polizeipräsident Manfred Schreiber."

211   "blow us both up.": Genscher, *Erinnerungen*, 151.

211   "into the election campaign!": Quoted in Prittie, *Willy Brandt*, 288.

211   any embarrassing interruptions.: On Chancellor Brandt's role in the negotiations, see Dahlke, *Der Anschlag*, 12–15.

211   "his life is safe.": Quoted in Ian Black and Benny Morris, *Israel's Secret Wars* (London, 1966), 270.

212   release of the hostages.: Klein, *Striking Back*, 55.

212   show had gotten under way.: BPA, September 5, 1972, B106/85168, BAK.

212   felt very vulnerable.: Foster, *Mark Spitz*, 210–11.

213   "ransom once again,": Reeve, *One Day*, 66.

213   sell the photo.: Brasher, *Munich 1972*, 73.

213   "How long could you stand that?": Moore, *Bowerman*, 293.

213   unfolding at the Israeli compound.: "Die Freude ist Ulrike Meyfarth vergangen,"
       Abendzeitung (Munich), September 6, 1972.

213   or as many as twenty-one.: Brasher, *Munich 1972*, 74.

214   "become spectator sports.": Mandell, *The Olympics of 1972*, 129.

214   globally televised act of terrorism.: Kay Schiller, "Death at the Munich Olym-
       pics," in *Between Mass Death and Individual Loss: The Place of the Dead in Twentieth-
       Century Germany*, ed. Alon Confino, Paul Betts, and Dirk Schumann (New York,
       2008), 129.

214   "have been in Lebanon.": Jim McKay, *The Real McKay: My Wide World of Sports* (New
       York, 1998), 7.

215   "history vis-à-vis the Jews": Genscher, *Erinnerungen*, 152–54.

215   "to bear immediately [in this crisis].": See text of Brandt appeal, September 6,
       1972, in B1/509, PAAA.

216   Germans could handle the matter themselves,: Klein, *Striking Back*, 55–56.

216   "its own forces": Genscher, *Erinnerungen*, 151.

217   miracle weapon immediately.: Guttmann, *The Games Must Go On*, 252.

217   code-named "Sunshine.": On Operation Sunshine, see "Sachverhaltsrekonstruk-
       tion"; Reeve, *One Day*, 70–72; and Klein, *Striking Back*, 63–64.

218   one hundred thousand peace demonstrators.: Schiller and Young, *The 1972 Mu-
       nich Olympics*, 199.

218   "more hysterical than in control.": Quoted in Reeve, *One Day*, 62.

218   "hostages with confidence.": Schiller and Young, *The 1972 Munich Olympics*, 297.

219   their complete cancellation.: BPA, September 5, 1972, B106/85168, BAK.

219   "useless."; "what *we* do.": Moore, *Bowerman*, 293.

219   agreement from Israel.: Serge Groussard, *The Blood of Israel* (New York, 1975), 201.

220   hostages would be executed.: According to a survivor's testimony, Issa explained
       this plan to his men, who genuinely believed they would get their plane and a
       flight to Cairo. See B141/30899, BAK.

220   protect its Israeli guests.: Genscher, Merk, Schreiber, and Brandt understood full
       well that, in light of Germany's recent past, Bonn simply could not allow Jews to
       be deported to hostile territory and possible death. See Hannes Burger, "Terror
       und Tod: Trauer und Trotz," in *Olympia 1972: München-Kiel-Sapporo*, ed. Harry
       Valèrian (Munich, 1972), 29.

221   "not wish to be involved,": "Bericht Henze," September 5, 1972, B2/191, PAAA;
       see also Dahlke, *Der Anschlag*, 15.

221   for the Israelis' safety.): BPA, September 6, 1972, B106/85168, BAK.

222   "stay with me forever.": Genscher, *Erinnerungen*, 156.

222   "dead back to life.": Quoted in Wolff, "When the Terror Began," 68.

Chapter 6: Battlefield Fürstenfeldbruck

224   copter pad by bus.: A useful documentary source for the Fürstenfeldbruck disaster
       is the above-cited report by the Bavarian Prosecutor's Office justifying its sus-
       pension of criminal proceedings against Munich police chief Manfred Schreiber
       and his assistant Georg Wolf: "Sachverhaltsrekonstruktion." For a report on the

operation by the Bavarian government, see "Bericht über den Ablauf der Polizeiaktion in München und Fürstenfeldbruck," JO Eté 1972, Correspondence Attentat, SG 1972, IOCA. Also invaluable is the time-line of the events of September 5/6 assembled in "Die Olympische Tragödie (Das Attentat)." Useful secondary sources include Klein, *Striking Back*; Reeve, *One Day*; and Dahlke, *Der Anschlag*.

224   "taken to the helicopters.": Klein, *Striking Back*, 69.

224   "number of terrorists wrong!": Klein, *Striking Back*, 69.

225   not relayed to the airbase.: "Sachverhaltsrekonstruktion."

225   scurried off the airplane.: Reich testimony, in "Sachverhaltsrekonstruktion."

226   for each of the terrorists.: Wolf testimony, in "Sachverhaltsrekonstruktion." See also Schreiber interview, "Mal der eine Falke, mal der andere Taube," *Der Spiegel* 38 (1972): 32–35; and "Bericht über den Ablauf der Polizeiaktion."

226   field in darkness.: "Mal der eine Falke," 34.

226   "What's happening?": "Die Olympische Tragödie (Das Attentat)," 3.

227   "all but paralyzed,": Reeve, *One Day*, 115.

227   "STOP FIRING!": "Die Olympische Tragödie (Das Attentat)," 3.

228   magazine was empty.: Adnan Al-Gashey testimony, September 19, 1972, B141/30899, BAK.

228   died of smoke inhalation.: Klein, *Striking Back*, 76.

228   operation of this magnitude.: Zamir's verdict on Bavarian police conduct at Fürstenfeldbruck was "absolute dilettantism." See "Ich werde heute noch für Palästina sterben," 32. See also Dahlke, *Der Anschlag*, 17.

228   "those of the Second and Third Reich."): General Alfred Gruenther quoted in David Clay Large, *Germans to the Front: West German Rearmament in the Adenauer Era* (Chapel Hill, N.C., 1996), 199.

229   order to fire into the bank.: "Ich werde heute noch für Palästina sterben," 33.

229   on foot into nearby fields.: McKay, *The Real McKay*, 13.

229   "All Israeli hostages have been freed.": McKay, *The Real McKay*, 13.

230   "might have come back.": Ahlers quoted in Reeve, *One Day*, 129. See also Arledge, *Roone*, 135.

230   "helicopter is burning!": McKay, *The Real McKay*, 14.

231   "thank me in the morning.": Arledge, *Roone*, 136.

231   "The Israelis.": McKay, *The Real McKay*, 16.

231   "*They're all gone.*": McKay, *The Real McKay*, 16.

231   at least partly, with Israel.: BPA, September 6, 1972, BIO6/85168.

232   harbored Palestinian terrorists.: "Empörung und Zorn in Israel," *SZ*, September 7, 1972.

232   "German Left can rediscover its identity.": Aust, *Der Baader-Meinhof Komplex*, 261. With their virulent hatred of Israel, West Germany's radical leftists certainly welcomed the Black September attack, but there is no evidence to support the late Tony Judt's supposition that "almost certainly, the killers had local assistance from the radical Left." See Tony Judt, *Postwar: A History of Europe since 1945* (New York, 2005), 473.

232   "poor man's weapon.": Jean-Paul Sartre, "La cause de people," *J'Accuse*, October 15, 1972, 3.

232   "murderous actions.": Rudolf Augstein, "Terror und kein Ende," *Der Spiegel* 38 (1972): 20-21.

232   from themselves on down.: For Schreiber's apologia, see his "Pressekonferenz Polizeipräsident Manfred Schreiber" and *Spiegel* interview, "Mal der eine Falke."

232   "hate-filled action.": dpa, September 6, 1972, B106/85168.

233   "freedom of action": "Die schlimmste Nacht der Bundesrepublik," *Der Spiegel* 38 (1972): 20.

233   "and what actually transpired.": Quoted in "Die schlimmste Nacht der Bundesrepublik," 21.

233   "Free State of Bavaria.": "Kanzler schießt scharf gegen den Münchner Einsatz," *Tageszeitung*, September 9/10, 1972.

233   "to build a Sing-Sing.": "Ich werde heute noch für Palästina sterben," 27.

233   "worst night . . . the Federal Republic.": "Die schlimmste Nacht der Bundesrepublik." See also "Hätte man doch Moshe Dajan geschickt," *Der Spiegel* 39 (1972): 83-90.

233   "shame and helplessness.": Grass to Brandt, September 7, 1972, Nachlass Willy Brandt, 6, Willy-Brandt-Archiv, Friedrich Ebert Stiftung, Bonn.

234   "positive experiences in Munich.": "Die Olympia-Arbeit des Presse- und Informationsamtes," September 12, 1972, B145/8061, BAK.

234   authorities had had to operate.: Holland's largest paper, *De Telegraph*, wrote sarcastically of "a masterful move by the German police." Quoted in dpa, September 6, 1972, B145/8061, BAK.

234   (inaccurate) good news.: For a West German commentary on foreign press treatment of the Munich tragedy, see "Verständisvoll und fair, tantenhaft und ungerecht," *SZ*, September 9/10, 1972.

234   "plagued this year's Games.": "Terrorism at Munich," *Chicago Tribune*, September 6, 1972.

234   erupted at the airport.": David Binder, "9 Israelis on Olympic Team Killed," *NYT*, September 6, 1972.

234   matters of law and order.: BPA, September 7, 1972, B106/85168.

234   early days of the festival.: BPA, September 7, 1972, B106/85168.

234   "entry of foreigners.": "The Blackest September," *Economist*, September 9, 1972, 32.

234   "fit to control a country.": "Black for Brandt, Too," *Economist*, September 9, 1972.

234   "ghosts of Munich's past.": Quoted in dpa, July 6, 1972, B106/85168, BAK.

235   "foreign sportspeople in Munich.": Quoted in "Ost-Berlin Rundfunk," July 6, 1972, B106/85168, BAK.

235   "shadow over Munich.": "Schatten über München," *ND*, July 9, 1972.

235   "Israeli air-pirates . . . refugee camps": "SED Hauptausschuß," September 16, 1972, DY16/178, BAB.

235   "employ force to that end.": Quoted in "Horror and Death at the Olympics," *Time*, September 18, 1972, 30.

235   "close to Dachau.": "Ich werde heute noch für Palästina sterben."

236   "West German officials.": Quoted in BPA, September 6, 1972, B106/85168.

236   deal with the problem.: "Hätte man doch Moshe Dajan geschickt," 83.

236   "are trying together.": Quoted in BPA, September 6, 1972, B106/85168.

236   "murdered our people,": Na'ama Sheffi, "Wagner in Israel. Vom Verbot bis zur Schaffung eines politischen Symbols 1938-1997," in *Richard Wagner und die Juden*, ed. Dieter Borchmeyer, Ami Maayani, and Susanne Vill (Stuttgart, Germany, 2001), 335-36.

237   "before the Munich disaster.": Kopel Report quoted in Klein, *Striking Back*, 249.

238   "admission of political responsibility": Steltzer to AA, September 7, 1972, in *Akten zur Auswärtigenpolitik der Bundesrepublik Deutschland*, ed. Institut für Zeitgeschichte (Munich, 1972-1974), 2:258-59.

238   failing to resolve the crisis peacefully.: "München: Ein Sieg der Partisanen in Nahost?" *Der Spiegel* 39 (1972): 100-103; "Die schlimmste Nacht der Bundesrepublik," 20.

238   "full responsibility": Steltzer to AA, 259.

238   "by German bullets.": "Die schlimmste Nacht der Bundesrepublik," 21.

238   "domestic consumption": Steltzer to AA, 258.

238   "Israel against the Arabs.": *Achbar el Yom* quoted in "Harte Ausfälle gegen Bonn," *SZ*, September 16, 1972.

238   "German-Israeli conspiracy"; near future.: "Wutausbruch arabischer Nationalisten," *SZ*, September 7, 1972; also dpa, September 7, 1972, B106/85168.

239   "war begins in earnest.": Quoted in "München: Ein Sieg der Partisanen in Nahost?" 100.

239   "status with U.S. Jews.": Quoted in Robert Dallek, *Nixon and Kissinger: Partners in Power* (New York, 2007), 417.

239   "cold war politics."): "McGovern Blames Egypt and Lebanon in Slayings," *NYT*, September 7, 1972.

239   Arabs and benefit the Soviets.: Henry Kissinger, *White House Years* (Boston, 1979), 1299.

239   Henry Kissinger on September 6.: Nixon-Kissinger quotations from "Partial Transcription, Conversation 771-2," September 6, 1972, 8:13 a.m.-9:48 a.m., Oval Office, Presidential Tapes, NA.

240   "invite Soviet military help."): Kissinger, *White House Years*, 1299.

241   "measures to counter terrorism.": Kissinger, *White House Years*.

241   "set back indefinitely": "A New Mideast 'War' Opens—Unofficially," *SZ News in English*, September 11, 1972.

241   "infallibility and invincibility.": "Israel: 'Abwehr allein reicht nicht!'" *Der Spiegel* 40 (1972): 102-3.

242   "conscience of an agonized world.": Bush quoted in Bruce Maxwell, *Terrorism: A Documentary History* (Washington, D.C., 2003), 7-8.

242   targets were not known.: "Terroranschläge arabischer Untergrundbewegungen," September 6, 1972, B106/85194, BAK.

242   "especially sharp scrutiny": "Ein- und Ausreise von Arabern," September 5, 1972, B106/85194, BAK.

242   be expelled immediately.: "Maßnahmen gegen Ausländer," September 6, 1972, B106/85194, BAK.

242   few were actually deported.: "Verhaftungswelle unter arabischer Studenten," September 27, 1972, B106/86168, BAK.

242   "not to be trusted.": "Der Araber—dem ist nicht zu trauen," *Der Spiegel* 39 (1972): 27.

242   "all out of Germany!": *FAZ* quoted in "Der Araber—dem ist nicht zu trauen."

243   "shifted from Jews to Arabs.": "*L'Orient Le Jour*: 'Araber Feindlichkeit in der BRD,'" October 5, 1972, B106/85168, BAK.

243   Village recreation center.): "Spiel ohne Staat—das geht nicht mehr," *Der Spiegel* 38 (1972): 87.

243   "failed to prevent its actions.": Organizing Committee, *Die Spiele*, 1:38.

244   than originally scheduled.: Quoted in Guttmann, *The Games Must Go On*, 254.

244   "greatest moment of his life.": Quoted in Guttmann, *The Games Must Go On*, 254.

244   "loyalty to the Olympic ideal.": BPA, September 6, 1972, B106/85168, BAK.

244   only 8 percent against.: Hartmut Becker, "Die Beurteilung der XX. Olympiade München 1972 durch die Bevölkerung der Bundesrepublik," *Sportunterricht: Monatsschrift zur Wissenschaft und Praxis des Sports* 22, no. 6 (June 1973): 204.

244   "find it difficult": BPA, September 6, 1972, B106/85168, BAK.

244   "in memory of the dead.": Mansfield quoted in BPA, September 5, 1972, B106/85168, BAK.

245   "continue the 1972 contests.": "Munich, 1972," *NYT*, September 6, 1972.

245   "dance at Dachau.": *Los Angeles Times* quoted in Foster, *Mark Spitz*, 209.

245   "as if nothing has happened?"; "You didn't help.": JO Eté 1972, Correspondence, commentaries, protestations, 1972, IOCA.

245   "killed or tortured.": JO Eté 1972.

245   "stupefaction and incredulity": Report by Agence France quoted in BPA, September 6, 1972, B106/85168, BAK.

245   "rape of the Olympic spirit,": "A Day of Mourning and Sorrow," *NYT*, September 7, 1972.

245   "another victory.": Ladany, *King of the Road*, 318–19.

245   solidarity with the Israelis.): BPA, September 6, 1972, B106/85168, BAK. In Britain, former prime minister Harold Wilson called for Britain's immediate withdrawal from the Games. See "Mr Wilson's Statement on Olympics Angers Sir Alec," *Times*, September 11, 1972. Several Dutch ministers also demanded the withdrawal of their nation's team.

245   "peoples [was] still possible.": "Spiel ohne Staat—das geht nicht mehr," 87.

246   "an athletic victory?": "Trauer, die sich schnell verflücht," *SZ*, September 9/10, 1972.

246   "colleagues have been murdered.": Quoted in Reeve, *One Day*, 149.

246   "Ping-Pong."; "political profit.": "Olympic Personalities: Is the Olympic Flame Going Out?" *NYT*, September 10, 1972.

246   win to Israel.: "Trauer, die sich schnell verflücht," *SZ*, September 9/10, 1972.

246   "I'd go,": Moore, *Bowerman*, 296.

247   "what they [the terrorists] want.": Kenny Moore, "Munich's Message," *Sports Illustrated*, August 5, 1996, 31.

247   "that phosphorous conflagration.": Moore, "Munich's Message."

247   to save the lives of Jews.: "Ein Opfer in Kampf gegen Gewalt," *SZ*, October 9, 1972.

248   sacrifice for the Arab cause.: Dobson, *Black September*, 87.

248   "all ears deaf to us?": Quoted in Dobson, *Black September*, 87.

Chapter 7: The Games Go On

249   around the Olympic Village.: "Einsatz des Bundesgrenzschutzes zum Schutz Olympischer Bauten und Anlagen," September 9, 1972, B106/88817, BAK.

249   returned to Tel Aviv.: Top Olympic officials like Daume and Brundage also had body guards assigned to them. See "Höchste Alarmstufe der Polizei," *SZ*, September 11, 1972.

249   "Rumors of threats": "Security in the Olympic Village: Minutes of the Meetings of the Executive Board," September 9, 1972, IOCA.

250   "no longer wanted.": "Spielstraße-Künstler protestieren," *Nord-Rhein Zeitung*, September 11, 1972.

250   "peaceful demonstration": "IRA Cyclists Invade Olympics," *NYT*, September 8, 1972.

250   "piece of nonsense,": "Reports of Gunshots Close Olympics," *Los Angeles Times*, September 11, 1972.

251   "symbol of insensitivity.": "Trauer, die sich schnell verflüchtigt," *SZ*, September 9/10, 1972.

252   4 × 400–meter relay team: "Matthews Winner in 400 Showdown," *NYT*, August 25, 1972.

252   into the Munich Games: "House Money Sends Runner Matthews to Munich," *New York Herald Tribune*, July 12, 1972.

252   "and leave in peace?": Matthews, *My Race Be Won*, 335.

253   left the podium.: "Munich Fans Boo Americans," *NYT*, September 8, 1972.

253   "pornography out of it.": "Matthews Takes a Stand and It Brings Him Trouble," *NYT*, September 8, 1972.

253   "patriotic people, period.": Matthews, *My Race Be Won*, 340.

254   "don't think we do.": Matthews, *My Race Be Won*, 356.

255   "white man's world.": Matthews, *My Race Be Won*, 357–59.

255   all further Olympic competition.: "Minutes of the Executive Board," September 8, 1972, IOCA.

255   "the athletes in question.": Brundage to Buck, September 8, 1972, ABC, Box 183, UIA.

255   and competitive apparel.: Buck to Matthews, September 9, 1972, ABC, Box 183, UIA.

256   "in their actions.": "Statement by the President of the United States Olympic Committee," September 15, 1972, ABC, Box 183, UIA.

256   "and enjoy it?": Quoted in Moore, *Bowerman*, 289.

256   "and our country.": Dowd to Buck, September 12, 1972, JO Eté 1972, Cojo Comité d'Organisation, IOCA.

257   are in trouble.: Accurso to IOC, September 11, 1972, JO Eté 1972, Cojo Comité d'Organisation, IOCA.

257   "as our countrymen.": Tunis to Brundage, September 12, 1972, JO Eté 1972, Cojo Comité d'Organisation, IOCA.

257   in the 4 × 400-meter relay: "IOC Strafe trifft US-Staffel hart," SZ, September 10, 1972.

257   "we got jobbed,": "Bowerman: Regrets about Munich," Track and Field News, October, 1972, 26.

258   "that much inside me.": "Prefontaine's Workouts Are So Good They Scare Him," NYT, August 24, 1972.

258   "seemed missing.": "Matthews Takes the 400-Meter Dash and Boos," NYT, September 8, 1972.

259   "on the inside"): Smit, Sneaker Wars, 102.

260   "at the Olympic Village,": "Matthews Takes the 400-meter Dash and Boos."

260   "morale of the U.S. team,": "Olympic Personalities," NYT, September 8, 1972.

261   not "a Commie" after all.: Wallechinsky, The Complete Book, 325.

262   new world record.: "World Record for Russian in Decathlon," Guardian, September 9, 1972.

262   actually died trying!: David E. Martin and Roger W. H. Gynn, The Olympic Marathon (Champaign, Ill., 2000), x.

264   for a podium finish.: Martin and Gynn, The Olympic Marathon, 279–81; "Munich Here We Come," Newsweek, July 24, 1972; "The Long and Shorter of Distance Racing," NYT, August 31, 1972.

265   "and World War Two.": Quoted in Smit, Sneaker Wars, 102.

265   by some thirty seconds.: For accounts of the race, see Martin and Gynn, The Olympic Marathon, 284–88; Moore, Bowerman, 299–303; "U.S. Wins First Olympic Marathon since 1908," NYT, September 11, 1972; "Frank Shorter läuft Marathon im Alleingang," SZ, September 11, 1972.

266   crossing the finish line.: On the Südhaus stunt, see Martin and Gynn, The Olympic Marathon, 288; "Cruel Hoax Deprives Shorter of Cheers," Times, September 11, 1972.

266   "don't usually have time to do."): "Cruel Hoax."

266   "use of their legs.": Brasher, Munich 1972, 78.

267   "and better brains.": Quoted in "U.S. Track and Field Showing in Games No Cause for Panic," Los Angeles Times, September 12, 1972.

267   "an unhappy team.": Brasher, Munich 1972, 91.

267   "to the track and field.": "U.S. Track and Field."

267   "like Alexander the Great": Dave Zirin, "What's My Name Fool?": Sports and Resistance in the United States (Chicago, 2005), 165.

268   (26–21) at halftime.: For accounts of the game, see Wallechinsky, The Complete Book, 1079–1081; "Soviet Five Ends U.S. Olympic Reign with Disputed Last Shot 51–50," NYT, September 10, 1972; and "Title Changes Hands in Three Seconds," Sportsworld, August 27–September 10, 1972, 41. Useful also is the film :03 Seconds from Gold (2002). For an analysis of this film, see Chris Elzey, ":03 Seconds from Gold," Journal of Sports History 29, no. 3 (Fall 2000): 518–22.

269   originally requested his timeout.: "Basketball Krimi nach Mitternacht," sid, November 10, 1972; see also Jones testimony before the IOC, "Minutes of the IOC Executive Board," November 10, 1972, IOCA.

269   "until they got it right.": Bill Gaffey, "1972 Munich Olympics, USA vs. USSR Basketball Game," *Hoops*, accessed August 4, 2011, http://www.pahoops.org/1972olympics.htm.

270   "gross irregularities": See copy of the U.S. protest, Olympics Basketball Tournament, in ABC, Box 185, UIA.

270   "the hands of the FIBA administration.": USOC press release, September 11, 1972, ABC, Box 185, UIA.

270   received their silver medals.: "United States Refuse Silver Medal," *Guardian*, September 11, 1972.

271   "violations of official basketball rules.": Buck to Killanin, January 18, 1973, in "United States Refuse Silver Medal."

271   "Great Gold Heist": Tito Steven, "The Great Gold Heist," *San Juan Star*, September 11, 1972.

271   for anti-U.S. sentiment.: Felice to IOC, September 14, 1972, JO Eté 1972, Correspondence, 1970–1972, IOCA.

271   "American basketball invincibility.": "Soviet Writers Glorify Russian Cage Triumph," *Los Angeles Times*, September 12, 1972.

272   "The Revenge Tour,": On this series, see Chris Elzey, "Cold War on the Court: The 1973 American-Soviet Basketball Series," *Proceedings of the North American Society for Sport History* (2001), 17–25.

272   "violent [hockey matches] in history,": James Cooke and John Goodbody, *The Olympics of 1972* (London, 1972), 111.

272   tore up their dressing room.: "Die Pakistaner dürfen nicht mehr antreten," *FAZ*, September 12, 1972.

273   keep their silver medals.: "Die Pakistaner dürfen"; see also "IOC Impose Life-Ban on Pakistan Team," *Times*, September 12, 1972; "Die Pakistani sorgen für einen Skandal," *SZ*, September 11, 1972.

273   "International Hockey matches.": "Die Pakistaner dürfen"; Cooke and Goodbody, *Olympics of 1972*, 111–12; Noorudin to Killanin, September 11, 1972, JO Eté 1972, Correspondence 1970–1972, IOCA.

273   first gold medal in Olympic football.: "Poles Stop Hungarian Hat-Trick," *Sportsworld*, August 26–September 10, 1972, 69; "Polens Fußballer erstmals mit Gold," *SZ*, September 11, 1972.

274   the Americans had done.: "Unolympisches Fußball-Reglement," *SZ*, September 11, 1972; "Poland Ends Hungarian Hopes for a Record," *Times*, September 11, 1972.

274   "lost their nerve": "Ganz unjapanisch gefreut," *FAZ*, September 11, 1972.

275   "could have been expected,": "News from the U.S. Olympic Committee," October 1972, ABC, Box 185, UIA.

275   in the athletic cold war.): Hoffer, *Something in the Air*, 237.

275   return to East Berlin.: "Erich Honecker gratulierte unseren Medaillengewinner," *ND*, September 11, 1972.

276   "painful loss of prestige"; "closed society,": "Uns fehlt der Schwung," sid, September 10, 1972, DSHA.

276   "[the virtues of] regimentation.": "Man for Man, East Germans Were Tops," *Los Angeles Times*, September 12, 1972.

276   "going soft.": Large, *Nazi Games*, 292–93.

277   "weaknesses had been exposed.": "Lessons Must Be Learnt," *Times*, September 12, 1972.

277   "Carefree Games.": "Schlußfeier der XX. Olympischen Spiele," *SZ*, September 10, 1971.

278   wars of the twentieth century.: "Schlußfeier," September 10, 1972, B106/30673, BAK. On early plans for the closing ceremony, see also "Die geplante Eröffnungs- und Schlußfeier der Olympischen Spiele 1972 in München: Eine kritische Analyse," File 3.3 Eröffnungsfeier, Schlußfeier, Siegerehrungen, DSHA.

278   "hours of deepest darkness.": "Schlußfeier im Schatten des Dramas," *SZ*, September 13, 1972.

278   another, even more heinous, act of terror.: On the bomb threat at the closing ceremony, see "Die bange Stunde unterem Regenbogen," *SZ*, September 11/12, 1972; "Im Zweifel runtergeholt," *Der Spiegel* 39 (1972): 49–50.

279   *internal* security crisis.: "Im Zweifel."

280   "must end seriously.": Quoted in Mandell, *The Olympics of 1972*, 174.

280   throughout the ages.: "Frivolity, Sorrow Blend into Olympic Closing Ceremony," *Los Angeles Times*, September 12, 1972.

280   "For He's a Jolly Good Fellow.": "Frivolity, Sorrow"; see also Mandell, *The Olympics of 1972*, 174. For all the criticism of Brundage in many parts of the world, including his native country, most Germans remained grateful to him for his efforts in bringing three Olympic festivals to Germany: Garmisch-Partenkirchen and Berlin in 1936 and Munich in 1972. ZDF Television broadcast a homage to the outgoing IOC president entitled "Auf Wiedersehen Mr. Brundage." A transcript of the film can be found in the papers of Brundage's long-time assistant, Frederick J. Ruegsegger, Box 1, Folder 38, UIA.

281   "naked political blackmail.": "The Games that Lost Their Soul," *Sportsworld*, October 1972, 4.

281   "botch of this one.": Red Smith, "Six Days Late, the Gasman Cometh," *NYT*, September 11, 1972.

281   "of athletics overall.": "Olympics Awards," *Los Angeles Times*, September 12, 1972.

282   keep the Games safe.: "Montreal Weighs Its '76 Olympics," *NYT*, September 8, 1972.

282   "as well—of the hosts.": Dick Pound, *Inside the Olympics* (Toronto, 2004), 87.

282   outlay for Mexico City.: Volker Kluge, *Olympische Sommerspiele. Die Chronik III, Mexiko Stadt 1968–Los Angeles 1984* (Cologne, Germany, 2282), 232.

282   and national prestige.: "Erste Bilanz der Spiele," *SZ*, September 11, 1972.

283   "wake them up to do it.": Jim Murray, "Olympic Awards," *Los Angeles Times*, September 12, 1972.

283   corrupt and meaningless circus.: "Olympic Changes Are Overdue," *Los Angeles Times*, September 12, 1972.

283   "springboard for politics": Christman to Brundage, August 26, 1972, ABC, Box 182, UIA.

283   "relatively small.": "Judging at the Olympics," ABC, Box 182, UIA.

284   taken against them.: "Das Sebstbild wurde zerschossen," SZ, September 12, 1972.

284   not yet be detected.: "The Future of the Olympics," Times, September 12, 1972.

284   "grotesque shadow hanging over the competition": "Protests Cloud Contests," Guardian, November 12, 1972.

284   "accelerate the fight.": Pound, Inside the Olympics, 55.

284   "closer to the dark side.": Ken Mannie, "Doping Déja Vu," Coach and Athletic Director, October 2006.

285   "hear our national anthem played.": "Medaillen gewonnen—Verkrampfung verloren," SZ, September 11, 1972.

286   "with the local population.": "Medaillen gewonnen."

286   clearly took on new meaning.: "Olympic Notes," Los Angeles Times, September 12, 1972.

287   favored the proposal.: "Erste Bilanz der Spiele," SZ, September 11, 1972.

287   "will be raised again.": "Killanin: More Women Events for Olympics," Los Angeles Times, September 11, 1972.

288   "seen in ten days.": Cooke and Goodbody, Olympics of 1972, 21.

288   90 percent of the available seats.: Kluge, Olympische Sommerspiele, 228.

288   "of the Junkers": Murray, "Olympic Awards."

288   "in the contemporary era?": Becker, "Die Beurteilung," 204.

289   "to have been wrecked.": "Das Selbstbildnis wurde zerschossen."

Epilogue

292   on West German soil.: "Auslieferung nach Israel," September 7, 1972, B141/30899, BAK.

292   methods of entering West Germany.: "Vernehmungen in Stadelheim and Kaisheim," September 14, 1972, B141/30899, BAK; see also "Vernehmungsprotokoll Badran."

292   "psychological torture": "Auswärtiges Amt. Prozeß gegen Palästinischen Terroristen," September 14, 1972, B141/30899, BAK.

292   be dismissed forthwith.: "Ergebnisvermerk der Dienstbesprechung vom 8.9.72," B106/146540, BAK. See also Dahlke, Der Anschlag, 20.

292   all its thirteen occupants.: Dahlke, Der Anschlag, 20–25; Reeve, One Day, 155–59.

293   completely on their own.: AA Vermerk, October 29, 1972, "Gespräch zwischen Herrn Dg31 und dem Leiter des Büros der Arabischen Liga in Bonn," Dr. Khatib, B36/501, PAAA.

294   terror on German soil.: Klein, Striking Back, 127–28.

294   "surprisingly low figure.": Reeve, One Day, 158.

295   agrees with this interpretation.: Klein, Striking Back, 125–28.

295   "problem of Palestine.": Quoted in Bird, Crossing Mandelbaum Gate, 254.

295   simulated "hijacking.": Klein, Striking Back, 127–28.

295 "judicial reckoning is possible,": Fernschreiben, BSMJ to AA, November 2, 1972, B36/501, PAAA.

295 "a serious crime.": "Auslieferung der Attentäter aus Libyan," November 13, 1972, B36/501, PAAA.

296 "flown to Libya.": Golda Meir, *My Life* (New York, 1975), 399.

296 "by the German decision.": Quoted in Feldman, *The Special Relationship*, 185.

296 "with the Nazi era.": "Jüngste Entwicklungen der deutsch-israelischen Beziehungen," undated, B36/525, PAAA.

296 "and the Jewish people.": "Jüngste Entwicklungen." For a vivid example of Israeli anger over the release of the Palestinian terrorists, see a letter by Israeli track coach Debra Markus, who complains bitterly of Israel being forced to "stand alone" because it has been "sold out" by her supposed friends. Markus letter in JO Eté 1972, Correspondence Attentat, SG 1972, IOCA.

297 "do it all over again,": "Planner of Munich Olympics Attack Dies," Daoud obituary, Associated Press, July 4, 2010. Israel's journalists had long made much of Daoud's close relationship with Yasser Arafat (a.k.a. Abu Mazen), claiming that the funding for the Munich attack came directly from Arafat. See, for example, Tom Gross, "A Leader 'Uncompromised by Terror'? Abu Mazen, the Munich Massacre and Other Attacks," June 8, 2003, http://www.tomgrossmedia.com/.

299 disposal of West Germany's individual states.: Genscher's order is mentioned in "Mr Dayan in Munich during Attempt to Rescue Hostages," *Times*, September 11, 1972.

299 led the police operation.: "Strafanzeige gegen die Verantwortlichen," *SZ*, September 11, 1972.

299 proposition as absurd.: "Eine neue Kontroverse über das Olympia-Massaker," *Der Tagespiegel* 1 (1973).

300 failings in the hostage crisis.: BSMI, "Erfahrungsbericht über die Vorbereitung." See also the voluminous three-part report put out jointly by the press offices of the federal and Bavarian governments: "Bericht über: 1/Die Sicherheitsmaßnahmen in München und im Olympischen Dorf; 2/Die Bemühungen nach dem Überfall . . . ; 3/Den Ablauf der Polizeiaktion in München und Fürstenfeldbruck," September 19, 1972, JO Eté 1972, Correspondence Attentat, SG 1972, IOCA.

300 slain Israeli Olympians.: "Hintenrum verteilt," *Der Spiegel* 46 (1972): 80.

300 "more diligent [in protecting Israelis during the Games],": Quoted in "Terror zerstört die heiteren Spiele," *SZ*, September 5, 1973.

300 "reward" to Israel.: Reeve, *One Day*, 223.

300 as the shooting ended.: Reeve, *One Day*, 232; see also Reuters report, "Olympic Massacre Victim Died Later," September 8, 1972, JO Eté 1972, Correspondence Attentat, SG 1972, IOCA.

301 compensation in any amount.: "Terror zerstört die heiteren Spiele."

301 been killed by police bullets.: Reuters report, "Munich Finds Disputed 1972 Olympic Documents," October 9, 1972, JO Eté 1972, Correspondence Attentat, SG 1972, IOCA.

301   "'truth' being hushed up.": Reuters, "Munich Finds Disputed."

302   terrorists' grenades or bullets.: Reeve, *One Day*, 224–32.

302   years of seeking compensation.: "Munich Olympics Families Scorn German Offer of DM 6 Million," *Ha'aretz*, May 1, 2001.

302   "I'm furious,": "Munich Olympics Families."

302   "a humanitarian gesture.": "Germany's Compensation for Munich," *NYT*, September 7, 2002.

303   "those unfortunate occurrences.": "Terror zerstört die heiteren Spiele."

303   for a major memorial.: "Terror zerstört die heiteren Spiele."

303   "out of tragic history.": "Terror zerstört die heiteren Spiele."

303   and postwar eras.: Lamm's idea was enthusiastically embraced by the Federal President's Office as a boon "for the FRG's image abroad." See "Bundespräsident to Bundesministerium für Forschung und Technologie," April 17, 1973, B106/35483, BAK.

303   "slammed in my face.": "Terror zerstört die heiteren Spiele."

304   "for further German initiatives": König letter, June 5, 1973, B106/35483, BAK.

304   "of international understanding.": FAZ, December 31, 1973, quoted in B106/35483, BAK.

304   at close quarters.: "Gedenken an den schwarzen Olympiatag," *SZ*, November 5, 1974.

304   intrude upon the Games.: "IOC Remains Silent on Remembering Munich," *USA Today*, February 10, 2006.

304   King Memorial in downtown Atlanta.: "Munich Dead Get Belated Olympics Memorial," *Jerusalem Report*, May 30, 1972.

305   and injured 111.: "Echoes of Munich's Nightmare," *NYT*, July 28, 1996.

305   "was lost long ago."; "bomb went off.": "Memorial for Munich Victims," *NYT*, July 29, 1996.

305   upcoming Sydney Games.: "Ceremony Silence Call for Munich Victims," *Australian*, November 27, 2305.

305   "nor forgive them.": "Sydney Memorial to Munich Olympics Unveiled," dpa, November 26, 2306, Clippings File, DSHA.

306   outlay for Munich.: Roman Czula, "The Munich Olympics Assassinations: A Second Look," *Journal of Sport and Social Issues* 2, no. 1 (Spring/Summer 1978): 21.

306   approximately $300 million.: "Munich Legacy: Tight Security," *USA Today*, November 4, 1992.

306   "the party atmosphere": "Echoes of Munich's Nightmare."

306   "worked in the past.": Dan Yaeger, "How Safe Will It Be?" *Sports Illustrated*, August 2, 2004, 20.

306   city's Muslim areas.: "Experts Say Greek Verdicts Don't Dispel Olympic Threat," *NYT*, October 17, 2003; "Stepped-up Police Activity Irks an Arab Area in Greece," *NYT*, April 26, 2004.

306   "extra [security] measures,": Jenny Hazen, "Israeli Athletes Let the Games Begin," August 8, 2004, http://www.ujc.org/.

307   obviously much impressed.: "An Amazing Display of Security Vigilance," *Jerusalem Post*, August 8, 2008.

307   analogies between the two events.: "Wie Partisanen überall angreifen," *Der Spiegel* 41 (1980): 38–44.

307   "lessons of Munich": "Munich Massacre Remembered," Associated Press, September 1972, Clippings File, DSHA.

308   "It's all very painful.": "Perspective: A Stark Reminder Reverberates Worldwide," *NYT*, September 16, 2001.

308   "you never shake.": "Perspective."

308   "fuse that ignited Arab terrorism.": "ABC Returns to Munich Olympics," *USA Today*, August 29, 2002.

308   "be forever cursed.": "Perspective."

308   "something to consider.": "ABC Returns to Munich Olympics."

309   on the '72 Games.: For an analysis of Spielberg's film and other cinematic treatments of the Munich terror attack, see David Scott Diffrient, "Spectator Sports and Terrorist Reports: Filming the Munich Olympics and (Re)imaging the Munich Massacre," *Sport in Society* 11, nos. 2/3 (March/May 2008): 311–29.

309   "prayer for peace": "His Prayer for Peace," *Time*, December 12, 2005, 70–71.

310   "convenient fable.": "Sie gehen nicht an, die Lichter," *Der Spiegel* 35 (1972): 57.

310   irregularities in the OC's books.: "Der Staat als Verschwender," *Rheinischer Merkur*, November 27, 1972.

310   an entire television studio.: "Nachspiele—nicht mehr ganz so heiter," *SZ*, August 25/26, 1973. Retailers of Olympic souvenirs found themselves sitting on some DM 50 million worth of unsold items—a full half of their original inventories. Even the Waldi toys had not exactly jumped off the shelves. See "Sozusagen Abfall," *Der Spiegel* 46 (1972): 85.

310   and minimal accoutrements.: "Ernüchterung nach dem großen Fest," *SZ*, January 10, 1974; "Bavarian Gamesmanship over Olympic Village," *Guardian*, December 7, 1972; "Zu klein, zu kalt," *Der Spiegel* 43 (1972): 60–62.

310   who should pay the upkeep costs.: "Die letzte Olympia-Entscheidung fällt der Richter," *SZ*, July 17, 1973.

310   drop into the buildings.: "Olympiadach wird braun und schrumpft," *SZ*, June 28, 1973.

311   stay on their construction schedule.: "Verdunklungsmanöver um Zeltdach-Verfärbung?" *SZ*, August 24, 1973.

311   its best quality.: "Bleiben die Olympia-Hallen Dunkelkammer?" *SZ*, October 12, 1973.

311   gloomy atmosphere inside the buildings.: "Das Zeltdach wird verdunkelt," *SZ*, April 20/21, 1974; "Verdunklung kostet 2,1 Millionen," *SZ*, July 13/14, 1974.

311   last until the year 2050!: "Die Skeptiker behielten nicht recht: Olympia-Dach stabil wie am ersten Tag," *MM*, July 22, 1980.

311   "no events at all.": "Ernüchterung nach dem großen Fest."

312   DM 2 billion estimated in late 1972.: "Münchner Olympia-Schlußbilanz in Bonn," *SZ*, February 20, 1976.

312   "a sensible investment": "Stolze Zahlen beim Olympia-Kassensturz," *SZ*, June 25/26, 1977.

312   "the big winner": "München war der große Gewinner der Olympischen Sommer-
       spiele 1972," *Sport-Kurrier*, June 27, 1972.
313   Munich had not.: "Millionen Besucher im Olympiapark," *FAZ*, August 19, 1977.
313   "urban life."; "Olympic Mountain.": "Das Olympiadorf fast ausverkauft," *FAZ*,
       January 17, 1979.
313   "agendas of all Münchner": "Die Entscheidung hat sich gelohnt," *Münchner Stad-
       tanzeiger*, July 20, 1982.
314   "highest moment" in their lives.: "Große Parade der Goldmedaillen-Gewinner,"
       SZ, September 13, 1972.
314   "West Germany's sports capital.": "München zog aus Olympia größten Gewinn,"
       SZ, July 23, 1993.
315   "other relevant officials.": Hans-Jochen Vogel, *Nachsichten: Meine Bonner und Ber-
       liner Jahre* (Munich/Zurich, 1996), 20–21.
315   "significantly sharpened.": "Strauß empfiehlt nochmalige Olympiabewerbung
       Münchens," *SZ*, March 19, 1973.
316   "imperialistic machinations"; "willfully allowed": "Olympia '72 in der Sicht von
       Ost und West," *Welt der Arbeit*, June 8, 1973, 13.
316   "and stacking toilet rolls.": "Opposition spricht von einem Racheakt," *SZ*, Janu-
       ary 19, 1981.
317   "cups in his cupboard?": "Opposition spricht."
317   "in the general populace.": "Anlaß zu Mißdeutungen," *Der Spiegel* 5 (1980): 71.
317   "out like a candle.": "Das gab's nur einmal—das kommt nie wieder," *SZ*, August
       21/22, 1982.
318   "all set to go": "Die blutige Spur des schwarzen September," *SZ*, September 4/5,
       1982.
318   "'not with me!'"; "dignified and appropriate,": "Und dann sind sie weg aus dem
       Dorf," *SZ*, November 5, 2002.
318   "formulation of a politician": "Und dann sind sie weg."

Index